Tension Areas
in World Affairs

WADSWORTH CONTINUING EDUCATION SERIES

Leonard Freedman, General Editor

Armament and Disarmament: The Continuing Dispute

edited by Walter R. Fisher
and Richard D. Burns
Los Angeles State College

Contemporary Communism: Theory and Practice

edited by Howard R. Swearer
and Richard P. Longaker
University of California, Los Angeles

Contemporary Moral Issues

edited by Harry K. Girvetz
University of California, Santa Barbara

Issues of the Sixties

edited by Leonard Freedman
University Extension
University of California, Los Angeles
and Cornelius P. Cotter
University of Wichita

Metropolis: Values in Conflict

edited by C. E. Elias, Jr.,
James Gillies, and Svend Riemer
University of California, Los Angeles

Politics 1964

edited by Francis M. Carney
and H. Frank Way, Jr.
University of California, Riverside

Tension Areas in World Affairs

edited by Arthur C. Turner
University of California, Riverside
and Leonard Freedman
University Extension
University of California, Los Angeles

Tension Areas in World Affairs

edited by Arthur C. Turner
University of California, Riverside
and Leonard Freedman
University Extension
University of California, Los Angeles

Wadsworth Publishing Company, Inc., Belmont, California

"The purpose of foreign policy
is not to provide an outlet for our sentiments
of hope or indignation;
it is to shape real events in a real world."

President John Fitzgerald Kennedy at
Salt Lake City, September 26, 1963

Second printing, July 1965

L.C. Cat. Card No.: 64-25027
Printed in the United States of America

Preface

Tension Areas in World Affairs provides a combination of elements not previously available in publications for college classes and continuing education programs. In the experience of the editors, such a combination has long been needed. Therefore, this anthology possesses certain special characteristics:

(1) It focuses upon the major international problems of our time in the context of *specific countries or topics.* We make no effort to be all-inclusive. Rather, within each of the major theaters of international tension we have endeavored to select countries (such as Egypt in the Middle East), international organizations (such as the Common Market in Europe), or large-scale projects (such as the Alliance for Progress in Latin America) that we believe to be representative of the region as a whole.

(2) It deals with these countries and problems in the *contemporary* setting. But ours is not an ephemeral approach that pursues the day-by-day headlines. Our concern is with the major international trends established or emerging in the mid-1960s. Although some details included here may change, the readings have been carefully selected to provide analyses that will not soon become outdated.

(3) It emphasizes the *controversies* surrounding the great problems that confront the world today, while it presents a substantial amount of basic information and analysis. Since there is a wide range of opinion on the key questions around which this book is built, we have provided contrasting and sometimes conflicting views to encourage thought and discussion.

(4) It taps sources from *several countries.* We have included selections by British, French, Russian, Chinese, Indian, Pakistani, Egyptian, Israeli, South African, Nigerian, Ghanaian, and Mexican spokesmen in order to encourage an examination of ideas not widely considered within this country. The book, however, has many selections from U.S. sources, since we also focus on the implications of the issues for our own foreign policy.

The editors worked together throughout the book, but divided the primary responsibility for writing introductory essays, selecting material, and editing specific chapters. Arthur C. Turner is responsible for Chapters 1, 2, 3, 4, 6, 8, and 9, and Leonard Freedman for Chapters 5, 7, 10, 11, and 12.

Thanks are due to many people. The editors greatly appreciate the courtesy of the authors and publishers who gave their permission for the selections used here. Much of the basic research for this book was carried out with skill and insight by James Bell, Dr. Freedman's research assistant. Dr.

Turner wishes to express his thanks to his research assistant, Linda Mercer, and to his secretary, Susanne De Filippo. The maps have been admirably executed by James Wright.

A.C.T.
L.F.

Contents

1. Introduction: The World of the 1960s
Arthur C. Turner 1

Part One: Europe

2. The Common Market: Inward or Outward Looking? 14

The Interest of the United States in the European Economic Community, Philip H. Trezise 20

It Means the End of Britain as an Independent European State, Hugh Gaitskell 27

President de Gaulle Reads Britain Out of Europe, Charles de Gaulle 30

There Is Now a Deep Division of Policy, Edward R. G. Heath 33

America Gets an Unexpected Break, Henry S. Reuss 36

3. NATO: Is It Still Necessary? 45

Need for the Closest Coordination in the Defense of the Atlantic Community, Robert S. McNamara 50

The Demise of NATO, Ronald Steel 54

Total U.S. Commitment to the Defense of Europe, John F. Kennedy 60

What Price Conventional War in Europe? Bernard Brodie 66

The Need for Disengagement, H. Stuart Hughes 74

In the Long Run de Gaulle Cannot Win, Louis J. Halle 79

4. Berlin and the German Question 83

A Hopeful View of the Role of Germany, W. W. Rostow 87

We Can Now Make a Deal on Berlin, Charles W. Thayer 94

Recognize the Oder-Neisse Line, but Do Not Yield on Berlin, H. R. Trevor-Roper 103

The Present Impossibility of Unifying Germany, Claiborne Pell 108

Germany Gives Rise to Vast Uncertainties, Hans J. Morgenthau 114

5. Eastern Europe: Polycentrism and U.S. Policy 119

The East European Satellites: Variations on a Soviet Theme, Paul Kecskemeti 121

Moscow's Satellites—in and out of Orbit, Anatole Shub 130

COMECON, Michael Gamarnikow 136

Colonialism in Eastern Europe, Ferenc Nagy 144

The State Department View, W. Averell Harriman 150

Part Two: Africa

6. Africa: Dissension and the Quest for Unity 156

Africa Is Poised on the Razor's Edge, Waldemar A. Nielsen 159

Apartheid in South Africa: Defiance of the United Nations, U.N. Special Committee 165

The Truth That Hurts, Eric H. Louw 175

Toward African Unity, Organization of African Unity Charter 185

Needed: A Central Authority, Kwame Nkrumah 187

We Must Be Realists about African Unity, Sir Abubakar Tafawa Balewa 190

Part Three: The Middle East

7. Egypt and Arab Leadership 196

Nasser's Decade, Alfred Sherman 199

Nasser's Foreign Policy, Charles D. Cremeans 207

Arab Socialism, Leonard Binder 215

On Peace, Neutrality, and Israel, Gamal Abdel Nasser 222

Israel's Security, David Ben Gurion 226

Part Four: Asia

8. China, The U.N., and the Sino-Soviet Conflict 232

United States Rejects Soviet Proposal to Seat Communist China, Adlai E. Stevenson 235

A Two-Chinas Proposal, Eustace Seligman 239

Keep the Door Open to the Possibility of Change, Roger Hilsman, Jr. 245

Wars of National Liberation Are Not Dangerous, Central Committee, Chinese Communist Party 250

World War Can Be Averted, Central Committee, Soviet Communist Party 253

The Great Schism: On Sino-Soviet Conflicts, Hugh Seton-Watson 255

9. India: The Prospects for Democracy 266

A Splendid Exception to All Our Generalizations, Clinton Rossiter 269

The Most Dangerous Decades, Selig S. Harrison 275

The Challenge to India's Integrity, Chanakya Sen 281

The Pakistan-American Alliance: Stresses and Strains, Mohammed Ayub Khan 289

10. Vietnam: Military or Diplomatic Solution? 295

Vietnam: Free-World Challenge in Southeast Asia, George W. Ball 297

Vietnam—Another Korea? Hans J. Morgenthau 302

We Should Go Over to the Offensive, Thomas Dodd 310

Our Options in Vietnam, Bernard B. Fall 316

Part Five: Latin America

11. Cuba: Communism in the Western Hemisphere 328

Cuba and the Nuclear Risk, Walter Lippmann 330

Cuba Must Be Freed, Freedom House 334

The Case for Reconciliation, Maurice Zeitlin and Robert Scheer 346

Castro, Latin America, and the Sino-Soviet Conflict, Ernst Halperin 354

12. The Alliance for Progress 357

Objectives of the Alliance for Progress, Charter of Punta del Este 359

The Alliance and Its Accomplishments, Teodoro A. Moscoso 361

The Latin-American Oligarchy, Peter R. Nehemkis, Jr. 368

Development before Reform, John Paton Davies, Jr. 371

Revolution, Yes! Carlos Fuentes 378

The Contriving of Reform, Albert O. Hirschman 385

1

Introduction: The World of the 1960s

Arthur C. Turner

Prophecy, the attempt to estimate at least the general character of the future, to extrapolate into the unknown the curves of the present, is proverbially subject to error but unavoidable in practice. Prophecy—risky or not—is, after all, as essential an element of statesmanship as it is of intelligent attempts to discuss contemporary affairs. But students of world affairs have an interest in their subject matter that is not altogether abstract; it is, in part—and rightly—pragmatic. They want to know not only what the situation is and how it came to be, but also what the alert and aware citizen ought to do, as well as think, about it. In a world of change, governments must try to shape policy to meet the emerging needs of the future as well as the pressing needs of the present. It is almost forty years since H. G. Wells suggested that every government should have a Ministry of Foresight. The suggestion was not, perhaps, altogether a happy one; for every department of government in the modern world ought to try to exercise foresight in regard to its own specific problems.

Such considerations are, however, idealistic, and it would be absurd to pretend that governments in general live up to them. Even where foresight is attempted, it is all too rarely exercised with skill. Facts are distorted, or used selectively, to justify predetermined conclusions. The love of symmetry and repetition, tinged perhaps by superstition, enters into it too. Sir Lewis Namier, the great Anglo-Polish historian, remarked tersely in one of his essays, "One would expect people to remember the past and to imagine the future. But in fact . . . they imagine the past and remember the future"—an epigram obscure, profound, and, even when understood, not at all comforting. But it explains a good deal in the actions of people and governments. It explains, for example, why France was brilliantly prepared in 1939 for the defensive trench warfare of 1914–18; why Mr. Neville Chamberlain, ex-Lord Mayor of Birmingham, was convinced that Hitler could be bought off by specific material concessions; why many Americans in the 1950s regarded Russia as a threat precisely equivalent to that posed twenty years earlier by Hitler's Germany; and why Britain for years held herself aloof from active participation in the movement for European integration.

Different Character of the 1950s and 1960s

In the early 1950s, the world scene in terms of politics and power was a relatively simple one, commonly capable of interpretation by the concept of *bipolarity*. Undoubtedly, this concept was an oversimplification; yet, in a rough-and-ready way, it was adequate, and it did not involve any great distortion. In the aftermath of World War II, two countries—the United States and the Soviet Union—did, indeed, dominate the world's politics like colossi. Most of the other countries of the world grouped about one or the other of these two political poles, and for several years bipolarization became more and more accentuated. The Soviet Union consolidated its hold on the countries of Eastern Europe, adding Czechoslovakia in 1948 to its satellites. In 1949, communism gained its largest triumph when it succeeded in taking over all mainland China.

The United States, meanwhile, in a complete reversal of its historic policy of isolationism, set about organizing defensively all the rest of the world that was willing to be so organized. The North Atlantic Treaty of 1949 initiated a whole complex of regional alliance systems that ringed the globe. In every case, the essential features were U.S. membership and American willingness to defend the area against communist aggression. The treaties—NATO, the Southeast Asia Treaty, the ANZUS pact with Australia and New Zealand, and others—created permanent organizations, usually complete with secretariats and headquarters. The most elaborate was the NATO structure, both civil and military, based in Paris and extending throughout all the Western European states covered by the treaty. Along with the organizations went the creation of military bases by the United States, mostly air force bases but also a considerable number (especially in Europe) for ground forces and naval power.

Thus, for a time, it appeared that world politics, whatever its complexities, had at its core as the only question that really mattered: the relative strengths of the two great blocs. Of any country, any region, it seemed enough to know whether it was enrolled under the banner of the West or that of the communist camp, or whether it was maintaining neutrality—a status presumably both precarious and temporary. In the high noon of this period—when President Eisenhower and Secretary of State Dulles were in office and the ghost of Stalin had not yet been exorcised—world politics might be said to have had a motto borrowed from Shakespeare's *Henry IV*: "Under which king, Bezonian? Speak, or die!"

The Erosion of Bipolarity

Alas for the lovers of simplicity and the short, clear explanation—as most of us are at heart—the world's Bezonians neither declared themselves nor died. Instead, as the years passed, they became even more assertive in their expressions of neutrality; and their numbers, instead of diminishing, increased. The world picture, rather than proceeding through progressive stages of clarity to a final resolution, reverted toward further complexity, multiplicity, and subtlety. History, of course, seldom proceeds by abrupt transitions from one situation to another. The seeds of decay in the "bipolar" world were already present in its heyday; indeed, the breakup was already occurring in the middle 1950s. The conflict between communism and democratic ideals is still a major factor—perhaps the major factor—in world politics. Yet, in recent years, the world picture has been transformed in large measure as a result of three major developments. These three main, discernible trends have a certain parallel character, and they have all acted either to break the cohesion of the two great embattled camps or to create new forces outside such an alignment altogether.

Weakening of the Communist Bloc

In the first place, the world communist movement no longer has only one headquarters—Moscow—from which one worldwide effort may be traced through a tightly organized hierarchy of power and to which all members unquestioningly look for leadership and doctrinal guidance. The earlier identification of a world ideological movement with Russian national interest (perhaps always inherently implausible and unstable, though it seemed appallingly successful as long as it endured) has suffered grave and possibly irreparable damage. The first crack in the structure antedated the high tide of bipolarity: such is the untidy nature of the world. The breach between Yugoslavia and Russia in 1948, nonetheless, seemed for long an isolated and anomalous event rather than the harbinger of a general trend.

The middle and late 1950s saw the beginnings of much graver breaches in the monolithic communist world. In November 1956, simultaneous events in Poland and Hungary threatened the existence of the whole East-European Russian satellite empire. Paradoxically, the more extreme of the two movements was the less striking in its long-term results. Hungary attempted to cut itself loose from the Warsaw Pact—the Russian counterpart of NATO. Such independence within the zone of Russian suzerainty apparently could not be tolerated; the Hungarian strike for an independent policy was crushed in the streets of Budapest by Soviet military force. The Western world looked on, emotionally involved but militarily aloof, and took no action whatever to assist the Hungarian fighters for freedom. The Dullesian theme of "Liberation"—that the aim of U.S. policy was to liberate the satellite countries from communist rule—forthwith ceased to be believable except as an exceedingly long-term velleity unrelated to actual political or military acts in any probable future. And in no very long time, of course, a policy of liberation becomes perfectly meaningless, because a new generation grows up that never lived under the former regime and has no memory of it.

The desire to be rid of the communist yoke was at least as strong in Poland as in Hungary, but in 1956 the Poles displayed an ability, unprecedented in their heroic and often tragic history, to judge with precision the limits of the possible. An impressive display of national unity exacted from Russia a certain measure of "home rule" for Poland within the communist empire. Wladyslaw Gomulka took office as director of this curious experiment in national communism. His regime and the Roman Catholic Church in Poland showed cautious tolerance of each other, and Poland for some years enjoyed a far greater degree of freedom of discussion than any other European satellite. In the economic sphere, the trend toward collectivism in agriculture was reversed, and the overwhelming bulk of farm land was allowed to revert to the hands of peasant owners, though not, it goes without saying, to the hands of the landowners from whom it had been filched in 1945.

As 1956 receded into the past, and particularly from 1962 onward, Poland to some extent lost her advantage. A steady nibbling at the position of the Church recommenced, and freedom of speech was again restricted. But, in general terms, there still is a far greater degree of national autonomy within the Soviet East-European system than there was in the early 1950s. Russia has once more to take very seriously into account national differences and national aspirations. The satellites vigorously resist Russian attempts to channel their trade within the system of COMECON (the communist counterpart of the Common Market), and so far they have resisted successfully.

An even graver breach in the communist system has been created by the open clash between Russia and China. This division appeared to be on the brink of occurring for several years; it finally arrived in 1963. Although it has important ideological features, the split may be said primarily to demonstrate a triumph of traditional factors in power politics and nationalism over ideological kinship. China, with its enormous population, could not accept forever a role subordinate to Russian leadership. Ideologically, the triumph of communism in China, thirty-two years more recent that its triumph in Russia, is vastly more virulent and dangerous. Chinese policy has been far more adventurous in the 1960s than Russian policy, and it increasingly demonstrates racialist overtones when bidding for support in Africa and Asia.

Thus, in little more than a decade, the Eisenhower-Dulles policy of "Liberation" became indistinguishable in practice from the previous, Truman-Acheson policy of "Containment." The policy of containment, first enunciated in a celebrated article in 1947 by George Kennan, might be summarized roughly by saying that if communist power can be prevented from expanding and adding to the area it dominates, it will, in the long run, necessarily undergo internal changes that will make it less dynamic and less hostile.

Oddly enough, this possibly not very inspiring belief that if only the Western world could hold fast long enough in a defensive posture, *something* would happen, has been in considerable measure justified by events; for, in the long run, something *did* happen. Rather, several things began to happen, whose consequences will continue to unfold themselves. Polycentrism took the place of centralism in the communist world, and within the Russian orbit there appeared a greater autonomy of the various satellites. Simultaneously, in the Russian orbit and in independent but communist Yugoslavia—though not, or not yet, in Communist China—came some betterment of the conditions of everyday life, some diversion of resources in the direction of consumer goods, and some softening of a philosophy that thought formerly only of very long-run goals and not at all of immediate human desires and human hopes.

Weakening of the American Alliance System

In a curiously parallel and synchronous way, the same years have seen a weakening of the international system of Russia's great rival. The great system of American alliances that bound the whole free world in one network, of which the United States was the linchpin, is all too clearly not what it once was. Perhaps a skeptic might put it that it never was what it appeared to be; at any rate, it has come to have a certain air of the obsolescent, if not of the obsolete. The United States' allies do not accept her leadership as unquestioningly as once they did. They have become restive and independent in policy.

Though such restiveness is a worldwide phenomenon, it is perhaps most noticeable in three areas. Western Europe is increasingly independent in its attitudes. In the Far East, the economic revival of Japan has likewise enabled it to end its dependence on U.S. assistance and guidance. In Latin America, the situation is somewhat different, for there has been no achievement of economic strength; but there is increasing resentment of U.S. political and economic domination of the Western Hemisphere, so that whereas the Latin American nations once almost automatically followed the U.S. lead, they now have to be cajoled and persuaded to do so—and not always successfully. In addition, the Castro regime in Cuba constitutes an enormous and dangerous breach in the former system of virtual U.S. hegemony in the Americas. In the north, even Canada, friendliest of allies and the greatest trading partner of the United States, has shown in recent years symptoms of regret that she is yoked so inescapably to the U.S. economy and the U.S. defense system.

By far the most significant of these developments is the revival of Europe as an independent center of power and not just a series of American satellites. Here, the American system was at its strongest, with the North Atlantic Treaty Organization as its very centerpiece and symbol. Even had nothing else happened in recent years beyond the end of Western Europe's economic dependence on the United States—and the questioning, especially by de Gaulle, of the American domination of NATO—one would still be justified in saying the American system had eroded. But more has happened. A number of developments have begun to call in question the rationale of the whole system.

Essentially, the American system of military alliance and economic aid are anticommunist in purpose; the former is more narrowly and explicitly so. The alliances are basically guarantees (expressed in varying formulas, all designed to circumvent the fact that the Senate alone can authorize a declaration of war) that the United States will assist certain states in the event of communist aggression against them. Many of these areas—those in CENTO or SEATO, for example—are places of little military strength. The United States grouped these countries in alliances to make it easier to plan in advance for action in the contingency of communist aggression, and, by giving military aid and modernizing their armies, to create in such countries a degree of military strength to deter aggression. Similarly, the program of economic aid aims at creating sounder and more productive economies that will offer less of a target for communist propaganda and infiltration. A second benefit, that more prosperous countries will also be more friendly toward the United States, has also been hoped for.

However, the acceptability of this whole program to America's subordinate partners in it has been steadily dwindling in recent years. First, American economic aid is not limited to those who pursue policies friendly to America or her allies. A Sukarno or a Nasser, however derisive his attitude to the United States, however obnoxious the policies he pursues, can apparently continue to count on receiving massive aid. Why, then, be a docile ally? Furthermore, the American thesis that Russia constitutes an overt *military* threat to Western Europe and the states on her own southern border (Turkey, Iran) has never been as self-evident in Europe as it has seemed in the United States. Since the late 1950s, skepticism about this thesis has increased to the point of downright disbelief. The policy of Russia, internally and toward her satellites, and the policy of Russia and her satellites toward the West have undergone modification. There is now considerable trade and tourist traffic between Eastern and Western Europe. The "Iron Curtain" is a phrase whose appropriateness has passed. Perhaps the same is true of the "Cold War."

More serious, and contributing more to the decay of the American alliance system, is how narrow are its definitions and objectives. The fact that American alliances guarantee support against no other contingency than overt aggression by Russia or China constitutes an increasing ground of grievance. There is a natural human tendency to consider, or to hope, that alliance is more or less equivalent to friendship or a general promise of support. It has not proved so for America's allies. If President de Gaulle has been the first to draw the necessary conclusions and take an absolutely cold-blooded look at the profit-and-loss consequences for France of the American alliance, he will not be the last. And, since these alliances were in fact constructed by the United States to further the U.S. national interest, we cannot in reason object if the other partners measure them by the yardstick of their various national interests.

Such an appraisal shows that any nation linked to the United States by an alliance makes a very bad guess if it looks for assistance, or even general support, in any international situation not concerned with repelling a communist onslaught. (And outside the Far East no situation involving a communist onslaught has in fact arisen.) In the Suez crisis of 1956, Britain received no help, only equivocation from Secretary Dulles throughout a summer of negotiation; and when, in November, Britain, France, and Israel went to war in what could be argued to be an essentially defensive action for the maintenance of established treaty rights, the result was an unholy alliance of the United States and Russia browbeating Nasser's opponents into withdrawal to give him the prestige of a victory that he had not won. Portugal, a NATO ally, got little sympathy and no help in 1961 when India crudely invaded and annexed the ancient Portuguese territory of Goa; Portugal also will hear no protests from the United States about the fact that the unrest in her African colony of Angola is kept alive only by assistance from other areas of Africa. France received no assistance from the United States to maintain order in Algeria (though Algeria is included in the NATO guarantee). Most curious of all was the attitude of the United States to Sukarno's desire to incorporate Netherlands New Guinea in Indonesia. Despite the fact that he had no real claim to it, the United States not only did not assist the Netherlands but positively hampered its defense efforts by refusing to afford the transit facilities normally available at all times to aircraft of friendly powers. When—as is fully predictable—Sukarno's insatiable appetite leads him toward the acquisition of the Australian half of New Guinea, it will be interesting to see whether the ANZUS Pact of 1951, by which Australia substituted a basic reliance on America for her security in place of her previous reliance on Britain, can demonstrate its validity.

Non-European allies of the United States also find in disputes with non-European countries that they need not look for U.S. assistance, but are lucky indeed if U.S. neutrality is the worst they experience. Pakistan, a member of both CENTO and SEATO, has never been able to stir up any American support of her case against Indian occupation of Kashmir. Malaysia is learning in her fight for life against Sukarno just how myopic the United States can be about aggression committed by a nonwhite country, despite the fact that Malaysia is progressive, economically sound, and pro-Western (the only new nation to fight a war against communist guerrillas and win; moreover, for what it is worth, Malaysia is linked by alliance with the West).

In any of these cases, U.S. policy may have been wise, well calculated, and in the best long-term interests of the free world and general stability. But what is hardly open to debate is that such incidents do not make much of a case for the continuing validity of the U.S. alliance system. For, ultimately, membership in that system is not a condition of U.S. aid in the event of actual communist aggression. India has always spurned the whole system, and continues to do so; but aid to her when a border war with China broke out in 1962 was prompt and generous.

The "Third World": The Underdeveloped Nations

All this does not amount to saying that the American alliance system is dead. The periodic meetings of its councils continue to take place; the military staff committees make contingency plans; all the routines are continued. But to many of the world's statesmen and in the opinion of many commentators the system has not so much died as become irrelevant to the major developments of the present decade, and in particular to two of them. These two are polycentrism within the Soviet sphere, and the many new independent countries of Africa and Asia.

The latter is one of the most extraordinary developments in modern history and indeed may be regarded as marking the end of an era. It constitutes the termination of that period of European political domination of the world—domination that began some four-and-a-half centuries ago, in the period of the great explorations, and reached its culmination about the beginning of the twentieth century. At that point, virtually the whole world could be put either into the category of the European powers and their transplants overseas (e.g., the United States, Canada, and Australia) or into that of their dependencies: the vast colonial areas of Africa and the rimland of Asia, plus innumerable island possessions. The exceptions were not many: a few nonwhite states had managed to preserve their independence (Siam, Abyssinia); a few derelict non-European empires had been preserved, not so much by their own strength as by the jealousy of their potential partitioners (Turkey, Persia, China); and one unique case, Japan—a nonwhite state that had successfully adopted European techniques in government, economics, and war—turned itself into an imperial power.

With remarkable speed this set of political arrangements has utterly dissolved. Even before World War II, the more enlightened imperial powers were planning the eventual independence of their subject populations and were preparing them for it (the history of the British connection with India is the best example); but mostly this development is a matter of the postwar period, and even, indeed, of the past four or five years. A few former colonies gained their independence in the late 1940s (e.g., India, Pakistan, Ceylon, the Philippines, and Indonesia). In the late 1950s, the trickle of new independent states became a torrent.

This astonishing, huggermugger windup of the age of European imperialism deserves more explanation and study than it has yet had time to receive. In the late 1950s, why did the European colonial governments suddenly and almost unanimously (the exceptions were Spain and Portugal) decide that they must get rid of their colonies—to which they had hitherto granted independence only slowly, cautiously, and reluctantly? The most striking example of this change of policy was the Belgian Congo: there, the decision was made by Belgium in January 1960, only six months before it was put into effect.

No complete answer can be given now. But, clearly, the decision was not due to the strength of the independence movements or the military weakness of Europe. To say that the colonial areas "won" their independence is, in regard to most of them, a polite fiction. The strength of the European states in relation to that of their colonies was still overwhelming, had the will to exercise it been there. But, quite suddenly, the European colonial powers grew tired of responsibility, tired of being exposed to criticism in the United Nations, and decided to make an end of the situation. The basic reason seems to be that they perceived no advantage in retaining colonies. The history of Western Europe in the 1950s was one of great prosperity and unprecedented economic expansion, accelerated by the beginning of the Common Market (January 1958), but starting well before that. Yet this prosperity was increasing at a time when many colonies had already been given independence. Before this expansion, the theory that Europe's wealth and importance depended on its possession of extensive overseas colonies had been a generally held article of faith, subscribed to both by Marxists—perhaps one should say Leninists—and their most determined capitalist opponents. Suddenly, the theory was defeated by the most convincing of refutations—a pragmatic demonstration of its falsity in the real world; and it simply collapsed. The consequence was a hasty sloughing-off of colonial burdens with great speed, and, one might add, with an almost total disregard of all those responsibilities and not altogether imaginary reasons for caution and gradualness that until recent years had figured so prominently in the public statements of the colonial powers. Thus, the Belgian Congo collapsed into widespread bloodshed and near chaos; and the Algerian problem was "solved" by sacrificing the interests of one tenth of the population, the million European Algerians; similarly, the British government sacrificed the interests of white settlers in Kenya; and a Zanzibar known to be on the brink of revolution was given independence. Once independence for colonies was decided upon by the European powers, no other considerations were allowed to stand in its way.

This mass achievement of independence has entirely altered the world's political picture. In 1960, the high tide of the movement, seventeen new sovereign states emerged in Africa alone. Mainly because of this achievement of independent statehood by formerly dependent areas, the membership of the United Nations has risen from the 51 of 1945 to the 113 of the spring of 1964. More than forty of the members added since 1945 belong in the category of the "new nations" of the Afro-Asian bloc.[1]

The existence of these newly independent states poses great problems for Western, and particularly for American, policy-makers. The new states have a number of features common to most of them. They are poor, they are non-white, and they are inexperienced actors on the world scene who are anxious

[1] Difficulties of classification make it pointless to try to be more precise in numbers. Is Israel a "new nation"? Is Thailand? Though Jamaica and Trinidad are former colonies, one has serious doubts whether Sir Alexander Bustamente wishes to be regarded as a member of the Afro-Asian bloc. There are also, on this topic, difficulties of nomenclature. "New nations" is clear but often inaccurate. Old colonial boundaries, which are the boundaries of the new states, generally disregarded African realities, so that most new African states (e.g., the Congo, Nigeria) are not really nations. "Underdeveloped nations" is accurate for most of them, but clumsy. "Developing nations" is a euphemism: some, like Indonesia and Ceylon, are going backward in an economic sense. One admires the directness of Barbara Ward (Lady Jackson), who, in a book title, has simply called them "the poor nations." The French phrase *Le Tiers Monde* is gaining increasing acceptance in its English form, "The Third World."

to play an important part. They now exist, however, as independent entities and must be wooed, not coerced. A policy of mere indifference toward them is, for good or ill, not a possible option. The structure of the United Nations, in whose General Assembly each of them has one vote, gives them a political importance in any situation short of war out of all proportion to their power—which in most cases is very small indeed.

American policy toward the new states so far has not been strikingly successful, particularly in regard to nudging them in the direction of responsible external behavior. Too often, it seems that a kind of paralysis seizes Washington that inhibits its dealings with the actions, even when totally irresponsible, of a Nasser, a Sukarno, a Nehru. We even have a curious tendency, one suspects, *not* to favor those in the underdeveloped world who have been ready to stand up and be counted on our side—an Ayub Khan, an Abdul Rahman. This paralysis, of course, is self-induced and need not be a permanent feature of our foreign policy, which it hamstrings in many important situations. It is a feature of our foreign policy that is an irrelevant carry-over from domestic considerations. It reflects the uneasiness of Washington about the treatment of minorities in the United States, not a just and cool assessment of the outside world.

The Problems of This Decade and the Next

All of these three factors, which have fundamentally altered the world picture within the past ten years, have one thing in common: they demonstrate the continuing and almost unequaled power of nationalism in world politics. It is nationalism that has disrupted the communist bloc, nationalism that has led France and other states to question American leadership, nationalism that has brought about the end of colonial empires. This, too, is paradoxical; for only a few years ago it was assumed that nationalism was a diminishing force in human affairs, and, indeed, technological conditions make it highly inappropriate and awkward. These conditions call for political organization into larger areas and units; but, at present, technology and dominant political forces are at cross purposes. Even in Europe, where the drive for political integration was recently at its strongest, it has now been stalled if not actually reversed.

One of the most disquieting features of the contemporary world is the tendency of new states to exhibit many of the phenomena formerly characteristic of European nationalism: frontier conflicts, irredentist claims to territory that will be of no real advantage even if gained—many all-too-familiar themes from the past have their new versions in Africa and Asia today. Such episodes as the passionate Indian determination *not* to hold a plebiscite in Kashmir; the frontier disputes of Morocco and Algeria, of Ethiopia and Somalia, of Ghana and Togo; the more fundamental quarrel of Indonesia and Malaysia—all these, and others that might be mentioned, have a depressingly familiar sound. Precisely when Europe is apparently beginning to renounce such unprofitable follies, the new states embark with gusto on the same. For the present, such disputes will presumably not have important consequences—but the prospect of the possession of nuclear weapons and missiles by a large number of states is good ground for apprehension.

This latter point underscores the fact that ours continues to be an extraordinarily precarious era. No nuclear power has yet made a move toward the dismantling of any but the most obsolete parts of its armory. The great arsenals of missiles are still poised, still capable of destruction on a scale unprecedented even when measured against the vast horror of twentieth-century wars. Now, other nations clamor to join the "club." France's accession to substantial nuclear status may not add any major element of danger. But, if our response to de Gaulle's nuclear ambitions is one of mere irritation, we are bound to view China's aspirations in this field with profound anxiety.

On the other hand, it does not follow that despair is the only realistic reaction. A partial nuclear-test-ban treaty was, after all, achieved in July 1963. It was a very limited step indeed. Yet it was more than many students of world politics had predicted; and those who contend that it signifies little if anything might consider how much higher tensions would have been today if the negotiations had collapsed and if the U.S. and U.S.S.R. were still testing thermonuclear weapons in the atmosphere. Conceivably, the supreme tension of November 1962 taught both sides the inescapable lesson, so that we are less likely to go so close to the brink in the future. Moreover, it can be argued that the process of diffusion of power just described represents a healthy departure from monolithic-bloc confrontations. That there is greater confusion in the world today than there was ten years ago is discouraging to those who are comfortable only with sharply defined issues, but it may mean a better prospect for survival.

These various arguments support either deep uneasiness or careful optimism. But these are general attitudes that must be tested in specific contexts. This book provides eleven such contexts—countries, areas, and problems—in which tension exists in varying degrees. The reader must determine for himself, in each case, how grave are the problems created by these tensions for U.S. policy and for mankind in the ever more complicated world of the 1960s.

part one

Europe

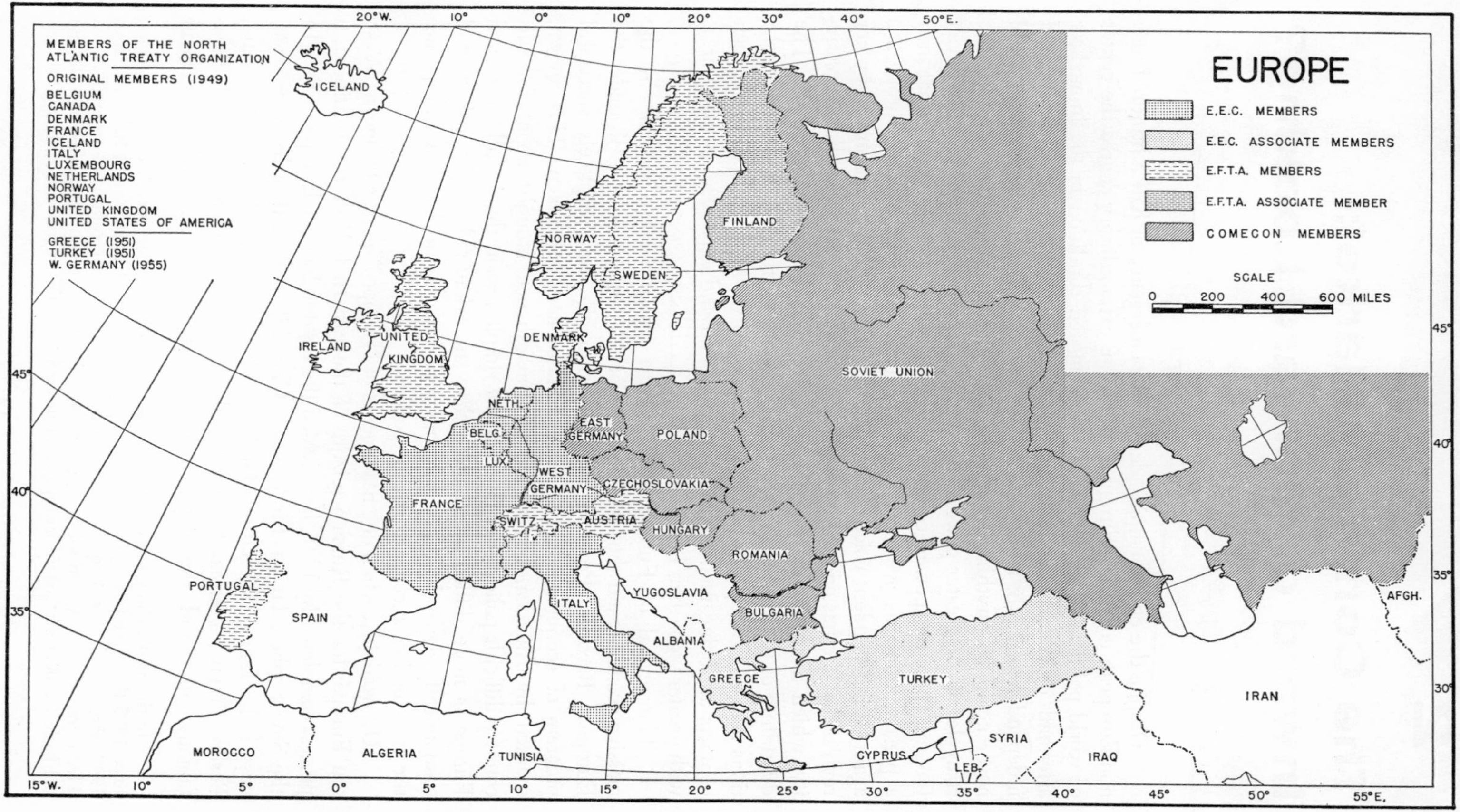
EUROPE
E.E.C. MEMBERS
E.E.C. ASSOCIATE MEMBERS
E.F.T.A. MEMBERS
E.F.T.A. ASSOCIATE MEMBER
COMECON MEMBERS
SCALE
0 200 400 600 MILES
MEMBERS OF THE NORTH ATLANTIC TREATY ORGANIZATION
ORIGINAL MEMBERS (1949)
BELGIUM
CANADA
DENMARK
FRANCE
ICELAND
ITALY
LUXEMBOURG
NETHERLANDS
NORWAY
PORTUGAL
UNITED KINGDOM
UNITED STATES OF AMERICA
GREECE (1951)
TURKEY (1951)
W. GERMANY (1955)
ICELAND
NORWAY
SWEDEN
FINLAND
DENMARK
IRELAND
UNITED KINGDOM
NETH.
BELG.
LUX.
EAST GERMANY
POLAND
WEST GERMANY
CZECHOSLOVAKIA
FRANCE
SWITZ.
AUSTRIA
HUNGARY
ROMANIA
SOVIET UNION
PORTUGAL
SPAIN
ITALY
YUGOSLAVIA
BULGARIA
ALBANIA
GREECE
TURKEY
IRAN
AFGH.
SYRIA
LEB.
IRAQ
CYPRUS
MOROCCO
ALGERIA
TUNISIA
20° W.
10°
0°
10°
20°
30°
40°
50° E.
15° W.
10°
5°
0°
5°
10°
15°
20°
25°
30°
35°
40°
45°
50°
55° E.
45°
40°
35°
30°

2

The Common Market: Inward or Outward Looking?

Despite the end of empire, despite the emergence of half a hundred new non-European countries, Europe is still to an extraordinary degree the center of world politics. From a chaotic and exhausted condition in the immediate aftermath of World War II, it has risen again to prominence, prosperity, and independence. Little more than a decade ago, it seemed that Europe could never again be anything more than a theater in which were decided the struggles of the greater powers on its wings, the United States and the Soviet Union. These two powers could now agree gloomily at least on this: that such a presumption was overhasty and has been falsified by events. Europe has again an independent voice. More than that, Europe has demonstrated by her revival that she has enormous resources in economic skill and political creativity, which the other parts of the world need and cannot do without. The dwindling of the European empires has not meant the end of economic relations between Europe and the underdeveloped world. On the contrary, such contacts are being maintained or reestablished and expanded in many areas with greater vigor than in the heyday of imperialism.

The revival of Europe was in large measure made possible by the massive economic aid that the United States has given since 1948 under the European Recovery Program, the one genuinely and completely successful program of economic aid the United States has undertaken. This revival, sparked by America, has as a later consequence brought about for this country difficult policy questions, for the simple reason that a fully recovered Europe is more difficult to handle than an exhausted, impoverished, and economically dependent Europe. America's present problems in Europe are the fruit of her successful earlier policies.

Unavoidably, when one now speaks of "Europe," he usually means Western Europe; for the Russian seizure of the eastern half of the continent, a process completed by 1948, has divided the historic body of Europe in two. In the Soviet sphere lay (as Sir Winston Churchill said, with a historian's sadness, in his famous speech of March 5, 1946, at Fulton, Missouri) "Warsaw, Berlin, Prague, Vienna, Budapest, Belgrade, Bucharest and Sofia, all these famous cities and the populations around them. . . ."[1] The movement

[1] In this melancholy roll call Vienna and Belgrade no longer stand, the former being since 1955 the capital of an independent though neutralized Austria, and Belgrade, since 1948, the capital of a Yugoslavia that is communist but not controlled from Moscow. The degree of Moscow control in all cases is less, but not so much diminished as to restore the basic freedom of Eastern Europe or to make Churchill's regret out of date.

toward European integration, in its various manifestations, is limited to Western Europe. But Eastern Europe, though it enjoys no such prosperity as Western Europe, has also had some degree of revival; and the success of the Eastern European countries in winning a measure of freedom from Russian control is an indication of the continuing vitality of the historic nations of Europe.

Western Europe has experienced since the early 1950s an extraordinary and unprecedented economic boom that has raised the general standard of living and introduced into everyday life many goods formerly regarded as luxuries. This boom has been associated with the creation of new international organizations that have brought about a new degree of international economic integration. It is hard to say whether or not the great economic expansion was caused by the new organizations; in all probability, they accelerated an economic expansion that would have occurred in any event.

Of these new organizations the most important—the very symbol of the new Europe—is the European Economic Community (EEC), also known as the Common Market. Its prototype was the European Coal and Steel Community (ECSC), which came into being on August 10, 1952, following a treaty signed on April 18, 1951. The ECSC linked France, Western Germany, Italy, Belgium, the Netherlands, and Luxembourg in an international organization with strong central institutions to create a common market for coal and steel products. The six states greatly broadened the area of their functional cooperation when on March 25, 1957, they signed the Treaty of Rome to create two other communities on the model of ECSC: the European Atomic Energy Community (which for a number of reasons has not so far proved very important) and the European Economic Community. The Treaty of Rome went into effect on January 1, 1958.

EEC has proved a phenomenal success. Internal tariffs on goods among the member states have been cut by 50 per cent, and both their external trade and their internal productivity have expanded greatly. The gross product of the community as a whole expanded 30 per cent in the six years between January 1958 and January 1964; the comparable figure for the United States over the same period was 22 per cent, and for the United Kingdom 16 per cent. The founders of the three communities had always been explicit that economic integration was intended to lead to political integration, and in the first years of EEC it seemed that advances along this road, too, might well prove fast—in which case the founding of EEC would, indeed, prove a historic landmark for Europe. Latterly, however, the attitude of de Gaulle, who is skeptical about any political constructs above the level of the national state, has thrown grave doubt on the likelihood of any moves in this direction during his lifetime (or, more precisely, during his tenure of power; but the two seem likely to be coterminous).

The success of EEC has proved to have an attractive power for the other states of Western Europe. The most important convert was Britain. British policy had badly misjudged the chances for success of the European integration movement. It had failed to assume the leadership of the movement in the late 1940s (when British leadership would have been most gratefully received); it had failed to join the Coal and Steel Community when afforded the opportunity in 1950; and it had failed in 1955–57 to take up an invitation to join the negotiations that eventuated in the Common Market. Throughout 1958, Britain pushed in vain the idea of an outer ring of European states, linked with the Common Market but not accepting all its conditions, specifically the common external tariff. French hostility defeated the plan, seeing in it an attempt to have the best of both worlds—which essentially it was. Britain then improvised the European Free Trade Association (EFTA), or "Outer Seven," linking the United Kingdom with Austria, Denmark, Norway, Portugal, Sweden, and Switzerland, a less binding economic association whose object is the elimination of customs duties and other obstacles to trade between the members. EFTA came into being on May 3, 1960, and Finland joined as an associate member on March 27, 1961. EFTA has kept its tariff reductions in step with those of EEC to facilitate eventual union of the two groups. Within its limits, EFTA has been successful; but the United Kingdom's partners are too small in economic importance to form any substitute for EEC.

On July 31, 1961, Harold Macmillan, then Prime Minister of the United Kingdom, announced his government's intention to seek full membership in EEC. This decision took great political courage, and its rightness has been the subject of prolonged debate. The existence of EEC has indeed evoked an amusing number of international paradoxes and historical ironies. For Russia, EEC constitutes a most unwelcome demonstration of the continuing vitality of capitalism, and Russia has attempted (belatedly and unsuccessfully) to imitate it in Eastern Europe by trying to breathe some life into COMECON, the Common Market's East European counterpart. Britain, which for a decade had viewed with ill-judged skepticism the movement toward European integration, found herself, in the end, a humble petitioner for membership in EEC. Within British politics, the ironies were even more pronounced. The decision to seek membership, even at some sacrifice of Commonwealth trade patterns, was made by a Conservative government, the party *par excellence* of patriotism, of Empire, of Commonwealth. The decision was strongly opposed by Hugh Gaitskell (1906–1963), then leader of the Labour Party, a party that combines the theoretical internationalism typical of the Left with a strong suspicion of foreigners in concrete matters. As his selection in this chapter demonstrates, his speech against British membership in the Common Market (given at the Labour Party Conference of October 1962) used a patriotic imagery whose more normal home would have been a conference of Tories: "We, at least, do not intend to forget Vimy Ridge and Gallipoli."

Gaitskell's eloquent speech is notable because the case against British participation in the Common Market is less familiar on this side of the Atlantic. It is worthwhile, however, to consider the reasons that impelled Macmillan and his cabinet to make what must have been an agonizing decision, amounting as it did to a wholesale reversal of historic attitudes, not only for the party but for the country as well. Essentially, it was due to a sense that the large-scale economic arena opened up by the Common Market offered an opportunity and a stimulus that the British economy, which has notoriously lagged behind that of other states of Western Europe in the postwar period, badly needed.

Macmillan justified his decision in a pamphlet[2] published in October 1962, which, for an official document, contained a good deal of plain speaking. He acknowledged that the government had "taken what is perhaps the most fateful and forward-looking policy decision in our peacetime history. . . . an unprecedented departure from the past." He argued that British membership in the European Community would be "a source of new strength, not only to this country, but to the Commonwealth as a whole." It was "a complete misreading of the situation" to regard it as "a choice between the Commonwealth and Europe"; for "We are dealing with two entirely different types of organization."

Macmillan indicated that although the sterling area provided an economic link in most cases, "the Commonwealth is not a single economic unit. Nor, to be honest, is there any practical possibility of making it one." The clear trend of his argument, moreover, was that there was less and less chance of making it one.

> Conditions in the Commonwealth have greatly changed since the Ottawa Agreements were signed some thirty years ago. . . . Just as one example, before the last war we in Britain took five times as much wool from Australia as Japan did, but today Japan takes twice as much as we do. . . . As a result of all these changes, although total Commonwealth trade has greatly increased, the proportion of total Commonwealth trade done with other Commonwealth countries has fallen. . . . We have to consider the state of the world as it is today and will be tomorrow, and not in outdated terms of a vanished past.

Britain was rediscovering that she was inescapably European:

> We in Britain are Europeans. That has always been true, but it has now become a reality which we cannot ignore. In the past, as a great maritime Empire, we might give way to insular feelings of superiority over foreign breeds and suspicion of our neighbours across the Channel. . . . if we had not turned away from Europe in the Imperial heyday of the late 19th and early 20th centuries, it is even possible that the slaughter of two world wars might have been avoided. Are we now to isolate ourselves from Europe, at a time when our own strength is no longer self-sufficient and when the leading European countries are joining together to build a future of peace and progress . . .?

[2] *Britain, the Commonwealth and Europe* (London: Conservative and Unionist Central Office, 1962).

On Commonwealth trade, he frankly said, "Our entry into the Common Market would mean an end to the present system of free entry and preferential treatment for imports from the Commonwealth." But an increasing proportion of Commonwealth trade was now with countries outside the Commonwealth. There was a necessity to move toward new, worldwide agreements on trade.

> There are people who fear that the Commonwealth will never be the same again, if Britain goes into Europe. But it is not the same today as it was ten or even five years ago. It is a continuously developing organism. The essential long-term interests of Britain, Europe and the Commonwealth are inseparably linked. . . . We are faced with a tremendous issue. This is no time to bury our heads in the sands of the past and take the kind of parochial view which regards Europe with distrust and suspicion. . . . We want to see Britain taking the lead in building a new future and working towards that unity of the world which is the ultimate vision of mankind. The European Community is a signpost to that future and we must play our part.

The negotiations regarding the British application for membership in EEC occupied eighteen months. They were terminated by the decision of French President de Gaulle in January 1963. The outcome did not depend on the difficulty of the negotiations, which were in fact nearing a successful conclusion. It was a political decision. De Gaulle's view of Britain's relation to Europe is stated in the selection from his famous press conference vetoing British membership.

In a larger sense, however, the debate over British membership is suspended, not concluded. The other five members of the Six cannot override the French veto, but all wish to see Britain a member. The excellent reception given Mr. Edward R. G. Heath's speech before the Council of Europe on May 7, 1963, reflects the attitude of all the Western European states except France. His remarks, excerpted here, recommend an expanding EEC in contrast with the restrictive concepts of de Gaulle. In order to maintain contacts and harmonize economic policies as far as possible, France's EEC partners have been able to insist on periodic meetings within the framework of Western European Union—a body created in 1955 to ease Germany's accession to NATO, and which includes the Six plus Britain.

Whether or not de Gaulle's policy is well judged, at least two of his generalizations are undoubtedly correct. First, the Six of EEC have more in common than other European countries, and they have a sound basis for unification. They are, in a sense, the core of Europe. They constitute almost exactly the area that in the ninth century comprised the empire of Charlemagne. Second, the question is not really, or exclusively, the question of British membership. The British application was followed by a rush of applications from other EFTA members and from Ireland. British membership would bring in its train perhaps half a dozen other new members and demand rethinking of EEC policies in an expanding economic context.

President de Gaulle seems to view with extreme distaste the prospect of economic unity of the Atlantic world. Others find repugnant the alternative that de Gaulle appears to favor: the prospect of a European Economic Community increasingly turning in upon itself and developing intra-Community trade at the expense of outside competition. The hope of moving world trade in an expansionist rather than a restrictivist direction rests chiefly on the trade negotiations known as the "Kennedy Round," which began in May 1964. Despite the flexibility in negotiation enjoyed by the U.S. under the Trade Expansion Act of 1962, the "Kennedy Round" will be difficult and may take years to conclude.

EEC's greatest problem is agriculture. The hard-won agreements of January 1962 on agricultural policy were only an outline. Fundamentally, France, alone among the Six, enjoys a sizable export surplus of agricultural produce. For France, the price of allowing German industry to compete freely in the French market is to allow French agriculture free access to the German market. However, German farmers (like some others) exert an influence over their government out of proportion to their numbers, and the German government is forced to fight a slow, rearguard action on this basic point. It is important to notice that France is insisting on the development of EEC according to its basic program, while Germany is dragging her feet.

For a number of reasons, discussed in the readings that follow, and particularly in the survey by Philip H. Trezise, the path from the present stage of development to an ultimate Atlantic Community, freely trading and politically cooperating, will not be an easy one; it seems to be much more difficult than expected, say, two years ago. Every project of unification has both an inward and an outward face. Increasing unity within may be accompanied by new defenses against the rest of the world. For this reason, as Henry S. Reuss suggests in his article, with its novel viewpoint, our uncritical welcoming of increasing integration within EEC may have been overhasty. Even an Atlantic Community with institutions that implement its existing cultural unity will not necessarily be advantageous to the world as a whole unless it steers clear of being a cartel of industrialized nations for the purpose of bargaining with the underdeveloped. The most hopeful sign is that these dangers are at least being recognized.

The Interest of the United States in the European Economic Community*

Philip H. Trezise

First, I propose . . . to suggest the perspective in which the Common Market needs to be viewed. Second, I will take up the considerations that operate to pull ourselves and the Common Market countries together. Finally, I will discuss in some detail the issues that are currently giving us difficulty with the Common Market.

As to the matter of perspective, it is just as easy to expect too much from the European Common Market as it is to expect and ask for too little. We are going to need a measure of restraint and wisdom in dealing with what is, after all, a brand-new development in world affairs.

We should remember that ever since the fall of imperial Rome—that is, for a period of about 16 centuries—Western Europe has been broken up into rival national states. In this small piece of land, where physical barriers between regions are much less forbidding than in our own country and where people share a common culture and background, there developed over the years the most appalling and sanguinary differences of policy and interest between neighboring countries. Our histories are full of accounts of the military struggles that took place in Western Europe. Even our legends find their inspiration mainly in Europe's endless series of wars.

Until only a few years ago, efforts to unify Western Europe were confined almost entirely to adventures in military conquest. It is helpful to recall that only three of the conquerors—Charles the Great, Napoleon, and Hitler—even came close to success. Their failures were attributable to the strength of national feelings in Europe.

Now, after a millennium and a half of separatism, Western Europe has taken the first steps to accomplish what the military conquerors could not do. We must look at the Common Market against this kind of background.

In the United States we are given to comparing the development of the Common Market with the creation of the federal union of the United States under the Constitution in 1787. This is a natural comparison, and there are in fact certain likenesses. But the differences between these two situations are

* Address made at Atlantic City, N.J., on June 3, 1963, published in *Department of State Bulletin,* June 23, 1963, pp. 971–976. Mr. Trezise is Deputy Assistant Secretary of State for Economic Affairs.

very great. These differences help us to understand the character of recent European events.

The 13 States of our original confederation had just completed a successful revolutionary war against a common enemy. There were almost no significant differences of language or historical experience among them. Sectional interests had not yet become deeply established. The period during which each of our States had acted as sovereign republics had been so short and so unsatisfactory that very few people had any compelling reason to wish to continue a system of separate economic and political units on this continent. On the contrary, the political and intellectual leaders of that time were acutely aware that we could have neither prosperity nor security without federation and unity.

By contrast, the six countries which form the nucleus of a united Europe have been divided in countless ways. They have behind them individual national histories and a tradition of devastating national rivalries. The two principal members, France and Germany, were bitter enemies for almost a century. Instead of having just emerged from a war against a common enemy, the Six had been engaged in a savage war with one another only a short time ago. In each of the six countries, businessmen and farmers had long been accustomed to separate national economic systems. Within the Six, Belgium, Holland, and Luxembourg were low-tariff, free-trading countries. West Germany, and particularly France and Italy, were in one way or another high-tariff and protectionist. In terms of living standards there were wide disparities as between, say, southern Italy at one extreme and Holland at the other. When the Common Market began to be talked about, many people in Europe could reasonably have expected to lose, or at least to be exposed to unwelcome competition, if their countries proceeded to merge their economies with the other European states.

In these circumstances it was not in prospect that union in Western Europe was going to be accomplished in one single stroke, as was done in Philadelphia in 1787. Unlike our Constitution, the Treaty of Rome did not create a sovereign nation of its signatories. At the most, it set in motion a process of unification. That process has already gone some distance. As we see, however, it is subject to interruption and delay. National interests have not by any means been generally subordinated to the common interest.

It would be unreasonable, realistically speaking, to expect that they would have been. At this point, however, the continued existence of the Common Market is not in doubt. The progress toward unification obviously is not going to be as fast as seemed possible only a few months ago. Equally, the durability of the existing structure is not in serious question.

The movement toward unity in Europe has had consistent and powerful support from the United States. General Marshall's historic speech at Harvard in 1947 made it clear that we believed that European recovery would have to be organized as a common effort. In the Congress there was strong pressure throughout the years of the Marshall Plan for European integration.

It is fair to say that at every point in time the attitude of the administration in power in Washington has been one of benevolence and encouragement toward the drive for unification in Europe.

Our interest in European unity has been impelled by motives of self-interest, but self-interest in the most enlightened sense. Originally it seemed to us that Europe could not overcome the economic and political consequences of World War II unless national barriers were reduced and national differences moderated. The threat to European freedom from the East obviously could not have been resisted by individual countries standing alone. We were concerned that the longstanding enmity between France and Germany should not reappear and become the source of another intra-European struggle that might set the world on fire.

These were and are sound reasons for promoting the integration of Western Europe. As time has passed, moreover, we have come to see that we have other interests which engage us closely with Europe, interests that can be prosecuted more effectively in partnership with a united Europe than in relationship with a series of individual national states.

One of these lies in the problem of dealing with the poor countries of the world, the so-called less developed areas. Possibly the most complex and difficult task that the world now faces is that of achieving a satisfactory level of economic and political progress in Africa, Asia, and Latin America over the next two or three decades. This is something we cannot back away from, for it bears directly on the question of peace and war. At the same time, its magnitude and its sheer complexity are such that nobody at this point can know how and when a measure of success can be attained.

Almost the entire burden of financial aid for the less developed countries inescapably falls on the countries of North America, Western Europe, and Japan. These same areas must provide the largest part of the market for an expanding volume of exports from the less developed countries. It is a real question whether the richer countries can find the political genius to assure that aid and trade will be forthcoming in sufficiently generous measure to give the less developed countries a chance for satisfactory economic progress. A strong and prosperous Europe can make an immense contribution in these respects. We need Europe as a partner in this enterprise; Europe in turn needs us.

A second field of increasingly mutual interest is that of financial and monetary affairs. The Common Market countries together have monetary reserves of about the same magnitude as our own. At the present time Europe is in a very strong balance-of-payments position, while we are not. Our balance-of-payments deficit, in fact, finds its reflection mainly in the large European surplus. Flows of capital from the United States to Western Europe have been large. Counterflows have been, comparatively, small.

These relative financial positions could be changed very rapidly. It was not very long ago that the overriding problem was the shortage of dollars in

Europe. And, although a new dollar gap appears remote enough, a net European deficit could certainly reappear within a few years.

The central point, in any case, is that we both stand in need of an international monetary system which will enable countries to handle temporary deficits without imposing undue limitations on trade or on internal economic growth. We have made some progress in this direction in the form of the new $6 billion borrowing arrangement within the International Monetary Fund. It ought not to be beyond the wit of man to move from there to further measures for international financial cooperation among the chief monetary and trading nations, which is to say the United States, the United Kingdom, Western Europe, and Japan. Here again, the Common Market, when and as it reaches its goal of a common monetary policy, can be a more effective partner than can six key European nations operating individually.

As we have known all along, the Common Market offers a potential trading partner of great consequence. Even now the Common Market comprises the largest single element in world trading. Last year, when our imports and exports taken together amounted to about $35 billion, the Common Market total was in excess of $40 billion.

Potentially this new trading unit could be an exceedingly expansive one. Incomes in Europe have been rising very rapidly as a result of high rates of economic growth. The possibilities for a new pattern of consumption are obviously very great. For example, the United States has four times as many radios, five times as many automobiles, seven times as many TV sets, four and a half times as many refrigerators and washing machines as Europe. In some things, such as telephones installed, Western Europe is where we were in 1912.

There is already under way a great expansion of consumer demand in Europe. This takes the form of demand for consumer durables and for variety and upgrading in food (packaged and precooked foods) and clothing. Somebody is going to have to produce these things, as well as the machinery and raw materials that are needed for them.

It is most important, therefore, that the Common Market should be an outward-looking, liberal trading community. If it were to elect to live behind a high tariff wall, the result would be to encourage European producers to take over the new areas of demand, even though outsiders could provide many of these things more cheaply and efficiently.

Already progress toward a common tariff is affecting other countries. Take electric computers: The French duty on German computers has been cut to 10 percent from an original 20 percent. On American computers, thanks to our negotiations in 1961, it is down to 17.3 percent. Eventually, if nothing is done about it, the external tariff will be 14 percent against everybody, while there will be no internal duty. In short, the producers within the Common Market will enjoy an advantage of $14 per $100 of product to add on to lower transportation costs and other advantages. In some lines a tariff differential of this kind can be prohibitive. In all cases it will hurt the exports of outside producers.

Our concerns on this score go beyond our own exports. A commercially restrictive, inward-looking Europe would have a disastrous impact on the attitudes of Latin America, Japan, the British Commonwealth, and many others. The inevitable tendency among these areas would be to set up rival trading blocs. This is not the way to make the free world richer. Nor is it the road to political well-being and cooperation.

As you all know from the newspapers, our chief present problems with the Common Market are precisely in the field of trade. There are three matters on which we have had differences of more or less serious proportions.

One is agriculture. We need to be clear that everybody is a sinner in agricultural trade. No country in the world has shown any disposition to allow market forces to work on agriculture. We all have some form or another of special supports and subsidies for agricultural producers, and we all in turn have devices for insulating the domestic producer from import competition. We are not the worst offender in these respects, although we have not on the whole provided a shining example either. Now, however, we have undertaken to try to check and, if possible, to reverse the whole postwar trend toward restrictionism in agriculture. We have served notice on Western Europe and on our other trading partners that another round of tariff negotiations is going to require that agricultural trade be an integral part of the process.

This is a matter of no small direct consequence to our own producers. We have been selling more than a billion dollars of agricultural goods to the Common Market countries, almost a quarter of our total agricultural exports. A third or more of these exports could be endangered immediately or over the longer run by Common Market agricultural policies. It is our interest, of course, to hold this market if we can. It is the European interest, one might add, that the cost of its basic foods should not be unnecessarily high, and this in turn depends on reasonable freedom for efficient producers to sell in Europe.

Apart from our own direct and commercial interest, it has become increasingly apparent that a world trading system which has one set of rules for industrial products and a radically different set for agricultural products is not a tolerable or tenable one for the agricultural exporters. Countries which depend heavily on agricultural exports for their foreign exchange earnings—and these include most of the less developed countries as well as Australia, New Zealand, and Canada—have become more and more vocal in their complaints about the way in which the system operates. Even if our own trading interests were not so directly engaged, it would be the part of leadership for us to seek to remedy this state of affairs. For our larger concern must always be with the construction and expansion of an orderly and efficient international trading system as an indispensable part of the structure of a peaceful and prosperous world.

At Geneva a few days ago we managed to move ahead in respect to agriculture. The Common Market negotiators agreed that agriculture would be a part of the next round of trade negotiations. We shall be starting this month to examine in more detail the possibilities for general understandings on trade in cereals and meats. These are going to be very difficult discussions and negotiations. It would be exceedingly rash to predict their outcome. All that can be said so far is that we have made a beginning.

Another difference between ourselves and the Common Market had to do with trade with the less developed countries. At Geneva we considered a proposal for substantial and rapid reductions in barriers to trade in primary products and agricultural commodities from the less developed countries. This proposal included the suggestion that high consumption taxes imposed on such commodities as coffee and tea also be reduced or eliminated. On our part, we took the position that special tariff and trade preferences to some less developed countries should be phased out. We all agreed that we should not ask the poorer countries to provide full reciprocity in tariff reductions.

The outcome of our discussions on these matters was, frankly, not entirely satisfactory. The Common Market countries, for reasons which we can understand even if we do not agree with them, are disposed to go much more slowly than we think is necessary. The whole subject has been set aside for further study and discussion at the technical level in Geneva. It is evident that the supporters of our position have their work cut out for them in moving the matter ahead. But we must persevere, for this is an issue of abiding significance.

The third of our differences with Western Europe had to do with the basic character of the next tariff negotiation. In simplest terms, we took the position that it was in everybody's interest for us to be able to use the tariff negotiating authority contained in the Trade Expansion Act of 1962, that is, to cut tariffs generally by up to 50 percent. This, as a practical matter, implied that tariff reductions would be linear or across the board.

The initial reply of the Common Market was to the effect that the main problem lay in the wide range of our tariff levels. It is the case, of course, that we have a good many more duties above 30 percent, say, than does the Common Market, where tariffs have been averaged as a part of the movement toward a common commercial policy. The Common Market's counterproposal to our suggestion of a general linear cut was that tariffs should be harmonized. By harmonization it was meant that we would establish common tariff levels toward which all trading nations would move by degrees. On industrial products, for example, the suggested goal was a 10-percent level. Everybody would be asked to cut tariffs in excess of 10 percent by one-half, as a kind of first installment toward the eventual goal.

The European counterproposal had two fatal disabilities from our point of view. For one, it could not be reconciled with the plain intent of Congress in passing the Trade Expansion Act, since we would thereby have been required to cut more deeply than the Common Market on most items but would not be entitled to credit for our rates that already were below 10 percent. For another, it would have resulted in very modest reductions in trade barriers, in the order of a 10-percent or 12-percent tariff cut rather than something up to 50 percent.

As you know, our differences were negotiated out after some very strenuous bargaining. We have an understanding in principle on our linear approach, with provision for special rules to take account of trade distortions that might be caused by very wide tariff differences. Here, too, we have a difficult technical job to do in translating this generalized agreement into detailed negotiating rules. Once again, however, we have passed the first and perhaps the chief obstacle.

Coming back to my earlier comments, it is clear that our relations with the Common Market are not going to be free of differences any more than will be the case in our relations with other parts of the free world. We are impelled by reasons of interest, including domestic political interest, in certain directions. It is necessary to recognize that Europe is similarly impelled, and sometimes in directions different from those that we consider binding. There is no reason to expect that this state of affairs will be radically changed in the years ahead.

On the other hand, there are the strongest kinds of pressures operating to make both ourselves and the Europeans find bases for resolving our differences. Together with the United Kingdom and a few other countries, we make up the bulk of the free world's economic power. Working in reasonable harmony, we are able to command and deploy most of the resources—whether you look at them from the point of view of total output, monetary reserves, or trading potential—of the world. If we can operate in cooperation, many of our domestic problems can be managed more easily.

More than that, of course, is the omnipresent threat of the Soviet Union and the Communist bloc. The truth is that our cherished institutions, which we have in common, are mutually endangered by Soviet ambitions. We have had to find means for military collaboration against Communist expansionism. It is just as much in our common interest that we use our combined economic capacities to strengthen the economic base on which, in the end, our survival as free peoples depends.

It Means the End of Britain as an Independent European State*

Hugh Gaitskell

I will quote the conclusion of Sir Donald McDougall, the Deputy Director of the N.E.D.C. . . . "There is no really compelling economic argument for Britain's joining unless it is thought that, without being exposed to the blast of competition from the Continent, she will never put her house in order." . . .

Britain's entry into a Customs Union—such as the Economic Community of Europe—has a double effect. The barriers go down between us and the six countries of Europe. But they go up between us and the Commonwealth. We shall find it easier to sell in the markets of the six, because we shall no longer be faced with tariffs against our goods. How much are they now? Ten to fifteen per cent. But we shall be at a disadvantage in the rest of Europe compared with our position today, because in the European Free Trade Area we now have a tariff advantage over and against the six countries, which we shall lose if we go in. And since it would be rash to assume that the advantages which the Commonwealth countries give us in their markets will be retained by us when we deprive them of the advantages they at present have in ours, we shall also lose in Commonwealth markets for the same reason.

What does all this amount to? In 1961, 16.7 per cent of our exports went to the Common Market countries; 13.1 per cent—not so very far off it—to the rest of Western Europe—the E.F.T.A. countries, and 43 per cent went to the countries of the Commonwealth Preference System. We would gain in markets where we sell less than one-fifth of our exports and lose in markets where we sell about half our exports. . . .

Of course, these are not the only arguments in the economic field. There is the question of the size of the market. Is it not tremendous to have a home market of 220 million people? Will not this make it possible for our firms to expand and to reduce costs, and so become much more efficient? There is something in this argument. I do not deny it for a moment, but in my view it is considerably exaggerated. The idea of the world being divided up in this way so that, as it were, you only sell in a market where there are no tariffs and

* From *Britain and the Common Market.* Text of speeches made at the 1962 Annual Conference of the British Labour Party, October 3, 1962 (London: Labour Party, 1962), pp. 3–23. The late Rt. Hon. Hugh Gaitskell, M.P., was leader of the British Labour Party from 1955 until his death in 1963.

never sell anything anywhere else is, of course, rubbish. We sell to the world, not just to Europe. . . .

And if we are to take firms, I do not think you can judge their efficiency simply by the size of the country to which they belong. Some of the most efficient firms in the world are from small countries, from Switzerland, Holland and Sweden, with no large home market at all. . . .

The emphasis on "dynamic Europe" has played a large part in this controversy. It is an attractive idea. If indeed it could be shown that the establishment of the Common Market had produced the remarkable industrial expansion in Europe in recent years this would be a most compelling reason. But this cannot be shown. Nor is it true. As a matter of fact, the rate of expansion in Europe, however you measure it—by industry, by exports, by gross national product—was faster in the five years 1950–55 than it was in the five years that followed. Indeed one can hardly say that as yet the Common Market, which is only in its early stages, has had any effect. The truth is that the reasons for European expansion are different. I will not bother you with them. I can assure you, however, that it is not mainly because of the Common Market that Europe has had this remarkable growth recently. . . .

We must be clear about this: it does mean . . . the end of Britain as an independent European state. I make no apology for repeating it. It means the end of a thousand years of history. You may say "Let it end" but, my goodness, it is a decision that needs a little care and thought. And it does mean the end of the Commonwealth. How can one really seriously suppose that if the mother country, the centre of the Commonwealth, is a province of Europe (which is what federation means) it could continue to exist as the mother country of a series of independent nations? It is sheer nonsense.

I referred to the Liberals. Of course, the Tories have been indulging in their usual double talk. When they go to Brussels they show the greatest enthusiasm for political union. When they speak in the House of Commons they are most anxious to aver that there is no commitment whatever to any political union. I do not often sympathise with Dr. Adenauer, but I am bound to say in the recent exchanges with Mr. Macmillan I was all for him.

But let me come back to what Britain's role should be. To start with, do not let us confuse the question of whether we think it is good or bad for the Europeans to get together in Western Europe and form their federation with the question whether we should be in it. The first question is their affair and it may well be the answer to their problem. It is not necessarily the answer to ours. For we are not just a part of Europe—at least not yet. We have a different history. We have ties and links which run across the whole world, and for me at least the Commonwealth, the modern Commonwealth, which owes its creation fundamentally to those vital historic decisions of the Labour Government, is something I want to cherish.

It comes to this, does it not? If we can associate ourselves with Europe, with the other states in Western Europe, in a larger community with our links with the Commonwealth fully maintained, if by so doing we can achieve that influence upon European development which has so often been urged upon us and which I fully accept as very desirable, this would be a fine ideal: it would be the building of a bridge between the Commonwealth and Europe. But you cannot do that if at the beginning you sell the Commonwealth down the river. . . .

Fourth, there is foreign policy, the right to maintain as at present our own independent foreign policy. I have discussed this already and I will state simply what I think should be said and made clear. That is this. We need to lay down, if we go into the Common Market, that there is no commitment whatsoever by going in which involves any political institutional change of any kind. The right of veto in this matter is imperative and must be maintained. We must be free to decide whether or not we want any further political development. And I think we should say a little more, in all honesty, than perhaps the Government are inclined to say. I do not believe the British people now, at this stage, are prepared to accept a supranational system, majority decisions being taken against them, either in a Council of Ministers or a Federal Parliament, on the vital issues of foreign policy. . . .

I am the last person in the world to belittle what we might call the old Commonwealth. When people say, "What did we get out of New Zealand; what did we get out of Australia; what did we get out of Canada?" I remember that they came to our aid at once in two World Wars. We, at least, do not intend to forget Vimy Ridge and Gallipoli; we, at least, do not intend to forget the help they gave us after this last war. Harold Wilson will remember the loans from Canada, the willingness of New Zealand and Australia to accept very low food prices to help us out year by year.

Then we have the new Commonwealth. Why, what a comment it is that some people should be ready, no sooner is it created, to cast it aside! It means something to us and to the world. Where would our influence be in the world without the Commonwealth? It would be very much less. And I believe with all my heart that the existence of this remarkable multi-racial association, of independent nations, stretching across five continents, covering every race, is something that is potentially of immense value to the world. It does matter that we have these special relations with India and with Pakistan, with the African states as well as with Canada, Australia and New Zealand; for together we can, I believe, make a great contribution to the ending of the cold war. . . .

It is said, of course, that the young are in favour of [the Common Market]. The young are idealists; they want change; we know that. We welcome it, and I have no desire to belittle this. But if I were a little younger today, and if I were looking around for a cause, I do not think I should be quite so certain that I would find it within the movement for greater unity in Europe. I think I would find it outside in the world at large. I would rather work for the Freedom from Hunger campaign; I would rather work for War on Want. I would rather do something to solve world problems. And if we look for examples here, we can find them, as a matter of fact, in the United States.

Sometimes ugly things happen in that country. But surely we can all of us pay tribute to the fact that today no less than 10,000 young men and women from America are working and living at the same standard of living and speaking the same language after six months rigorous training, teaching and practising agriculture in the underdeveloped countries of the world. That is the Peace Corps and it is a fine concept.

You may say: "You can have this in Europe, too." Yes, but only on our conditions, only if Europe is a greater Europe, only if it is an outward-looking Europe, only if it is dedicated to the cause of relieving world poverty, only if it casts aside the ancient colonialisms, only if it gives up, and shows that it gives up, the narrow nationalism that could otherwise develop.

There is that possibility. But there is another side in Europe and in the European Movement—anti-American, anti-Russian, pro-Colonial; the story of the Congo and Algeria, the intransigence over Berlin. We do not know which it will be; but our terms present what I believe to be the acid test. . . .

If we could carry the Commonwealth with us, safeguarded, flourishing, prosperous; if we could safeguard our agriculture, and our E.F.T.A. friends were all in it, if we were secure in our employment policy, and if we were able to maintain our independent foreign policy and yet have this wider, looser association with Europe, it would indeed be a great ideal. But if this should not prove to be possible; if the six will not give it to us; if the British Government will not even ask for it, then we must stand firm by what we believe, for the sake of Britain, and the Commonwealth and the World; and we shall not flinch from our duty if that moment comes.

President de Gaulle Reads Britain Out of Europe*

Charles de Gaulle

Concerning this very important question of the European Economic Community and also that of the possible membership of Great Britain, it is the facts which must be considered first. Sentiments, favorable as they might be and as they are, cannot be put forward in opposition to the real factors of the problem. What are these factors?

The Treaty of Rome was concluded between six continental States,

* From the text of President de Gaulle's seventh press conference, held in Paris at the Elysée Palace on January 14, 1963. Translation supplied by the French Embassy.

States which economically speaking are, in brief, of the same nature. Whether in terms of their industrial or agricultural production, of their foreign trade, of their commercial customs and clients, or of their living and working conditions, there are many more similarities than differences between them. Moreover, they are adjacent, they interpenetrate, they are extensions of each other through their communications. The very fact of grouping them and linking them together in such a way that what they produce, buy, sell and consume, they produce, buy, sell and consume by preference within their own grouping thus conforms to reality . . . There is a feeling of solidarity between them, first owing to the awareness they have of together possessing an important part of the origins of our civilization, and also with regard to their security, because they are continental countries and they are confronted by the same single threat from one end of their territorial grouping to the other. Finally, they have a feeling of solidarity because not one of them is linked on the outside by any special political or military agreement.

Thus it has been psychologically and materially possible to organize an economic community of the Six. Moreover, this was not without difficulty. When the Treaty of Rome was signed in 1957, it was after long discussions, and once concluded, so that something could be accomplished, it was necessary for us French to straighten ourselves out in the economic, financial and monetary domain. And this was done in 1959.

From that time on, the Community was workable in principle, but it was then necessary to implement the Treaty. Now this Treaty, which was quite specific and complete on the subject of industry, was not at all specific and complete on the subject of agriculture. And yet, it was essential for our country that this be settled. . . .

And some of these arrangements are still being worked out. I will note in passing that, in this vast undertaking, all the decisions taken were taken by the Governments, for nowhere else is there any authority or responsibility. . . .

Then Great Britain applied for membership in the Common Market. It did so after refusing earlier to participate in the community that was being built, and after then having created a free trade area with six other States, and finally—I can say this, the negotiations conducted for so long on this subject can be recalled—after having put some pressure on the Six in order to prevent the application of the Common Market from really getting started. Britain thus in its turn requested membership, but on its own conditions.

This undoubtedly raises for each of the six States and for England problems of a very great dimension.

England is, in effect, insular, maritime, linked through its trade, markets and food supply to very diverse and often very distant countries. Its activities are essentially industrial and commercial, and only slightly agricultural. It has, throughout its work, very marked and original customs and traditions. In short, the nature, structure and economic context of England differ profoundly from those of the other States of the Continent.

What is to be done so that Britain, such as it lives, such as it produces and such as it trades [may] be incorporated into the Common Market such as it has been conceived and such as it functions?

For example, the means by which the people of Great Britain nourish themselves is in fact by importing foodstuffs purchased at low prices in the two Americas or in the former dominions, while still granting large subsidies to British farmers. This means is obviously incompatible with the system the Six have quite naturally set up for themselves.

The system of the Six consists of making a pool of the agricultural products of the entire Community, of strictly determining their prices, of forbidding subsidizing, of organizing their consumption between all the members and of making it obligatory for each of these members to pay to the Community any savings they might make by having foodstuffs brought in from outside instead of consuming those offered by the Common Market.

Once again, what is to be done to make Britain, such as it is, enter that system?

One was sometimes led to believe that our British friends, in applying for membership in the Common Market, agreed to change their own ways even to the point of applying all the conditions accepted and practiced by the Six, but, the question is to know if Great Britain can at present place itself, with the Continent and like it, within a tariff that is truly common, give up all preference with regard to the Commonwealth, cease to claim that its agriculture be privileged and, even more, consider as null and void the commitments it has made with the countries that are part of its free trade area. That question is the one at issue.

One cannot say that it has now been resolved. Will it be so one day? Obviously Britain alone can answer that.

The question is raised all the more since, following Britain, other States which are, I repeat, linked to it in the free trade area, for the same reasons as Great Britain, would or will want to enter the Common Market.

It must be agreed that the entry first of Great Britain and then that of those other States will completely change the series of adjustments, agreements, compensations and regulations already established between the Six, because all these States, like Britain, have very important traits of their own. We would then have to envisage the construction of another Common Market. But the 11-member, then 13-member and then perhaps 18-member Common Market that would be built would, without any doubt, hardly resemble the one the Six have built.

Moreover, this Community, growing in that way, would be confronted with all the problems of its economic relations with a crowd of other States, and first of all with the United States.

It is forseeable that the cohesion of all its members, who would be very numerous and very diverse, would not hold for long and that in the end there would appear a colossal Atlantic Community under American dependence and leadership which would soon completely swallow up the European Community.

This is an assumption that can be perfectly justified in the eyes of some, but it is not at all what France wanted to do and what France is doing, which is a strictly European construction.

Then, it is possible that Britain would one day come round to transforming itself enough to belong to the European Community without restriction and without reservation, and placing it ahead of anything else, and in that case the Six would open the door to it and France would place no obstacle in its path, although obviously the mere membership of Britain in the Community would completely change its nature and its volume.

There Is Now a Deep Division of Policy*

Edward R. G. Heath

What in fact we are really debating is whether or not there is going to be a greater European unity; and if there is to be, what form it is going to take. . . . Earlier debates [in the Council of Europe] were animated by the belief that there was in Europe a will to erect European unity and . . . that what was presenting the difficulties . . . were the technical problems of trade or politics or defence. . . . The tragedy of the present situation is that just when so many countries in Europe have come to recognize the possibilities of closer integration, and to face the technical problems and had created the will to solve them, they were prevented from doing so in Brussels in January. . . .

We are in a completely new situation . . . because it is now clearly demonstrated that there is not the will to unity in Europe today. This is fundamental and cannot be disguised or overlooked. . . . It has been said . . . that this problem of European unity could immediately be solved if only Britain were prepared "to sign the Treaty of Rome," to use the exact words which are being spoken. This, of course, has now become a sort of simple, easily played gramophone record which is used constantly in order to cover the noise of the repeated breakings of the crockery. . . . It has been said that "one day England may manage to transform herself sufficiently to become part

* Address to the 15th Session of the Consultative Assembly of the Council of Europe, Strasbourg, May 7, 1963. Text from *Commonwealth Survey*, IX, No. 12 (June 4, 1963), 492–496. The Right Hon. E. R. G. Heath, M.P., was Lord Privy Seal in Mr. Macmillan's Cabinet and in charge of British negotiations with EEC. Under Sir Alec Douglas-Home he was made Secretary of State for Industry, Trade and Regional Development and President of the Board of Trade. Mr. Heath was awarded the Charlemagne Prize of the Council of Europe on May 23, 1963, for distinguished services to Europe.

of the EEC." Therefore it is very important that we should look quite clearly at the situation to see what the position is. . . .

Everyone knew when we went to Brussels on 14th January [1963] that matters had been brought to a degree of ripeness at which we could sit around the table and negotiate a package deal, which is the method by which the Community itself works. Why, then, were the negotiations broken up? It is said that we are an island. Naturally, when I heard this in Brussels, I treated it as a very grave statement. I at once referred the matter to Whitehall for advice. They, of course, consulted the Commonwealth and our EFTA partners about this matter of great importance, and finally they came back and advised me that we are, in fact, an island. They also pointed out, however, that we were an island when the negotiations started on 10th October, 1961. It did not, therefore, seem to be a very sound reason for breaking up the negotiations.

It is also stated that Britain has very insular characteristics. What are our insular characteristics? They are, apparently, that we indulge in world trade. I therefore looked up the figures. I see that the Federal Republic [of Germany] sends 16 per cent of its gross national product abroad in world trade. The United Kingdom, rather to my regret, sends only 14 per cent of its gross national product in world trade. The Federal Republic has 10.7 per cent of world trade altogether. The United Kingdom, slightly to my regret, has only 9 per cent. The Federal Republic sends 64 per cent of its exports outside the Community and 28 per cent of them to EFTA. We in the United Kingdom send only 14 per cent of our exports to EFTA. The fact that we indulge in world trade would therefore not seem to be a very sound reason why we should not be considered eligible as a member of the Community.

This of course overlooks the fact that the Treaty of Rome is an open treaty. It starts by saying that it is "determined to establish the foundations of an even closer union among the European peoples." All of this, therefore, was in flagrant breach of the Treaty of Rome, Article 237 of which states that any European State may apply to become a member of the Community. It does not say "any European State except islands." . . .

On 10th October, 1961, in Paris, I accepted the Treaty of Rome in its entirety, together with the protocols to the treaty. There is, therefore, no justifiable argument that Britain ought to accept the Treaty of Rome, and that, then, all would be well. I hope that we shall never hear this argument again. Statements to the effect that Britain has not accepted the common tariff, the common agricultural policy or the financial regulation of the Community, or that the EFTA position is unclear, are equally unfounded.

Then it was said that the club was still developing, which made it very difficult for anyone to join. This seemed strangely in contradiction with the offer to Denmark, almost the next day, of membership straight away. If, however, this is the position, does it mean that no new members can join until the end of the transitional period in 1970? Does it mean that new members then will not get a transitional period at all because it will not be allowed for in the Treaty of Rome? Or does it mean that the Community is simply to remain as six countries from now on? These are very fundamental questions but they lead us to the conclusion that there was another reason for the break-up of the negotiations.

The fundamental reason is . . . that two clear and very different views of what Europe ought to be have emerged. The British conception is . . . of a Europe consisting of the members of the Community who are already there and those who would adhere, probably the United Kingdom, Denmark, Norway and Eire, that would make ten as a hard core. We never felt that ten members was too large a number on which the Community could operate. Associated with it would be those countries which were already associated or in process of becoming associated, Greece and Turkey and the other members from EFTA, Portugal, Sweden, Austria and Switzerland. They would have economic arrangements but they would not take part, as they did not wish to do so, in any political or defence matters. This larger Europe would have its connections right across the globe with all those countries which had been formerly in any way associated with the member countries. That meant for the existing members the eighteen associated states.[1] For us it meant the Commonwealth and the dependencies. For any new members it meant those countries which were associated with them. Thus we foresaw that Europe would be able to exercise its influence right across the world because of the friendly relations and the connections which it had with all those countries which I have described. Such a Europe would obviously be outward-looking, taking part in tariff reductions for the increase of world trade. . . .

The other conception of Europe is . . . one of a much more limited number of countries which endeavor to become self-sufficient in supplying their own needs and which are protectionist, and have to be, in their approach. This implies, in our view, that an independent European defense policy, possibly separate from the Atlantic Alliance, can arise, leading to many suspicions and fears of moving towards a third force. Some of these suspicions and fears may not be justified. These ideas may not be in the minds of those who sponsored the conception but the difference between the two conceptions is perfectly clear now for all to see. It is apparent that most of the countries in Europe . . . support the first concept and the wish to see the large Community and the outward-looking Europe which I have described, rather than

[1] The EEC Treaty provides (mainly at the insistence of France) for special economic relations of the Community with Associated States—ex-colonies. A second Convention of this kind (the first having completed its five-year term) was initialled on December 20, 1962, in Brussels and signed on July 20, 1963, at Yaoundé, Cameroun. The signatories of this Convention of Association between the EEC and the Associated African States and Madagascar are, in addition to the EEC: Burundi, Cameroun, Central African Republic, Chad, Congo (Brazzaville), Congo (Leopoldville), Ivory Coast, Dahomey, Gabon, Upper Volta, Madagascar, Mali, Mauritania, Niger, Rwanda, Senegal, Somalia, Togo.

The possibility of such association for British tropical African ex-colonies was one of the concessions won by Britain in the negotiations. However, when the possibility of such a status was offered to the Commonwealth Members concerned at a Commonwealth Prime Ministers Meeting in September 1962 it was unanimously rejected.

the smaller and more limited approach. There are those who say, to sum up here, that Britain is not European. What is really meant is that we are not European in the second sense which I have described . . . but there can be no doubt whatever that we are European in the first sense. . . . So there is now a deep division of policy and what is plain is that there cannot be greater unity in Europe until this problem is settled.

We are not prepared to turn our backs on Europe. . . .

One further initiative which affects all our countries is the "Kennedy Round" of tariff negotiations. Britain will give her full support to those negotiations. We do not share the view of those who believe that the object is to allow American domination of the countries of Europe. We hope to see a balanced negotiation between all the parties in order to reduce tariff barriers and allow an increase of world trade. If this can be achieved, then we can reduce the discrimination which exists and is bound to grow between the Community and EFTA. But this . . . is in my view the first real challenge to all those, whether members of the Community or outside it, who want to see Europe developing in an outward-looking way. We must recognize that this is the challenge and it will be seen as such not only by our own peoples but by all the peoples of the developing countries as well.

America Gets an Unexpected Break*

Henry S. Reuss

Instead of cursing de Gaulle, we ought to thank him for compelling us to reexamine the goals of our foreign policy. For the past two years we have uncritically supported the Common Market, although it was bound to impair Free World trade by discriminating in favor of the insiders and their former colonies, and against those on the outside looking in.

Our vision was warped. For, in fact, since World War II our goal should have been nothing less than a community of the entire Free World. In such a community, the industrialized countries—Western Europe, the United States, Canada, Australia, New Zealand, Japan, and perhaps some others—would strive together for full employment and rapid growth within their own borders. They would also work toward the removal of trade barriers which separate them from each other and from the developing nations. And they

* *Harper's Magazine,* May 1963, pp. 37–42. Reprinted by permission of the author. Mr. Reuss is a U.S. Congressman from Wisconsin.

would seek a mechanism of international exchange and payments which would avoid crises and permit each country to progress socially and economically. The industrialized countries would achieve full employment and at the same time provide their partners, the developing countries, with growing export markets and a dynamic source of public and private capital.

From time to time there have been glimmerings from official Washington that we were dedicated to such a large concept. But mostly we have been preoccupied with a particular view of Europe, centered on the Common Market. European regionalism should have been seen as merely a means to an end. Instead we have allowed it to become an end in itself. When Common Market policy collided with Free World policy, the former nearly always won out.

Immediately after World War II it made sense to concentrate on rebuilding war-torn Europe as a step toward a Free World community. We invented the Marshall Plan. We encouraged regional institutions, such as the Organization for European Economic Cooperation, the Council of Europe, the Coal-Steel Community, and Euratom. The Common Market of France, Italy, Germany, and the three Benelux countries (often called the Six) was part of this pattern.

In the beginning its entirely valid purpose was to strengthen the economies of its members by giving them a mass market and the spur of competition. Another sound objective was the ending of animosity between France and Germany. These things have now been done.

Curiously, the most significant steps toward Free World unity were taken in the immediate postwar period, when emphasis on Europe was amply justified by the need to fend off chaos. At Bretton Woods in 1945, we laid the foundation for a world-wide monetary order. In 1948 we convened the countries of the Free World to establish the multilateral tariff-cutting procedures of the General Agreement on Tariffs and Trade known as GATT. With the Point Four program in the early 1950s, we gave direct aid to the developing nations. Those programs have not been matched by any comparable efforts since the mid-'fifties. European regionalism has had top priority in our foreign policy. Ironically, as Europe came to need less of our concern and the Free World more, we gave Europe more and more and the Free World less. In effect, we turned our backs on the larger goals and, as a result, little progress toward them has been made since the promising postwar beginnings.

We knew, for example, that the Free World needed a better system of international payments. But we were unwilling to go to France and other prosperous European countries and frankly ask for needed help. So we staggered along with monetary arrangements that have remained at best precarious.

Likewise we recognized that the developing countries needed economic assistance. But until very recently, we allowed the Europeans to drag their feet on foreign aid. And, although we paid lip service to the principle of multilateral, liberalized trade, we hailed the Common Market, with its obvious discriminatory features, as a great progressive step.

Strangely, hardly anyone questioned the assumptions that led to our single-minded concern with Europe. In the Great Non-Debate, few people pointed out that the Common Market was encouraging a European particularism rooted in the ancient dreams of unity of Charlemagne, Dante, and Henry IV at just the time in history when speedy communications and the aspirations of rising peoples everywhere required a Free World generalism.

To understand how great a mistake this was, let us see just how the Common Market works, and who gets hurt.

First of all, *we* do. Unless our surplus of exports can be increased to offset our deficit items such as military expenditures overseas and investments abroad, we face continuing deficits in our balance of payments. Incomes are rising in the Common Market countries. They could be our fastest-growing export area. But if the Common Market continues on its recent inward-looking course, we will lose rather than gain exports. The Common Market aims to insulate its members against the rest of the world with an external tariff averaging 11 per cent and no tariff wall between its members. Such discrimination will hurt us.

Metal lathes provide a case in point. In 1958, the last pre-Common Market year, we exported $1.5 million of metal lathes to Germany, and $3 million to France. The German tariff was zero; the French tariff 11 per cent. The Common Market external tariff is now 9 per cent. The increase in the German tariff from zero to 9 per cent is likely to cut us off from that market entirely. And the decrease in the French tariff from 11 to 9 per cent is not likely to help us, since the Germans can ship their lathes into France duty-free. Thus even if Americans were to lead a Spartan life, keep wages and prices stable, and make admirable gains in productivity, our export possibilities to the Common Market could be largely gobbled up by its own members.

Consider, for instance, our consumer durable-goods industry, which produces such things as washing machines, driers, refrigerators, dishwashers, garbage-disposal units, and lawnmowers. Market studies show that these commonplace amenities of the American home have been rare luxuries abroad. Now, however, there is a shortage of domestic help in Europe due to full employment. There is a huge new market for every kind of appliance from clothes driers to dishwashers. And we could easily meet this demand, for our appliance plants have vast idle capacity while over 6 per cent of our labor force is unemployed.

Yet the new Common Market external tariffs effectively exclude most United States appliances (the tariffs are: electric percolators, 18 per cent; dishwashers, 19 per cent; vacuum cleaners, 18 per cent). Were it not for this tariff wall, exports of our consumer durable goods to Europe could match the spectacular sales in America of Europe's compact cars, which have been admitted under our low (6.5 per cent) automobile tariff.

The man from Mars might well clutch his forehead and wonder: Why don't these foolish mortals put some of the unemployed in the United States back to work making and exporting these household appliances which Europeans now want and can afford? This would not merely spur the U.S. economy and create jobs for Americans. It would also help the European countries. At present, a wage increase in Europe can cause inflation because higher purchasing power will compete for roughly the same amount of consumer goods. If Europe were to let down her trade barriers, new imports could sop up this excess purchasing power. And these sales of our products abroad would help wipe out the U.S. international payments deficit and Western Europe's payments surplus, to the advantage of the whole Free World. Only thus can the dollar—the international currency of Europe and the U.S.—become stable once again.

The discriminatory tariffs of the Common Market imperil not only our exports of manufactured goods. Our farm exports face at least an equal threat from the Market's policy of agricultural protectionism. For other countries of the Free World—including the European countries left out of the Common Market—the prospect is ominous.

Exports are the economic lifeblood of Sweden, Switzerland, Austria, and other members of the European Free Trade Association. A large share of their exports have traditionally gone to the Common Market countries.

Denmark's efficient farmers, for example, have earned about half of the nation's export income. A major market for their products has been West Germany. However, as the Common Market agricultural policy goes into effect, Denmark is already beginning to feel the pinch. The Danes must anticipate the probable loss of $150 million yearly in export trade.

Israel as well as Canada, Australia, New Zealand, and other British Commonwealth countries also face serious problems of discrimination from the Common Market, although they are breathing a momentary sigh of relief at Britain's failure to join it.

Israel, for example, has staked her economic future on expanding trade with Europe. Sixty per cent of her exports now go to Britain and the Six. She sells oranges, her principal export earner, to Britain at a nondiscriminatory tariff of 10 per cent—that is, the same tariff paid on oranges from any other country. This enables Israel to compete successfully with other orange-growing countries. If Britain joins the Common Market, Israel would have to pay a tariff of 20 per cent to sell her oranges in Britain. It would be hard to compete with oranges from Italy and North Africa, which are members of the Common Market and thus pay no tariffs.

Or take Canada, Australia, and New Zealand. They sell vast quantities of grain, meat, dairy products, and fruit to Britain duty-free, or at a low tariff. Britain fought for a provision that would safeguard the present level of Commonwealth exports to Britain, and this insistence proved a major stumbling block to British entry.

Grave as is the threat to the other industrialized nations, the most damage will be done to the developing countries. A few former French and Belgian territories will receive preferential entry for their products into the Common Market. But to most of Latin America, Asia, and Africa the Common Market looks like a rich man's club designed to make the rich richer.

Argentina, for example, will be hurt if the Six proceed to eat French duty-free grain rather than Argentine grain that must pay the Common Market external tariff. Brazil will be hurt when the former French African colonies increase their coffee production and export it to the Six duty-free. Ecuador faces the same problem as cocoa production shifts to former French Africa. What the United States gives to Latin America through the Alliance for Progress it can take away by failure to bargain away the Common Market's discriminatory policies.

Some time ago our policy makers perceived that the Common Market could become a threat as well as a blessing. We then decided that Britain must be helped to join in order to leaven the lump of the Six with the yeast of British democracy and free-trade philosophy. Future historians may well dispute whether Britain's entry might not instead merely have enlarged the area of the Common Market's discrimination against the outside world.

But whatever the merits of the Britain-must-join-at-all-costs position, the method we used to pursue it did a disservice to ourselves and to the rest of the Free World. We distorted and crippled the tariff-cutting power of President Kennedy's Trade Expansion Act of 1962 to make it a lever to push Britain into the Common Market. The key and much-publicized provision of this Act was the power to abolish tariffs entirely on many major industrial commodities, such as consumer durable goods, machinery, chemicals, and paper. Not only the United States but the whole Free World stood to benefit. But this power was conditioned on Britain's joining the Common Market. The intent was to convince all concerned that if Britain failed to join, there could be no effective tariff-cutting negotiations. Now that Britain is out, we awaken to find the Act's zero-bargaining clause "full of sound and fury, signifying nothing."

A second result of our fixation on the Britain-must-join policy has been the postponement of the negotiations made possible by the Trade Expansion Act. There is no reason why these negotiations should not be taking place now. But State Department spokesmen have let it be known that bargaining must be delayed until at least 1964 while we wait for the British position to be "clarified."

What should the United States do now? To pursue an outworn policy would be the worst folly. It could result in a revival of American protectionism and isolationism. Such a course would make it impossible for us and other advanced countries to meet our responsibility to developing nations. This is a forbidding prospect.

But where there is danger there is also opportunity. De Gaulle's veto of Britain may shake us out of our obsession with the Common Market and its enlargement and cause us to concentrate on the logical goal—a Free World community—in trade, in international payments, in economic growth, and in aid. We should take positive steps toward that goal now. This means that we must use the Trade Expansion Act to reduce Free World trade barriers quickly and multilaterally, for our own benefit and for everyone else's.

When? Instead of a business-as-usual approach to negotiations, we should start tomorrow.

With whom? Our main bargaining partners, hopefully, will be the Common Market and the Free World's other industrialized nations. If the Common Market refuses to negotiate, we should immediately conduct aggressive bargaining with the other industrial nations. We should extend the benefits of these negotiations to the developing countries, but not to a noncooperating Common Market. This would require an amendment to the present GATT "most-favored-nation" clause, under which tariff reductions negotiated between any countries accrue to the benefit of all other GATT members.

How deep? We should enact the Douglas-Reuss amendment to the Trade Expansion Act, which will give us the power to abolish tariffs on major groups of commodities. At present, Administration policy is to the contrary. At his February 7, 1963, press conference, when he was asked whether he planned to seek passage of this amendment, President Kennedy said:

"No, we haven't planned to ask the Congress, because we do have the power, under the Trade Expansion bill, to reduce all other tariffs by 50 per cent, which is a substantial authority. We lack the zero authority."

It is true that a 50 per cent tariff-cutting power is better than none at all. But it is far from sufficient to stimulate a large expansion in world trade. In fact we had this 50 per cent tariff-cutting power several times under the old Reciprocal Trade Agreements Acts of the 1930s and 1940s which President Kennedy consigned to limbo on January 24, 1962, when he sent the Trade Expansion bill to Congress. "The Trade Agreements Act," he said at that time, "must be replaced by a wholly new instrument. A new American trade initiative is needed to meet the challenges and opportunities of a rapidly changing world economy."

The President went on to request the special authority to *eliminate* tariffs: "To be effective in achieving a breakthrough agreement with the EEC so that our farmers, manufacturers, and other Free World trading partners can participate," he said, "we will need to use both the dominant-supplier authority (to eliminate tariffs) and the general authority (to reduce tariffs by 50 per cent) in combination."

The President, it would now seem, was right the first time—in his 1962 trade message rather than in his 1963 press conference. In the modern industrial world, a vestigial tariff of a few percentage points can effectively block trade.

There is an even more important reason why we need the power to eliminate, not just reduce by 50 per cent, the Common Market's tariff wall. The Common Market internal tariffs will shortly be at zero. Discrimination against countries outside it can be eliminated only if the Common Market's external tariff is also reduced to zero. Unless we likewise have the power to reduce our own tariffs to zero we lack the leverage to get rid of those aspects of the Common Market which threaten us and the whole Free World. Regardless of the benefits of the Franco-German rapprochement and a new market for the Six, our initial support of the Common Market made sense only if we were prepared to try to bargain away its threatening features as soon as possible.

As the Trade Expansion Act now stands, we are in effect saying: "Since France has kept Britain out of the Common Market, we are going to punish ourselves. We will make it impossible to bargain effectively for the entry of American goods into foreign markets."

Clearly this position makes very little sense. Instead, our first order of business should be to invigorate the Trade Expansion Act by including down-to-zero bargaining power. This would be helpful in many ways.

We in the United States, with our lagging growth rate, our persistent balance of payments deficits, our chronic unemployment, will benefit particularly.

The United Kingdom, the European countries not in the Common Market, Canada, and Japan, seriously damaged by the Common Market's protectionism, would also gain. They would welcome U.S. leadership in bargaining down tariffs.

Similarly, the developing nations of Latin America, and the Asian and African countries not affiliated with the Common Market, would profit. They need expanded outlets in the industrialized world for both their raw materials and their growing manufactures. American initiative in eliminating tariffs would be a major step in opening up such markets.

Even the nations of the Common Market themselves would be aided in their economic progress, if not in the political aspirations of some of their leaders. An attempt at autarchy does not make the best use of the resources of the Six or of their former colonies associated with them. They would do far better by concentrating on the items which they are best suited to produce, rather than by using protective tariffs to make uneconomic enterprises profitable.

As U.S. trade policy shifts from its Common Market fixation to a Free-World-wide orientation, we must take other steps to advance the prosperity of the Free World community.

Foremost, our rate of economic growth must be stepped up. We are already committed to this objective. President Kennedy's tax reduction is to be the prime mover. But this measure must be supplemented by the vigorous trade policy I have outlined here. It will serve to make our industry better able to compete in the world market and also give us some new customers.

Additionally, we need a more durable system of international payments. As the Joint Economic Committee of Congress has pointed out, the present policies of the Treasury and the Federal Reserve System to protect the dollar are inadequate. Our foreign creditors could still start a run on the dollar. Because of this possibility, the Federal Reserve is anxious to make bank loans harder to get, and interest rates higher, all "to protect the dollar." This threat of renewed tight money could mean continued stagnation for our economy.

Fortunately, a way out of this dilemma exists. The countries of Europe should be asked to do for us what we helped them do for each other in the 'fifties: form a payments agreement under which capital that flows from one country is matched by compensating credits from the others. With such an agreement in effect, the Federal Reserve would have no excuse for restricting growth "to protect the dollar," since the dollar would be protected by our international partners. If France's financial authorities have acquired the habit of saying "No" from France's President, and oppose such an agreement, we should go ahead and negotiate one without France.

At the same time we must continue to push all the industrialized nations to increase their foreign aid efforts in the developing countries. A good start in this direction has been made by the Organization for Economic Cooperation and Development. It should be energetically encouraged. However, I believe that a healthy economic relationship between the industrialized countries—with freer trade, an adequate system of international payments, and full employment—will actually help the developing countries more than any amount of direct aid they are likely to get.

Will the kind of Free World community I am proposing involve the surrender of sovereignty by its members? The answer is surely: not much. Existing political machinery—like GATT, for trade; the International Monetary Fund, for payments; the Organization for Economic Cooperation and Development, for growth and aid—can do the job for a long time to come.

Indeed, elaborate political machinery might do more harm than good. If it is less broad than the Free World—just Sixes or Sevens or Atlantic powers—it may merely divide the Free World. I do not think we need another supranational organization now. It would be far better, I believe, for parliamentarians and ministers from the industrial countries of the Free World to meet from time to time to debate trade or payments or growth or aid. If new institutions are needed they should be allowed to evolve organically from progress in economic and social cooperation rather than from an advance blueprint.

Obviously the Free World community cannot be born without the cooperation of other industrial nations. Cabinet ministers must agree to mutual tariff-cutting, to buttress each other's currencies, and to share the foreign-aid burden. Such agreements, our own standpatters may say, are unlikely. Perhaps the Belgians will balk, or the Germans will refuse, or the French will once again say "No." How foolish, our pessimists will argue, to make requests that are bound to be turned down, to everyone's embarrassment.

I do not agree. I think we should go ahead and make our requests. Ministers in democratic countries come and go, but public opinion remains. If we place our proposals before the world, public opinion just might bring public officials around, sooner or later.

Sometimes, when the cause is just, the result comes sooner rather than later. In 1962, for instance, Congress had before it the bill to reimburse Philippine citizens for war damage caused by U.S. Armed Forces. On May 9, the House unexpectedly voted the bill down, 201–171. The Philippine government stuck to its guns, saying very publicly that the bill was a just one and ought to pass. President Macapagal canceled his June trip to the U.S. The Philippine Independence Day was changed from July 4 to June 12. The American people and then Congress got the message. On August 1 the House passed the bill, 194–35, and it became law on August 30.

Similarly if we develop a just proposal for a Free World community, it is better to make it publicly, and to take our chances that it will one day prevail. To keep quiet about it is simply to insure failure.

A summit conference of the heads of the Free World's industrialized nations might well serve to get us all moving toward the goal of community, and away from interim means that have failed. The sooner we can fix our minds on that goal, the better the chances that the Free World will avoid shaking itself apart over U.S.-European political or military disputes—over who joins or does not join the Common Market, for instance, or over who should have nuclear weapons and how they are to be controlled.

These disputes will continue to occur. They may become more heated as, in one European country after another, power is transferred from the old men who now wield it to younger hands. But these disputes need not be fatal if the Free World has a larger purpose to hold it together.

From the standpoint of domestic politics, the goal of a Free World community is one the American people can grasp. Once they understand, they will give more support to programs designed to end our economic lag and unemployment at home. For Americans respond best when they can see the connection between domestic and foreign policy, between individual measures and broad goals, between practical means and idealistic ends.

3

NATO: Is It Still Necessary?

NATO is the most important of the many regional alliances of the United States. It is the formal bulwark of free Europe, the area regarded as the most vital, outside North and Central America, to the security of the United States.

The alliance came into being in the most intense period of the Cold War. This fact in itself explains why the question is often raised whether, in the changed circumstances of the middle 1960s, the alliance is still necessary, or whether, if still necessary, it is in need of a radical overhaul. Questions and comments, as this chapter demonstrates, run the gamut from fundamental skepticism about the necessity for NATO to technical and detailed suggestions about how it can be improved to serve better its basic purposes. The breadth, depth, and, even more, the continuity of the controversy, however, leave no doubt that NATO is at least important.

NATO was created to organize the defense of Western Europe against possible Soviet aggression. It was the equivalent, for the more advanced and basically stronger societies of Western Europe, of the unilateral guarantees by the United States to Greece and Turkey embodied in the "Truman Doctrine" of 1947. Although NATO involved active cooperation by the Western European nations (and Canada), its core was a U.S. guarantee of the territorial integrity of all the member states. But it did not involve any guarantee of their colonial territories or their extra-European interests.

The Communist take-over of Czechoslovakia in 1948 caused the United States to abandon its historic line of policy, to decide that Jefferson's warning against "entangling alliances" was no longer appropriate, and to enter a permanent, peace-time alliance. The U.S. Senate, on June 11, 1948, recommended the "association of the United States with such regional and other collective arrangements as are based on continuous self-help and mutual aid, and as affect its national security." The North Atlantic Treaty[1] was signed in Washington, D.C., on April 4, 1949, by the United States, Canada, the

[1] The North Atlantic Treaty was in effect an enlargement of the Brussels Treaty of March 17, 1948, which linked France, Belgium, the Netherlands, Luxembourg, and the United Kingdom in what was called "Western Union." Western Union merged with NATO, but after France rejected the European Defense Community Treaty in 1954 it became the means whereby German membership of NATO was rendered acceptable and, presumably, less dangerous. Western Germany and Italy acceded to the Brussels Treaty, which was amended to impose certain restrictions on German rearmament. This was known as "Western European Union" (WEU). After France's rejection of British membership in EEC, WEU provided a convenient framework within which British contacts and negotiations with the Six could be maintained.

United Kingdom, France, Belgium, the Netherlands, Luxembourg, Iceland, Denmark, Norway, Italy, and Portugal. To these twelve were added, in 1951, Greece and Turkey and, in 1955, the Federal Republic of Germany.

The fifteen-member alliance has its structural oddities. It straddles the Atlantic, with two members in North America. One member, Iceland, has no armed forces. The alliance has two members (Greece and Turkey) that are remote from Western Europe and whose defense by land or sea is entirely different from that of Western Europe. Portugal, likewise, is physically separated from the other members; moreover, it can by no stretch of imagination be called a democratic state. But, after all, the test for NATO membership was not cultural homogeneity or sound constitutional government but readiness to take an active part, under U.S. leadership, in confronting the Soviet threat at a certain moment in European and world history.

Stalin evoked NATO—unintentionally, of course; and Khrushchev has maintained its cohesion, especially by his actions in Hungary in 1956. The Korean War converted the rather sketchy North Atlantic Treaty (a short and simple document) into a full-fledged organization with a physical headquarters, a large staff (civilian and military), and a military and naval structure with an elaborate series of commands to cover the whole area of the alliance's concern. So rapid was the growth of NATO that critics feared it might even supersede the United Nations in the minds of Western policy-makers as the most important of international organizations, or hoped, since it envisaged other forms of cooperation than the military, that it might become a vehicle for international integration in the social and economic fields.

However, NATO has been confined in practice—and rightly—to its military role. Other activities toward European integration have been developed by means of other international bodies that are more appropriately and specifically designed: intensive economic integration through EEC and EFTA; general economic cooperation of the Atlantic Community through the Organization for European Economic Cooperation (OEEC), later restructured as the Organization for Economic Cooperation and Development (OECD); and general discussion and formulation of long-term goals through the Council of Europe.

NATO has seemed to be in a state of semipermanent crisis; for perhaps ten years commentators have produced phrases about "critical reconsideration of its role" or about its being "at the crossroads." Nor have all its troubles been imaginary. Perhaps, indeed, it never did regain the spirit of urgency or of willing cooperation in a common cause that it possessed at the Lisbon meeting of the North Atlantic Council in 1952. The early quotas for forces to be made available to the Supreme Allied Commander, Europe (SACEUR) have never been met; furthermore, SACEUR, who has been in effect an American viceroy in Europe, must exercise a military-political expertise that has already strained the talents of a distinguished line of officers: Eisenhower, Ridgway, Gruenther, Norstad, and Lemnitzer. The civilian side of NATO, headed by the Secretary-General (an office created in 1952; SACEUR has existed since

1950), has never developed to the point where it can take over the political and diplomatic functions that properly pertain to it and leave the Supreme Commander to the sufficiently exigent tasks of international military command.

Nevertheless, the present situation of NATO merits more serious consideration than did the less genuinely critical stages of the past. The phrase "in disarray," applied by Walter Lippmann in the spring of 1963, is now frequently used. The case against NATO is made eloquently by Ronald Steel in his article "The Demise of NATO," which argues that the alliance is the superfluous legacy of the age of American dominance. Doubts about the alliance have arisen fundamentally from the revival of the European economy, which has led to increased self-assertion of the Western European states and to restiveness under American leadership. A second factor, reinforcing the first, is the end of the American nuclear monopoly. Since Russia has atomic weapons and delivery systems approximately on a level with the United States, confidence in American nuclear retaliation has lessened, even though the retaliation principle has been frequently and emphatically restated by American leaders—as in President John F. Kennedy's Frankfurt speech, included in this chapter.

The problems of NATO center about three main questions. The first concerns its basic necessity. Some critics maintain that there never has been any threat of Russian aggression against Western Europe, but that Russia is concerned only with the security of her glacis, Eastern Europe, and that her interest there is by no means new. And, as far as Western Europe is concerned, Russian interests can be regarded as limited to hopes of embarrassing its democratic governments, or perhaps of taking over by an internal political coup. Against such a development NATO offers no security at all. This argument, however, tends to ignore the central, unsolved question in Europe: the question of Germany, and within Germany that of Berlin. In regard to these questions sheer military power is not irrelevant. Some of these critics would agree that an American-organized defense of Western Europe was perhaps necessary in the past—say, during Stalin's rule—but is not necessary now. Many Western European politicians seem to lean in this direction. A further variation, which has been under discussion for half a dozen years and would involve substantial abandonment of NATO in its present form, is the Rapacki Plan, named for its originator, the Polish foreign minister. The Rapacki Plan—advocated in the essay by H. Stuart Hughes—would seek to reduce the risk of war in Central Europe by banning nuclear weapons from a broad belt including East and West Germany, Poland, and Czechoslovakia, and by withdrawing American and Russian troops from that area—a feature known as "disengagement." This plan has many attractive features, especially from the European point of view—both Eastern and Western. The most attractive is that it would eliminate that nightmare for Europeans, the nuclear rearmament of Germany. The Rapacki Plan, however, depends on an agreement between Russia and the United States, of which there is no sign. For both great powers, such a plan would involve a fundamental reappraisal of policy. But reappraisals are always agonizing, and they are always avoided if possible. The continuation of established policies is the virtually inescapable tendency of all states at all times—escapable, indeed, only by great positive initiative and political courage.

The second question concerns the strengthening of NATO's capacity to wage war by conventional, or non-nuclear, means in order to allow the West the choice of nuclear or conventional retaliation. To make the latter choice reasonable, there must be a possibility of doing so successfully. The article by Bernard Brodie discusses—in a somewhat skeptical spirit—the possibilities of what he calls CWE (conventional war in Europe). Brodie's skepticism, of course, is not based on the illusive argument that the West cannot field as many troops in Europe as Russia has available. In fact, the population figures of the NATO allies vis-à-vis those of Russia and her satellites show that there is no such impossibility, provided only that the Western allies have the political will to field troops, a will of which there is so far no sign.

The third question, and certainly the most crucial today, concerns the various ramifications of the problem of nuclear weapons within NATO. Basically, it is not a matter of military necessity but of European pride and political sensitivity. President Kennedy commented in his press conference of July 5, 1962, that

> stronger pressures have arisen in Europe for a European nuclear force not as dependent upon the United States as the present one. What we have suggested is that this is a matter that Europe should consider carefully; that we would, of course, be responsive to any alternative arrangements that they wish to make. . . .

He said that the United States regarded the present arrangement as giving "full and sufficient guarantees for the integrity of Europe," but that "if Europe does not agree with that . . . then we'd be prepared to discuss an alternate arrangement."

As far back as 1961, President Kennedy indicated his willingness to make available to NATO the five nuclear-armed Polaris submarines stationed in the Holy Loch on the Clyde estuary near Glasgow, Scotland. This transfer was made in 1962, though the vessels remained fundamentally under American command. But the question entered its present acute stage in December 1962 during the Nassau meeting of Kennedy and Macmillan, at which (as a *quid pro quo* for the decision to drop the development of the Skybolt missile) the President agreed to make Polaris missiles available for British submarines. This decision meant that Britain would acquire a nuclear submarine fleet in addition to the nuclear bomber fleet that it already had; it exacerbated de Gaulle's suspicion of the "Anglo-Saxon" inner group of NATO, and was possibly the fundamental reason for his veto, one month later, of Britain's membership in the Common Market.

The Nassau communiqué also envisaged making available to NATO part of the national nuclear forces already available, and, more crucial, the creation by NATO of a Polaris-armed, multilateral, mixed-manned naval force; i.e., one in which the crews would be of mixed nationality. This force was first thought of as a submarine force, but early in 1963 it was modified to plans for a surface fleet of missile-carrying ships. This project was rejected by de Gaulle out of hand, but in October 1963 a seven-nation agreement was signed to begin the training of crews for the first of the planned twenty-five mixed-manned Polaris ships. This project, though almost an invitation to skepticism on the grounds of impracticability, would afford the NATO states collectively a greater share in the system of deterrence than they have ever previously had. The ultimate control of the force is still open to discussion; there are some indications that the United States would be prepared, in the long run, to see it become purely European.

Meanwhile, the problem of revived nationalism within NATO is symbolized by France under de Gaulle. The French president seems more and more inclined not merely to withhold participation in projects that call for increased cooperation, but to withhold even that degree of cooperation that he had previously accorded. He has greatly stressed the creation of an independent French striking force. At the end of July 1963, de Gaulle withdrew the French fleet from NATO command in order to employ it (eventually with nuclear warheads) as an independent organ of French foreign policy. On October 9, 1963, Paris announced that an undisclosed number of Mirage IV supersonic bombers with nuclear bombs now constituted the beginning of France's independent *force de frappe*. The motivation of all this willfulness is clearly national pride; for, if it is doubtful that the President of the United States would risk a nuclear war over a possibly ambiguous European issue, it is not plausible to assume that de Gaulle would bring down upon France much more complete and certain destruction for the sake of some non-French issue such as Berlin. In the jargon of the day, an independent nuclear force is for de Gaulle a *status symbol,* not a real factor in military calculations. The case against dispersal of nuclear weapons within the Western alliance was made by Secretary of Defense Robert S. McNamara in his Ann Arbor speech.

De Gaulle's wish to restore the greatness of France has led to a number of gestures, especially foreign visits. More serious is his abandonment of consultation and cooperation with other NATO members in shaping foreign policy; such consultation and cooperation was one of the most hopeful and positive aspects of NATO. The recognition of Communist China by France (January 31, 1964) is the most striking example of this decision; by linking up the two most notable dissidents of the two great camps, it superbly symbolizes the end of bipolarity.

De Gaulle's policy is not, or is not yet, neutralism; in the Cuban crisis, he stood firmly by the United States; nor is it adopted frivolously. But we may ask whether, in contemporary circumstances, it is not mistaken. As Dean

Acheson, the architect of NATO, said on December 21, 1963, "The idea that there are national, or European, or North American interests which can be safely pursued in disregard of a common interest belongs to that past which has brought us all such loss and suffering." De Gaulle's emphasis on the greatness of France, and by implication on the unchallengeable importance of the nation-state, runs counter to that of men like Monnet, de Gasperi, and Schumann, who strove so creatively to make the new Europe; and it will effectively hamstring the attempts of NATO to solve its current problems in any fashion acceptable to all fifteen members. In the last of the articles that follow, Louis J. Halle discusses this basic question of whether de Gaulle's attitude toward NATO and similar matters does not run counter to the tide of history in ways that are dangerous and possibly pernicious for the West as a whole.

Need for the Closest Coordination in the Defense of the Atlantic Community*

Robert S. McNamara

The North Atlantic alliance is a unique alinement of governments. The provision for the common defense of the members has led to a remarkable degree of military collaboration and diplomatic consultation for a peacetime coalition. The growth of the alliance organization has accelerated as the task of defending the treaty area has increased in scope, size, and complexity. NATO has had its stresses and strains, but it has weathered them all.

Today NATO is involved in a number of controversies, which must be resolved by achieving a consensus within the organization in order to preserve its strength and unity. The question has arisen whether Senator Vandenberg's assertion is as true today as it was when he made it 13 years ago. Three arguments have raised this question most sharply:

It has been argued that the very success of Western European economic development reduces Europe's need to rely on the United States to share in its defenses.

It has been argued that the increasing vulnerability of the United States to nuclear attack makes us less willing as a partner in the defense of Europe and hence less effective in deterring such an attack.

* Address at the University of Michigan, Ann Arbor, June 16, 1962. Text from *Department of State Bulletin,* July 9, 1962, pp. 64–69. Mr. McNamara is Secretary of Defense.

It has been argued that nuclear capabilities are alone relevant in the face of the growing nuclear threat and that independent national nuclear forces are sufficient to protect the nations of Europe.

I believe that all of these arguments are mistaken. I think it is worthwhile to expose the U.S. views on these issues as we have presented them to our allies. In our view, the effect of the new factors in the situation, both economic and military, has been to increase the interdependence of national security interests on both sides of the Atlantic and to enhance the need for the closest coordination of our efforts.

A central military issue facing NATO today is the role of nuclear strategy. Four facts seem to us to dominate consideration of that role. All of them point in the direction of increased integration to achieve our common defense. First, the alliance has overall nuclear strength adequate to any challenge confronting it. Second, this strength not only minimizes the likelihood of major nuclear war but makes possible a strategy designed to preserve the fabric of our societies if war should occur. Third, damage to the civil societies of the alliance resulting from nuclear warfare could be very grave. Fourth, improved nonnuclear forces, well within alliance resources, could enhance deterrence of any aggressive moves short of direct, all-out attack on Western Europe.

Let us look at the situation today. First, given the current balance of nuclear power, which we confidently expect to maintain in the years ahead, a surprise nuclear attack is simply not a rational act for any enemy. Nor would it be rational for an enemy to take the initiative in the use of nuclear weapons as an outgrowth of a limited engagement in Europe or elsewhere. I think we are entitled to conclude that either of these actions has been made highly unlikely.

Second, and equally important, the mere fact that no nation could rationally take steps leading to a nuclear war does not guarantee that a nuclear war cannot take place. Not only do nations sometimes act in ways that are hard to explain on a rational basis, but even when acting in a "rational" way they sometimes, indeed disturbingly often, act on the basis of misunderstandings of the true facts of a situation. They misjudge the way others will react and the way others will interpret what they are doing.

We must hope—indeed I think we have good reason to hope—that all sides will understand this danger and will refrain from steps that even raise the possibility of such a mutually disastrous misunderstanding. We have taken unilateral steps to reduce the likelihood of such an occurrence. We look forward to the prospect that through arms control the actual use of these terrible weapons may be completely avoided. It is a problem not just for us in the West but for all nations that are involved in this struggle we call the cold war.

For our part we feel we and our NATO allies must frame our strategy with this terrible contingency, however remote, in mind. Simply ignoring the problem is not going to make it go away.

The United States has come to the conclusion that, to the extent feasible, basic military strategy in a possible general nuclear war should be approached in much the same way that more conventional military operations have been regarded in the past. That is to say, principal military objectives, in the event of a nuclear war stemming from a major attack on the alliance, should be the destruction of the enemy's military forces, not of his civilian population.

The very strength and nature of the alliance forces make it possible for us to retain, even in the face of a massive surprise attack, sufficient reserve striking power to destroy an enemy society if driven to it. In other words, we are giving a possible opponent the strongest imaginable incentive to refrain from striking our own cities.

The strength that makes these contributions to deterrence and to the hope of deterring attack upon civil societies even in wartime does not come cheap. We are confident that our current nuclear programs are adequate and will continue to be adequate for as far into the future as we can reasonably foresee. During the coming fiscal year the United States plans to spend close to $15 billion on its nuclear weapons to assure their adequacy. For what this money buys, there is no substitute.

In particular, relatively weak national nuclear forces with enemy cities as their targets are not likely to be sufficient to perform even the function of deterrence. If they are small, and perhaps vulnerable on the ground or in the air, or inaccurate, a major antagonist can take a variety of measures to counter them. Indeed, if a major antagonist came to believe there was a substantial likelihood of its being used independently, this force would be inviting preemptive first strike against it. In the event of war, the use of such a force against the cities of a major nuclear power would be tantamount to suicide, whereas its employment against significant military targets would have a negligible effect on the outcome of the conflict. Meanwhile the creation of a single additional national nuclear force encourages the proliferation of nuclear power with all of its attendant dangers.

In short, then, limited nuclear capabilities, operating independently, are dangerous, expensive, prone to obsolescence, and lacking in credibility as a deterrent. Clearly, the United States nuclear contribution to the alliance is neither obsolete nor dispensable.

At the same time, the general strategy I have summarized magnifies the importance of unity of planning, concentration of executive authority, and central direction. There must not be competing and conflicting strategies to meet the contingency of nuclear war. We are convinced that a general nuclear war target system is indivisible and if, despite all our efforts, nuclear war should occur, our best hope lies in conducting a centrally controlled campaign against all of the enemy's vital nuclear capabilities, while retaining reserve forces, all centrally controlled.

We know that the same forces which are targeted on ourselves are also targeted on our allies. Our own strategic retaliatory forces are prepared to respond against these forces, wherever they are and whatever their targets. This mission is assigned not only in fulfillment of our treaty commitments but also because the character of nuclear war compels it. More specifically, the United States is as much concerned with that portion of Soviet nuclear striking power that can reach Western Europe as with that portion that also can reach the United States. In short, we have undertaken the nuclear defense of NATO on a global basis. This will continue to be our objective. In the execution of this mission, the weapons in the European theater are only one resource among many.

There is, for example, the Polaris force, which we have been substantially increasing and which, because of its specially invulnerable nature, is peculiarly well suited to serve as a strategic reserve force. We have already announced the commitment of five of these ships, fully operational, to the NATO Command.

This sort of commitment has a corollary for the alliance as a whole. We want and need a greater degree of alliance participation in formulating nuclear weapons policy to the greatest extent possible. We would all find it intolerable to contemplate having only a part of the strategic force launched in isolation from our main striking power. . . .

With the alliance possessing the strength and the strategy I have described, it is most unlikely that any power will launch a nuclear attack on NATO. For the kinds of conflicts, both political and military, most likely to arise in the NATO area, our capabilities for response must not be limited to nuclear weapons alone. The Soviets have superiority in nonnuclear forces in Europe today. But that superiority is by no means overwhelming. Collectively, the alliance has the potential for a successful defense against such forces. . . . The number of U.S. combat-ready divisions has been increased from 11 to 16. Stockpiled in Europe now are full sets of equipment for two additional divisions; the men of these divisions can be rapidly moved to Europe by air.

We expect that our allies will also undertake to strengthen further their nonnuclear forces and to improve the quality and staying power of these forces. These achievements will complement our deterrent strength. With improvements in alliance ground-force strength and staying power, improved nonnuclear air capabilities, and better equipped and trained reserve forces, we can be assured that no deficiency exists in the NATO defense of this vital region and that no aggression, small or large, can succeed. . . .

The security provided by military strength is a necessary, but not sufficient, condition for the achievement of our foreign policy goals, including our goals in the field of arms control and disarmament. Military security provides a base on which we can build free-world strength through the economic advances and political reforms which are the object of the President's programs, like the Alliance for Progress and the trade expansion legislation. Only in a peaceful world can we give full scope to the individual potential, which is for us the ultimate value.

A distinguished European visited the United States last month as a guest of the President. André Malraux, French Minister of State for Cultural Affairs, is an eminent novelist and critic. He led an archeological expedition to Cambodia and fought in the Spanish Civil War and the French Resistance Movement. Malraux paid a moving tribute to our nation when he said:

> The only nation that has waged war but not worshipped it, that has won the greatest power in the world but not sought it, that has wrought the greatest weapon of death but has not wished to wield it. . . . May it inspire men with dreams worthy of its action.

The Demise of NATO*

Ronald Steel

Today NATO is floundering in a permanent state of crisis, for the two conditions on which it was built—American invulnerability and European weakness—have virtually disappeared. The nuclear stalemate has erased the significance of American atomic supremacy, while the evolution of military technology has made the United States directly vulnerable to attack. Europe, for its part, has reconstituted itself into a stable and powerful economic force, one which is eager to assert its independence and potentially capable of defending its own interests. In combination, these two changes in the world power structure have undermined NATO's foundation and thrown its future into doubt.

In its original conception NATO was meant to be a simple guarantee pact between the United States and Europe. It held out the promise that America would intervene if necessary to prevent Western Europe from falling under Communist control. Thus it was, in effect, an extension of the Monroe Doctrine from the Western hemisphere to Europe, with a repudiation of that provision which forbade our interference in European affairs. For the Europeans, the pact with America offered the promise of a desperately needed breathing space to help them weather the early postwar period of social unrest and economic hardship. Behind the shield of NATO—and with the stimulus of the Marshall Plan—the Europeans would build up their own economies so that they might become secure from subversion within and strong enough to protect themselves from without. The alliance, then, appeared to be in everyone's interest: it gave the Europeans an opportunity to reconstruct their economies without the burden of a large-scale arms program; and it gave America

* *Commentary,* May 1963, pp. 397–402. © 1963 by the American Jewish Committee. Reprinted by permission. Mr. Steel is a political journalist and a Congressional Fellow of the American Political Science Association.

the assurance that the resources of Western Europe would not drop by default into Russian hands.

But if the avowed purpose of NATO was to serve as a military adjunct to what was essentially an economic aid program—the idea being that the Marshall Plan would ultimately pay itself off in the ability of the Europeans to provide their own defense—there was also another view of the relative priorities of American military and economic involvement in Europe. The Truman administration, in fact, was split in two over the issue. On the one side were those who saw the Soviet threat as primarily political-economic and only secondarily military; for them NATO was a fence behind which Europe could rebuild its shattered house. On the other side were those who conceived the alliance as a military counter-force to the Soviet presence in Eastern Europe, and as a device for securing advanced bases for American power. In this view, Soviet aggression was believed to be imminent, and NATO was therefore seen only as the prelude to a vast rearmament program designed to achieve parity on the Continent with the Russians.

These two views were quite irreconcilable because they rested on totally different interpretations of Europe's needs and Russia's intentions. The conflict, however, was soon resolved in favor of those who regarded NATO as the framework for a powerful military counter to the Soviet Union. Accordingly, the alliance was transformed from a simple guarantee pact, under which America promised to come to Europe's defense in case of a Soviet attack, into an integrated military force pooling the resources of Europe and America. Within less than two years after the treaty was signed, Secretary of State Acheson called for the rearmament of Germany and the incorporation of ten German divisions into a European land army.

Despite this change, however, the alliance continued to rest—as it had rested since its inception—upon the strength of the American nuclear deterrent. The nuclear guarantee was the ultimate line of Western defense, and—despite token military integration—control of the deterrent lay entirely in American hands. So far as the Europeans were concerned, this meant that there was always the danger that the United States, for reasons of its own safety, might one day decide to withdraw the guarantee, thereby leaving the Continent vulnerable to Russian aggression. American involvement in Europe was too recent a phenomenon for Europeans to take for granted; more vivid in their minds was the long history of American isolationism. Nor could the creation of a European land army solve this problem, for even with a large conventional army Europe could not deter the Russians from using their nuclear weapons if there were no fear of American nuclear reprisal. Thus, the Europeans were obliged to find some means of making sure that in the event of Russian aggression against the Continent, the United States would be committed from the very start.

The answer lay in the American troops stationed in Europe as a contribution to the NATO land forces. The presence of these soldiers served, in a way that no promise or treaty possibly could, to guarantee that the United States would be immediately drawn into any military struggle in Europe. In other words, these troops were simply American hostages to Europe. Whatever additional functions they may have had, this was—and still is—their primary purpose, and it explains why our European allies have always been determined to keep them there. Unable by themselves to hold back any serious Soviet assault, the American divisions in Germany are the only tangible proof that the American nuclear guarantee really does extend to Europe.

Obviously, neither American nor European strategists could openly admit this, not even to each other. Such an admission would have horrified the United States Congress (which had been persuaded that NATO was the first step toward a mystical trans-Atlantic brotherhood), and it might have led to a new sweep of isolationism—exactly what the Europeans were bent on preventing. Consequently, elaborate theories were designed to account for the American land forces in Germany: they were there because the Europeans were outnumbered by Russian "hordes" (although census figures revealed this to be nonsense) or to serve as a "trip wire" which would bring an immediate nuclear response to any Russian land probe (although the Europeans could have played the same role themselves—if they had trusted the American guarantee).

So the Europeans got their hostages—but only at a price. The price was the creation of sizable land armies which were larger than the token commitments they had originally been prepared to make to NATO. Faced by labor shortages, material scarcities, and public hostility, the governments of Western Europe nevertheless restored the draft and devoted a considerable proportion of their scarce resources to building an army that was larger than they wanted and one for which NATO strategy could assign no function.

But the American hostages in Germany not only assured the Europeans that the United States was inextricably involved in the fate of the Continent; they also made the American nuclear deterrent more credible to the Russians. America's strategic nuclear arsenal, plus the tactical atomic weapons at the front, together formed the backbone of European defense. If the Russians relied upon their superior conventional forces to start a westward probe, they would be decimated by American short-range tactical weapons. And if they should be so foolish as to launch an all-out attack on Western Europe, America's strategic nuclear force would be unleashed in terrible retribution against the Soviet Union itself.

This strategy was reasonable so long as the United States retained a monopoly on tactical atomic weapons. But the whole picture changed when the Russians incorporated tactical atomic weapons into their army as well. From that point on, any confrontation of forces in Central Europe promised to escalate into a full-scale nuclear holocaust, and NATO's pledge to use atomic weapons in defense of Europe would only be realizable at the cost of transforming the Continent into a radioactive charnel-house. While the distinction between a nuclear war fought with tactical weapons and one fought with strategic weapons may be relevant to residents of Chicago, it is of little significance for the millions of people concentrated in the narrow land corridors of Europe.

In short, despite the missile bases, despite the nuclear stockpiles, despite the troops trained in the use of atomic weapons, NATO's nuclear strategy ceased to make sense on the day the Russians equipped their own forces with tactical nuclear weapons. At that moment it became unmistakably clear that America's vast nuclear force, all protestations to the contrary notwithstanding, could only be used to *deter* the Russians from launching an attack on Europe—but never to fight battles on the Continent once war had erupted. If deterrence ever broke down, there could be no nuclear defense of Europe that would not also mean the destruction of Europe. Yet to have admitted this would have been to demolish the entire foundation on which NATO's elaborate structure for defense had been built.

It was to cope with the new situation and restore a lost credibility to NATO that the Kennedy administration proposed an increase in the alliance's land forces from 23 to a total of 30 divisions. In the eyes of its advocates this proposal offered the prospect of a conventional NATO response to any Soviet land probe in Central Europe without the suicidal resort to nuclear weapons. By an unfortunate coincidence, 30 was exactly the number of divisions which NATO had earlier claimed was the bare minimum necessary to support a strategy relying on the very tactical weapons that it now proposed to circumvent. How the same 30 divisions could serve either strategy equally well was a mystery no one cared to explain.

This increased land force would have to come from the Europeans themselves, giving them the task of countering any Russian land attack by conventional means. As its part in the new strategy, the United States would continue to keep its troops as hostages in West Germany, but its principal contribution would be the awesome nuclear arsenal which it harbors for the joint defense of the West. From an American point of view, this division of labor—European manpower plus the American nuclear deterrent—seemed an ideal solution to NATO's defense problems: at long last the old Dulles doctrine of "massive retaliation"—so bold in phrase, so meaningless in effect—could be put to rest. From the European point of view, however, the new strategy has come too late and promises too little. For the advent of the intercontinental missile, by making the United States itself vulnerable to Russian nuclear power, has brought the credibility of our guarantee to Europe into even more serious question than before.

Nations are often loyal to one another; sometimes they will even fight on their friends' behalf. But nuclear weapons have made war qualitatively different from anything nations have experienced in the past. Nobody can be sure that a nation will deliberately commit suicide in response to an attack on its allies. The Europeans know that "never" and "always" have been said too many times in the history of alliances for any nation to count upon them; and they well remember Czechoslovakia in 1938 and Budapest in 1956. De Gaulle voiced a widespread underlying fear in Europe when he said:

> America and Soviet Russia are able to strike one another directly and no doubt reciprocally able to destroy one another. It is not certain that they will risk it. No one today can know when, or how, or why one or the other of these great atomic powers will use its nuclear arsenal. One has only to say this in order to understand that as far as concerns the defense of France, the battle of Europe, and even the world war such as they were imagined when NATO was created, all is brought into question.

For the supreme task of nuclear deterrence, then, alliances have ceased to be psychologically credible, although they remain useful for other purposes. Only a political confederation can give the assurance that an attack upon one really is an attack upon all. But the "Atlantic community," however laudable a goal, is still little more than rhetoric, and the disintegrating NATO alliance appears increasingly unlikely to furnish a stable base for a political union between America and Europe—one which neither partner seems willing to translate from hyperbole to reality.

Apart from all this, the new emphasis on conventional forces in Europe is no solution to the disagreements within the alliance because it consigns the Europeans to an inherently inferior role. Europe today is an emerging great power, the economic equal of America, and potentially capable of defending itself. Caught up in the vision of European union, a vision which we ourselves encouraged them to form, and impelled by the very economic recovery that we ourselves fostered in order to make them self-sufficient once again, the Europeans are no longer content to leave the ultimate decision between war and peace concentrated exclusively in American hands. There should be nothing surprising in this. "It is," as Henry Kissinger has pointed out, "against all reason to expect our European allies to integrate their conventional forces in a joint command and to place increased reliance on a conventional defense, while one partner reserves for itself a monopoly on the means of responding to the Soviet nuclear threat and freedom of action in employing nuclear weapons."

In sum, it is not simply that certain defense policies have become outdated, but rather that the whole structure of the alliance has become anachronistic, and is not likely to be revitalized by gimmicks such as nuclear multilateralism and missile-carrying cargo ships. Multilateralism, under which the United States and the European allies would both contribute to a pool of nuclear weapons, is simply a device for side-stepping the basic question of who shall control the West's nuclear forces. If the projected joint nuclear force were to be controlled by a committee of nations operating under majority rule, it would have the power to pull the United States into a nuclear war proposed and that no Congress would permit. If, on the other hand, the joint nuclear force is to be subject to an American veto—as the administration has admitted—then there is little hope that it will satisfy the desire of the Euro-even against its own will—a situation that no American President has ever peans for a greater role in their own defense. All it offers them is the dubious privilege of paying for expensive American-made weapons which they cannot control, for which even Pentagon strategists can find no military justification, and which promise to make Germany the fulcrum of a powerful nuclear missile force in a spasmodic effort to block France's modest nuclear efforts.

NATO's strategic crisis might be less severe if the only point of contention between the United States and the Soviet Union were centered in Europe. Then it might be reasonable to suppose that American and European interests were identical, and it might reasonably be argued that it is in Europe's best interest to continue relying on the American nuclear monopoly. But unfortunately, the struggle between the United States and the Soviet Union is not confined to Europe. Latin America, Southeast Asia, and Africa are all implicated too, and the events of the past few years have shown that the interests of our European allies in these areas often differ from our own. Latin America is peripheral to Europeans' concerns; our involvement in Vietnam elicits either their disinterest or disapproval; and in the long Congo crisis we learned that our closest allies were most opposed to our policies. NATO, whatever the pretensions of its enthusiasts, is not a global alliance; it is only a pact between America and Europe for the defense of Europe. Beyond that it may have great expectations but little substance.

The interests of the two partners, as they conceive them, have diverged significantly in the past, but perhaps never so greatly as during the recent Cuban crisis. The importance of this episode can hardly be exaggerated, for, as nothing since the Suez landings in 1956, it brought home to the Europeans the full extent of their bondage to American strategy and their total inability to influence that strategy. It revealed the true balance of forces within the alliance, showing the difference between power in being and power in theory, and it demonstrated how NATO really works in times of crisis.

To most Americans, the handling of the Cuban crisis seemed at once brave and judicious, authoritative and magnanimous—a triumphant display of military power tempered by political wisdom. While it may indeed have been all of these things, the Europeans viewed it from a different perspective. For them there were two crucial lessons to be drawn from the Cuban crisis. The first was that the United States was ready to risk the nuclear obliteration of its allies in defense of American interests, although the United States would not allow itself to be drawn into danger in defense of European interests—as its actions in the Suez landings demonstrated. The second lesson was that the two nuclear giants would impose whatever settlement they saw fit upon weak third nations involved in their power rivalry.

The showdown between America and Russia was *Realpolitik* on a grand scale, the most naked military confrontation they had yet engaged in. To Washington officials, their intoxicating victory seemed to indicate that the Europeans had even more reason than ever to put their faith in American diplomacy and American protection. But the Europeans—who were neither consulted in advance nor allowed to assume that they could in any way influence the course the United States had embarked upon—interpreted this victory quite differently: they saw themselves in the place of Cuba, forced to accept a settlement imposed upon it by two great nuclear powers acting in concert. It was, so far as they were concerned, Suez all over again, with Cuba the victim instead of Britain and France. From this point of view, the moral of the Cuban crisis was that when the chips are down nations without nuclear weapons will always be forced to acquiesce in the will of the nuclear powers. Rather than undermining the European desire for an independent nuclear deterrent, as Washington imagined, Cuba only reinforced it.

By acting unilaterally in Cuba, the Kennedy administration did everything that was consistent with the interests of a great power, and everything inconsistent with the maintenance of an integrated alliance. It is not that its actions were wrong; a great power must pursue its interests even at the expense of alienating its allies. But these actions revealed that the alliance, for all the rhetoric about interdependence, is still made up of one powerful nation and a group of its protectorates. Such an alliance of unequals, based upon an outdated political vision of the world, and structured upon the permanent dominance of one of the partners, cannot outlast the disappearance of the conditions which originally led to its creation. NATO is faced with a crisis it can no longer avoid. In an age where alliances are becoming obsolete, it must either be replaced by something completely different—that is, an Atlantic community to which the United States would relinquish its sovereignty, its control of nuclear weapons, and its diplomacy—or else the alliance will dissolve as Europe constitutes itself as a great power with its own independent system of defense. Considering the sad history of military alliances based on external threats, and the tendency of nuclear weapons to reinforce rather than undermine national sovereignty, it seems that NATO is in process of joining that long and distinguished list of disintegrated alliances.

Total U.S. Commitment to the Defense of Europe*

John F. Kennedy

One hundred and fifteen years ago a most learned parliament was convened in this historic hall. Its goal was a united German federation. Its members were poets and professors, and lawyers, and philosophers, and doctors and clergymen, freely elected in all parts of the land. No nation applauded its endeavors as warmly as my own. No assembly ever strove more ardently to put

* "Defense of the Atlantic Community Is Indivisible." Address by the late President John F. Kennedy in the Paulskirche, Frankfurt, Germany, June 25, 1963. Text from *Department of State Bulletin,* July 22, 1963, pp. 118–123.

perfection into practice. And though in the end it failed, no other building in Germany deserves more the title of "Cradle of German Democracy."

But can there be such a title? In my own home city of Boston, Faneuil Hall—once the meeting-place of the authors of the American Revolution—has long been known as the "Cradle of American Liberty." But when, in 1852, the Hungarian patriot Kossuth addressed an audience there, he criticized its name. "It is," he said, "a great name—but there is something in it which saddens my heart. You should not say American liberty. You should say liberty in America. Liberty should not be either American or European—it should just be liberty."

Kossuth was right. For unless liberty flourishes in all lands, it cannot flourish in one. Conceived in one hall, it must be carried out in many. Thus the seeds of the American Revolution had been brought earlier from Europe, and they later took root around the world. And the German revolution of 1848 transmitted ideas and idealists to America and to other lands. Today, in 1963, democracy and liberty are more international than ever before, and the spirit of the Frankfurt Assembly, like the spirit of Faneuil Hall, must live in many hearts and nations if it is to live at all.

For we live in an age of interdependence as well as independence—an age of internationalism as well as nationalism. In 1848 many countries were indifferent to the goals of the Frankfurt Assembly. It was, they said, a German problem. Today there are no exclusively German problems, or American problems. There are world problems—and our two countries and continents are inextricably bound together in the task of peace as well as war.

We are partners for peace, not in a narrow bilateral context, but in a framework of Atlantic partnership. . . .

That is why our nations are working together to strengthen NATO, to expand trade, to assist the developing countries to align our monetary policies and to build the Atlantic Community. I would not diminish the miracle of West Germany's economic achievements. But the true German miracle has been your rejection of the past for the future—your reconciliation with France, your participation in the building of Europe, your leading role in NATO, and your growing support for constructive undertakings throughout the world.

Your economic institutions, your constitutional guarantees, your confidence in civilian authority, are all harmonious with the ideals of older democracies. And they form a firm pillar of the democratic European community.

But Goethe tells us in his greatest poem that Faust lost the liberty of his soul when he said to the passing moment: "Stay, thou art so fair." And our liberty, too, is endangered if we pause for the passing moment, if we rest on our achievements, if we resist the pace of progress. For time and the world do not stand still. Change is the law of life. And those who look only to the past or the present are certain to miss the future.

The future of the West lies in Atlantic partnership—a system of cooperation, interdependence and harmony whose people can jointly meet their burdens and opportunities throughout the world. Some say this is only a dream, but I do not agree. A generation of achievement—the Marshall Plan, NATO, the Schuman Plan, and the Common Market—urges us up the path to greater unity.

There will be difficulties and delays, and doubts and discouragement. There will be differences of approach and opinion. But we have the will and the means to serve three related goals—the heritage of our countries, the unity of our continents and the interdependence of the Western alliance.

Some say that the United States will neither hold to these purposes nor abide by its pledges—that we will revert to a narrow nationalism. But such doubts fly in the face of history. For 18 years the United States has stood its watch for freedom all around the globe. The firmness of American will, and the effectiveness of American strength, have been shown in support of free men and free governments, in Asia, in Africa, in the Americas; and above all, here in Europe we have undertaken, and sustained in honor, relations of mutual trust and obligation with more than 40 allies. We are proud of this record, which more than answers doubts. But, in addition, these proven commitments to the common freedom and safety are assured, in the future as in the past, by one great fundamental fact—that they are deeply rooted in America's own self-interest. Our commitment to Europe is indispensable—in our interest as well as yours.

It is not in our interest to try to dominate the European councils of decision. If that were our objective, we would prefer to see Europe divided and weak, enabling the United States to deal with each fragment individually. Instead we have and now look forward to a Europe united and strong—speaking with a common voice—acting with a common will—a world power capable of meeting world problems as a full and equal partner. . . .

This is in the interest of us all. For war in Europe, as we learned twice in 40 years, destroys peace in America. A threat to the freedom of Europe is a threat to the freedom of America. That is why no administration in Washington can fail to respond to such a threat—not merely from good will but from necessity. And that is why we look forward to a united Europe in an Atlantic partnership—an entity of interdependent parts, sharing equally both burdens and decisions, and linked together in the task of defense as well as the arts of peace.

There is no fantasy. It will be achieved by concrete steps to solve the problems that face us all: military, economic and political. Partnership is not a posture but a process—a continuous process—a continuous process that grows stronger each year as we devote ourselves to common tasks.

The first task of the Atlantic Community was to assure its common defense. That defense was and still is indivisible. The United States will risk its cities to defend yours because we need your freedom to protect ours. Hundreds of thousands of our soldiers serve with yours on this continent, as tangible evidence of this pledge. Those who would doubt our pledge or deny this indivisibility—those who would separate Europe from America or split one ally from another—would only give aid and comfort to the men who make themselves our adversaries and welcome any Western disarray.

The purpose of our common military effort is not war but peace—not the destruction of nations but the protection of freedom. The forces that West Germany contributes to this effort are second to none among the Western European nations. Your nation is in the first line of this defense—and your divisions, side by side with our own, are a source of strength to us all.

These conventional forces are essential, and they are backed by the sanction of thousands of the most modern weapons here on European soil and thousands more, only minutes away, in posts around the world. Together our nations have developed for the forward defense of free Europe a deterrent far surpassing the present or prospective force of any hostile power.

Nevertheless, it is natural that America's nuclear position has raised questions within the alliance. I believe we must confront these questions—not by turning the clock backward to separate nuclear deterrents—but by developing a more closely unified Atlantic deterrent, with genuine European participation.

How this can best be done, and it is not easy—in some ways more difficult to split the atom politically than it was physically—but how this can best be done is under discussion with those who may wish to join in this effort. The proposal before us now is for a new Atlantic force. Such a force would bring strength instead of weakness, cohesion instead of division. It would belong to all members, not one, with all participating on a basis of full equality. And as Europe moves towards unity, its role and responsibility, here as elsewhere, would and must increase accordingly. Meanwhile, there is much to do. We must work more closely together on strategy, training and planning. European officers from NATO are being assigned to Strategic Air Command headquarters in Omaha, Nebraska. Modern weapons are being deployed here in Western Europe. And America's strategic deterrent—the most powerful in history—will continue to be at the service of the whole alliance.

Second: Our partnership is not military alone. Economic unity is also imperative—not only among the nations of Europe, but across the wide Atlantic.

Indeed, economic cooperation is needed throughout the entire free world. By opening our markets to the developing countries of Africa, Asia and Latin America, by contributing our capital and skills, by stabilizing basic prices, we can help assure them of a favorable climate for freedom and growth. This is an Atlantic responsibility. For the Atlantic nations themselves helped to awaken these peoples. Our merchants and our traders ploughed up their soils—and their societies as well—in search of minerals and oil and rubber and coffee. Now we must help them gain full membership in the 20th century, closing the gap between the rich and the poor.

Another great economic challenge is in the coming round of trade negotiations. Those deliberations are much more important than a technical discussion of trade and commerce. They are an opportunity to build common industrial and agricultural policies across the Atlantic. They are an opportunity to open up new sources of demand, to give new impetus to growth, and make more jobs and prosperity, for our expanding populations. They are an opportunity to recognize the trading needs and aspirations of other free countries, including Japan. . . .

Trade expansion will help us all. The experience of the Common Market—like the experience of the German Zollverein—shows an increased rise in business activity and general prosperity resulting for all participants in such trade agreements, with no member profiting at the expense of another. As they say on my own Cape Cod, "A rising tide lifts all the boats." And a partnership, by definition, serves both partners, without domination or unfair advantage. Together we have been partners in adversity—let us also be partners in prosperity.

Beyond development and trade is monetary policy. Here again our interests run together. Indeed there is no field in which the wider interests of all more clearly outweigh the narrow interest of one. We have lived by that principle, as bankers to freedom, for a generation. Now that other nations—including West Germany—have found new economic strength, it is time for common efforts here, too. The great free nations of the world must take control of our monetary problems if these problems are not to take control of us.

And third and finally, our partisanship depends on common political purpose. Against the hazards of division and lassitude, no lesser force will serve. History tells us that disunity and relaxation are the great internal dangers of an alliance. Thucydides reported that the Peloponnesians and their allies were mighty in battle but handicapped by their policy-making body—in which, he related "each presses its own end . . . which generally results in no action at all . . . they devote more time to the prosecution of their own purposes than to the consideration of the general welfare—each supposes that no harm will come of his own neglect, that it is the business of another to do this and that—and so, as each separately entertains the same illusion, the common cause imperceptibly decays."

Is this also to be the story of the grand alliance? Welded in a moment of imminent danger, will it disintegrate into complacency with each member pressing its own ends to the neglect of the common cause? This must not be the case. Our old dangers are not gone beyond return, and any division among us would bring them back in doubled strength. . . .

It is only a fully cohesive Europe that can protect us all against fragmentation of our alliance. Only such a Europe will permit full reciprocity of treatment across the ocean, in facing the Atlantic agenda. With only such a Europe can we have a full give-and-take between equals, an equal sharing of responsibilities, and an equal level of sacrifice. I repeat again—so that there may be no misunderstanding—the choice of paths to the unity of Europe is a choice which Europe must make. But as you continue this great effort, undeterred by either difficulty or delay, you should know that this new European greatness will be not an object of fear, but a source of strength, for the United States of America.

There are other political tasks before us. We must all learn to practice more completely the art of consultation on matters stretching well beyond the immediate military and economic questions.

Together, for example, we must explore the possibilities of leashing the tensions of the cold war and reducing the dangers of the arms race. Together we must work to strengthen the spirit of those Europeans who are not now free, to re-establish their old ties to freedom in the West, so that their desire for liberty and their sense of nationhood and their sense of belonging to the Western community over hundreds of years, will survive for future expression.

We ask those who would be our adversaries to understand that in our relations with them we will not bargain one nation's interest against another, and that the commitment to the cause of freedom is common to us all.

All of us in the West must be faithful to our conviction that peace in Europe can never be complete until everywhere in Europe, and that includes Germany, men can choose, in peace and freedom, how their countries shall be governed, and choose, without threat to any neighbor, reunification with their countrymen.

I preach no easy liberation and I make no empty promises, but my countrymen, since our country was founded, believe strongly in the proposition that all men shall be free and all free men shall have this right of choice.

As we look steadily eastward in the hope and purpose of new freedom, we must look—and ever more closely—to our transatlantic ties. The Atlantic Community will not soon become a single overarching superstate. But practical steps toward stronger common purpose are well within our means. As we widen our common effort in defense, and our three-fold cooperation in economics, we shall inevitably strengthen our political ties as well. . . . In the far future there may be a great new union for us all. But for the present, there is plenty for all to do in building new and enduring connections.

In short, the words of Thucydides are a warning, not a prediction. We have it in us, as 18 years have shown, to build our defenses, to strengthen our economies, and to tighten our political bonds, both in good weather and bad. We can move forward with the confidence that is born of success and the skill that is born of experience. And as we move, let us take heart from the certainty that we are united not only by danger and necessity, but by hope and purpose as well.

For we know now that freedom is more than the rejection of tyranny—that prosperity is more than an escape from want—that partnership is more than a sharing of power. These are, above all, great human adventures. They must have meaning and conviction and purpose—and because they do, in your country and in mine, in all the nations of the alliance, we are called to a great new mission.

It is not a mission of self-defense alone—for that is a means, not an end.

It is not a mission of arbitrary power—for we reject the idea of one nation dominating another. The mission is to create a new social order, founded on liberty and justice, in which men are the masters of their fate, in which states are the servants of their citizens, and in which all men and women can share a better life for themselves and their children. That is the object of our common policy.

To realize this vision, we must seek a world of peace—a world in which peoples dwell together in mutual respect and work together in mutual regard—a world in which peace is not a mere interlude between wars, but an incentive to the creative energies of humanity. We will not find such a peace today, or tomorrow. The obstacles to hope are large and menacing. Yet the goals of a peaceful world—today and tomorrow—must shape our decisions and inspire our purposes.

So we are all idealists. We are all visionaries. Let it not be said of this Atlantic generation that we left ideals and visions to the past, nor purpose and determination to our adversaries. We have come too far, we have sacrificed too much, to disdain the future now. And we shall ever remember what Goethe told us—that the "highest wisdom, the best that mankind ever knew" was the realization that "he only earns his freedom and existence who daily conquers them anew."

What Price Conventional War in Europe?*

Bernard Brodie

Just as the "massive retaliation" doctrine characterized the main thrust of the Eisenhower administration's defense policies, so that of the Kennedy administration has been marked by persistent emphasis on very nearly the opposite theme. That theme is briefly stated as follows: although we will not voluntarily relinquish the nuclear ascendancy now enjoyed by the United States, prudent anticipation of the coming nuclear stalemate requires us to return to conventional forces for the tactical defense even of Europe. . . .

The new American school of thought, which exists in several variants on the part of advocates both in and out of government, possesses no label com-

* "What Price Conventional Capabilities in Europe?" *The Reporter,* May 23, 1963, pp. 25–33. Reprinted by permission of The RAND Corporation. Mr. Brodie is former Professor of International Relations, Yale University, and is a senior staff member of The RAND Corporation.

parable in pithiness to the Dulles "massive retaliation" tag; but we shall call it here the Conventional War in Europe philosophy (CWE).

The administration's authentic views on the subject of CWE have not been readily available to the public. There was some reference to them in Secretary of Defense Robert S. McNamara's Ann Arbor speech of June 16, 1962, but a later and much better source is his book-length statement before the House Armed Services Committee on January 30, 1963. The relevant comments are characteristically lean, but their significance is clear.

After pointing out that ". . . we must continue to strengthen and modernize our tactical nuclear capabilities to deal with an attack where the opponent employs such weapons first, or any attack by conventional forces which puts Europe in danger of being overrun," Mr. McNamara went on to say: "But we must also substantially increase our non-nuclear capabilities to foreclose to our opponent the freedom of action he would otherwise have, or believe he would have, in lesser military provocations. We must be in position to confront him at any level of provocation with an appropriate military response. The decision to employ tactical nuclear weapons should not be forced upon us simply because we have no other way to cope with a particular situation. . . .

"Although we are still a long way from achieving the non-nuclear capabilities we hope to create in Europe, we are much better off in this regard than we were two years ago. Today the NATO forces can deal with a much greater range of Soviet actions, without resorting to the use of nuclear weapons. Certainly, they can deal with any major incursion or probe. But we must continue to do everything in our power to persuade our Allies to meet their NATO force goals so that we will possess alternative capabilities for dealing with even larger Soviet attacks." . . .

However, on this issue as well as on several others, our major allies have for some time shown themselves markedly resistant to our persuasion. Following the French veto on Britain's admission to the Common Market, the NATO alliance has been in a state of shock. France's rejection of American leadership in military and other matters has been violent and extreme. . . . And, however much the French behavior is regretted by our other allies, the latter are not about to respond with a larger conventional effort.

In trying to understand this attitude, one must first remember that the view our government is now advancing as the only reasonable one is the reverse of the idea that our leaders were preaching only a few years ago. . . .

The purposes of achieving a very large conventional capability are generally given as follows:

> It should discourage the enemy from thinking that our unwillingness to be the first to use nuclear weapons, or to see nuclear general war visited upon the world, gives him opportunities to achieve limited but important victories by local non-nuclear aggression. He must not suppose that he can outbid us quickly and decisively in non-

nuclear strength. Making it clear that he cannot will add materially to deterrence.

If he nevertheless becomes involved through "miscalculation" in an attack on us and finds that, because of our resistance, he has applied most or all of his non-nuclear strength, he will have a chance to pause and reconsider what he is risking. If he then continues his aggression, the onus for bringing in nuclear weapons will be on him.

It may be we who want to take the diplomatic and even military initiative, and it will make all the difference in our willingness to do so if we can make some meaningful move without nuclear weapons.

There is also the conviction that at least by 1970 there will be no such thing as a meaningful superiority in strategic nuclear capabilities. Thus, the threat of strategic nuclear war as the ultimate backstop to a diplomatic position will be unavailable.

In any case, the enemy is to receive the clearest warning that we will not accept a loss of territory or other comparable defeats. We remain committed to introducing nuclear weapons not only if the enemy does so but also if we find ourselves losing significantly. The aim of keeping war in Europe non-nuclear is considered terribly important, but nonetheless secondary to the aim of not losing.

We should distinguish this CWE philosophy from several other ideas which have become current of late and which I do not wish to challenge. At this date few persons professionally involved in defense doubt the need for some conventional forces for the contingencies of limited war such as might easily occur outside Europe and conceivably inside Europe as well. The spelling out of the specific requirements is difficult and controversial, but on the point of principle there is not much argument.

We should also distinguish various current doctrines of discriminate or controlled general war, especially that which not only stresses counter-force targets but which adds special and positive emphasis to sparing cities. Avoidance of city bombing, except in direct reprisal, probably has sufficient justification, apart from other obvious interests, in the elementary and familiar proposition that enemy cities have far more strategic significance as hostages than as ruins.

It is also true and important that our allies have made promises to NATO which they have not met and which, until the pertinent agreements are changed, we are justified in pressing them to fulfill. Although the commitments to these force levels were made under the explicit assumption that any outbreak of war in Europe between the Soviet bloc and the West would be almost immediately nuclear, there is no need to deprive available forces of all capability for fighting with conventional weapons.

What we shall be questioning, at least by implication, is, first, the image of the world reflected in the fervor and the zeal—and the excessive goals—behind what is up to a point a reasonable idea, and second, the evident impatience with the misgivings and contrary ideas of allies whose views are habitually dismissed on the ground that they just don't understand the basic facts of nuclear life.

CWE advocates feel, with some justice, that the United States is carrying a disproportionate share of the NATO defense burden. They argue also that American contributions to nuclear capabilities in a general war are more than adequate and should not be duplicated. They usually consider tactical nuclear capabilities in Europe dangerous and illusory. Therefore, according to them, obligations to the common defense by our European and Canadian allies can only and should only take the form of providing greater conventional capabilities.

This idea is hard to put across in Europe. The situation naturally varies from country to country. The smaller NATO nations seem quite content to go along with our views, but they also feel, as small countries have always felt, that what they can contribute is not going to make a critical difference in NATO strength anyway, so why exert themselves unduly? The British and French governments have different ideas from ours about the value to them of independent nuclear capabilities. The French especially have long been determined to go ahead with their program regardless of American objections—partly, perhaps, because they know the United States cannot withhold from France the protective covering accorded Europe, but mostly because they are bent on rejecting the status of a satellite.

The British seem to be less concerned about nuclear dependence on the United States, and among the many who have professed willingness to give up the independent nuclear deterrent is the new leader of the Labour Party, Harold Wilson. However, we should remember that many Britons who take that position do so for reasons that are not necessarily reassuring to the government of the United States. In Britain rejection of the nuclear deterrent often goes with neutralism . . .

Thus, appeals to our NATO allies to increase their military effort must be based on something more objective than the fact that we have shifted to a new strategic philosophy, especially one that must appear to them to cost more and at the same time diminish deterrence. Our insistence that it will increase deterrence is based on premises and assumptions which may be valid under some circumstances but which are certainly not unchallengeable. Our assumption that the new philosophy would demonstrate its superior merits *if* war breaks out will be weighed against the European presumption, however debatable, that the resulting stance could make it *easier* for war to break out—by appearing to push our nuclear strength into the background. Besides, our allies are deeply suspicious of alleged American efforts to get them to provide the "men-at-arms for the American nuclear knight"—to quote one German formulation for a thought that gets served up repeatedly in different verbal flavorings. In any case, their readiness to accept unquestioningly American tutelage in military and strategic matters is considerably less today than it was five or ten years ago.

Those CWE advocates who urge that we should put ourselves in a position to be able to stem at least for a time a full-scale non-nuclear attack by the Soviet forces have in general advanced a startlingly modest view of the extra effort required.

Present promises to NATO would, if fulfilled, raise existing strength on the Central Front from something like twenty-four divisions to something like thirty. NATO may yet conceivably get those thirty divisions, but they are not likely to be well-equipped and full-strength divisions with adequate logistic backing. . . .

There is another point to be considered. If estimates of Soviet ground forces have been exaggerated, it is clearly desirable to cut them down to proper size. Obviously, we want to evaluate *any* forces correctly, whether they be enemy or allied. In pointing out inherent enemy weaknesses, however, we should be careful not to gloss over our own; for example, the inherent weakness of having a force structure stemming from fifteen different nations, with an allocation of commands designed as much to accomplish political as military ends. Whatever the number of divisions available to NATO, their effectiveness must surely fall short, perhaps markedly, of being comparable to a good single-nation army having the same number of divisions.

Anyway, the substantial reduction in Russian ground forces between 1955 and 1961 was a somewhat tardy adjustment to what the Soviets considered the requirements of the nuclear age (as well as, let us add, the absence of any strong urge to conquer a nuclearly defended Western Europe). They stopped further planned cuts in 1961, apparently in response to our build-up. Experience since then suggests their readiness to move up with us to maintain their relative advantage in ground forces in Europe. Their reasons for doing so may or may not be very sophisticated, but it is the one kind of tangible superiority they feel able to maintain.

As Sir Winston Churchill once wrote, concerning the planning for a particularly ill-starred offensive: "However absorbed a commander may be in the elaboration of his own thoughts, it is necessary sometimes to take the enemy into consideration." In the spinning of military theories, it is really remarkable how seldom that is done. In the present case the "enemy" should be considered under both of two guises. First, there is the shrewd opponent familiar in war-gaming rooms, blessed with a free-ranging imagination and showing no biases other than those we share with him. He is shrewd, skillful, and aggressive; he has to be, or one cannot have a challenging and interesting game. The other is the real Soviet opponent, with whom we have had prolonged experience which is available for study but which only a few people do in fact study. He is the opponent who we know has very special ways of looking at things—in other words, who has strong biases, some of which are fundamentally different from ours. This is the opponent who not infrequently blunders but who always shows a deep respect for our strength.

Concerning the CWE school's argument that the enemy will be more deterred by a strong conventional force than he would by a somewhat lesser force committed to using nuclear weapons at a relatively early stage: this can only be the war-game opponent. Certainly the argument requires some quite singular assumptions. One is that the Soviets will boldly make large forays against our nuclear power with non-nuclear arms. According to this line of reasoning, the determination of ourselves and our allies to resist clear aggression will collapse if there is any hint that tactical nuclear weapons may have to be used, and the Russians will know it. In fact, they will be so confident of our restraint that they will take what would otherwise be the most monumental risks! Actually, the question of "credibility" so effectively raised against the Dulles massive-retaliation doctrine hardly applies in Europe—and we are not talking massive retaliation anyway, but tactical nuclear defense. It would probably take much persuasion on our part to shake the Soviet leaders from their apparent conviction that in the event of a substantial attack by them the nuclear weapons available to NATO forces in Europe would quickly be used. Why should we attempt to shake that conviction?

Another critical and dubious assumption is that the enemy will almost certainly refrain from using nuclear weapons if we refrain. Presumably it is "in his interest" to play the game that way—to make war locally but not to risk general war. But there is overwhelming evidence that he fears that *any* war in Europe is in great danger of escalating to general war, and that he rejects the notion that the introduction of nuclear weapons tactically makes all the difference.

Soviet military thinking continues to reject those refinements of military thought that have now become commonplace in this country—concerning, for example, distinctions between limited war and general war, between "controlled" and "uncontrolled" strategic targeting, and between nuclear and non-nuclear tactical operations. The kinds of civilian specialists who have given rise to most of the relevant ideas in this country do not even exist in the Soviet Union. The new Soviet manual of strategy written under the direction of former Chief of Staff Marshal V. Sokolovsky expresses scorn for the "modern school of American economists who consider that it is possible to juggle with nuclear warfare." . . .

Clearly the proposed strategy offers no inducement to the Russians to stay non-nuclear in an all-out premeditated attack with their ground forces. Proponents of the CWE philosophy repeatedly assert that we will not allow ourselves to be beaten. Since in tactical operations with nuclear weapons first use is extremely important—for example, by accomplishing the quick destruction of the opponent's supporting air forces—our determination to introduce such weapons rather than accept defeat tells the enemy, if he believes us, that *he* must introduce them. . . .

The idea that the entire Russian field army could become involved in non-nuclear conflict as a result of an "accidental" outbreak of local violence is perhaps worth a place in the list of contingencies that a planner wishes to think about. But that we should consider the possibility strong enough to let it set a goal for our conventional build-up is fantastic. Anything that could properly be called "accidental war" has been extremely rare historically. What should make it more common in a nuclear age? . . .

In view of the lessons we must draw from the Cuban crisis of 1962 concerning our position in Berlin, it is a mischievous interpretation to hold that the outcome was determined *mostly* by our local conventional superiority. If local superiority in conventional arms made all the difference, why did not Khrushchev make some face-saving retaliation in places where he was superior, as in Berlin? Many indeed predicted that he would. On the contrary, Khrushchev and Ulbricht began, on top of the abject surrender in Cuba, to be sweetly reasonable over Berlin. The significance of this seems to have been completely missed by most observers, who apparently accepted it simply as a bonus. And when the Chinese Communists castigated Khrushchev for retreating from a "paper tiger," his public reply was, "The paper tiger has nuclear teeth."

Surely all can agree that the Cuban episode demonstrated the great aversion of the present Soviet leaders to *any* direct hostilities with the United States. It indicated strongly that they fear even small outbreaks of violence between them and us, no doubt because they consider such outbreaks too likely to proceed rapidly to nuclear war. What surprised and sobered Khrushchev was our readiness to confront him. Our previous behavior had apparently led him to believe we would tolerate his installing the missiles; when he found that we were not that tolerant, he rushed to get them out—apparently unimpeded with any worries about "humiliation."

Still another assumption of the CWE school is that having greater conventional strength would permit us occasionally to take the diplomatic and military initiative where we would not dare do so if we had only nuclear weapons to work with. . . .

Since the end of the Second World War we have at no time taken or *seriously contemplated* any kind of military initiative that was not prompted by some external military aggression by the opponent. Concerning the uprisings in East Germany and in Hungary and the building of the Berlin Wall we did nothing, and our reasons could hardly have hinged on a shortage of conventional forces. In Korea we responded to a direct aggression against a protégé, and in Cuba we responded to a gambit aimed directly at ourselves.

There are many reasons why we are not more given to initiating crises where a clash of arms might be involved, but surely one is the same that caused Khrushchev to surrender in Cuba: violence between great opponents is inherently difficult to control, and it cannot be controlled unilaterally. We therefore save confrontations for the opponent's aggressions.

The most important ingredient in deterring Soviet aggression in Europe is our known readiness to oppose it. For support of this policy, our force structure has been in no important respect inappropriate. Stout hearts and a sense of Soviet methods have been and will surely continue to be more necessary than a conventional build-up. . . .

There are other considerations. The Germans know that not much territory can be yielded before they have yielded all of theirs. The French have pointed to our CWE philosophy as evidence, among other things, of the beginning of American withdrawal from the commitment to defend Europe even at the risk of total nuclear war. To them it confirms their foresight in aspiring for a national *force de frappe*. However wrong that deduction may be, we have needlessly given them much leverage for making it.

When charged that their philosophy looks toward making a new war in Europe resemble the Second World War, CWE advocates answer that it would be a lot better for Europeans than a tactical nuclear war—the implication being that they should jump at the chance. But most Europeans have a different way of looking at the present choice of alternatives. To contribute more men and money in order to make it possible to enjoy another Second World War strikes them, at the very least, as too much relinquishment of the nuclear deterrent. They are abundantly convinced that our staunchness and readiness to use the kind of force we already have in Europe is quite enough to keep the Russians at bay. They seem to hold the same to be true of keeping our position in West Berlin—which makes them willing to follow our lead, though we should be clear that for our non-German allies Berlin is not the best issue for inspiring them to greater sacrifice. . . .

The real issues are much more political than technical. Our experience with the Russians, crowned by the Cuban episode of last October, tells us that the Soviet opponent is not ten feet tall in the moral intangibles of power—as he would have to be to do some of the bold things he does in war games. Even in the Berlin "blockade" of 1948–1949, when we failed altogether to test the Soviets' resolve to deny us access on the ground, they did not attempt to interfere with our airlift, as they could easily have done simply by jamming our Ground Controlled Approach radar system. Why should we go on postulating a kind of behavior that is radically different from what they have demonstrated over a long time? After all, the Soviet leaders have now openly broken with the Marxist-Leninist philosophy of inevitable war, avowedly on the ground that nuclear weapons do matter.

Those weapons have vastly affected the expectation of major war in Europe, and it is absurd not to make the most of that change. It is illogical to propose that the NATO powers should add substantially to their defense burdens in order to exploit a probably slim chance for moderating a possible future European war—which, however, the present dispositions make highly improbable.

It is one thing to exhort our allies to see that their contributions of forces maintain reasonable standards of efficiency, which certainly ought not to exclude a capability for limited conventional operations. It is quite another to invoke fantasies of great modern armies locked in desperate combat in Europe with never a nuclear warhead going off between them. The one attitude invites credit for our political sense as well as for our strategic thinking; the other merely discredits us in both respects.

The Need for Disengagement*

H. Stuart Hughes

The problems of "disengagement" and military alliances in Europe cannot be discussed independently of the political and economic situation in that area. American policy is currently based on assumptions that have long outlived their usefulness and that have acquired a false air of permanence . . . At NATO's inception . . . this policy made sense, and both partners in the coalition—the Truman administration and the European governments, which shared a "left-center" ideology—believed in it. Today this is no longer true. From the military standpoint, NATO has become something quite different from what it was at the start. It is no longer a military coalition in the familiar European tradition, provided with sufficient *conventional* ground forces to act as a deterrent to Soviet expansion. It has become little more than a trip wire for "massive retaliation." The United States' decision to supply its European allies with nuclear warheads has robbed NATO of its military *raison d'être*. It has destroyed the earlier concept of an old-fashioned ground army that would make the Soviet Union hesitate to incur the losses and the international opprobrium which overrunning Central and Western Europe would entail, and it has substituted for it a new theory which reduces Europe to the status of an advanced outpost of the United States in the planning for general nuclear war.

Thus the NATO powers are currently trying to carry out a policy in which they have no real trust. In Britain the campaign for unilateral disarmament has split the Labour party, with a majority of the delegates to the national conference urging abandonment of nuclear weapons. It is true that in Parliament two thirds of the Labour M.P.s remain faithful to the American alliance as currently defined; but even the right wing of the party is committed to advocating universal disarmament, a position which is hard to reconcile with the present theory of NATO. Moreover, the anti-nuclear campaign extends far beyond the adherents of Labour; it is attracting young people of the most varied political allegiances and activating those who have previously been apolitical. In Scandinavia, too, neutralism is a force to be reckoned with, and both government and opposition would like to redefine the alliance in terms that would make it more compatible with the idea of disengagement.

* "Disengagement and NATO," by H. Stuart Hughes, from *The Liberal Papers*, edited by James Roosevelt, pp. 303–312. Copyright © 1962 by James Roosevelt. Reprinted by permission of Doubleday & Company, Inc. Mr. Hughes is Professor of History at Harvard University.

In Italy, Germany, and the Low Countries, loyalty to NATO runs deeper, but here also there are strong crosscurrents of dissent. In Italy the left-wing Socialist party opposes American missile bases. Beyond that, the reliability of France itself within the alliance is far from clear. . . .

De Gaulle has struck at the whole concept of the alliance, making no secret of his belief that the proper organization for Europe should be a loose league of sovereign states under the leadership of his own country.

The logical consequence of such an idea—joined to the prospect that in the near future all the larger powers will be able to manufacture their own nuclear weapons—would be a competition in weaponry *within* the NATO alliance. If each major nation possessed its own bombs and missiles, in addition to those provided by the United States, the distinction between the two types would tend to disappear. As the proud possessor of ultimate weapons, each nation would be a law to itself, and the concept of the alliance would become less and less meaningful.

If one adds to these political and military considerations the current economic split within the NATO powers between the "inner six" and the "outer seven," one can only conclude that the alliance as originally devised a decade ago is falling apart at the seams. In this crisis of NATO, nationalism and neutralism reinforce each other. The first is largely a conservative tendency, the second is characteristic of the democratic left, but they both in effect work against the NATO alliance. For when a nationalist like De Gaulle exploits his countrymen's nostalgia for past grandeur and concentrates his attention on France's African "mission" and on restoring great power status through an independent atomic capability—when France, which was to have been the key pin of NATO, goes off on a nationalist tangent, then internationally minded Europeans are far less likely to seek their salvation in a military alliance, and far more inclined to trust to disarmament, disengagement, and even neutrality for their future preservation.

Since NATO can scarcely be preserved in its present form, the real question is: Should it be transformed by some new principle or should it be abolished? The first would seem the more prudent—although a change of name might well be in order—since the sudden abolition of NATO might entail a crisis of European confidence. In either case, however, the prime goal should be to keep Europe out of the nuclear race by progressively enlarging a Central European area of military disengagement. The idea of disengagement—of removing the hostile forces of East and of West from direct contact with each other—can be formulated in two different ways. In its more cautious form it proposes merely to forbid the deployment of nuclear weapons in a specified area. In its more thoroughgoing form it suggests that the area in question be neutralized and hence removed from the East-West struggle. The proposal of the latter sort advanced by George F. Kennan in his Reith Lectures over the BBC in 1957 occasioned widespread discussion both in Europe and in this country, where it first familiarized the public at large with disengagement possibilities.

This goal can be fully realized only as part of a wider settlement with the Soviet Union. But there are certain things that can be negotiated right away. Among them the most important are the establishment of an initial zone of disengagement and the denial of nuclear weapons to further powers.

The logical place to start negotiation on disengagement is some version of the Rapacki Plan—which has gone through various modifications, but which has usually had as its central feature the nuclear demilitarization of East and West Germany, Poland, and Czechoslovakia. It is far from sure that Khrushchev is currently ready to accept this plan, and it is quite certain that both De Gaulle and Adenauer are against it, but it has great appeal both for Britain and for the Soviet satellites. Above all, the fact that it has been under informal discussion for so long a time has made it appear less threatening than any alternative proposal to both sides in the power struggle. At the very least, an announcement by the American government that it was ready to begin negotiations on this basis would offer two important advantages—it would give evidence that we had serious intentions of reducing military tension in Europe, and it would quite clearly suggest that our policy was no longer tied to the views of our conservative allies.

Moreover, the Rapacki Plan presents a realistic alternative to the "liberation" of East Central Europe about which Republican politicians have talked so much and done so little—witness the failure to give aid to the Hungarian revolution of 1956. On the one hand, its adoption by the United States would offer assurance to the Communist rulers of the Soviet Union and the satellite states that we had abandoned any intention of overthrowing their regimes by subversion or force of arms. At the same time, it would clearly convey to the peoples of East Central Europe that we had not lost interest in their fate—rather, that we were substituting for a purely rhetorical notion of "liberation" a more workable policy for relieving direct military pressure on them and thereby for strengthening the liberal tendencies within their borders.

The Rapacki Plan has the final advantage—as the person of its author, the Polish foreign minister, implies—of "disengaging" two of the Soviet satellites with the strongest Western ties. Thus it offers the most coherent proposal that has appeared to date for bridging the gap between the Western and the Soviet spheres. Currently this is no more than a faint hope. But some partial version of the Rapacki Plan might at least run a chance of acceptance on a trial basis. If, for example, the United States and the Soviet Union were to agree on demilitarizing a relatively small but contiguous area including one province of each of the four states in question—say, Bavaria, Saxony, Bohemia, and Silesia—it could be the beginning of a disengagement by stages that would finally include the whole four-nation zone.

The denial of nuclear weapons to fifth or sixth powers—which means preventing Western Germany and Communist China from joining the present "nuclear club"—is absolutely crucial and grows more urgent with each passing month. Since the French bomb test in the Sahara, there have been reports that the Germans have similar plans afoot, and no one knows exactly what nuclear capabilities exist in the Communist camp. One authoritative estimate—that of a committee of the American Academy of Arts and Sciences, published in 1959—suggests that nineteen nations have the technical capability of producing nuclear weapons in the foreseeable future. It should be obvious, then, that on this single matter at least the United States and the Soviet Union have a common interest in closing the nuclear club while there is yet time.

An obvious corollary to such a recommendation is strong opposition to any German plans for nuclear armament . . . a neutralist Germany would be far preferable to a nationalist one.

The rearmament of Germany has aroused fears in Eastern Europe that are justified and that extend far beyond Communist opinion. The revival of German nationalist feeling and the return to positions of influence of many of the same individuals and groups that supported Nazi expansion represent a real danger to the peace.

If the United States should advance a serious proposal for disengagement, it would immediately relax tensions aroused by the Berlin issue. More specifically, the Western powers might even go as far as offering diplomatic recognition to East Germany and proposing a United Nations guarantee for Berlin's future status. The guiding principle in these concessions should be a frank recognition of the fact that West Berlin in its present situation is both untenable and an international anomaly. The problem it presents for us is far more human than it is military—that is, we should not be primarily concerned with maintaining an advanced outpost in power politics, but rather with honoring our pledges to two million West Berliners by seeing to it that their lives, their livelihood, and their liberties remain secure.

The final aim, then, in the case of Germany, would be equality of international status for the two German states, which would both eventually be disengaged from military alliances and left free to form some sort of loose federation. At the start at least, within this federation two contrasting political and economic systems would continue to exist—communism in the East, capitalism in the West. But in the end it would almost certainly be the institutions and practices of West Germany—which would have behind them the bulk of the population and resources of the whole country—that would come to predominate.

So much for immediate goals. How do these proposals leave the long-range situation of NATO and of Europe in general? Here it is important to distinguish between NATO in its strictly military aspect, and the integration of Western Europe on the economic and cultural planes.

From the military standpoint, the logic of the above proposals is a drastic reduction in NATO's scope. A "disengaged" West Germany would cease to be a member. At a subsequent date Italy and Scandinavia might also prefer neutrality. Similarly France might be left to follow its own nationalist course: the policy recommendations I have made obviously imply a loosening of American ties with De Gaulle. Indeed, the logic of such a position might lead to an eventual neutralization of the whole six-nation area. This would leave NATO a truly Atlantic alliance based on the United States, Canada, and Great Britain.

Even within the reduced NATO area a change in armaments policy would be advisable. Should Labour, for example, ever win an election in Britain, the new government might well request the dismantlement of NATO missile or Polaris bases. The United States should be psychologically prepared for this and should begin right now to close down these bases throughout Europe. Currently they are not contributing to the *defense* of the West in any realistic sense; they are simply increasing tension and the danger of an accidental explosion that might bring on general nuclear warfare. Ultimately the defense of Western Europe should be reduced to conventional weapons alone. Kennan's Reith Lectures offer an imaginative suggestion for recasting the Western continental armed forces as strictly defensive units of a paramilitary or territorial-militia type.

From the wider standpoint, the former NATO powers could still form an economic and cultural unit. Indeed the release of military pressure might enable them to discuss more amicably their economic disagreements. Here the tactful mediation of the United States could be of crucial influence in reconciling the "six" and the "seven." Similarly American cultural interchange with Europe would become more fruitful once its military concomitants were removed. The progressive dismantling of NATO's present overexpanded structure need not suggest a loss of American interest in Western and Central Europe. On the contrary, as with the substitution of disengagement for "liberation" in our policy toward the Soviet satellites, the new American attitude toward the West would mean putting realism in place of arrangements which no longer correspond with the facts. And this change would further suggest that by abandoning a sterile and nearly exclusive emphasis on military measures our country was attempting to re-establish a hierarchy of values closer to the Europeans' own conception of their contemporary role.

Nor would the economic and cultural integration of Western Europe necessarily intensify the current cleavage between East and West. Indeed, it might do the very opposite by helping to convince the Soviet Union and its satellites that the Western nations were shifting from military to economic concerns. In this context a disengaged and federated Germany would be transformed from the constant source of contention that it is today into an economic and cultural bridge between East and West—as Poland and Czechoslovakia would be serving in a similar capacity on the other side of the ideological divide. And should this sort of economic and cultural interchange prove rewarding, the Soviet Union might be willing to take further steps toward relaxing its grip on its satellite states.

The basic contention in the above proposals is that it is to the interest of the United States to decrease cold-war tension by drastically reducing the military emphasis of its European policy, by curtailing the nuclear aspirations of its allies, and by encouraging the constitution of a disengaged zone or zones. If we should take the initiative in such proposals, then there would be a good chance that the Soviet Union would respond in similar fashion by recognizing that disengagement and a nuclear truce are in its interest also.

In the Long Run de Gaulle Cannot Win*

Louis J. Halle

The present is saturated with the past and pregnant with the future.
—Leibnitz

We shall not truly understand the political dilemmas that confront our world in the immediate present unless we can see them in terms of the long historical perspective. We must see them in the context of a swelling movement that began to gain momentum two or three centuries ago and is today bearing all mankind forward into a future that will surely be different from anything known before.

The immediate dilemmas of Franco-American relations, of nuclear defense, of the Atlantic alliance, of European integration—these and a host of others arise only because of the direction that the stream of history has taken, and the increasing speed of its movement. Already it is so rapid that we find our international political arrangements are obsolete as soon as we have made them. We are like the parents of a boy who is growing so fast that he outgrows new clothes before there is time for him to break them in.

This is poignantly evident in the field of weapons and military strategy. The revolutionary new weapon that the Pentagon orders today is likely to be obsolete by the time it has been designed, developed, put into production and made operational. By the time we had adopted the strategy of "massive retaliation" for local aggressions in 1954, the Russians had rendered it unworkable by breaking the nuclear monopoly. We were deterred from carrying out our threat of "massive retaliation" for aggression against Dienbienphu because Moscow, in effect, now held our own cities and those of our allies hostage.

What applies to weapons and strategy applies as well to the political organization of the world and its international arrangements. Just as the Rus-

* "Why de Gaulle Cannot Win," *The New York Times Magazine,* June 2, 1963. Mr. Halle is a former member of the State Department Policy Planning Staff and teaches foreign affairs at the Graduate Institute of International Affairs in Geneva.

sians are finding that the satellite system developed by Stalin at the end of World War II won't work in today's conditions, so we in the West are finding that our defensive-alliance system of the nineteen-fifties, its military arrangements still uncompleted, won't work in the nineteen-sixties.

Why won't it work any more in the nineteen-sixties?

President Charles de Gaulle put the matter bluntly in his press conference of Jan. 14, 1963. France, he said, had been able to rely on the United States to come to her defense with nuclear weapons, in accordance with the terms of the NATO alliance for as long as the United States could use such weapons with impunity. However, now that the Russians had acquired the means to destroy American cities in retaliation, France could no longer be sure that the United States would use its nuclear armament in response to an aggression against territory remote from its own.

"In these conditions," he said, "no one in the world, and especially no one in America, can say whether or where or when or how or to what extent American nuclear weapons will be used to defend Europe."

Surely he was right. No one can be certain that we would invite the destruction of perhaps a third or one half of our population, and our permanent disablement, in order to punish a state that had committed aggression against a distant ally. At the same time, since a potential aggressor could not be certain that we wouldn't, our nuclear armament still has a deterrent effect that is essential to the defense of Europe, as President de Gaulle acknowledged.

For over 5,000 years, the old-fashioned defensive alliance has worked because unlimited disaster was not implicit in its implementation. Since this is no longer the case, there is reason for regarding it as a device made obsolete by the power of the new nuclear armaments.

So far so good. It is when we confront President de Gaulle's proposed alternative that we have cause for dismay—for, if anything, it is even more anachronistic. He is like a mother who, seeing that her son has already outgrown his newest clothes, proposes that he get out the clothes he had before, recalling how well they had once fitted him.

France, he has said, cannot rely for her national defense on any nuclear armament that is not her own, that is not exclusively in her possession and control. As her sovereignty and independence require it, he is therefore proceeding to create such a national armament.

This argument would obviously apply as well to every other state that cherishes its sovereign independence. If France cannot entrust her defense to a nuclear force in foreign hands, neither can Germany, nor Belgium, nor Egypt. Cuba, which has just experienced the limits to which it is able to depend on a foreign nuclear force, would not find President de Gaulle's arguments inapplicable to its own situation.

What he has proposed in effect, as an alternative to the alliances that have become unsatisfactory in the nuclear age, is an international anarchy that the nuclear age has rendered even more unsatisfactory—that the nuclear age has, in fact, rendered intolerable. One must ask, then, whether complete dependence on alliances or the adoption of President de Gaulle's alternative is the only choice open to the world.

Because five of his Cabinet Ministers did not think it was, they resigned all together on May 15, 1962, when de Gaulle gave a press conference in which he derided a proposed third course to which they felt themselves committed.

The issue between the President and the dissidents of May 15 was simple in its essence. He explicitly said in his press conference of that date that any proposals which were not based on the persistence of what he called *"l'Europe des Etats"* was unrealistic. "There is not," he said, "and cannot be any other possible Europe than a Europe of States. . . ."

The statement is categorical and applies to a future without end. Its context leaves no doubt that the "States" to which he refers have sovereign independence as their essential attribute and he rejected any limitation on it. And here was where the dissident members of his Cabinet disagreed.

There are others who also do not agree—including statesmen and scholars who, far from having the reputation of utopians, have for a generation been under sustained attack as cynical "realists" unable to see beyond power politics. The question they raise today is whether what is obsolete in the nuclear age is not precisely the system of sovereign nation-states—that international anarchy which our present world has inherited from an utterly different world in the historical past.

The context of their argument is not the largely imaginary issue of world government but such specific matters as the future of the Common Market, the future of the already advanced movement for European unification and the future of our ancient but rapidly developing Atlantic community. The essential problem is how to control the danger of war while achieving an effective defense of individual freedom.

Many of us have come to the conclusion that the States in President de Gaulle's *Europe des Etats* are simply too small to function as sovereign entities in the new landscape that opens before us as we are borne forward by the stream of history. Their present boundaries are more relevant to the 15th century, in which they first began to take shape, than to the 20th century. . . .

President de Gaulle's "Europe of States" would, by his own logic, be a Europe in which every state ought to have its own nuclear establishment. A federated Europe, however, would need only one such establishment and such an establishment as it could provide, with the Continental resources available to it, would be many times as effective in the defense of all Europeans as any number of small, primitive national establishments, such as de Gaulle's France is projecting for herself. Most important of all, it would be far less dangerous for everyone. It is when we think of nuclear defense, therefore, that we see how obsolete the idea of a "Europe of States" has become.

The direction in which history is so rapidly bearing us makes the increasing unification of the primitive nation-states that have come down to us from the past a virtual necessity. What, however, should the area of unification be? Should it be confined to continental Europe? Should it include Great Britain? Should it embrace the vague area that we refer to as the Atlantic community?

We deceive ourselves when we pose these questions as either-or alternatives. All of us live in the midst of concentric circles of community, from our tight local communities through wider and looser national communities to the widest and loosest of all—such communities as we refer to when we talk of "Christendom" or "the West." One would like to see Europe form a unified community, with the British as an integral part—one that was outward-looking and constructively involved with the rest of the world and that had its own European nuclear defense. Such a union would accord with the policy of the United States, which has identified itself with the effective defense of Europe, and which could deal more happily toward that end with a Europe that was strong and united than with a Europe in fragments, each asserting its sovereignty by brandishing its own nuclear armament.

Since European and American defense are integral, the United States of America and a United States of Europe would properly be drawn to each other in a partnership of equals or, eventually, in some even closer association. The strength of such an Atlantic association would then exert a liberating effect on Communist Europe. It would also have a constructive influence for guiding and assisting the development of the new nations, and of the underdeveloped world generally.

There is no reason why there should not be, simultaneously and in their different degrees, a little Europe, a big Europe, an Atlantic community and even wider associations. There is every reason why this should be the direction of development.

Looking at the long historical perspective in which the events of our present are but passing incidents, we cannot say where we may eventually get to or chart the exact road by which we will get there. What is clear is direction. If history is any guide, then there will be detours and switchbacks in the road that takes us in this direction. We shall be repeatedly delayed and frustrated and set back; we shall be in constant danger of a disaster that may terminate the whole historic enterprise. The direction, however, remains clear: it is away from the 19th-century nationalism of which Charles de Gaulle is the last great representative. This is why he will surely fail in his efforts to assume the leadership of Europe. The Europeans outside France are ready to rally around a genuinely European standard, but they are not ready to fall in line behind the flag of France.

4

Berlin and the German Question

Most great wars end with the imposition of some general peace settlement, which redraws the map of Europe until, in a generation or so, the revival of the defeated state (possibly aided by dissensions that spring up in the course of years among the victorious powers) enables it to question the settlement. World War II is unique in the modern history of Europe in its complete failure to conclude in this normal way. Some temporary arrangements improvised in the closing months of the war have achieved that paradoxical permanence that the provisional sometimes does. Even though they have in fact never worked as originally intended, they constitute, even after two decades, all the German settlement there has been. German peace treaty there has been none.

The basic document—the protocol of September 12, 1944, between the United States, the Soviet Union, and the United Kingdom—provided that Germany would be "divided into three zones, one of which will be allotted to each of the three Powers, and a special Berlin area, which will be under joint occupation by the three Powers." This protocol supplemented by another on November 14, specified the boundaries of the three zones and of the Berlin area, and, within Berlin, the parts to be occupied by each of the three powers. A later agreement, of May 1, 1945, found room for France among the occupying powers (over Russian protests) and established the control machinery for the occupation of Germany and Berlin: for Germany, an Allied Control Council for the coordination of administration in the four zones, and for Berlin, a four-power *Kommandantura* to be the actual government of the city.

In view of later developments, the most fascinating aspect of these documents is that, although U.S., British, and French troops were to be stationed in Berlin, and although Berlin was an enclave of Allied-occupied territory in the Soviet zone, the documents contain no provision whatever for rights of access by U.S., British, and French troops to Berlin; indeed, the question of access is not even mentioned. (There is an ironic contrast in the U.S. care to obtain detailed guarantees of rights of access to the port of Bremen, a U.S. enclave in the British zone.) The documents have been available in print since 1955 in the official volume on the conferences at Malta and Yalta in 1945. The papers show that lack of foresight was no monopoly of the State Department, for on page 118 is this staggering footnote:

> An undated appendix to J.C.S. 577/28 consists of a draft of a message to the Secretary of War and the Secretary of the Navy as follows:
>
> "The Joint Chiefs of Staff recommend you advise Secretary of State that there are no reasons from a military viewpoint why the draft Protocol of European Advisory Commission relative to Zones of Occupation in Germany and Administration of Greater Berlin should not be approved."[1]

The fatuity of this advisory opinion surely earns it an immortal place in the gallery of the egregious.

The U.S. government rejected a proposal to redraw zonal boundaries so that all zones would be wedge-shaped and converge on Berlin as a common point; it also dismissed, after brief consideration, a British proposal for a guaranteed corridor through the Russian zone to Berlin.[2] It is far from clear why the U.S. government turned down these suggestions, each quite sensible in its way. There may have been valid objections to them; but nearly any would be trivial compared to the objections that can be leveled against what was actually done. For what was done left Western troops isolated in West Berlin, without any physically sure means of access, without even any legally impregnable claim to access: a situation consistently affording Russia an easy means of harassing and embarrasing her ex-allies at any moment that she wishes. The Western neck was perpetually stretched out under the guillotine. Against Russian aggression on the Western position in Berlin there is, and can be, substantially no local defense. Western troops there are essentially hostages or symbols. Aggression against them is prevented only by consideration of what the consequences might be in the larger context of international relations.

The fundamental question of access was not in the first instance settled at an intergovernmental level at all. Western routes to Berlin were conceded by General Zhukov in conversations at his headquarters in Berlin (beginning on June 29, 1945) with General Lucius D. Clay and Robert D. Murphy of the State Department, then General Eisenhower's political adviser for German affairs. These provisional arrangements—which in their details were far from satisfactory to General Clay—were not put in writing. They were confirmed, in a more satisfactory form, by the Allied Control Council on November 30, 1945.

So far as Germany as a whole was concerned, the Western allies were confronted in the summer of 1945 with unilateral Russian actions regarding Germany's eastern frontiers. Russia, in effect, shifted Poland westward. A large tract of eastern Poland was annexed to Russia, and parts of Germany,

[1] *Foreign Relations of the United States: Diplomatic Papers: The Conferences at Malta and Yalta 1945* (Washington: United States Government Printing Office, 1955), p. 118.

[2] See mention of both proposals in Karl Loewenstein, "The Allied Presence in Berlin: Legal Basis," *Foreign Policy Bulletin,* XXXVIII (February 15, 1959), 82.

lying east of the rivers Oder and Neisse, were annexed to Poland. The southern half of the detached German territory of East Prussia was also annexed to Poland, and Russia took the northern half. The Western allies refused to regard these moves as a definitive arrangement, saying that they must await confirmation as part of a general settlement.

The first postwar German crisis occurred when the Russians imposed a blockade of West Berlin in June 1948. It was frustrated by the improvised "Berlin airlift" and ended when the agreement of May 4, 1949, was made with the Russians. Meanwhile, the Allied Control Council (for Germany) and the Allied *Kommandantura* (for Berlin) had broken down, both ceasing to meet in the spring of 1948.

As Western policy in Europe diverged more and more from Russian policy, the conviction grew in the West that the revival of industrial Germany was essential for the general economic revival of Europe, and, moreover, that a revived Western Germany was an essential part of an anti-Soviet grouping in Europe. France, in favor of extreme decentralization in Germany, at first followed these Anglo-American policies rather reluctantly. However, the Federal Republic of Germany, a new German state comprising the former American, British, and French zones of occupation, was brought into being in 1949 and given sovereign status by the agreement signed in Paris on October 3, 1954, which also cleared the way for West German entry into NATO. The agreement reserved to the allies "the existing rights and responsibilities . . . relating to Berlin." Russia (which of course had no share in these changes in the status of West Germany, and protested them) retaliated by recognizing in an agreement of September 20, 1955, the sovereignty of East Germany ("German Democratic Republic"). East Germany, however, is regarded by the Western allies as a Russian satellite, and they have never recognized its sovereignty.

The present phase of the Berlin question began on November 27, 1958, when the U.S.S.R. denounced the presence of the Western allies in West Berlin as an anachronism, requested negotiations within six months for their withdrawal, and offered Berlin the status of a "free city" with autonomy. At the same time, Russia gave notice that it considered as having become null and void the agreement of September 12, 1944, and the other agreements relating to the zones of occupation in Germany and the joint administration of Berlin. Further, the Soviet government announced its intention to transfer to East Germany the functions and powers exercised up to that time by Russia under those agreements.

The Western reply stated that these denunciations of agreements were invalid, and claimed that the situation in regard to Berlin was essentially unaltered. No negotiations were initiated. The situation entered a new stage in August 1961, when East German authorities suddenly built a wall to separate the eastern sector of Berlin from the Western-held sectors, and more rigidly to control traffic between the two parts of the city. Up to that time, traffic had been unhindered, and many East Berliners had earned their livings in West

Berlin, where the pay was much higher. Thus, Berlin had been a thorn in the side of the Communist Eastern European system by affording a window through which the "seductions" of the Western way of life could be glimpsed and even, to a limited extent, enjoyed. This anomaly ended with the building of the "Berlin Wall," which evoked no Western reaction beyond the verbal. Contingency plans had apparently not foreseen this contingency.

Since the building of the Berlin Wall, neither the Berlin situation nor the German situation has altered in any important way. The original "deadline" that Khrushchev announced in 1958 has been repeatedly postponed, and the preoccupations of the Soviet chief, particularly in regard to the deepening differences between Russia and China, have apparently kept him from tautening tensions in Berlin and Germany to the breaking point. Yet it remains in Soviet power to turn the Berlin situation into a first-rate crisis at any moment, and this potential of trouble will remain as long as Western troops are in the city and as long as its free status, to whose maintenance the West is pledged, continues to be as vulnerable as it is. Various ways out of this dilemma have been suggested, such as making Berlin the seat of the United Nations under international guarantee or simply of making it a free city under U.N. guarantee. Despite the plausibility of these suggestions, no long-term solution of the Berlin problem seems possible outside a general solution of the German problem. The great obstacle here is the commitment of the West to the proposition that the only tolerable solution is that of a *unified* Germany, free to make its own decisions in foreign policy as well as internally free (i.e., democratic). But freedom of decision means freedom to join NATO, and there is no reason whatever to suppose that Russia will ever accept such an outcome.

There is no easy way out of this dilemma. In the readings that follow, Charles W. Thayer suggests some possible approaches to a "deal" on Berlin and Senator Claiborne Pell insists that the first stage is to abandon the worship of "aims" that have more kinship with myth than reality.

One of the central issues is whether there is any *safe* way of arming the Germans and using them as a bulwark against Russia.[3] The Germans are so numerous, so industrious and industrialized (which is to say both wealthy and powerful), and so centrally placed in Europe that if they are unified they cannot easily, and in all probability cannot at all, be made simply a tool of someone else's policy. The same is true even of West Germany alone, which now contains about three quarters of the German population and the preponderant part of its industry. Moreover, most European peoples are far from sure that the Germans have really "reformed." W. W. Rostow takes an optimistic view in this respect, citing the success of democratic government in West Germany today. Hans J. Morgenthau remains doubtful about the extent of the

[3] Cf. A. J. P. Taylor's remark: "How can we build up Germany as a Great Power and use her as an ally against the Soviet Union without risk to ourselves? The answer is simple: it is not possible, and those who attempt the impossible will sooner or later pay the price." *The Course of German History*, 2nd ed. (New York: Capricorn Books, 1962), pp. 9–10.

reformation, seeing plenty of ominous signs that the old domineering spirit is still there.

There is an uncomfortable conviction in Europe that one of the first foreign-policy aims of either a unified Germany or a Western Germany armed with nuclear weapons would be the restoration of the 1939 frontiers of the *Reich*. No German government spokesman has ever accepted the Oder-Neisse line. Every official West German map continues to show these eastern territories as part of Germany—merely tinted a lighter shade. On March 22, 1964, in one of his first major policy statements, Chancellor Ludwig Erhard said that Germany could not abandon its claim to these territories. Yet there is no way in which the Western powers could undo the Oder-Neisse line peacefully. Russia, which created it, could of course undo it and thereby, in theory, have an easy way to purchase the good will of a unified Germany. However, the indications are that Russia sees little attraction in such a possibility, inasmuch as she sees little attraction in a reunited Germany from any point of view. The basic Russian aim seems to be to secure Western acceptance of a permanent division of Germany.

The question, then, is whether such an outcome may not be in the general interest, as well as Russia's interest. Russia's interest, after all, may on occasion coincide with the interests of the United States and Britain. Senator Pell makes this point in developing his own proposals. H. R. Trevor-Roper, on the other hand, argues that, although we should recognize the Oder-Neisse line, we must not surrender to the Russian desire for a Germany permanently divided.

A Hopeful View of the Role of Germany*

W. W. Rostow

I have come here today to talk to you about the role of Germany in the evolution of world politics.

If one looks at contemporary Germany and thinks back over the history of this century, it is clear that the internal condition of the Federal Republic of Germany and its role on the world scene represent an extraordinary achievement—certainly one of the greatest achievements of the postwar generation.

* Address made at the University of Dayton, Dayton, Ohio, on Sept. 18, 1963. Published in *Department of State Bulletin*, October 7, 1963, pp. 536–542. Mr. Rostow is Counselor and Chairman of the Policy Planning Council, U.S. Department of State.

I am not referring here simply to the miracle of German economic recovery, in which a devastated nation, with an important part of its territory temporarily withdrawn, absorbed some 11 million refugees and then went on to rebuild itself and to create new levels of economic and social life for all its people.

I am thinking, rather, of the emergence of a stable, democratic government, rooted in a broad national consensus on foreign and domestic affairs transcending the major parties, freed of much of the bitterness and fragmentation which have marked democratic politics in parts of Europe in the past.

I am thinking of the steady loyalty of the Federal Republic of Germany to the concepts of both European integration and the Atlantic partnership.

I am thinking of the expanding role of Germany as a constructive force in many parts of the world outside of Europe.

And I am thinking, too, of the combination of poise and determination with which the German people look to their ultimate reunification by peaceful means in the face of steady Communist provocation and the Communist attempt to portray their just concern for their fellows and their just aspiration for national self-determination as a desire for bloody revenge for defeat in the Second World War.

To understand the scale of this achievement, one must look back at the history of modern Germany and the four major elements which converged to make that history difficult—difficult for Germany, for its neighbors, and for the world.

First, Germany was formed late among the modern nations. France, Britain, Russia, even the United States, had acquired a clear sense of national identity and nationhood when the German peoples were still struggling in the mid-19th century to form an effective union. This accident of history tended to give Germany a sense that it had a lot to make up in a hurry before it could assume its rightful place in Europe and on the world scene. It made Germany at once less certain and more assertive in defining its national destiny.

Second, in its initial phase, German unity was dominated by the province of Prussia. That northeastern region had an old history of militarism, and it had been somewhat distant from the liberal currents of thought and feeling which ran through Western Europe, including Western Germany, in the late 18th century and, especially, during the French Revolution and its aftermath. There is a sense in which contemporary Germany represents the victory—and I believe the final victory—of the men who organized the liberal Frankfurt Parliament in 1848, although the revolution of 1848 was at the time captured by Prussia and the German nationalists.

Third, there is the simple fact of German energy, competence, and will to express its national feeling and identity in a large way on the world scene. In the context of European power politics between, say, 1860 and 1945, this thrust periodically created the greatest problems, since German ambitions clashed head-on with the vital interests of other nations, although there were substantial intervals when Germany found peaceful channels for the expression of its talent and national ambitions, enriching international life in many directions—for example, in science, education, literature, and every other dimension of Western cultural life.

Finally, there is the fact of geography: Germany is located astride the balance of power in Europe. It represents a critically important area, population, and concentration of resources between the East and the West. In the past some Germans have been able to dream of using that position to dominate Europe. From the Communist point of view, in the pursuit of world power, Germany remains the greatest possible prize.

Taken together, these elements of history, national gifts, and geography have been the cause of severe difficulty . . .

We in the United States made important mistakes in our European policy between the two world wars and also had painful lessons to learn and to apply. By not joining the League of Nations and by not making our presence and military potential a steady factor in European security calculations, we helped create a situation which made it possible for Hitler to dream of German domination of Europe and European domination of the world. As I recall the diaries of Count Ciano, with their detailed account of the diplomacy of the Axis in the 1930's, there were virtually no references to the United States. Hitler and Mussolini dreamed their dreams and made their plans as if the United States did not exist as a factor in Europe's power balance. Our isolationism between the wars helped encourage this tragic parochialism.

Reading this lesson in the immediate postwar days, the American Government sought to make a policy toward the European Continent which would avoid the mistakes of earlier times. . . . And we went forward in support of European integration. Behind this decision was an act of faith—faith that the ultimate logic of the Atlantic connection, already tested in two world wars and then under a third test by Stalin, would prevail and that a united Europe would build its policy on the fundamental overlap in our respective interests, not on the potential cross-purposes and divergencies—which were, and are, evident enough.

It was on this view of the problem of Europe and Germany that we built the Marshall Plan. We played our part in constructing NATO; we backed the Coal and Steel Community and EURATOM; and we supported the Common Market. It was within this policy, to which German leadership creatively responded, that the Federal Republic of Germany has found its way back to a role of dignity, equality, and leadership within Western Europe itself, in the councils of the Atlantic community, and on the world scene.

I believe the German people and their political leaders understand better than most that the real problems they confront and we in the West confront can only be solved by integrated European action and Atlantic partnership.

In terms of history, they have—with authentic insight and sincerity—put aside the old rivalry with France and made the Franco-German *rapprochement* a major long-term object of policy, to be achieved within the framework of an integrated European Community and sound Atlantic partnership.

In military affairs the Germans live, after all, on an exposed frontier of the free world. They understand that the protection of that frontier and of West Berlin has been achieved over the years, not by gestures or by self-imposed Communist restraint, but by a massive mobilization of military resources and an evident will to use them. They understand that the military strength of the United States—in underground silos, in Polaris submarines under the seas, on aircraft carriers, alert on airbases all over the world, standing in ready reserve in the United States—is a critical and irreplaceable component of their security, along with the United States garrison in Berlin and United States troops side by side with their own on German soil, and with all the other contingents and commitments that NATO represents.

With their economic life interwoven intimately with that of every part of Europe, they understand that their prosperity hinges on an outward-looking policy of trade, with policies that widen rather than narrow the areas embraced within a low-tariff trading system. They have supported the concept of genuine economic integration in Europe—common organs with substantial powers of decision—and have been willing to make substantial sacrifices to make it work.

They have, moreover, seen economic integration as a way station to other forms of European unity, involving political as well as economic relations among the other European states.

Shorn of colonies by history, and freed in this generation from the responsibilities and burdens of helping manage the great transition from colonialism, Germany has been able to approach the problems of the underdeveloped countries on a worldwide basis and with a fresh vision of the task and its opportunities.

With some quarter of a million American troops located in Germany for the defense of an essentially common frontier, the German Government has understood the strain on our balance of payments imposed by our commitment to the collective defense of the free world and has been sympathetic and helpful in cushioning some of its consequences.

Finally, looking to the East and to those 18 million Germans still held against their will within an essentially occupation regime, but understanding also the nature of the nuclear age, the Germans have pursued the struggle for self-determination and for national unity by peaceful means and as part of the Western coalition.

In short, reading the lessons of their experience and the common experience of this century, looking soberly at their problems as a nation, studying modern military technology and the nature of modern communications, the Germans have understood that none of us in the West—including, of course, the United States—can solve our problems unless we make common cause, unless we build policies on a common loyalty to Western values and the great Western tradition of which we are all a part. They have understood that the task with which we have been confronted since 1945, and which we still confront, includes, but transcends, older concepts of nationalism, national defense, and national destiny.

We have every reason to believe that the cast of German policy is firmly set in all the major political parties and in the minds and hearts of the German people—including the younger generation now emerging, which never really knew the days of Hitler. But the modern world is so intimately interwoven that we in the United States bear a part of the responsibility for maintaining the continuity of German policy.

First, we must remain not merely a reliable ally to Germany but a true partner with Germany in helping maintain within NATO the defense of the Western frontier, including West Berlin. The German contribution to its own and to Western defense has expanded and matured. We are both engaged, with some of our NATO allies, in exploring the setting up within NATO of a multilateral nuclear force, which would offer European nations self-respecting participation in nuclear deterrence without leading to national nuclear proliferation. We are both engaged with all our NATO allies in refining our strategic doctrine, in moving toward an agreed NATO defense policy for the nuclear age, and in designing the courses which would make that doctrine steadily effective.

The stability of German policy hinges on the continued success of the collective defense of Western Europe and on Germany's role as a respected senior partner in that effort.

We have demonstrated in the past two years in the Berlin and Cuban crises that the commitment of the United States to collective defense has survived the Soviet acquisition of nuclear weapons and the Soviet ability to damage the United States grievously in a nuclear war. The Soviet tactics of nuclear blackmail mounted in 1958 against Berlin, and pursued down to 1962, failed. The first condition for the stability of the West is that such tactics continue to fail, should they be again attempted.

Second, in a period when we are seeking to reduce the dangers and tensions of the cold war and to establish how far we can move safely toward the control of armaments, it is essential that we consult in greatest intimacy with our allies where their interests may be involved. It is for that reason that we resisted in Moscow all pressures to link the nuclear test ban to a nonaggression pact between NATO and the Warsaw powers. The Atlantic partnership is more than a defensive alliance. It is a group of nations with a common heritage and large abiding common interests. We are evidently prepared to fight together. But we must learn to work with equal intimacy in exploring the opportunities for moving gradually toward a more peaceful world.

We consulted almost daily, in the greatest operational detail, in dealing with the Berlin crisis of 1961–62. We intend to consult with equal intimacy in exploring the possibilities which may open up in the months ahead for easing the dangers and tensions of the cold war. And in these consultations the issue of Germany still split, its people still denied the rights of self-determination, must be dealt with by Germany and Germany's allies with the greatest concern and seriousness.

Third, we must support Germany, within whatever degree of unity Europe comes to achieve, to play a maximum role in all the great creative enterprises of the free world, already extensive but still expanding: in the adventure of aid to the underdeveloped countries; in designing policies of trade, not merely within Europe and as between Europe and the United States but on a world basis, where all of us must find ways of creating a trade framework beneficial at once to the more developed and less developed nations of the free-world community; and in monetary affairs, where we must fashion in the 1960's new ways of underpinning a flow of trade and capital movements which is increasing much faster than the world's gold supply.

Although our bilateral relations with Germany are intimate and intensive—and they should be, since together we bear a very high proportion of the burden of European defense—we are ultimately bound together by loyalty to a larger vision. The vision has three parts: the unity of Europe; the building of the Atlantic community; and the systematic deployment of the energies and the resources of the Atlantic community for the larger purposes of world peace and prosperity. . . .

It should neither surprise nor dismay us that movement toward these goals—supported equally by all three of our postwar Presidents—should be slow. This is the biggest piece of international architecture ever undertaken at a time of peace by sovereign nations. Great issues are at stake in each country, reaching deep into both their history and their current politics.

But as President Kennedy made clear on his trip to Europe in June of this year, we remain firmly committed to support the highest degree of European unity Europeans themselves can organize, within the larger framework of an Atlantic partnership. . . .

Although this policy took shape in response to Stalin's immediate postwar effort to take over an impoverished and disheartened Western Europe, it is not dependent, in our judgment, on the persistence of active Soviet thrusts against the West of the kind we have seen, for example, over Berlin in the period 1958–1962. We need a unified Europe working in partnership across the Atlantic for reasons that go deeper into the times in which we live and the problems we shall face.

The nature of military technology—and Communist nuclear capabilities—decrees that the Atlantic community is about the smallest unit which can organize a rational and effective defense of Europe. . . . We can see nothing but danger to us all if Europe should separate itself from the United States or if it should regard its great prosperity and the recent easing of tensions with Moscow as an occasion in which old-fashioned nationalism can again be given free rein.

Communist authorities have said two things which are worth noting about the recent period of relaxed tension. First, that there shall be no ideological coexistence. This means that they conceive of the present negotiations as limited to one phase—one important phase—of the cold war; namely, efforts to reduce the danger that a nuclear war might come about which would be neither to their interests nor to ours. It means also that the Communists intend to persist, with every other means at their disposal, to press for the expansion of Communist power and influence. All the information at the command of the government, watching the behavior of Communists in every quarter of the globe, suggests that they have in no way reduced their efforts to expand their power and influence at the expense of the West.

The second thing they have said is that they hope and expect in a period of slackened tension that what they call the "inherent contradictions" of the West will increasingly assert themselves. They hope and expect that, with the crises in Berlin and elsewhere somewhat less acute, we in the West will not have the wit to stick together; and they evidently intend to exploit any schisms among us that might open up.

These are warnings we should take seriously; and they relate to the maintenance within Germany of the kind of politics and policy which, as I said earlier, represents one of the greatest collective achievements of the postwar.

I am confident that Germans and German policy will remain loyal to the concepts of European unity and the Atlantic partnership and to the collective defense of the values of Western civilization which underlie that policy. But this means that Germany's allies in Europe and North America must also remain actively committed to this policy.

The issues on our common agenda in the West have changed in recent months, as indeed they have often changed over the period since about 1947, when the present policy was launched. The policies of the Atlantic nations have exhibited in these two decades a great resilience. We have survived problems and crises of many kinds, leaving the bone structure of NATO still intact and the impulse toward European unity still vital. We have dealt with problems of economic reconstruction in Europe and foreign aid in the developing nations, with a wide range of issues in trade and monetary affairs. We have dealt with thrusts against Turkey and Greece and twice with major thrusts against Berlin. We have adjusted our common strategy from a time when the major threat was the Red Army on the ground to the increasing complexity of an era when the Soviet Union commanded a nuclear arsenal and the means to deliver it with missiles. We are in the process of moving from a time of U.S. nuclear monopoly to one where the burdens and responsibilities of nuclear defense are increasingly shared. We have seen moments close to war and have had substantial intervals of relatively relaxed tension between Moscow and the West. We have seen relations between the West and Eastern Europe move from the black despair of Stalin's time to a period where men on both sides of the Iron Curtain can look forward with greater hope to increasing degrees of national independence and human freedom in the East, and to rebuilding old lines of connection that derive from the common religions and cultural bases of Eastern and Western Europe. We have seen Western Europe survive a series of difficult crises in the old colonial areas and move toward new relations of association and partnership with the former colonies and with other nations now emerging into the world under the banners of national independence and modernization.

All of these adjustments have not gone easily; and being democratic societies, the difficulties have been there for all to see. Our debates are out in the open. But we have every reason for faith that the policies, machinery, and attitudes of mind built up in the past generation will evolve in ways which will enhance the unity of the West—not fragment it.

To this end Germany has now a great role to play. No nation has a greater stake in the success of a collective policy in the West or more capacity to give it substance. Germany's postwar security, prosperity, domestic tranquillity, and growing stature on the world scene are rooted in that policy; and what Germans and Germany have already achieved now makes it possible for them actively to lead in carrying it forward into the next phase of Western history. But so interconnected is the world in which we live that the steadfastness of one is dependent on the steadfastness of all. In particular, we in the United States—still the inescapable leaders of the West—must remain steadily on course.

If we retain as a nation our loyalty to the large objectives of European unity and the Atlantic partnership—which the President so strongly reaffirmed on his trip to Europe in June—we can feel confident not merely of the stability of German policy but of the steady progress of the cause of freedom in every quarter of the globe.

We Can Now Make a Deal on Berlin*

Charles W. Thayer

It is high time for us to reconsider our longstanding policy on Berlin and face the reality of two Germanies—a reality we have so far denied by refusing to consider diplomatic relations of *any* kind with the East German regime. The need is urgent: a realistic policy might considerably strengthen our position in Europe if it is carried out soon. But a diplomacy based on

* "We Can Now Make a Deal on Berlin" by Charles W. Thayer. *Harper's Magazine,* June 1962, pp. 27–32. Copyright © 1962, Harper & Row, Publishers, Incorporated. Reprinted by permission of Brandt & Brandt. Mr. Thayer has lived in Germany periodically for nearly a decade since he resigned from the U.S. Foreign Service.

illusions—and our East German policy has been pinned to an obvious illusion—is bound in the long run to end in humiliation, or worse.

Not long ago at an American embassy in a small Balkan capital, an experienced European diplomat was criticizing Washington's policy on Berlin. "You Americans keep insisting on maintaining the status quo," he said. "Yet you are unwilling to recognize one of the fundamental facts of that status—the existence of Herr Ulbricht's East German government."

The American Ambassador objected that Ulbricht's regime was not a sovereign state but a Soviet colony.

"Haven't you already recognized plenty of Soviet colonies?" the European retorted.

Fortunately we still have time to alter our position. If we examine the costs closely we shall find them small, except perhaps for broken illusions; and many of these bear the unmistakable label, "Made in West Germany."

As the Rusk-Dobrynin conversations opened in mid-April, the State Department showed an encouraging trend toward a more rational approach to Berlin's problems. Its proposals (leaked, significantly, from Bonn) for more formal contacts between East and West Germans and for East German participation in the regulation of access to Berlin are steps in the right direction. But they still fall considerably short of what is necessary for a satisfactory solution.

Bonn's politicians—fearful of being accused of helping perpetuate the division of their country—are only partially to blame for our reluctance to abandon the rigid diplomacy we inherited from a less flexible era. American public opinion, confused by meaningless arguments about "hard" and "soft" lines and equally fearful of accusations of disloyalty to our German allies, sometimes exhibits an admirable but misplaced faith in such slogans as "no retreat" and "no more Munichs."

But while we remember Munich, where the West capitulated to Hitler, we should also recall another historic city, Stalingrad, where Hitler himself suffered an enormous defeat because he was unwilling to order a strategic withdrawal. In dealing with the Russians, we are rightly warned of Lenin's famous dictum that it may be necessary to take "one step backward" in order to gain "two steps forward"—but this formula need not be a monopoly of the Communists. If we are willing to readjust our lines today, we can prevent a headlong retreat tomorrow—and we may well enhance the prospect of taking two steps forward the day after.

At first view, the arguments for standing fast may appear formidable. Many Americans as well as Germans concerned with the Berlin problem warn of what they call Khrushchev's "salami tactics"—the plot to cut away at our rights in thin slices until nothing remains. Exasperated by our failure to retaliate effectively when the wall caught us by surprise last August, these people grimly predicted that the Kremlin would accelerate its slicing tactics. Unless we stood firm, they warned, we would lose Berlin altogether and then Khrushchev would turn his attentions to Frankfurt and Bonn.

The standfasters have been shown wrong. First, the acceleration they predicted has not yet taken place, and second, they overlook the sad fact that the erection of the wall did little more than consolidate the Communist position which the Kremlin had acquired in the East Sector as a result of negotiations during the war and later extended by its own legally unjustifiable interpretations of the wartime agreements. The wall did not essentially affect the rights of the West in the area where the West had actually been able to assert its rights—West Berlin. The wall was motivated, not so much by a desire to encroach, as by the necessity of stopping the steady flight of East Germany's labor force. It did, of course, curtail certain vestigial legal rights of the Western allies in the East Sector, but these were of little practical value. And it cruelly penalized both East and West Berliners by splitting up families, disrupting friendships, and incarcerating nearly two million East Berliners in the giant concentration camp which is the Communist empire. But these measures, however despicable, meant consolidation, not encroachment. The salami Khrushchev swallowed on August 13 had already been sliced fifteen years before when the generals ruled Berlin.

Much of the argument against a change in our position comes from lawyers both in Washington and Bonn, and indeed our strictly legal position may seem unassailable. The lawyers argue that our "original rights" to be in Berlin would be seriously compromised if we extended any form of recognition to the Eastern regime. We are, they point out, committed by the Paris Treaty of 1954 to the recognition only of Bonn as representative of Germany, and to the reunification of Germany as the fundamental aim of our policy. Finally, they note that our wartime agreements prohibit any settlement of Germany's boundaries until the signing of a final peace treaty for World War II. Hence, to recognize the East German state would be to betray the German people, to renounce the goal of reunification; and it would mean accepting the Oder-Neisse Rivers as the eastern boundary of East Germany. Russia's establishment of this boundary after the war placed Germany's easternmost provinces inside Poland—a loss of German territory which some Germans are naturally loath to accept.

The Adenauer regime, in fact, has taken a position which is even more drastic than Washington's. It has maintained that any state recognizing Ulbricht's regime will be "unrecognized" by Bonn. This threat, however, failed to impress the only independent Communist state in Europe when Tito established an embassy in East Germany.

The Yugoslav defiance of Adenauer is significant, because it points up a confusion between diplomatic reality and law which has become widespread in recent decades, and is particularly strong in Germany, where a legal education is almost obligatory for anyone seeking a diplomatic career. In assessing the force and importance of the legal arguments against recognition, we would do well to keep two things in mind:

First, while legal and diplomatic relations between East and West Germany outrage the lawyers in Bonn, trade relations do not seem to disturb them at all. The Adenauer government has often sought to demonstrate its loyalty to the West by pointing out that 95 per cent of West German trade is with the West and only 5 per cent with the East. So, when the Communists erected the wall last August and the cry for retaliation was raised, it was widely suggested that Bonn cut off its Eastern trade. But Bonn refused. Perhaps, Bonn suggested, the *United States* would reduce its trade with the East. The trade between the two Germanies goes on and the often complex relations between manufacturers, shippers, and purchasers seem to run smoothly enough.

Secondly, we must always remember that legal niceties designed for Western consumption often provide Moscow with pretexts for attacking Western positions—*but seldom do they serve as restraints on Soviet actions.* Soviet diplomacy is determined by Soviet national interests as interpreted from the perspective of Marxism-Leninism—not by Anglo-Saxon jurisprudence. And the Kremlin's policy toward Germany will be governed, not by the juridical relationships between the West and East Germany, but by what Moscow thinks is best for Communism—regardless of law, ethics, or any other bourgeois consideration.

What of the Germans themselves? Americans in Bonn and Berlin often seem deeply impressed by grim predictions that the German people will react violently, drastically, to any compromise with the East German regime. One of the most eloquent exponents of this theme is Sebastian Haffner, a native Berliner and a British subject, whose writings are widely published abroad. A passionate believer in the desirability of integrating Germany with the West, Haffner warns that the German people have stronger historical grounds for hating the West than for loving it. Every precaution, he warns, must therefore be taken to nurture the fragile bonds that tie the West Germans to the European community. Narrow American or Western European interest must not be allowed to frustrate the legitimate German yearning for reunification. Any form of recognition of the Eastern regime, he believes, would put an end to all hope of recreating the German state. Thus betrayed by the West, German public opinion would be so exasperated that it would demand that Bonn withdraw from NATO and the Common Market, thereby destroying the nucleus of European integration.

Official spokesmen of the Adenauer government have gone even further than Haffner in private conversations with Americans. They suggest that American recognition of Ulbricht would mean not only the breakup of the Western alliance but a "flight to Moscow." Germany, they say, would not necessarily lead but would inevitably follow the less stalwart members of the community, such as Italy, in seeking some kind of alliance in the East.

Are these dark prophecies the crude threats or naive attempts at blackmail which they appear to be? Do the German people really believe they have anywhere to go but West? Have they so quickly forgotten their history and their own personal treatment at the hands of the Russians since 1941?

Publicly, few German politicians—Christian Democrats, Social Democrats, or Free Democrats—would dare contradict such predictions. They are repeated incessantly in Germany and some seem so mesmerized by them that they have come to believe them. Others, frustrated by the failure of the Adenauer-Dulles prescription for reunification, seek a kind of refuge in visions of calamity. Others merely believe that to oppose them would mean political suicide at the polls. But they are not, I believe, the product of sober, rational analysis of the realities of the German dilemma; and they are certainly not shared by the German public beyond the confines of Bonn.

A knowledgeable Western diplomat, who has served longer in Bonn than most of the German politicians presently residing there, has estimated that the views of the Federal Republic's government penetrate German public opinion to a depth of approximately fifteen miles. Beyond that distance from the capital, the passions that stir the politicians are replaced by other more immediate and practical concerns. For the mass of Germans, the making of money, personal security, economic stability, and regional rivalries take precedence over the distant dream of a national government seated once more in Berlin.

Except for a handful of extreme nationalists—chiefly refugees from the lost provinces, who have been thoroughly repudiated at the polls—the German public has long since reconciled itself to the transfer of the territories east of the Oder-Neisse Rivers to Poland. One does encounter bitter political organizations like the one called "Undivided Germany"—but their active members remind one more of itinerant friars preaching the Second Coming than of serious statesmen. I am convinced that few Germans seriously consider reunification a reasonable possibility in the foreseeable future. . . .

Unquestionably, the erection of the Berlin wall roused most West Germans from their apathy toward their compatriots in Berlin and the East Zone. But within two or three weeks one got the impression that their consciences had not been troubled because they had theretofore neglected their less fortunate relatives and now were resolved to succor them. Rather, they seemed disturbed because they had forgotten to go to their relatives' funeral—a sin of omission which, because it was irreparable, had best be forgotten.

It would be a mistake to assume that the West Germans have completely abandoned their aspirations for a reunited and free Germany. They have, however, shown more realism than their politicians in Bonn publicly profess in understanding that these aspirations are not currently attainable. Khrushchev, they know, is not prepared to relinquish the East to a non-Communist West. And they also know the Western allies are not prepared to fight for its liberation.

Nor am I suggesting that the United States should repudiate its commitment to ultimate reunification. The festering sore of legitimate grievance in the heart of Europe is not in the interest either of America or Western Europe. Hence we cannot afford to overlook any realistic possibility of achieving that end.

Bonn's controversial Ambassador in Moscow, Dr. Hans Kroll, has suggested that, sooner than we may expect, Khrushchev will find himself at such odds with Peking that he may consider it expedient to give up East Germany in order to secure his western frontiers and free himself for action in the East. However attractive this prospect may seem, the reverse may come true much sooner. Long before Sino-Russian relations deteriorate to the point Dr. Kroll suggests, we may find we must establish some form of communication with East Germany or risk going to war. If this is the case, would it not be wiser to trade some sort of recognition in return for real advantages to ourselves—before we find ourselves under really tough pressures to give it away?

What, then, should we try to bargain for? What tangible advantages can we gain? Obviously there are a number of ways in which our position in Berlin could be improved. Let us begin with the most serious: our right of access. Whenever this issue is raised, East German Communists quote General Lucius Clay, General Eisenhower's deputy at the time the occupation started and until recently President Kennedy's special representative in Berlin. In his memoirs, *Decision in Germany,* Clay, describing the various documents pertaining to the occupation of Berlin in 1945, wrote: ". . . no one of them contained any guarantee of access or specific provision for truck, rail, or air right of way." (Subsequently an air agreement was concluded in writing.) Further along in his book, Clay suggests that it may have been a mistake not to get a written agreement at the start of the Berlin occupation on our right of access instead of relying on the Russians' verbal assurances.

I think it is doubtful that a written agreement would have altered Stalin's decision in 1948 to try to force us out of the city by the blockade. The usual Russian excuse for that action was not that we never had the right of access but that we subsequently forfeited it by creating the West German government and introducing a West German currency.

Nevertheless, the fact remains that today there is no written agreement between East and West on this vital point—a fact Khrushchev makes the most of to confuse world opinion on our Berlin position and to make life miserable for the West Berliners.

Since the Kremlin alone is responsible for violating the oral agreement, what possible advantage could we gain from a new agreement, this time in writing, which presumably could be torn up as soon as it had served the Kremlin's purpose—for example, Western recognition of its East German satellite? Obviously, agreements with the Kremlin, written or unwritten, are worthwhile only so long as they correspond with current Soviet interests and so long as breaking them is not too costly in terms of Russia's overall reputation in international negotiations.

There is considerable evidence that because of difficulties within the Soviet Union as well as within the Communist bloc, Khrushchev would welcome a respite on the German front and would find it to his interest to maintain it. His failures in agriculture, the ill-concealed differences with China, and the restlessness of his satellites culminating in Albania's open defiance—all indicate some of his vulnerabilities, and argue that he might well find stabilization of the German front desirable. Although none of these considerations are directly exploitable by the West, the proper recognition of their existence could easily redound to our advantage and open the way for the "two steps forward" in Lenin's formula.

Assuming we took the one step backward in the form of some sort of recognition of the Eastern regime, how could the next two steps bring us forward?

The city fathers and returning American officials have been making brave assurances that Berlin is flourishing, not only economically but also psychologically, and that young workers and college students are flocking into the city from West Germany. Nevertheless there is considerable evidence, aside from the huge subsidies necessary to keep it alive, that nervous tensions have reached dangerous levels particularly in those strata of the population on which a community depends for its spiritual viability. Recently a leading theatrical producer, for example, announced that he had moved his family to a West German city. He launched into an impassioned defense of his action:

"For sixteen years we have hung on and put up with every hardship," he said. "We have kept our nerves through every crisis in the hope that one day the division of Germany would come to an end. But instead of that we see our own city divided by the wall. This is no atmosphere in which to bring up a family. I shall remain but my children have gone."

A well-known Berlin novelist told me that the crisis of nerves had reached the breaking point. A pause, he said, was essential if Berlin was to continue as a viable city, and some recognition of the reality of the Ulbricht regime was not, he believed, too high a price to pay.

Perhaps a new access agreement and respite for West Berliners' jangled nerves and future plans are somewhat nebulous advantages to be purchased by recognition of the Eastern regime. But there is another possible advantage to be wrung from such a bargain. Ever since Stalin's death the specter of relaxation—some call it "liberalization"—has been stalking through the Eastern bloc. It appeared a few months after Stalin's death in East Berlin at the time of the July uprising. It appeared again in Hungary and Poland. Visitors to Moscow have encountered it right under the Kremlin's walls among young writers and intellectuals. In Poland it produced the Gomulka regime. In Hungary, it has at long last forced Kadar to admit that the vast majority of Hungarians are anti-Communists who can no longer be treated as criminals.

In East Germany, Ulbricht, a vicious old Stalinist himself, has been permitted to ignore the strictures against neo-Stalinism and the "cult of personality" only in order to restrain the growing popular demand for a less harsh dictatorship. But even Ulbricht has not been able to exorcise the liberal specter, whose followers include not only the 90 per cent anti-Communist majority but, I believe, a good proportion of the East German SED, or Communist party, as well.

Those "hard-core" East German Communists with whom I and other visitors to the East have had contact are strikingly different from their colleagues in Moscow. Although they hate the West, their hatred often seems to stem from feelings of inferiority which have been accumulating for a long time. "Why don't you consider us *salonfähig?*" they have asked in injured tones. "Why don't you recognize us as socially acceptable?"

Most of them have been Party members only since 1945. The older ones were brought up in the schools of the Weimar period when Goethe and not Marx reigned in the classrooms. Today they talk openly of "the attractions of Western liberalism" which have lured so many to the West. They fear Ulbricht but they do not respect him. "The trouble with Ulbricht is he has no sense of humor," one of them told me. The diagnosis may sound trivial but the admission that something is wrong with him is not.

Among Russian Communists Ulbricht commands something less than respect: "Poor Ulbricht," a Moscow Communist said to me, "he has a very tough row to hoe." Some of his Eastern Satellite colleagues evince very little compassion for him indeed. "He costs too much," one of them complained. "Three times he has gone bankrupt and each time Nikita Sergeyevich had to bail him out." (Since then he has been bailed out a fourth time.)

Some form of recognition would not of itself bring about Ulbricht's demise. But it is obvious that Khrushchev would be reluctant to replace him with a more able and less despicable creature so long as the Berlin situation remains so critical. Were the West to recognize the Eastern regime by maintaining some form of representation in East Berlin, it is not unlikely that the pragmatic Mr. Khrushchev would be disposed to risk the appointment of a Gomulka-type proconsul who, by making life a little less harsh in East Germany, would ease its political and economic problems. And any Western action which tended toward recognition of the Oder-Neisse line would probably elicit sighs of relief from the Eastern Europeans who suffered under Hitler during the war.

Furthermore, Western representation in East Germany would inevitably increase Western contacts with those lower-echelon members of the Communist party who now seem so resentful of their inferior status as East Germans; it is not unlikely that the new relationships might help to swing the balance within the Party itself against Ulbricht and in favor of someone whose authority does not rest chiefly on the condemned methods of Stalin, and whose reputation does not depend on the proscribed "cult of personality."

Such a replacement would not of course presage an early unification of Germany. It might well, however, lead to a modus vivendi between the two Germanies which in the course of time—perhaps a decade or two—would come far closer to that goal than the present policy of no retreat.

What it certainly would accomplish would be a mitigation of the hardships of the seventeen million East Germans at present subjected to all the brutalities of a neo-Stalinist regime. The possibility of persuading the Kremlin to force Ulbricht to tear down his wall is remote. The only alternative to removing it for the foreseeable future is to surmount it. West Berlin officials talk today of normalizing it—of making it possible for East and West Berliners to cross it. One high official has even suggested the possibility of an arrangement whereby East Berliners with temporary exit permits to enter the West would be sent home at the expiration of their visa. Others have suggested schemes for the reunification of families whereby families now split by the wall would be allowed to choose which side they would reunite in.

All of these possibilities suggest some of the advantages of a less rigid stand on the Berlin issue. Would this involve the establishment of formal diplomatic relations with Ulbricht and the maintenance of full-fledged embassies in the East Sector? Not necessarily.

Between the State Department's cautious proposals for more contacts between East and West Germans on the one hand and a formal recognition, with an exchange of Ambassadors on the other, there lies a wide area of maneuver. For example, it may be possible to negotiate a mutually satisfactory settlement by agreeing to set up commissions in East and West Berlin for the regulation of traffic in goods and people across the boundary. Perhaps it will be necessary to agree to the exchange of consular officers accredited not to the chiefs of state but to the local authorities.

But unless we are prepared to enter that area—now posted with "no trespassing" signs by shortsighted lawyers and politicians—we may soon find ourselves in another impasse or, worse still, forced by circumstances down a path leading in the opposite direction from our long-range goals.

Nor need any such step be irrevocable. It could be made contingent on the fulfillment by the Russians and East Germans of their pledges on the right of land and air access. If there were any interference with our access to Berlin, our representatives could be withdrawn and we could return to the status quo ante which we now have.

Whatever may happen, the fact remains that the policy of seeking for reunification by standing fast has thus far produced no useful results. And if that policy is continued, the dangers of crisis and dismal failure in our German policy will mount. Clearly, the time has come to explore another approach. The wall of Berlin is not like the wall of Jericho. If we are really sincere in our commitments to Germany as a whole we must do something more than stand beneath it shouting imprecations at Ulbricht and the surly Vopos who guard it.

Recognize the Oder-Neisse Line, but Do Not Yield on Berlin*

H. R. Trevor-Roper

The problem of Berlin epitomizes—has long epitomized—the problem of Europe. It has been acute for so long that we almost take it for granted. At times it becomes more acute. High words are then uttered; threats are made and even carried out. There was the blockade of 1948; there is the wall of 1961.

But in the end, after a great deal of coming and going, all sides return to what has come to seem "normality"—though "normality" is certainly an odd word for the economic and practical absurdity of a capital divided along an arbitrary line into two parts, with entirely different social and political systems, currency and culture; especially when this line is not even part of a larger frontier (as it is in Jerusalem, the only parallel) but leaves one half of the city a helpless island in a foreign, hostile sea.

However, the very permanence of the crisis, the fact that we can regard it as "normal," enables our attitudes to crystallize, and by now we can identify certain stock responses to the problem. Basically, there are three such responses. There is the Russian response, that the "anomaly" of West Berlin must be ended and the whole city absorbed into a permanent, separate, internationally recognized East German state. There is the "hard" Western view, that West Berlin must be maintained in its present form, even at the risk of nuclear war, pending the reunification of Germany. And there is the "soft" Western view that the problem of Berlin is detachable from the general problem of Europe and that, in order to avoid general war for an admitted anomaly, some compromise should be made with the Russians at its expense.

What I have called the "hard" Western view is held by many in America and by Right-Wing European politicians like Dr. Adenauer and General de Gaulle. The "soft" view is held by many European Socialists (outside West Berlin) and not only by Socialists in Britain. In considering these reponses, it is simplest to begin with the agreed facts and then to examine the different arguments about them.

For there are certain indisputable facts. Everyone agrees that the present position is anomalous. No one intended it to be permanent. In 1945 the East-

* "Berlin: The Large and Basic Issue," *The New York Times Magazine,* February 25, 1962. © 1962 by The New York Times Company. Reprinted by permission. Mr. Trevor-Roper is Regius Professor of Modern History at Oxford University.

ern and Western allies in Germany both envisaged a temporary division of the country, while it was under military occupation, but both looked forward, after the end of occupation, to reunion under an independent, "democratic," civilian government.

Unfortunately, behind this genuine, stated agreement, there was from the beginning an irreconcilable difference of ultimate assumptions which, precisely because they were irreconcilable, were never explicitly stated. The West assumed that the independent government of united Germany, when it came, would be a "Western democracy"; the Russians assumed that it would be a "people's democracy." From this profound, unstated difference all later policies have flowed.

Let us start with Russian policy. In 1945 Stalin was riding the crest of victory. He was full of hope. Where Lenin had failed, he believed that he was succeeding. Starting from a narrow but solid base in East Germany, he would build up a German Communist party at whose touch the feeble democracy of West Germany, once the Western Allies had left it and the inevitable slump had occurred, would dissolve.

As long as this hope lasted, Stalin naturally believed in German reunion. And German reunion would only be a stage in his triumph. With a Communist government in Berlin ruling all Germany, the victory of communism over all Europe would not be long delayed.

Unfortunately for him, Stalin's calculations went wrong. Western democracy was tougher than he thought. The slump did not occur. In 1948 the Communist advance in Europe was halted. Inside Germany, Western policy proved more successful than his own, and it soon became clear to the Russians that, as things had turned out, German reunion would mean not a Communist but a "Western" government of all Germany.

That was a prospect which they could not admit. They therefore changed their policy. They turned from aggression to defense. Half a loaf, they decided, was better than no bread: a Communist East Germany better than a "Western" all-Germany. So Germany must stay divided. After Stalin's death the facts and the consequences were made clear. First, there was the anti-Communist revolt in East Germany. Then Stalin's heirs recognized West Germany. No doubt they hoped that the West would respond by recognizing East Germany.

Khrushchev has carried on this new defensive policy. In an important speech at Leipzig in 1956 he made it quite plain. He was all in favor of German unity, he told the Communists of East Germany, provided it was Communist unity; but if that was impossible—and he admitted that it was now impossible—then let there be two Germanys.

However, if German division was to be permanent, certain consequences followed. "Anomalies" which were a source of weakness and irritation in East Germany, and which had only been accepted on the assumption of a temporary division, must be cleared away. The existence of the West Berlin enclave a hundred miles inside Communist territory was such an anomaly. Therefore, Khrushchev demanded, it must be eliminated.

The very same facts which have caused Khrushchev to reject German reunion have caused the anti-Bolsheviks of the West to press for it. No doubt if Stalin's earlier policy had succeeded—if the German Communists, from their base in East Germany, seemed likely to acquire the reunited provinces—the roles would be reversed. The West would then demand a continuation of the present division in order to keep West Germany, at least, safe for democracy.

But, in fact, this is not so. In fact, the West knows that East Germany is a rickety police state which would collapse without foreign support. If there were elections in all-Germany tomorrow, there can be no doubt that there would be a "Western" landslide. This being so, Western leaders naturally do not wish to give up their strong legal position. They insist, now as in 1945, that the division of Germany is a temporary measure which must be ended. And although they cannot end it without Russian agreement, which they will not get, they are determined not to jeopardize their legal right to it.

That right is publicly represented in the present status of West Berlin. Admittedly that status is anomalous, illogical, unpractical, physically indefensible. But it cannot be renounced, because it happens to be an essential part of a much greater right: the right to an ultimate German reunification which would in fact, as things are, bring Germany to the West.

So far the position is simple enough. The Russians, afraid of a "Western" all-Germany, want Germany permanently divided, which means the ending of the West Berlin "anomaly." The West, confident that reunion means a great accession of strength to itself, looks forward to the reunion to which, in 1945, all parties pledged themselves; and this means—for the time being—preserving the Berlin "anomaly." On the other hand, these opposite positions entail a practical deadlock. It is an inescapable fact that neither side will ever willingly agree to the reunification of Germany on the other's terms. It is out of this deadlock that the third attitude, what I have called the "soft" Western attitude, has arisen.

This third attitude can be reduced to the belief that German reunion, being unattainable, should be indefinitely shelved, and that the Berlin "anomaly" should be, in some way, "rationalized." Being Westerners, the advocates of this solution cannot positively urge that the West Berliners, who have so long maintained a Western life in their beleaguered citadel, be handed over to be communized by the contemptible Ulbricht regime. That would be morally intolerable.

But they suggest that some arrangement can be made whereby West Berlin retains its non-Communist freedom but changes its status, so that the Russians are no longer irritated by this alleged center of agitation in the midst of the Communist paradise. In this way they think that the fears of both blocs can be reduced and Europe "stabilized."

Now this program has undoubtedly a great emotional and rational appeal. It recognizes the hard fact of deadlock. It recognizes opposite points of view. It seems to reduce a great danger with a very small change. To detach the problem of Berlin from the problem of Germany might begin the dismantling of the cold war.

These are all very great advantages and they account for the wide acceptance of the program. We ought, therefore, to examine sympathetically the fundamental assumptions on which it rests.

These assumptions are basically simple. They are, first, that the Russians have a genuine fear of aggression from the West, which we should recognize and try to exorcise; second, that German unity under a "Western" government would greatly and legitimately increase that fear; third, that German unity is anyway, in itself, undesirable.

All these views seem to me reasonable in themselves. We should remember that each great invasion of Russia has come from the West. Three times at least—in 1812, in 1914, in 1941—great armies have advanced from Western Europe and almost destroyed the Russian state. If we in the West are afraid of an armed, united, Communist Germany, we should sympathize with the Russian fear of an armed, united, anti-Communist Germany.

And can we even be sure that such a Germany would be a safe neighbor for ourselves? Nazi Germany was, after all, anti-Communist. Nazism was not entirely invented by Hitler: it continued many earlier German characteristics and ambitions which have not necessarily died with it. How, then, can we trust a new united Germany, once again resentful of past defeat, conscious of present power?

These reasons are very strong. They are so strong that many people who are determined to resist communism in Western Europe are strongly tempted to yield to them. It certainly seems more rational to suppose that the Russians, like ourselves, are ultimately concerned with security than to imagine that they are intent on world conquest; to settle for what is attainable than to threaten nuclear war in defense of absurd positions; gradually to resolve than perpetually to maintain the cold war. Nobody who has suffered from the politics of united Germany, in the brief seventy-five years of its union, can deny that its re-division would be a small price to pay for the settlement of Europe.

On the other hand, if we look carefully, can we be so sure that we shall get settlement that way? We remember that Hitler's "last territorial demands" in 1938, though apparently reasonable in themselves, were soon shown to be only a beginning. We remember that very good reasons for meeting him were advanced, in Britain, by honest men who only wanted settlement in Europe: Socialists eager to divert resources from militarism to social reform; "Little-Englanders," weary of the effort required by an ambitious foreign policy; "imperialists" who saw the future in the Commonwealth, not in Europe. And we notice that in Britain, it is exactly the same classes who today support the "soft" policy toward Khrushchev.

And finally, we remember that what seemed to the "appeasers" of the

Nineteen Thirties a "rationalization" in Central Europe seemed to the Central Europeans themselves a discreditable betrayal. The consequences, both moral and practical, were disastrous. Instead of "detaching" an irritant "anomaly" from international relations, the men of Munich released an avalanche. This parallel is not at all comfortable; but it may also be instructive.

For if we follow it further, we find that the crucial fact, in the Nineteen Thirties, proved to be not the objective situation in Czechoslovakia but the character of Hitler. So today the crucial fact is not the situation in Berlin, but the character of Khrushchev, or his successors. If we could feel sure that they really wish to "stabilize" Europe, then the "soft" policy would no doubt be right. But if they are, as they profess themselves to be, Leninists, determined in peace or in war to conquer Europe for communism, then a whole new set of arguments must be faced.

We must then admit that the present Russian policy of keeping Germany divided may not be a permanent policy at all: it may be merely a response to the relative weakness of Russia in Germany at present. In that case, as soon as the balance of power in Germany is reversed, the response will be reversed, too: Khrushchev or his successors will revert to Stalin's policy of 1945–48.

The change is as easy one way as the other. As soon as the fusion of the two Germanys means not (as now) the collapse of communism in East Germany but the collapse of liberalism in West Germany, the Kremlin will call for German reunion—reunion which, in that case, will spell the doom of Western Europe.

And when will that moment come? We cannot tell. All we can say is that it may well be hastened, not postponed, by any Western decision to settle for permanent division. Those who advocate the permanent division of Germany often seem to forget the Germans. They suppose that the Germans will accept permanent division. I believe that the Germans may have to accept division in fact, but I do not believe that they will accept it in theory.

If the Western powers once say that they have accepted the permanent division of Germany, and prove that they mean it by recognizing East Germany and giving up their position in Berlin, whose sole political significance is as the guarantee of future reunion, then the confidence of West Germany will collapse. The West Germans will not become Communist, but they may well lose the will to resist.

At present West Germany is evidence of a marvelous Western victory. The marvel lies not only in its existence and its prosperity, but in its integration, as never before, into the West. The very division of Germany at present (since it is caused by Russian opposition to unity) is evidence of Western success. But once West Germany feels betrayed by the West, there may well be, as in 1938, a moral avalanche. If that happens, we can be sure that the Communists of East Germany will exploit the demoralization, just as Hitler exploited the demoralization of Weimar Germany during the Great Depression. Have we any reason to suppose that those who yielded so easily to Hitler will stand up to an equally determined successor?

All then depends on one great question: Is Khrushchev really or still animated by Leninist doctrine? I do not know the answer to this question; but I do feel certain of one thing. Those who made the greatest mistakes both about Hitler in the Nineteen Thirties and about Stalin in the Nineteen Forties were those who too easily supposed that those men did not really believe, or had ceased to believe, the doctrines they professed.

My own belief is that Khrushchev is not like Hitler. He is not a megalomaniac. He is not driven by a desperate fear that time is against him. He does not believe in the superiority of war. Therefore, it is possible to negotiate with him. But to act on the supposition that he has given up the articles of his faith would be folly. Even if he has, there are others who have not and who, even now, are striving to replace him.

What, then, must we do? In my opinion we must make every effort to reduce tension, to show that we are not encouraging West German irredentism. We should recognize the Oder-Neisse line. To that extent the Germans must pay, and pay finally, for their aggression and their defeat.

But on the essential point we must not yield. We must not give up our insistence on the old agreement to restore German unity within its agreed frontiers. That means we must not recognize the Ulbricht Government, or surrender the international status of Berlin. This may mean—probably will mean—a prolongation of deadlock. It may mean, in the end, two Germanys forever. But the permanent division of Germany by history is one thing; the same result by surrender is another; and, anyway, the division by surrender, if I am right, would not be permanent—it would be the prelude to Communist unity.

The Present Impossibility of Unifying Germany*

Claiborne Pell

Now that the Communist pressures appear temporarily eased upon Berlin, and our own national prestige is not presently under attack in that part of the world, it is the time for us to seek some sort of resolution of the Berlin problem. . . .

* From an address to the U.S. Senate, April 11, 1963. *Congressional Record,* pp. 6125–6127. Mr. Pell is U.S. Senator from Rhode Island.

I, for one, hope that our negotiators will at long last take the diplomatic initiative.

It is very much in our national interests to do so, since there is no situation in the world today where our forces and our flag occupy a more vulnerable position than in this island of freedom surrounded by Communist East Germany. And to seize the opportunity now when a few cracks seem to be appearing in the monolithic Communist structure might be particularly good from the viewpoint of our own American national interest. . . .

Now, let us briefly examine what are our own national interests there. Our national interests are the preservation of the freedom, of the liberty, and of the economic viability of West Berlin, along with our right of garrisoning West Berlin and, most important, our right of land access. At the moment, we have all of these except for the question of the right of access. And here, as a result of the somewhat fuzzy agreements drawn in good faith at the end of World War II, we did not press for any rights of specific land access to Berlin, instead preferring to have rights of general access. Moreover, the West Germans' right of land access to Berlin is presently subject to the whim of the East German authorities, a matter of very real concern to the Federal Republic.

What we must gain in any resolution of the Berlin problem is a clearly defined corridor of land access to West Berlin, backed up by ironclad guarantees for the freedom of West Berlin together with the West's complete freedom to garrison West Berlin. To achieve these ends, we can afford to acknowledge the continuing existence of the two German governments and agree upon the Oder-Neisse frontier. Such an agreement must equally spell out the right of land access to Berlin. In so doing, we would profit, since we would have gained what we have never yet had, the West's clearly defined and mutually agreed upon right of land access to Berlin, while the Communists would not have gained control over a single human being or a single square inch not already under their rule.

We would have gained in another way, too, since our present policy has led us to the ironic policy position that we depend upon the Russians staying in East Germany. Why? Because we refuse to deal with the East Germans, the de facto government of the area. By this refusal we strengthen the Soviet position that, not only do they want to remain in East Germany, but the United States makes it impossible for them to do otherwise. . . .

There are additional steps that could be taken, too, to help cool the temperature. The thought has been advanced of moving the United Nations headquarters to Berlin. I think that would be a bit difficult and extreme. However, there is no reason in the world why the European headquarters of the United Nations, presently at the Palais des Nations in Geneva, and the United Nations Educational, Scientific and Cultural Organization, presently in Paris, should not be moved to Berlin, preferably East Berlin. But, no matter if they were in East Berlin or West Berlin, the presence of these United

Nations' bodies would have a cooling-down effect upon the political temperatures in all of Berlin.

While the cruel Berlin wall is a permanent reminder of the failure of the Communist empire to retain the loyalty of its subjects, the present thinking in West Berlin is concentrating more upon amelioration and the improvement of conditions for the Germans on the other side of that wall. Of particular interest to the Berliners would be the seizing of the initiative in pressing far more vigorously for a relaxation of the Communist controls at the wall. As it is, East Berliners cannot cross to West Berlin to attend burials—only the coffin with its dead body is permitted through.

An additional cooling-down thought here, and a way of strengthening Mayor Willy Brandt's hand, would be to work out a revised status of forces agreement with West Berlin whereunder our American, British, and French forces would be garrisoned in West Berlin at the invitation of the West Berlin Government.

A further step in this direction would be to take the initiative in suggesting to the Communists in Berlin a mutual slacking off of propaganda and intelligence operations in each other's territory, in both East and West Berlin.

Along the lines of the cooling down of temperatures and the amelioration of relations between East and West would be the legitimization of today's almost half-billion dollars worth of annual trade that exists between Western Germany and Eastern Germany.

Actually, the West German Government is presently making efforts to normalize its own relations, especially its trading relations, with the satellite nations behind the curtain, particularly with Poland, Czechoslovakia, and Hungary.

Moreover, a reduction of tensions in Germany could result in a considerable reduction in the United States' present adverse balance-of-payments position, since at this time we are presently spending more than $50 billion a year in defense and supporting more than 400,000 men in Europe. All the other NATO members put together are spending less than $20 billion a year, none of them have a longer draft period, only two have as long a draft period and all the rest have either shorter draft periods or no draft at all. In addition, too, perhaps we could participate in some of the more than $4 billion trade in consumer, nonstrategic goods with the Soviet bloc which our NATO allies find so profitable.

Now, let us examine this question of a unified Germany. Some day, it will come. But, when that happy day comes, there will, in itself, no longer be a Berlin problem.

In fact, it is high time that we faced the impossibility of having a peacefully unified Germany in the near future. The present actual impossibility of unifying Germany is perceived by nearly all Europeans, Western and Eastern, many Americans, and quite a few Germans, though this thought is rarely uttered in public Why? Because, as so often happens in democracies, when we come to questions of foreign policy, we become frozen in our position.

Discussion of a change in direction becomes most difficult and, at times, very unpopular.

Yet, we should bear in mind what Lord Palmerston once said:

> We have no eternal allies and we have no perpetual enemies. Our interests are eternal and perpetual and those interests it is our duty to follow.

This means that policies must be determined by national interests, that national interests can and do change in a changing world, that it is the national interests which must be followed and which must determine policy and that the policies in themselves are not immutable. This sound advice should certainly apply to our American policy towards Germany. We must always ask ourselves the question, "where lies our American national interest?"

Original Western support for the concept of a unified Germany was based on the assumption that such a unified Germany would be neutral and would have neither arms nor the potential for making arms. When in September 1946, Secretary of State James Byrnes, in his "hand of friendship to Germany speech" expressed our national support of a unified Germany, the world had not yet become so polarized between the East and the West. We thought then that the unified Germany of the future would be a peaceful, unarmed Germany in a world at peace. Also, at that time, we hoped that we and the other nations of the world would disarm. We had proceeded to do so and had virtually dismantled our Armed Forces. But, the Soviets did not follow suit. Since then, we have had to rearm with the result that the death-dealing and destructive potential of weapons available to both West and East has increased fantastically.

More paradoxical, since 1954, we have urged the West Germans to build up their armed forces. With our support, they have established a strong army of 11 divisions of 253,000 men. It is actually the most effective and powerful land contribution to NATO and, excluding the Russians, the most powerful ground force in Europe. The West Germans also have a navy of 177 ships and 28,999 men and an air force of 90,000 men.

By the same token, East Germany has become the second leading industrial satellite nation today with an estimated gross national product of $19.5 billion in 1961, or $2 billion less than that of its leading satellite rival, Poland. It also has become a military power of some force with an army of approximately 200,000 or more, a 14,000-man navy and an air force of 10,000 men.

The present armed state of both East and West Germany is an existing fact. Moreover, in this time of world pressure, it is unlikely that any alliance will consent to give up any significant portion of its arms until the tensions between the East and the West have abated. The NATO nations certainly will not want Western Germany, the very bulwark of its land forces, to withdraw its troops from their strength. Nor will the Warsaw Pact nations, the Communist nations, permit East Germany, with all its industrial and military resources, to withdraw from the Communist orbit. In any event, it is a fact that nature abhors a vacuum, particularly in times of crisis. Hence, it is not likely that either the United States or the Soviet Union, the Western alliance or the Eastern bloc will agree on a disarmed, neutral Germany.

This being the case, would it not be better if we faced and accepted the fact of two separate German Governments until hopefully the international situation evolves to a more peaceful, temperate point where we can get agreement on a single, unarmed and democratic Germany?

Then, too, whenever the question of a rearmed and reunified Germany is discussed, there looms like a cloud in the back of our minds, the recollection that Germany has engaged in three aggressive wars within the past 100 years. Unfashionable as it is to mention today, this is a fact very much in the European mind. It is one of the reasons, too, for the general acceptance of the fact that Germany should not have nuclear weapons. From a long-term viewpoint, though, no one nation can be permanently pointed out in this connection, no matter what her history or whether or not she won or lost a war. Accordingly, there must be continued and strong emphasis on our present policy to prevent proliferation of those nations with the atomic weapons. This is perhaps the most important single policy that we and the Soviets share.

In Eastern Europe, the malaise concerning German rearmament is especially true. The people in the Eastern European countries, particularly Poland, Russia and Czechoslovakia, have almost traumatic fears of German rearmament. The fact that these fears are vociferated by the Communist governments of these countries does not obliterate the fact that the fears of these Eastern European people are genuine. They are fears derived not only from their brutal experiences and memories in World War II, but from centuries of prior unhappy attack and occupation by Germans. We must recognize the fact that the Eastern Europeans still fear the Germans even more than the Russians. The Poles know, too, that some of the West Germans calling most loudly for unification are thinking in terms of the next step, the regaining of the former German territories under Polish rule. For good or bad, only Poles live today in the Oder-Neisse Territories, scarcely a German is left there. Yet, even Dr. Adenauer recently said, "The Oder-Neisse line is not Germany's eastern frontier." Any attempt at reconquest by Germany certainly would produce a war with the Poles and probably turn Europe into an inferno.

A more strident West German minority has a third step in mind, the regaining of the Sudetenland in Czechoslovakia.

But, many Germans are aware of the dangers inherent in a reunited and armed Germany. In fact, the Social Democrats in 1959 advanced the Deutschland plan which accepted the Oder-Neisse frontier. Recently, Klaus von Bismarck, director of the North Rhine-Westphalia radio and grandson of the famous Iron Chancellor, and seven other leaders of German public opinion, advocated for the time being, the acceptance of the present West German boundaries and suggested that the emphasis of German policy be directed more toward the amelioration of conditions in East Germany and toward bringing more freedom to the East Germans, rather than upon reunification.

Historically, Germany has existed as a single country, united within her early-Hitler borders, for only one hundred of the past thousand years. Actually, if history and culture are to be used as criteria, West Germany has a greater affinity with Austria than with East Germany. They have certainly more cultural and social ties in common.

But, when thinking about Germany or any other problem in our world today, our paramount consideration must be that the Communists are the present main threat and danger to our lives and to our very civilization. The Communists are our No. 1 enemy, we are their No. 1 target. Those Communists who have the least to lose, like the Red Chinese, may well believe that war is their best means to attain world domination. Those with more to lose like the Soviets and their satellites, while still wanting world domination, may be more anxious to avoid war. In connection with the Communist threat, there are those in the West who believe that a rearmed and reunified Germany is the best bulwark against the Soviets. I submit that this is not necessarily the case. Twice before in the last half century, the Germans have made arrangements and understandings with the Kremlin so that they could concentrate their efforts on the West.

First, there was the Rapallo Agreement of 1922 and then the Ribbentrop Agreement of 1939. Perhaps, if there were a reunited and rearmed Germany with an awakened sense of lebensraum, this could happen again.

Accordingly, I think we should give our present policy toward Germany a critical reexamination with a view toward acceptance of the fact that Germany is divided as long as we have not reached the millennium of a world and a time when we can achieve a unified, unarmed Germany. From a tangible viewpoint, does such a de facto acceptance of a divided Germany give the Communists control over a single additional person or square inch? No. Nor would such action preclude our continuing to seek a solution for Germany which would result in the unified and unarmed Germany for which we all hope and where all its people might exercise their democratic rights.

Moreover, recognition of the Oder-Neisse frontier would have an exhilarating impact upon the Poles and a Pandora's Box effect of potential trouble and unrest for the Soviets. At present, while President de Gaulle has accepted the Oder-Neisse frontier, only the Communist countries formally recognize Poland's 283-mile western frontier. This recognition is highly important in influencing the ties of Poland to the Kremlin. If the West recognized the Oder-Neisse frontier as well, one of the main bonds tying Poland to Russia would have been cut. Poland's own restiveness and basic anti-Russian feelings could soon produce vehement outbursts against the Soviets.

Actually, de facto acceptance of East Germany and recognition of the Oder-Neisse line in exchange for concrete agreements for clearly defined land access to West Berlin and ironclad guarantees of its freedom would serve to hasten the day when a unified, neutral, disarmed and democratic Germany might be achieved. For, if these steps were taken, they would result in the relaxation of tension and alleviation of the anxiety of Europeans, Western or Eastern, friend or foe, that is the first conditon for such unification. . . .

Germany Gives Rise to Vast Uncertainties*

Hans J. Morgenthau

While the overriding fact of the seventies or eighties may well be the new power of China, the overriding fact of the sixties is the new power of Germany. The Soviet Union and the nations of Eastern Europe fear that new power; the United States and France compete for association with it. Yet all, many Germans included, are uneasy and apprehensive in the presence of that power. What does the new power of Germany consist of? Whence does it come? What makes us uneasy about it? And how ought we to deal with it?

Even in its present truncated state, Germany is again the foremost economic, military and political factor on the European continent. She has the highest gross national product and per capita income in Europe and has sufficient surplus resources to give economic and technical aid to scores of underdeveloped nations. Her industrial production in 1960 was 276 per cent above the level of 1936.

The German military establishment is already substantial and is rapidly growing. The German military budget has risen from 11.7 billion marks in 1959 to 19.7 billion in 1963. The German Army is today the backbone of the ground forces of NATO. In view of the defection of France and the military weakness of the other European allies, NATO tends to become the organizational superstructure for what is in substance an American-German alliance.

Politically, Germany has become the kingpin of the Atlantic Alliance. She is wooed like a highly desirable but reluctant bride. After de Gaulle and Adenauer had signed in January what looked like a marriage contract between Germany and France, President Kennedy had to go to Germany in June in order to demonstrate that, regardless of what France and Germany had signed, no one can love Germany more than America, and the President of the United States transformed himself in the process into a German ("I am

* *The New York Times Magazine*, September 8, 1963, pp. 21, 117–119. © 1963 by The New York Times Company. Reprinted by permission. Mr. Morgenthau is Albert A. Michelson Distinguished Service Professor of Political Science and Modern History at The University of Chicago. His *Politics among Nations* is one of the most influential general works on international relations published in recent decades.

a Berliner"). President de Gaulle had then to go to Germany in July in order to see and, if possible, to repair what was left of the Franco-German marriage after the passionate American interlude.

The limits of American policy toward the Soviet Union are determined by what is acceptable to the Government in Bonn. American policy is not being made in Bonn, but Bonn decides how far Washington can go. We have had but recently an illustration—unbecoming and irrational—of that strange relationship. Although the carefully worded text of the partial test-ban treaty precludes the possibility of even approaching recognition of the East German regime, the publication of the treaty created near-hysteria in Bonn. The President of the United States had to write a personal letter to Chancellor Adenauer. The Secretary of State had to go to Bonn. So did an Assistant Secretary of State and the Secretary of Defense.

The latter was lectured by Dr. Adenauer for almost an hour on the dangers of the test-ban treaty without being allowed to put in a word on his own. A hundred years ago, Bismarck would not have dared treat, say, the British Secretary of State for War like that; nor would the British Secretary, for that matter, have allowed himself to be so treated.

Whence does this crucial power of Germany come? It has two main sources. One is the circumstances which have dominated the European scene since Bismarck created a unified German state in 1871: the German people are, by dint of their natural endowments, the most populous, the most industrious, the most disciplined people of Europe, having at their disposal the most productive industrial plant on the continent. In consequence, if nature were allowed to take its course, Germany could make herself the master of Europe. But it is this mastery which the other peoples of Europe have refused to accept and which they have fought two world wars in this century to prevent. It is for this very same reason that both we and de Gaulle, in our different ways and with the support of Adenauer, have endeavored to integrate Germany into a larger whole, be it an Atlantic Community, a federated Europe, or a Europe dominated by a Franco-German combination.

The other source of Germany's strength lies in her own present circumstances. In consequence of the dispositions which the Allies made toward the end of the Second World War, Germany finds herself today divided into two states, while the provinces east of the Oder-Neisse line—Silesia, Pomerania, West and East Prussia—have been incorporated by Poland and the Soviet Union into their respective territories. The recovery of these provinces and the unification of the country are the two national objectives to which repeated official declarations and public opinion polls assign the highest priority. When Germany joined NATO in 1954 she did so with the understanding that her allies would support these aspirations, and the United States has consistently done so.

It is, however, obvious to all concerned that regardless of the opportunities which might have existed in the past and which might emerge in a distant future, there is in the foreseeable future no chance for the recovery of the eastern provinces and the unification of the country as long as the Soviet Union is opposed to this and has the power to prevent it. While all Germans will admit this in private, most of them—and particularly the politicians—are wont to talk in public as though they were convinced that the achievement of these two objectives is not only indispensable but can also be achieved by Western efforts.

Yet, while the West can only talk about unification and the recovery of the eastern provinces, there is one power which could achieve these two German objectives overnight if it wanted to, and that is the Soviet Union. The road to the realization of these objectives, then, leads through a German understanding with the Soviet Union.

The United States Government knows this, the German Government knows it, and—most importantly—Mr. Khrushchev is fully aware of it. He has before his eyes the vision of an eastern orientation of a united Germany. He hinted at this development in a memorandum submitted to the German Government in December, 1961, and has mentioned it to many visitors in recent years. "One day," he said to Mr. Paul-Henri Spaak in July of this year, "the Germans will want another Rapallo. It won't happen under Adenauer's successor, nor probably under his successor's successor. Later perhaps. But the day will come, and we can wait."

What is a pleasant dream in Moscow is a nightmare in Washington and a source of great political strength for Bonn. Bonn and Washington are verbally committed to the illusory proposition that their military alliance is the instrument for unification and the recovery of the eastern territories. Since the alliance is the cornerstone of its European policy, Washington cannot afford to pursue policies which entail the risk of weakening the alliance. It is this consideration which gives Bonn, for all practical purposes, a veto over the European policies of the United States.

More particularly, whenever Washington takes a step, however small and innocuous in itself, which so much as points in the direction of an accommodation with the Soviet Union on the basis of the European status quo, Bonn is likely to call Washington to order. The test-ban treaty is an example.

Such is the power, both natural and circumstantial, of Germany today. What makes us, the outside observers, as well as many Germans, uneasy in its presence? . . .

What is the political significance of the agitation for unification and the recovery of the eastern provinces? The agitation itself is an ubiquitous fact, ever present to the eyes and ears of the visitor. Listening to the radio on my first day in Germany I was startled to hear a reference to "*Mitteldeutschland*," which formerly was a geographic term like our "Middle West" and now signifies what we call "East Germany"—implying of course that the real East Germany lines beyond the Oder-Neisse line. Walking through the streets of the university city of Tübingen, I encountered at every turn big placards in screaming red, showing prewar Germany divided into three parts with the legend: "Thrice divided—never!"

What does it all mean? The Russians, the Poles, and the Czechs say it can mean only one thing: preparation for a war of revenge. On the other hand, all Germans to whom you put that question will tell you that it means nothing in concrete political terms, that it is a moral commitment, a sentimental aspiration, for the sake of which few would want to sacrifice much and nobody is ready to die.

One can accept that explanation for the present without closing one's eyes to the risks of the future. For it is an inherently unhealthy state of affairs for a political élite to commit itself in public to objectives which it admits in private cannot be realized in the foreseeable future. The moment of truth is bound to come. When it comes, will the leaders be capable of trimming the professed objectives down to the level of the means safely available, or will they embark upon risky policies in order to keep popular favor? . . .

What are the innate tendencies of German opinion? Have they become, if not democratic, at least rational and self-contained, or are they still dominated by that irrational expansionist urge of which Nazism was the most extreme manifestation? Is that quality of the German mind which gave rise to Nazism dead, or is it only dormant? . . . Unfortunately, the answer can only be ambiguous at best. Germany, as it were, still has to make up its mind.

On the one hand, there is the revulsion against the outrages and, more particularly, the failures of the Nazi regime; there are the attempts to atone for them; there is the indifference to, and even active aversion to, traditional nationalism on the part of large masses of German youth; there is a general retreat into the private sphere with the satisfaction of private needs taking the place of public concerns.

On the other hand, there is a new national assertiveness as a byproduct of newly acquired power and as a reaction to de Gaulle's new nationalism. There is a cynicism about democracy, politicians and the Bonn regime which expresses itself in thunderous applause whenever a nightclub comic makes a crack about them.

Finally, and most important, there is a kind of unnatural emptiness in the German mental landscape, a quiet before momentous events, a great people waiting for a new mission and perhaps a new leader. I watched the people of Frankfurt welcoming President Kennedy, hundreds of thousands of people filling the sidewalks from wall to curb, their eyes wet, their faces transformed in ecstasy, welcoming not so much a foreign statesman on a pragmatic mission as a savior sent from on high especially for them to set things right.

Had I ever seen anything like that before? I had indeed, decades ago. Everything was then exactly as it was now: the same ecstasy, the same passion, the same abandonment, the same irrational hopes. Only the recipient of those emotions was different then: he was a little man with hypnotically piercing eyes, a funny mustache, and an outstretched right arm.

What should American policy be in the presence of that new German power and our uneasiness about it?

The United States has one fundamental goal: the prevention of a drastic change in the world balance of power through an Eastern orientation of a united Germany. It has made common cause with Germany in maintaining the illusion that Germany's Western orientation will be the instrument for the realization of its national aims. This illusion has created schizophrenia in the German mind: It has set itself objectives which cannot be achieved by the means chosen.

America has also created schizophrenia for itself: Its commitment to the German nonrecognition of the European status quo is incompatible with its search for an accommodation with the Soviet Union. The United States has the extremely difficult task of disentangling itself from these two contradictions without impairing its relations with Germany and in the end driving Germany into the waiting arms of the Soviet Union.

No neat and simple formula can show the road to the achievement of that task. What is required is a patient, cautious and subtle endeavor, unceasingly pursued, of narrowing gradually and unobtrusively the gap that exists today between illusory verbal commitments and the facts of life.

This must be done by simultaneously toning down the verbal commitments and trying to restore the human contacts between the two Germanies. The former is indeed one of the preconditions for the latter; for the verbal commitment to the unification of Germany on Western terms and the restoration of the frontiers of 1937 has been one of the main factors in cementing the unity of the Soviet bloc and in making the realization of achievable Western aims impossible.

Paradoxically enough, if the United States should continue to be, in its verbal commitments at least, as intransigent as the most intransigent Germans, it is likely to find itself left behind by a new generation of German leaders who will, in one fashion or other, try to change circumstances rather than declaim against them.

Thus American policy must cope with two dangers: the remote one of a new Rapallo, the Eastward orientation of a united Germany, and the more immediate one of losing the initiative in the incipient realignment of positions in Europe. If it goes too far too fast in trying to narrow the gap it will increase the former danger; if it goes not far enough too slowly it increases the latter.

It is the measure of the new power of Germany that such are the difficult and risky choices with which it confronts the most powerful nation on earth.

5

Eastern Europe: Polycentrism and U.S. Policy

Is Eastern Europe any longer a "tension area" as suggested by the title of this book? Clearly it is not, if we are talking of vortices of the Cold War, of the East-West struggle. Cool, even unfriendly relationships are certainly involved; but not since Hungary in 1956 have any of the Eastern European countries been the occasion of a major international crisis.

Moreover, in 1963 the U.S. dropped its demand for the annual U.N. debate over Hungary. There have been gradual moves toward the normalization of diplomatic relationships between the U.S. and various Eastern European countries, and trade across the Iron Curtain is growing. And Tito, frustrated in his efforts to visit the White House in 1957 and 1960, finally got there in 1963. His reception publicly was less than effusive; but the invitation was sufficient to indicate that revisionism can occur in the United States as well as in Eastern Europe.

Still, if no international crisis currently stems from Eastern Europe, the area has its tensions. In large measure these can be summed up in the word "polycentrism"—the tendency toward many centers of Communist authority rather than one. Paul Kecskemeti traces the historical background since World War II of Soviet relationships with the East European countries and shows how some of the differences in approach developed. He sees this question primarily in terms of rivalries within the "top Party layer," and he makes the interesting point that Tito's expulsion from the Cominform came not because he was too friendly to the West but that, on the contrary, he attacked Stalin for being too accommodating to the West (in today's terminology, Stalin was not sufficiently "Stalinist"). Kecskemeti speculates on the possible emergence of more fundamental cleavages, but his approach is still that the current differences are no more than "variations on a Soviet theme."

Anatole Shub's interpretation of life in several of the Eastern European countries in 1963 goes further. He does not question the fact that communism is firmly established in each of these countries; but his account raises the possibility that nationalism may produce eventually not merely variations, but independent themes. Other recent observers of this region have confirmed Shub's impressions, and there are more and more references to greater toleration of dissenting views expressed by intellectuals; to jazz, the "twist," and buildings of modern glass; to pretty girls instead of tractors on the covers of magazines.

Economic factors play a significant part in the increasing tension between the claims of national autonomy and of Soviet leadership. This role is apparent in the experience of COMECON, Eastern Europe's answer to the Common Market. So far, at least, it has not succeeded in harnessing the various resources and capacities of its members for a major economic upsurge. (One indication of this failure is the fact that in 1963 and 1964 Czechoslavakia, Hungary, and Bulgaria, as well as Russia, have been compelled to purchase wheat in the West.) Khrushchev, as Michael Gamarnikow shows, has met strong resistance to his hopes for an international division of labor and a single unified market among the communist countries. The leaders of each of the countries concerned continue to think in their own national contexts. As a result, many of the recent economic developments in Eastern Europe have been taking place outside the institutions of COMECON, including the planned Rumanian-Yugoslavian navigation project at the Iron Gates on the Danube.

Rumania is a particularly fascinating case in point. The Rumanians' success in forcing the Russians to change their proposals for the division of heavy industry in Eastern Europe seems to have resulted from hints that they might go over ideologically to the Chinese. Now, the Rumanians, with $400 million a year in trade with the West and an eager desire for more, are very much in favor of closer ties with the West and of conciliatory moves on outstanding international issues. And yet, far removed though they were from Chinese views on world politics, they were able to use the Sino-Soviet split to embarrass the Russians.

All of this evidence of the desire of many communist nations not to be totally subservient to Russian interests has led the U.S. Administration to draw the policy conclusions expressed here by W. Averell Harriman. We should, he argues, use trade and diplomacy to try to open up a wider diversity in Eastern Europe and a greater receptivity to Western ideas.

Yugoslavia is often pointed to as illustrative of the advantages to be gained by this policy. It is true that Yugoslavia is not in our camp; that periodically the Yugoslav press gives vent to attacks on our policies in various parts of the world; that Tito and Khrushchev have exchanged cordial visits (Khrushchev even said that the Yugoslav workers' councils, through which much industrial decision-making has been decentralized, were very interesting, and that the Russians might well think about the idea; though the chances of this thinking going very far for the time being seem remote); and Tito is acquiring observer status in COMECON.[1]

Yet it is the view of the Administration that Tito is not in Khrushchev's pocket, in large measure because of the aid we made available in the past and the trade we are encouraging by including Yugoslavia in the "most-favored-nations" category for tariff purposes. (Poland receives this same tariff treat-

[1] He would like similar status in the Common Market.

ment; but it has not yet been extended to the other Eastern European countries.)

Opposition to this policy is based on the belief expressed here by Ferenc Nagy that differences among the Communists are not likely to be fundamental, and that close contact and trade with communist governments is immoral. The Congressional supporters of this view almost succeeded in depriving Yugoslavia and Poland of the most-favored-nation treatment. The Administration finally prevailed against this opposition, however, and current U.S. policy continues to encourage closer relationships with those Eastern European countries that show signs of wanting to loosen their ties with the Soviet Union.

It is unlikely that this policy will completely dislodge Soviet influence in Eastern Europe, or that the communist regimes there will be overthrown or converted to democracy. Clearly, Khrushchev would not tolerate any such results. In any case, communist leaders try to set limits to internal diversity and relaxation, as has been illustrated in Poland. Still, the U.S. intends to encourage a trend barely perceived until the last few years—the proliferation of polycentrism in the world of communism.

The East European Satellites: Variations on a Soviet Theme*

Paul Kecskemeti

At the end of the Second World War, a vast tract of East-Central Europe, running from the Baltic to the Adriatic and the Black Sea, came under Soviet political control, based mostly upon military occupation. Ever since then, the political history of the countries or country fragments involved (East Germany, Poland, Czechoslovakia, Hungary, Rumania, Yugoslavia, Albania, and Bulgaria) has been a set of variations on a common theme.

The unitary, common theme was the gradual imposition of totalitarian political regimes closely modeled upon Stalin's Soviet Russia. But there were also variations, departures from mechanical uniformity. This was inevitable. The process of sovietization started from initial conditions that differed widely from one country of the region to another, and also differed from those prevailing in Russia during the formative period of the Soviet regime itself. Moscow's pressure toward uniformity, massive as it was, did not succeed in effac-

* From the book *The Realities of World Communism,* edited by Dr. William Petersen, pp. 109–122. © 1963 by Prentice-Hall, Inc., Englewood Cliffs, New Jersey. Reprinted by permission. Mr. Kecskemeti is Senior Research Analyst with the RAND Corporation and Visiting Professor at the Russian Institute, Columbia University.

ing these initial differences. Thus, political developments in each country of the region proceeded along specific lines, reflecting variations in social structure, the degree of industrial development, national-political orientation, indigenous Communist strength, and so on. Because of these variations, no two countries of the region experienced the ordeal of sovietization in exactly the same manner. I shall briefly outline the various patterns of sovietization that emerged, the stresses generated by them, and the physiognomic differences now prevailing among the Communist regimes of the region as a result of the divergent historical paths they followed.

The withdrawal of the German forces from East-Central Europe in 1944–45 brought about the collapse of the German occupation regimes, puppet regimes, or Axis regimes that existed there, and gave the signal for the introduction of a new political order. This process took place under the general guidance of the Soviet Union. Nominally, the political transformation of the liberated areas was a joint responsibility of all the Allies, but this principle remained on paper. The decisive voice was Stalin's, and the execution of policy rested with the Soviet military authorities where Soviet forces were in occupation. In Yugoslavia and Albania, where local Communist partisan forces rather than the Soviet armies had displaced the Germans, Moscow exercised only remote control over political developments. The local partisans were nominally under Communist Party discipline, but they tended to ignore restraining counsel from the center.

In undertaking the political reorganization of East-Central Europe, Moscow deliberately ruled out the introduction of the integral Soviet form of government and instead adopted the "People's Democracy" as the standard pattern. Its main feature was shared power. Governments were to be formed by coalitions consisting of several parties certified as "antifascist" and "democratic." It was understood that such certification would be withheld from the parties of the Right, but the "democratic" coalitions were supposed to include, in addition to the Communists, non-Communist workers, peasants, and "national bourgeois" parties. In other words, the expansion of Communist control beyond the confines of the Soviet Union was started on a dualistic basis, providing for two distinct forms of rule—the Soviet system proper within the USSR, the People's Democracy elsewhere. This distinction is still being maintained in name, although in all People's Democracies as they exist today, the original multiparty coalitions have long given way to exclusive Communist control. . . .

The Soviet leadership's reasons for sponsoring People's Democracy were manifold and complex. To begin with, no full-blown one-party regime could be created at once in countries where the Communists had no organized mass following and hardly even any cadres—and this was true throughout most of East-Central Europe. Moreover, it was important for Stalin to convince the Allies that he was satisfied to share power with non-Communists in the areas liberated from the Germans. Any indication that exclusive Communist power was his ultimate goal risked provoking a strong Western reaction, barring the door to Communist expansion. In Western Europe, notably in France and Italy, this risk was particularly serious. There the Communists could enter the precincts of power by joining coalitions, but it was necessary for them to convince their partners of their democratic reliability. Playing the coalition game also in Eastern Europe, where the Soviet presence would have permitted a more ambitious course, served to clinch the point. . . .

Far from representing a distinct species, intermediate between the Soviet system and Western democracy, the People's Democracy was merely a pluralistic initial stage of a dynamic process that led to exclusive, totalitarian Communist control. The initial stage could be more or less far removed from the homogeneous end state; the People's Democracy concept was flexible in this respect. Stalin, at any rate, favored a good deal of initial diversity. Only Poland was singled out for special treatment.

Poland's case indeed was special: the wartime Polish government-in-exile, established in London, had repeatedly clashed with the Soviet Union over territorial and other issues. Hence Stalin insisted upon an integrally Communist-controlled Polish-front government from the beginning, and the Allies had to exert a considerable effort to induce him to lift his ban upon including representatives of the government-in-exile in Poland's first postwar government. But elsewhere, in Czechoslovakia, Rumania, and Hungary, for example, Stalin accepted genuinely heterogeneous multiparty coalitions, including "bourgeois" elements, as a starting point. He supported a similar policy for Yugoslavia; Tito was instructed to form a coalition government together with Subasic, the King's spokesman, but Tito disregarded these instructions. Using police terror, he made it impossible for the non-Communist parties to contest the elections set for November 1945. A single, Communist-sponsored front list was elected, so that Yugoslavia achieved the one-party regime already toward the end of 1945. In Albania and Bulgaria, developments followed a similar course. In the other East-Central European countries, however, the evolution of the Popular Democracies from permanent coalitions of independent parties to exclusive Communist control took several years.

The uniformity of the pattern of sovietization, then, was broken up right at the beginning by Balkan Communist leaders, notably Tito. Clearly, the tempo set by Stalin was too slow for them, and they saw no justification for Stalin's accommodating attitude toward the Western powers. Tito behaved as truculently as possible in dealing with the West, quarreling with Italy over Trieste and Venezia Giulia, aiding Greek Communist guerrillas, and shooting down American planes. All this amounted to open defiance of Stalin's foreign policy. The first rift in the Communist bloc was caused by Tito's radicalism.

It is noteworthy that Tito, the exponent of the radical, maximalist line, had spent the war years as an underground leader. Other local Communists with a background of underground activity, cut off from Moscow and unfamiliar with Stalin's political style and outlook, had generally taken it for granted that "liberation" by the Soviet army could mean only the rapid imposition of the dictatorship of the proletariat. They were disabused when the

Soviet military authorities, more or less ignoring them, organized coalition regimes instead, and gave the leading positions in the reconstituted Communist Parties to émigrés who had spent the past decade or two in the USSR. These "Muscovites"—Gottwald in Czechoslovakia, Rákosi in Hungary, Bierut in Poland, and so on—imposed the coalition policy over the radicals' objections.

Moderation vs. radicalism, however, was a self-liquidating issue in the Communist movement. Having secured control over the police, the courts, and other key positions, and sure of the backing of the Soviet authorities, the Communists lost no time in starting to wreck their coalition partners. Details varied, but by the spring of 1947, the movement toward exclusive Communist control was in full swing. At the same time, Soviet policy toward the West was stiffening. Communist expansion in the West was making no headway: the French and Italian Communists were forced out of the government in May 1947, and the Soviets were denied control over the West German economy. Since the results of Stalin's early postwar policy of cooperation had been disappointing, Soviet foreign policy and bloc policy veered toward radicalism, with Zhdanov as the chief spokesman of the new course.

The new forward policy was officially launched at the conference of Communist Parties held in September 1947 at Szklarska Poreba in Poland; this conference established the Cominform, an inter-Party bureau for publicizing joint ventures. Fittingly enough, the seat of the new bureau was Belgrade, the stronghold of Communist militancy. Barely restored on a radical basis, unity in the bloc collapsed over a different issue: Tito challenged Soviet organizational control within the international movement.

Having won his point on radicalism, Tito engaged on an ambitious empire-building venture: together with Dimitrov, the Bulgarian Communist chief, he undertook to confederate all East-Central European states. Greece, where the Communists, supported from Yugoslavia and Bulgaria, sought to seize power by force of arms, was to be added to the new empire. To Stalin, such a concentration of power in the hands of foreign Communists was anathema. To make things worse, Tito ejected the Soviet police agents planted in the Yugoslav apparatus. Stalin reacted with fury. He secured Yugoslavia's expulsion from the Cominform and sought to engineer an upheaval in the Yugoslav Party and put conventional Stalinists in control. But Tito was able to maintain himself by accepting help from the West. Yugoslavia, the erstwhile spearhead of Communist militancy, quickly adopted a neutralist course in foreign policy, still maintaining a "socialist" orientation but supporting only the most moderate policies advocated by Moscow. The first result of this startling reorientation was the collapse of the Communist forces in the Greek civil war. Deprived of Yugoslav support, they had to give up the struggle in 1949.

The initial stage of postwar political developments in East-Central Europe, characterized by multiparty People's Democratic coalitions, was liquidated in 1948–49. Communist intimidation and terror had broken up the existing "bourgeois" parties, and the Social Democrats had been forced to merge with the Communists. In most cases, the destruction of the multiparty system was a protracted, gradual affair, characterized by what Hungary's Stalinist boss, Mátyás Rákosi, called "salami tactics." In Czechoslovakia, however, the change was effected in an abrupt and violent manner: a *coup d'état* backed by armed factory guards imposed a Communist government on February 25, 1948.

Thus the stage was set for integral sovietization. This "second revolution," to use Seton-Watson's term, followed identical lines everywhere: the nationalization of all means of industrial production, the forced build-up of heavy industry, and the beginning collectivization of agriculture; terroristic regimentation of culture, education, and public life; and a hard line in foreign policy, reflected in stepped-up defense programs. New constitutions adopted throughout the region abolished political pluralism in all but name and made the Communist-controlled form of People's Democracy mandatory.

This virulent stage of sovietization caused enormous hardships and stresses. Forced industrialization drew manpower away from the countryside, and industrial workers were driven to exhaustion by constantly raised work norms. Rising industrial output, however, did not benefit the economy, because the biggest projects were planned without regard for economic needs, available sources of raw materials, or profitability. In the agricultural sector, the collectivization drives met with the peasants' determined passive resistance, which was so strong that by 1956 the socialized sector ordinarily ranged between only one-fifth and one-third of the area under cultivation. In Poland, where the regime did not push collectivization, the percentage was below ten; only in Bulgaria did the Communists succeed in bringing the collective sector up to nearly 80 percent by this date. In fact, the collectivization drives had to be kept within limits because contrary to all theory small peasant farms consistently turned out greater marketable surpluses than the large collective units. But even so, the countryside was not able to provide enough food for the increased urban populations. . . .

The ordeal of sovietization was peculiarly aggravated by the fact that the onset of the "second revolution" (1948–49) coincided with the Yugoslav crisis. This conflict, besides exacerbating the cold war and stimulating inflated defense expenditures, split all Communist Parties down the middle. Suffering from severe psychopathological delusions, Stalin concluded that Tito was in league with the West and sought to destroy him. Every Communist who had been friendly with Tito or leaned toward his side in earlier debates automatically became an enemy, and a colossal purge of Titoist "traitors" got under way. In the Soviet Union, Zhdanov's "Leningrad circle" was doomed; in the now-satellitized East European countries, the Stalinists started to liquidate "Titoist" deviants, notably including the former domestic underground. This campaign brought about the downfall of Gomulka in Poland, Rajk in Hungary, Kostov in Bulgaria, Patrascanu in Rumania, and innumerable lesser-known figures. Many were executed or sent to prisons and concentration camps on forged evidence and extorted confessions purporting to show that they were Western agents and spies. The purge was particularly fierce in Hungary, where the victims included not only the former underground cadres but former Social Democrats and Communists and fellow-traveling intellectuals with a Western background. This internecine warfare in the Party, which provided a lurid backdrop for the sovietization campaign, had critical political consequences in the sequel.

By early 1953, the satellite regimes' radical industrializing and collectivizing drives had led to a severe economic crisis over the entire region. Chronic shortages and inflationary stresses made it imperative to cut back sharply from the overambitious goals set for the satellites by the Stalinist leaders. Yet Marxist dogmatism, personified by Stalin, prevented any reconsideration and modification of policy: forced industrialization and collectivization was the only "correct" way to "build socialism," regardless of the consequences. Then, in March 1953, Stalin died.

Stalin's disappearance changed the course of bloc politics. Governmental power passed to a small group of oligarchs, Stalin's most powerful lieutenants, who were anxious to prevent any single member of their select company from eclipsing the rest and achieving one-man rule. Moreover, the successors had enough practical sense to recognize that the tempo of "building socialism" had to be reduced. The result was the proclamation by Moscow of a "New Course," stressing "coexistence," the relaxation of international tension, a retreat from unrealistic and overambitious economic goals, and the mitigation of terrorism.

In most of the satellite countries, the New Course was implemented without fanfare, but in East Germany and Hungary the incumbent Stalinist regimes were forced by Moscow to engage in public self-criticism, condemning their earlier radical course and announcing far-reaching changes. The East German regime demonstratively lifted a number of repressive measures that had been directed against the middle strata. In Hungary, the Stalinist boss Mátyás Rákosi was forced to abandon the premiership to Imre Nagy, known for his opposition to the collectivization of agriculture and to other harsh Stalinist policies. The result of this reshuffling was dual rule, for Rákosi remained leader of the Party.

The frank and abrupt introduction of the New Course in East Germany and Hungary had unexpected consequences. Seeing that the Communist leadership, discredited by its own admissions, made concessions to the middle strata while still insisting upon increased work norms, the workers rose in open revolt in Berlin and other centers (June 17, 1953). In Hungary, the peasants took the regime's self-criticism as a signal for a violent assault on collectivization. The East German revolt was put down by Soviet military force, and order was restored in Hungary by a mixture of repressive measures and concessions. But the Hungarian regime remained divided between Stalinists and moderates; the Party headed by Rákosi and the government led by Nagy were working at cross purposes.

This internal division was exacerbated by a policy that Moscow now strongly pushed, the rehabilitation of the victims of the Hungarian mass purges of 1949 and subsequent years. Official recognition that the entire purge had been based upon fictitious charges was a tremendous shock precisely to believers in the Communist ideology. Such admissions of error and mismanagement spread total disaffection among Communist intellectuals, who came to feel that Rákosi's continued presence at the head of the Party was morally intolerable. The opposition began a relentless campaign against the Stalinist Old Guard, denouncing its treachery against the Party and its alienation from the people. The writers succeeded in securing some public outlets for their charges, notably the *Literary Gazette,* the organ of the Communist Writers Union.

In other satellite countries, the New Course also led to ferment among Communist intellectuals, but where for one reason or another the purge could be kept quiet (that is, in East Germany, Czechoslovakia, Rumania, and Bulgaria), intellectual critique lacked a cutting edge. Outside Hungary, this issue produced a similar shock only in Poland. There, Moscow had not insisted upon rehabilitation, but the sordid truth about the framing of Gomulka and a host of other members of the home underground became known when revelations by a former high police official who had defected were broadcast from the West. In Poland, too, a campaign began within the Party to purify the regime and to remove the Old Guard. Radical opposition thus set Poland and Hungary apart from the rest of the bloc.

The New Course came to an end both in Soviet Russia and in the satellite countries with the fall of Malenkov early in 1955; thereafter, the Communist regimes were engaged in tightening controls. But a new shock was not long in coming: in Februrary 1956, in a closed session of the 20th Congress of the Soviet Communist Party, Khrushchev aired Stalin's crimes against the Party, and his revelations were soon made public by the U.S. State Department. In Poland and Hungary, the speech gave new impetus to the Party opposition, starting a chain of events that culminated in the revolutionary outbreaks of October 1956 in Warsaw and Budapest.

The two revolutions cannot be discussed here in detail; in the present context, they serve to point up the new, post-Stalin differentiation within the Communist bloc. While earlier the Balkan regimes had broken Communist uniformity by following a militant "Left" course, after Stalin's death Poland and Hungary drifted away from the other satellites in the "Right" direction. This differentiation still persists, although after a brief flurry of independence in October 1956, both Poland and Hungary were brought back into line.

The Polish revolution was less radical than the Hungarian: in Hungary, popular passion swept away the Communist regime and forced the revolutionary government to denounce the Soviet alliance, whereas the Poles were content with reforming the regime and preferred to stay within the bloc as their mainstay against the German threat to their new western boundary. The Hungarian revolution was suppressed in blood, and Communist restoration followed under Kádár. In Poland, the internal reforms inaugurated in October were gradually whittled away. Eventually, basic political institutions both in Poland and in Hungary reverted to the standard totalitarian type. In fact, Hungary in one respect carried sovietization further since 1956 than the earlier Stalinist regime had been able to do: now all the land is collectivized. Yet, the two post-October regimes stand in a clear contrast to those which had had no October experience.

In what does this contrast consist? The basic institutions, as indicated, are similar everywhere, and the post-October regimes cultivate no deviant ideologies. On the other hand, the personal backgrounds of the leaders deviate markedly: both Gomulka and Kádár had been in prison during the Stalin era, while the other satellite leaders are former Stalinists. But this difference in background has scarcely any relevance today: former Stalinists and anti-Stalinists have found common ground in Khrushchev's de-Stalinization policy. What really differentiates the post-October regimes from the others is not so much the leaders' outlook and basic orientation as the Party's standing within, and relation to, society as a whole. In the satellite countries which had no October, the Party, never having been seriously challenged, can still pretend to speak for the entire community. There, the "building of socialism" and the "transition to Communism" are presented as concerns shared by the whole people, and dissent is treated as an antisocial phenomenon, while the post-October regimes cannot put forward such claims. As the theoretical organ of the Hungarian party put it in a discussion of the new Soviet Party program: "It must be admitted that our country stands at a lower stage of social evolution than the Soviet Union." Since with the completion of Kádár's collectivization drive the Hungarian "social base" is about as "socialist" as in the rest of the bloc, the social "backwardness" noted by the Party organ must be understood to relate to the "superstructure," or, in this instance, to a lag in popular thinking. What is meant is that the people are by and large indifferent to the cause of socialism. Before October, such a diagnosis could not have been made public without a call for strong remedies: the intensification of the class struggle, the eradication of the remnants of bourgeois thinking. But the post-October regime just notes widespread popular indifference as a fact, for the time being unalterable. The same is true of Poland, as indicated by the regime's cultural, religious, and agrarian policies. In both countries, dissent is ignored as much as possible, rather than being treated as an antisocial phenomenon calling for stern rebuke and suppression. Isolated within their societies, the post-October regimes know they must trim their sails in order to keep things under control. Thus they make no issue of widespread deviant attitudes, as long as these are not expressed in an overtly defiant manner. In Soviet Russia and the other satellite countries, Communist controls are more relaxed than under Stalin, but they have a far wider scope than in the post-October regimes: the Party is less hesitant to set the line in politically sensitive cultural matters.

Another curious differentiation remains to be mentioned. Albania, the smallest and weakest satellite, is actively opposing the "coexistence" line standard in the European bloc, aligning herself with the militant Chinese position. It would be hard to explain this in terms of ideological preferences; Albania is not concerned with "building socialism" in the Chinese manner. Nor do the Albanian Communists have any stake in Chinese expansion *per se*. They do, however, feel threatened by their big neighbor, Yugoslavia, and this seems to be why they prefer a bloc policy that would, among other things, perpetuate the rift between Yugoslavia and the bloc. Behind Albania's condemnation of Yugoslav "revisionism," we may perceive a defensive reflex against Yugoslav expansionism.

In this paper the varying patterns of sovietization in East-Central Europe have been analyzed primarily in terms of happenings within the ruling circles—policy decisions made in Moscow, compliance or noncompliance by local Party leaderships, conflicts and rivalries within Communist groups, and the like. This emphasis is not meant to imply that such other factors as cultural traditions, national cohesion and self-assertion, and popular resentment of Communist regimentation had no significance. In fact, as we have seen, popular resistance to collectivization has been prolonged and effective. It is also noteworthy that the two "October" countries are the only ones in the area with a strongly anti-Russian national tradition. National self-assertion and security are the basic reasons for such developments as Tito's defiance of Stalin, Gomulka's success in keeping Poland within the bloc, and even Albania's pro-Chinese orientation. But the key to variations in Communist policy and in the degree of stability of the Communist regimes must be sought in the vicissitudes of the top Party layer. Had popular resentment been the dominant factor, we should have seen the most violent outbreaks around 1951–52, and this not only in Hungary and Poland but elsewhere, too. Actually, disturbances occurred only after controls were relaxed, and then mainly where the ruling group had become severely divided. Popular resentment broke through with elementary force once an opening was provided by division within the Party. Failing this, it remained contained. Czech, Rumanian, and Bulgarian quiescence after the 20th Congress, as contrasted with the Polish and Hungarian ferment, does not necessarily indicate a much higher degree of popular acceptance of Communism. Had a conflict within the leadership opened a crack in the protective wall of control, there would have been disturbances in those countries, too.

What does this imply for the future? Unity within the leadership remains a critical factor, and it is vital for the regimes within the Moscow orbit to close ranks against the Chinese heresy as long as the conflict between Peking and Moscow is not healed. Also, unity at the top will be endangered, with possible critical consequences for the stability of the Communist regimes, when the Soviet leader's position again falls vacant. Not that we can simply extrapolate from the succession crisis following Stalin's death: after Khrushchev, things will not look the same. Still, we can draw some tentative conclusions from the above analysis. A succession crisis involving mere personal rivalries need not undermine the stability of the Communist systems, but it would be different if the contenders were to invoke fundamental moral issues. In the past, terror was the most explosive moral issue, and this will not be relevant unless there is a resurgence of police terror. But less dramatic issues might also lead to deeply divisive splits.

In the satellite countries, political stability is guaranteed, first and foremost, by Soviet military power. The lesson of Hungary has sunk in: one cannot reckon with future attempts at self-liberation. But if the satellite governments are guaranteed by external pressure, it follows that they are isolated within their national communities, not only as an oppressive but also as an alien element. While the subject peoples cannot break loose from Soviet control by their own efforts, any internal weakening of the Soviet power system would release the centrifugal force of national self-assertion.

Moscow's Satellites—in and out of Orbit*

Anatole Shub

Shortly after the New Year, Communist Bulgaria demanded that the United States Legation in Sofia close its information display windows, containing photographs of Presidents Kennedy and Johnson and scenes of American life. The same week, Hungary's Communist Government authorized the United States Legation in Budapest to reopen its display windows, which had been shut since the 1956 revolution.

The timing was coincidental, but contrasts of this kind are becoming ever more common in Eastern Europe. More than at any time since the war, it is a region of increasing diversity and subtle change. Titoism, the Polish and Hungarian revolts, and now the Sino-Soviet split have all chipped away at the "monolithic bloc" which Stalin sought to create. With its dozen languages, half a dozen religions and divergent historical experiences, Eastern Europe is once again an intricate mosaic, patterned as much by its own national traditions as by Soviet fiat.

Of Stalin's eight original satellites, two—Yugoslavia and Albania—have already left the Soviet orbit. In the opinion of many observers, Rumania is now embarked on a similar path. Poland and Hungary, though still Russian allies, are in some ways more "revisionist" than Yugoslavia. Czechoslovakia is

* From *The New York Times Magazine,* March 15, 1964, pp. 22, 110–112. Mr. Shub is a Fellow of the Institute of Current World Affairs, and has lived and traveled in Eastern Europe since 1962.

the country in motion these days, strongly reminiscent of Poland and Hungary in 1954–55. Only East Germany and Bulgaria seem to be mired in the old vassal status.

In many basic respects, from darkened streets to guarded frontiers, the Communist countries continue to resemble one another more than any one of them resembles its non-Communist neighbors. Yet, to the Western visitor, the great surprise is not so much how Communism has altered the East European nations, but how they have managed to retain their historic identities and even, in varying measure, to transform Communism. Whether this process of change can be "stabilized" to Russia's advantage, or will lead to the eventual erosion of Soviet power itself, remains to be seen.

Poland

Closest to Moscow, seat of the Communist military alliance, Warsaw remains the freest of Eastern Europe's cities. Eighty-seven per cent destroyed by the Nazis, the city now has more churches than before the war—nearly all built or rebuilt with government funds. The Poles are probably the world's most ardent Catholics, for the faith inspired centuries of national resistance to Orthodox Russia and Protestant Prussia. The Communists are compelled to embrace the nationalist heritage in a myriad of ways. Only last year, for example, the regime sponsored elaborate anniversary celebrations of the 1863 uprising—which was directed against Russia and led by aristocrats.

Nationalism and Catholicism are only two aspects of the "Polish way." Equally striking are private agriculture (occupying 85 per cent of the land, with individual farms up to 122 acres) and cultural variety. Abstract art, twelve-tone music, "new-wave" films are commonplace; Polish sociology is decades ahead of anything comparable in the bloc; Western newspapers are available, and the Catholic Church continues to issue its own publications.

Sophisticated, witty, cosmopolitan, the intellectuals of Warsaw and Cracow look to Paris, not Moscow. Their private views and "desk-drawer" manuscripts range far beyond the official "revisionism" of Gomulka, Khruschchev or Tito, for they have had second thoughts—and incisive ones—about Marx and Lenin as well as Stalin. "The working class?" asked one of them recently. "A meteor that streaked briefly across the sky of history before drowning in the sea of automation."

Yet Warsaw and Cracow are not all Poland. The somnolent villages remain turn-of-the-century, while industrial towns like Lodz, Katowice and Nowa Huta are grim "Socialist" replicas of the early-capitalist squalor described by Marx. As for the so-called Western provinces annexed from Germany in 1945, to many they still look more German than Polish—and the Poles remain sensitive about them.

All this is not far different from historic Polish patterns: a brilliant aristocracy (now based on intellect rather than land), a rather sullen mass consoled by religion and alcohol, and continuing anxiety about the nation's survival between Germany and Russia.

Hungary

Hungary, too, seems to be repeating itself. After the defeat of its 1848 revolution, more prudent leaders gradually achieved most of the revolt's aims by 1867. Today's Hungarians also seem on the way toward realizing many of the original objectives of the 1956 uprising. Premier Janos Kadar's slogan is "Whoever is not against us is with us," which has meant greater opportunities for non-Communists. Symbolically, the old Stalinist leader, Matyas Rakosi, has never returned from his Russian exile, while the intellectual leaders of 1956, such as Tibor Dery and Gyula Hay, are free, published and permitted to visit the West.

In Budapest today, one can observe the rebuilding of the old Royal Palace, can dine in restaurants which consciously reproduce the aura of Hapsburg days, admire the most chic women in Eastern Europe, and listen alternately to gypsy fiddlers, progressive jazz, the *bossa nova* and Europe's best anti-Communist jokes. In food, drink, cosmetics and other amenities of personal life, Budapest is way out front—the result of more realistic economic plans as well as the pleasure-loving national tradition. One suspects that *la dolce vita* has already begun to take hold; in any event, the Fellini film (banned in Moscow, Bucharest, etc.) has been a smash hit.

Both Hungary and Poland are occupied by Soviet armies, and both are basically poor countries. Czechoslovakia and Rumania, on the other hand, have no Soviet troops and each is (for differing reasons) potentially rich; yet, paradoxically, they had for years the most stable Stalinist regimes in the bloc. This situation has now begun to change rapidly.

Czechoslovakia

Czechoslovakia, the most prosperous nation in Central Europe before the war, was also the only genuine democracy. With its advanced industry, skilled labor and egalitarian traditions, it might conceivably have become a Communist showplace. Instead, it is the living refutation of the theory that Communism's failures and "excesses" stem from the backwardness of the countries in which it has taken power.

The Czechs and Slovaks, with their "Good Soldier Schweik" traditions of passive resistance, gradually smothered the regime in a miasma of low productivity, withheld initiative and all-round pettifogging. The overextended Czech economy ground to a standstill in 1962, and the political crisis began.

The showing of "High Noon" in Prague a year ago may have been something of a landmark; it was the first "Western" seen there since 1948. Twist clubs and beatnik-type youth cafes appeared somewhat earlier. Kafka and other "modernist" writers were "rehabilitated" a few months later. One after another, leading Stalinists were removed, leading victims of Stalinism restored to positions of influence (if not yet of power). Unpopular aid to Cuba, Asia and Africa has been cut back. The Austrian border has been opened to large-scale tourism.

These and other measures produced a striking change in the Prague atmosphere in the course of 1963. The new year has begun with extensive economic reforms, and further "democratization" is considered inevitable.

Rumania

The Rumanians' historic legacy includes a unique talent for changing sides at opportune moments in great international conflicts. They came out of both world wars "victorious allies" even though, months before the end, they had been among the losers. Perhaps the greatest of Rumania's several paradoxes today is that it appears to be preparing the ground for at least the possibility of withdrawal from the Soviet bloc, yet without any of the ideological clamor that accompanied the Yugoslav and Albanian exits.

In the past four years, Rumania has reoriented its trade toward the West, defied the pressures of Comecon (the bloc's Council for Mutual Economic Assistance), and staked most of its future industrial projects on Western equipment. Rumanian cultural life has been quietly "de-Russified," while such non-Communist artists as Ionesco and Brancusi have been reclaimed for the national heritage. "We are Latins, not Slavs," the Rumanians now say again, for the first time since the war.

Yet the watchword has been nationalism, not liberalization. A Western movie in Bucharest is likely to be as dated and innocuous as *"The Great Waltz"*; the press is even less informative than Russia's; highway police still copy down the numbers of foreign license plates.

Parodoxically, too, the Rumanian economy seems to be the single extant example of "successful Stalinism." With rigid central planning, collective farms and all the rest, Rumania has been achieving consistently impressive rates of growth while most of the others have been faltering. Perhaps the explanation is that, because there were only a few hundred Rumanian Communists in 1945, the economy has been operated mainly by able young technocrats, who feel that the regime needs them more than they need it.

East Germany

There remain East Germany and Bulgaria, still politically depressed areas. Walter Ulbricht's German Democratic Republic is, as the saying goes, neither German, democratic nor a republic, but an occupation regime maintained by 20 Soviet divisions and (since 1961) the Berlin Wall. Some six million East Germans have already fled westward and more would follow if the Wall were removed.

Nevertheless, no regime has ever completely extinguished the German passions for technology, discipline and order. Thus, despite everything, East Germany is even today the most developed, densely populated and "European" of all Communist countries. It suffers by comparison, of course, with West Germany and West Berlin.

Bulgaria

Bulgaria—poor, pastoral and primitive—is the only European satellite which makes the Soviet Union appear advanced, and the only one which is Slav, Orthodox and traditionally pro-Russian. (A statue of Czar Alexander II still dominates Sofia's main square.) Bulgaria has had the additional misfortune of having been defeated, or diplomatically outmaneuvered by Yugoslavia and Rumania in every conflict of the last century; it still resents the loss of Macedonia to the former and the Dobruja region to the latter.

These traditions perhaps explain why its Communist leaders, while feuding constantly among themselves, have been so dependent on Moscow and why liberalization has never gone very far. The Georgiev spy trial . . . was a Stalinist performance of a kind inconceivable elsewhere in Eastern Europe since 1956. . . .

Despite these emerging differences among them, the Communist nations remain Communist. In each, the writ of the party central committee is law, leadership is self-perpetuating, the courts and press are politically controlled, the secret police is ubiquitous if no longer omnipotent. Voluntary association is sharply curbed, and travel remains a privilege rather than a right. In the domain of political freedom, the atmosphere at its best approaches that of Franco Spain.

In economic doctrine, the East European regimes remain committed, despite the vaunted de-Stalinization, to Stalin's concepts of Socialism. With varying intensity, they all continue to favor investment over consumption, machine-building industry over agriculture, hard goods over services, centralization over local initiative, administrators and technocrats over workers, peasants and craftsmen.

Private enterprise exists (the very gaps in Communist planning make it indispensable), but it is everywhere circumscribed if not penalized. In this sense, the most "revisionist" of Communist countries remain closer to the Soviet Union than to a democratic Socialist nation, such as Sweden.

The East European regimes remain linked to Russia in more formal ways as well. There is the Warsaw military pact, of which even Albania remains a member. There are Comecon and numerous bilateral arrangements which have tied the East European economies to Russia. There are endless consultations among the party functionaries, diplomats, propagandists and security police.

With the possible future exception of Rumania (which late last year voted twice against the Soviet Union at the United Nations), the satellite regimes back the Kremlin, chapter and verse, in international affairs, not only against the "Western imperialists" but in the more recent struggle against China. However, it also appears that Khrushchev, to an appreciably greater extent than Stalin, has had to tailor many of his policies to the views and needs of his East European allies, particularly in the struggle with the Chinese.

Has Eastern Europe's increasing variety made the Kremlin stronger or weaker? In the short run, the answer seems clear. The situation today is considerably less explosive than it was at Stalin's death. Economic conditions, by and large, improved; the Stalinist reign of terror appears to have ceased; the regimes in Hungary, Poland, Rumania and Czechoslovakia are more responsive to national sentiment than a decade ago. Moreover, a certain stability has been introduced by the demonstration, in East Germany (1953) and Hungary (1956), that Russia would—and the West would not—intervene in the event of anti-Communist uprisings. To the extent that Khrushchev has succeeded in avoiding the "worst," he can surely feel more secure.

However, the Soviet leader has purchased this relative security at the price of ideological disunity, the rise of nationalism and an unmistakable decline in Russian authority. Like Stalin with Yugoslavia, Khrushchev has shaken his finger at China and Albania, with even less effect; he has been trying to appease Rumania, with results as yet uncertain.

A dozen years ago, the late Klement Gottwald in Czechoslovakia was calling for "ever-greater utilization of Soviet experiences and ever-greater approximation of the Soviet example." No satellite leader, not even Ulbricht, talks quite this way any longer. The pressure now is in the opposite direction, as various features of East European life stir repeated controversy in Moscow—Soviet "liberals" demanding the showing of Polish films, for example, or "conservatives" fearfully censoring Khrushchev's own praise of Yugoslav workers' councils.

For Russia, the control of Eastern Europe has until now conferred indubitable benefits. Strategically, the area has served as a buffer against the West—specifically against Germany, which Russians high and low still fear. Economically, Eastern Europe has yielded important raw materials, from Polish uranium to Rumanian wheat, as well as advanced industrial goods—all on terms of trade which Moscow could not obtain elsewhere.

Perhaps of most significance, Communist rule in Eastern Europe has been an important ideological justification for the Soviet regime itself; the existence of the satellites is regularly cited in support of the Kremlin line that Leninism is a scientific historical doctrine, and Communist rule the irreversible "wave of the future."

It is in this ideological sense that a Russian loss of control in Eastern Europe might pose the gravest problems for the Kremlin. On what basis indeed could the harsh Russian dictatorship justify itself if, after half a century, the world Communist "wave" was clearly receding in the very heart of Europe? The repercussions in Russia of the Hungarian revolution—ranging from Moscow University student riots to the "anti-party group" battle in the Politburo—were a dramatic illustration of how much Soviet stability has hinged on a measure of order in its dependencies. In Russia today, one clearly senses the corrosive effects on Communist confidence of Chinese defiance, Yugoslav nonalignment, Rumanian opportunism and similar ideological strains.

Within Eastern Europe, the rise of nationalism, while relieving certain tensions, has also generated or revived others. Rumania has been restricting its Magyar minority; Hungarian publications refer to northeast Yugoslavia as "southern Hungary"; anti-Semitism looms large in Polish factional disputes; the Slovaks are resisting the Czechs. "In short," as a Warsaw wit observed, "Eastern Europe is itself again."

No one can predict how Mr. Khrushchev's revamped East European system will weather new shocks in the conflict with China, new economic dislocations, or the inevitable crisis of succession in the Kremlin itself. The developments are likely to be as complex and surprising in the next decade as they have been in the past one. But the underlying fact about Eastern Europe remains a simple one: none of its Communist regimes were popularly chosen; nor would they be so today, despite the reforms of the Khrushchev era.

A dissident Soviet writer was recently asked just what it was that he and his embattled colleagues really wanted in Russia; was it, perhaps, something like Yugoslavia? "Oh no," he replied disdainfully, "that's a *Communist* country! What we want is something like . . . Sweden."

So, in truth, do most East Europeans—which suggests that the changes we have witnessed thus far may be only a beginning.

COMECON*

Michael Gamarnikow

Of the world's many international organizations, perhaps the busiest is the Council for Mutual Economic Assistance. Its experts and functionaries, along with the various representatives of its member countries, are constantly on the move. Time and again they descend on all the larger cities of the Soviet bloc to "discuss," to "exchange experiences," to "prepare draft proposals," to "coordinate" or to "organize." During 1963, over 170 such meetings were held. They ranged from the summit meeting of the First Secretaries and Prime Ministers in Moscow in July to a conference of fashion experts and a meeting of specialists on water reserves.

What have been the practical results of this buzzing activity? In terms of the organization's objectives—very little. Even the communist press now admits that the COMECON regional specialization scheme will not become operative until the mid-seventies. One may say, in fact, that the feverish activity of the COMECON experts serves primarily as a smokescreen to hide the lack of any real progress in achieving COMECON's avowed aims.

* "COMECON Today," *East Europe,* March 1964, pp. 3–9. Reprinted by permission. Mr. Gamarnikow is an economist who specializes in Soviet-bloc affairs.

Those aims were clearly stated in a communiqué issued after the summit meeting of leaders of the COMECON member countries in May 1958, and in many subsequent policy declarations. They amount to the application of the principles of specialization and international division of labor to a single unified market embracing the whole communist bloc, or at least to that part of it which owes ideological allegiance to Khrushchev. This scheme, if carried to its logical conclusion, would eventually lead to the establishment of a unified and completely integrated bloc-wide economy, directed, planned and managed by a supranational authority. In an article published in the September 1962 issue of *Problems of Peace and Socialism* (Prague), Khrushchev indicated quite clearly that this was the ultimate aim of the COMECON integration scheme and his ultimate weapon for winning the peaceful competition with the capitalist West.

> Our aim is to build the socialist world economy as a single entity. But to accomplish this the socialist countries have no resources to draw on other than the accumulations created by each. It follows, then, that we cannot get on without agreement, even if only in general outline, on the policy of creating and utilizing accumulations on the scale of the Council. This presupposes, first, allocating funds for building common enterprises—a thing which we have just begun to do—and, second, agreed national investment plans which would take into account both the national and the common interests. . . .
>
> In the past the Council was not in a position to revise the system of coordinating plans generally and investment plans in particular on a new basis, because, first, according to the old statute it did not have the necessary powers and, second, it lacked the necessary planning instruments—material balances, comparable national-economic indices and unified statistics. The decisions of the June (1962) meeting will, however, enable the work of the Council to be organized in a new way. . . .
>
> Cooperation in the Council has now reached a point when it is necessary to decide the trend of the specialization in each country, that is, decide exactly which branches, in what complex and on what raw material base, should be built in each of the countries so as to meet our common needs in the most economic way. The time has come to draw up a balance sheet of production and consumption of the main types of manufacture in our countries for a period extending at least up to 1970, and in this way prepare a general scheme for inter-state specialization and coordination. The intention for the immediate years is to produce the more important types of manufacture on the basis of international specialization and coordination. . . .
>
> The greater international specialization and coordination provide a sound basis for long-term trade agreements. The Council is now faced with the job of drawing up a system which will ensure going over from bilateral to multilateral planning and regulation of the trade and accounting between the socialist countries.

On the face of it, Khrushchev's proposal was quite logical. It would obviously be impossible to integrate the centrally planned economies of the Soviet bloc without having a strong supranational authority to impose directives on the national governments with respect to planning and investment. Only such an authority could ensure proper coordination of the several national plans and the most effective allocation of common raw material resources, investment means and labor reserves among the member countries.

But the question of this supranational authority has sparked a bitter conflict within COMECON and virtually paralyzed all progress during the last 18 months. The conflict arises from the basic contradiction between national and community interests. The main point at issue is whether the member states should surrender a significant part of sovereign control over the development of their national economies in order to achieve greater economic efficiency for the bloc as a whole.

The problem has political aspects too. There is a contradiction between the obvious economic benefits of specialization and the grave political danger involved in the loss of economic sovereignty and in being too dependent on the USSR—which is bound to dominate the supranational authority of COMECON. This accounts for the fact that the East European communist leaders are obviously not quite sure whether they want to integrate their economies, at least to any significant degree.

The lesson of the Soviet-Albanian conflict has not been lost upon them. Khrushchev used the strongest possible methods of economic pressure, including a trade embargo and a virtual economic blockade, in an attempt to overthrow the Hoxha regime. The smaller countries are acutely aware of the fact that each consecutive step toward economic integration further erodes their economic independence, as well as their political autonomy, and exposes them progressively more and more to Soviet hegemony.

Until June 1962 COMECON had no central authority. The statute of 1960 did not provide for a policy-making executive. The highest organ was the Council of member states, represented usually by deputy prime ministers, which was to meet twice yearly. In practice this body was unable to make clear-cut policy decisions, because in the communist system such decisions are made by the party Politburos rather than on the governmental level. Besides, the COMECON statute had a built-in concession to the principle of national sovereignty. This was the unanimity rule, which in fact ensured the preeminence of national interests over those of the community as a whole. The unanimity rule and the practice of bilateral negotiations have been effectively used by dissenting COMECON members to prevent, or a least to delay indefinitely, measures which they considered contrary to their national interests.

At the summit meeting of the First Party Secretaries of the COMECON countries in June 1962 in Moscow, a decision was made to create a superior authority in the form of an Executive Committee with an alternating chairman, composed of the permanent representatives of all member countries—

again at the level of deputy prime ministers. This was clearly a compromise solution—an outcome of the conflict between the proponents of a supranational executive on the one hand and of national economic sovereignty on the other. But no sooner had the new Executive Committee been created than the conflict flared up again. The basic issue was that of the Committee's prerogative. Was COMECON to have a supranational planning and executive authority able to impose its own solutions and issue binding directives? Or were the essential problems of regional specialization to be negotiated bilaterally and on a national level—i.e., subject to the veto of individual party Politburos?

The controversy reached a peak when Khrushchev published the outline of his grand design—from which we have quoted above—in the September 1962 issue of *Problems of Peace and Socialism,* and elaborated on it in his speech to the November 1962 Plenum of the Central Committee of the CPSU. Khrushchev's grand design called for three major reforms in the COMECON economic integration scheme. First of all, the creation of a supranational planning authority, empowered to issue directives to the appropriate planning organs of the member countries. Secondly, the initiation of joint investment projects to develop raw material resources and other economic enterprises on a community-wide basis. This meant not only joint financing but also joint ownership. Finally, Khrushchev proposed full coordination of the investment plans of the member countries, which implied the free movement of capital according to the directives of the supranational planning authority.

Since the publication of these proposals, it has been apparent that the Executive Committee created in June 1962 had been conceived by the proponents of full integration as merely the political superstructure for what was to follow: the creation of a centralized planning authority that would take away from COMECON members the really significant part of their economic sovereignty. The power of making basic economic policy decision was to rest in the supranational, community-minded planning body, which was to be given full power to select investment projects for the whole COMECON area and allocate economic resources from the common pool, according to community rather than national priorities.

Apparently there had been little opposition to the creation of the Executive Committee, since its rules preserved the basic safeguard of national interests—the principle of unanimity. Moreover, the low level of representation on it precluded this body from making decisions without firm directives from the respective Politburos. But now, with the publication of Khrushchev's new proposals, the creation of the Executive Committee was clearly seen as the thin edge of the wedge, meant to ensure the predominance of community interest.

That is why a fierce conflict developed over the formal incorporation of the Executive Committee into the COMECON statutory organizational structure, as well as over the Committee's prerogatives. This conflict came to a head during the Seventeenth Session of the COMECON Council in Bucharest in December 1962, which ended in a complete deadlock. Because of a basic difference of opinion, no decision was made either on the prerogatives of the Executive Committee or on the establishment of a supranational planning body. The problem of coordinating investments was partly deflected along the lines of bilateral agreements, and partly postponed until 1965. Agreement has still to be reached on the necessary amendment to incorporate the already existing Executive Committee into the statutory organizational structure of COMECON. Thus, nearly two years after its creation, there is still no statutory provision for this body in the COMECON Charter, since any amendment of the 1960 statute would of necessity have to define its prerogatives.

The intensity of the conflict at the Seventeenth Session can be judged from the fact that the Polish chief delegate, Piotr Jaroszewicz, stated after his return from Bucharest that the decisions made by the Council "were based on a creative compromise." It is ironic that Jaroszewicz applied here exactly the same term Khrushchev had used less than two months earlier to describe his settlement of the Cuban crises. Clearly there is no need for "creative compromise" unless there is a basic conflict of policy and interests.

This major conflict turns upon four basic issues: (1) how to develop an economically rational basis for specialization and economic integration; (2) how to ensure adequate development of resources on a community-wide basis and at the same time an equitable distribution of the investment burden involved in this development; (3) what sort of over-all planning system to adopt; and (4) whether or not to accept the principle of a supranational authority. These disputed issues have been superimposed on the already existing conflicts and contradictions in the Soviet-bloc integration scheme. Their combined effect has been to reduce the progress of COMECON to a snail's pace. Another summit meeting in Moscow in July 1963, which again ended in a deadlock, amounted to a rejection of Khrushchev's grand design.

Indeed the only significant development in 1963 was in the opposite direction from that envisaged in Khrushchev's plan. This was the conflict between COMECON and Rumania over that country's plans for economic development. The Rumanians insisted on pursuing all-around industrial development in traditional communist fashion and in adapting their trade policies to their own design rather than to that of COMECON. Thus the Rumanian leaders challenged not only the principle that community interests should prevail over national interests, but the very concept of a division of labor based on *the present stage of economic development* of the Soviet-bloc countries.

The chief motive of the Rumanians was, perhaps, less the desire to maintain economic independence than the old-fashioned Stalinist belief that the development of a national base of heavy industry is the necessary prerequisite for building socialism. Although purely nationalistic appeals predominated in the propaganda put out by the Rumanian leaders for internal consumption, the strong Stalinist background of Gheorghiu-Dej and his closest associates suggests that autarkic economic concepts played at least an equal part in their strong and successful resistance to Khrushchev's grand design.

Whatever their actual motives, however, the immediate effect of the Rumanian opposition was to slow down and emasculate the COMECON integration scheme. Some steps taken by the Rumanians were definitely retrograde from the COMECON standpoint, since they led to a further duplication of productive capacity. New heavy industrial undertakings such as the Galati iron and steel complex manifestly contradict the basic principles of international specialization. But the main effect of the Rumanian revolt was to break the momentum in the progress of integration and in fact to introduce the element of national veto into an international system of planning. This voluntarism, which had been implicit in the practice of COMECON before 1962, has now been institutionalized by the Rumanian actions. This means that, at present, every COMECON member need accept only as much integration as it deems compatible with its national interests.

The Rumanians could not have succeeded in this without the Sino-Soviet conflict, which Gheorghiu-Dej cleverly exploited for his own ends. He judged quite correctly that Khrushchev could not afford still another open split in the world communist movement while he was engaged with the Chinese. The Chinese, in turn, helped Gheorghiu-Dej by denouncing Khrushchev's grand design as yet another revisionist sin and "a form of neo-colonialism." Other COMECON countries must have shared at least some of the Rumanian objections to Khrushchev's grand design, since the Rumanian viewpoint prevailed at the Moscow summit meeting of First Secretaries in July 1963. The final communiqué not only reaffirmed the national economic sovereignty of all COMECON members, but stated explicitly that "the best possible basis for a mutual coordination of economic plans is provided by *bilateral* consultations between member nations."

The net result of the Moscow summit meeting in July 1963 was not only a defeat for Khrushchev's supranational concept and the reaffirmation of those basic safeguards of national interest, unanimity and bilateralism, but a tacit acceptance of a slowdown and dilution of the whole COMECON integration scheme. Just as the speed of the convoy is determined by that of the slowest ship, so the pace and the extent of an international economic integration scheme is set by the most recalcitrant member country.

This does not mean that no progress at all has been achieved by the COMECON countries toward more international cooperation. But this progress ought to be described as *rationalization* rather than as *economic integration.* Although in certain cases a more rational use of existing resources can be a first step toward eventual integration, in others it can contradict the ultimate aim by perpetuating the duplication of productive capacity. An example of the first type of case is the creation of the COMECON bank; typical of the others are the bilateral specialization agreements made between member countries.

The agreement establishing the International Bank of Economic Cooperation was signed in Moscow last October, and the bank began operations on January 1, 1964. The creation of the COMECON bank, first proposed in Khrushchev's article in *Problems of Peace and Socialism,* should have been a positive development and a step forward in implementation of the bloc-wide integration scheme. But in practice, the existing conflicts of interest proved so powerful that the functions of the new bank had to be reduced to the lowest common denominator, acceptable to the most recalcitrant of the COMECON members.

Originally, the bank was to perform two basic tasks. One was important but purely technical, and the other was essential for the future development of the integration scheme. In the first place, as a clearing institution, the bank was to carry out multilateral settlements of outstanding trade balances. Secondly, as a credit-dispensing institution, the bank was to organize and supervise the joint financing of common industrial enterprises. Clearly, the first function—although a step forward from the stage of bilateral barter transactions—was purely technical and rationalistic in character. The other meant, at best, partial implementation of supranational control over investment schemes and financial capital resources.

But precisely for this reason the credit-dispensing function of the proposed bank was not acceptable to some COMECON members, which simply refused to allocate funds for joint investment purposes. No doubt the general scarcity of investment capital played a part in this negative attitude, but the predominant motive was most probably the fear of supranational control. Thus the function of dispensing investment credits had to be abandoned, at least for the time being. The newly created International Bank of Economic Cooperation will perform only technical multilateral settlements functions—just as the Bank of International Settlements in Basel has been doing for the West since 1930, without promoting the economic integration of Western Europe to any significant degree.

The introduction of multilateral settlements will, no doubt, help the growth of trade among COMECON members. In this sense the move must be regarded as a rational one. But the economic effects of the new multilateral clearing system will be entirely marginal, and will in no way hasten the general economic integration of the Soviet bloc.

It may be argued that even the mutilated COMECON bank is a first step toward the establishment of a credit-dispensing institution. But the second step cannot be achieved unless some agreement is reached on the principles of common financing of joint enterprises under supranational supervision. And the very principle of such joint financing is the source of a major conflict; until this conflict is resolved, there cannot be a second stage. Moreover, the charter of the new bank has built-in safeguards to protect national interests: the bank is governed by a Council on which each member country has three representatives, and all decisions of the Council must be unanimous. In practice, therefore, every member has a veto over any operation of the bank, present and future. In this way the opponents of joint financing have protected themselves in advance against any action on the part of the Council of the bank which they may consider contrary to their national interests. . . .

Bilateral trading patterns govern to a great extent the process of international division of labor which was, after all, to be the chief aim of the whole COMECON scheme. For this reason the progress achieved so far in the field of specialization has quite often been based on the continued duplication of productive capacity. It has amounted to a trading of products rather than their assignment to the most economic producer.

It must be recognized, of course, that to impose a rational specialization system on a group of countries which have followed a policy of independent industrialization for a long period of years has heavy costs: the scrapping of uneconomic plants and the shifting around of labor and capital to new production tasks. To convince local and national interests that closing a given plant or a whole branch of industry is essential for the welfare of the community as a whole is rather difficult without the objective evidence of comparative costs. For instance, the transfer of part of Hungary's radio production to Bulgaria has caused widespread criticism in the country, and even brought attempts to boycott radio sets imported from Bulgaria. In Czechoslovakia, proposals to reassign established production lines have resulted as a rule in an avalanche of protests. These examples suggest the degree of popular resistance to the shutting down of established production lines or factories in the interests of bloc-wide specialization. But because of the costs involved in the reorganization of existing industries the communist leaders themselves have not been too keen about it, and so little has actually been done. . . .

Purely technical specialization predominates in COMECON's temporary arrangements. Industrial assignments are allotted to individual countries by bilateral agreements in the course of an often haphazard give-and-take. Since these arrangements pertain to specific products and not to whole industrial lines, they tend to perpetuate the duplication of productive capacity. Moreover, because of the bilateral trading patterns, this type of purely technical specialization tends also to produce some degree of overlapping.

No doubt even this purely technical specialization increases over-all efficiency and is therefore an advance over the previous ideal of national self-sufficiency. On the other hand, it perpetuates the mislocation of capital resources in the bloc, where an acute shortage of investment funds is already the main brake on economic progress. But the worst feature of the purely technical type of specialization is its clearly temporary character. In whatever direction COMECON evolves, a redetermination of economic tasks will someday be inevitable. And the resultant scrapping, reconversion and dislocation is bound to involve an enormous economic loss.

Thus, although the bilateral specialization agreements tend to increase economic efficiency in the short run, from the long-term point of view they make the task of economic integration more difficult and complex. Khrushchev's proposal for a supranational planning authority was meant to overcome this contradiction. But the principle of national control has prevailed, and so specialization has been deflected along the line of temporary bilateral arrangements. The supranational allocation of economic tasks on a purely rational basis was clearly regarded by East European leaders as politically too dangerous.

This is why the main progress has been in ventures which presented no new threat to national economic sovereignty. The best example is the recently completed Friendship Pipeline, outwardly a shining example of international cooperation. But the Friendship Pipeline is simply a technically better method of transporting crude oil from the Soviet Union to Poland, Czechoslovakia and East Germany. These countries were already heavily dependent on Soviet oil supplies transported by rail. Consequently there were no political drawbacks to offset the obvious economic advantages.

The basic problem of COMECON remains the conflict of national vs. common interests. It is this conflict which prevented Khrushchev's grand design from getting off the ground. The only way to resolve it and to promote real integration would be the issuance of arbitrary directives by a supranational authority armed with effective prerogatives and a right to control. But can such an authority be set up now, when the autonomy of individual communist parties is growing? There is another basic contradiction here, namely that between the centralist economic spirit of Khrushchev's grand design and the trend toward political decentralization which is the reality of the Soviet bloc in the nineteen sixties.

Colonialism in Eastern Europe*

Ferenc Nagy

I appear here as the chairman of the Assembly of Captive European Nations, the organization which is comprised of the national representatives living in the free world of the nine countries behind the Iron Curtain.

I therefore feel that I cannot limit myself to deal only with the problem of one country, my homeland, but that in my statement I must examine the situation now prevailing in Central and Eastern Europe as a unit.

I would like to deal in my remarks with two points. First, the internal situation in these nine Eastern European countries; and second, the stand that the problem of these nine countries have taken in international politics.

* "Captive European Nations." Hearings before the Subcommittee on Europe, Committee on Foreign Affairs, House of Representatives, June 6–September 19, 1962 (Washington, D.C.: Government Printing Office, 1962), pp. 219–227. Mr. Nagy, a former Prime Minister of Hungary, is Chairman of the Assembly of Captive European Nations.

First of all I think it necessary to point out a few facts in connection with the Central and Eastern European nations which are, in general, well known, yet bear repeating from time to time.

One such fact is that there is not a single country in Central or Eastern Europe which established Soviet colonial rule and Communist government through the will and support of the people. Communism came to power in every country of Eastern Europe through the military and political intervention of the Soviet Union.

My other statement is this: Communism did not usurp the power in any single country of Eastern Europe from so-called conservative or reactionary elements. In every case Communism crushed the existing democratic regimes in order to insure its own rule and Soviet influence in these countries.

War itself eliminated the conservative political, economic and social forces. Democratic coalitions were established in every country of Eastern Europe, without exception, after the war. These coalition governments included the representatives of the peasantry, the workers and the working intellectuals. Communist and Soviet power, therefore, eliminated democratic governments in the countries of Eastern and Central Europe and subjugated their independence as democratic countries to Soviet oppression.

I thought it necessary to mention this, since it is an accepted practice in political and diplomatic statements, in newspaper articles, in various studies and political plans to refer to satellite nations, whereas these do not exist in reality—there are only satellite governments. . . .

The leaders of the Communist minority in certain countries naturally did not secure the support of the Soviet Union without paying the price for coming into power and remaining there. These Communist leaders must pay the Soviet Union for achieving their local dictatorial positions. Without exception, these Communist leaders are paying by sacrificing the well-being of their people and by accepting the dictates of the Soviet Union. They were forced, in every country, to eliminate the democratic constitutions and to accept the constitution of the Soviet Union; they had to close their borders toward the free countries; they had to accept Communist doctrines as their governing ideology; they had to end private ownership; their churches are subject to gradual liquidation; their citizens are forced to give up their individual rights and human dignity; their economic systems were integrated into the Communist world empire; and finally they had to participate in an alliance with the Soviet Union within the framework of the Warsaw Pact.

The nations of Eastern Europe had to sacrifice a great deal more for the benefit of the Soviet Union than any other former or present colony of the West, simply because the countries of Eastern Europe had more to give up and more which they could give the oppressor than any of the colonies of the underdeveloped world.

Naturally, the greatest blow to the Central and Eastern European countries was the separation from the Western World.

These countries, in general, had belonged for almost a thousand years to the Western political, cultural and economic community. Their general culture, their political and economic system, even though it varied with the individual countries—absolutely bound them to the Western World. But with the spread of the rule of the Soviet Union to Central Europe, this tie has practically ceased.

To the 100 million civilized people living in the Central-Eastern European sphere, it is the greatest hardship to feel that a foreign Eastern power wants to force foreign ideas and doctrines upon them, creating an Eastern character for peoples who belong to Western civilization with every fiber of their being.

This Soviet aspiration is causing more individual and national suffering to the peoples of Central and Eastern Europe than Western colonization has caused to the colonized peoples of Asia and Africa. With few exceptions, the Western colonial powers never strived to change the character of the peoples of their colonies by their colonial rule.

The suffering is increased manifold since these people resist and often fight against the aspirations of the oppressor. As a result, the prisons, the concentration camps and the gallows have become the most important institutions of the state life.

Even though the persecution of the individuals has lessened somewhat in certain Eastern European countries, this only means that, because of the consolidation of the regimes, there is no longer a necessity for the former degree of persecution, but does not, in any event, indicate a change of the system.

The conquest of the countries of Central and Eastern Europe have naturally meant more of a gain to the Soviet Union than the conquest of similarly populated colonies have meant to any former colonial power.

The Soviet Union by its conquest and occupation of Eastern Europe did not acquire underdeveloped countries which, at the most, produced only food and raw materials for the conquering power, but countries which were culturally, politically, and economically much more progressive than the Soviet Union herself. While the old colonial powers had to process industrially the raw materials received from the colonies, the more developed industry of the countries of Eastern Europe are able to convert the raw materials of the Soviet Union herself, and are thereby aiding Communist economic and military power. . . .

Much greater than the economic gains made by the Soviet Union are those of a political and military nature. In the first place, for the first time in history, the Soviet Union reached the territory west of the Carpathian Mountains, which had always been the ancient and natural defense line of southeastern Europe. The troops of the Soviet Union now stand in the heart of Europe. If ever there should occur a conflict, even transitorily, between the Communist system and that of the free world, this would mean an immeasurable danger for Western Europe.

This great strategic gain of the Soviet Union can be lessened only by the fact that in the event of a catastrophic conflict the peoples of Eastern Europe would not fight with the Soviet Union, but against her, and would endanger rather than insure the communication lines of the Soviet Union toward Western Europe.

Similarly to the strategic position, the Soviet Union has gained a great deal from a political viewpoint with the conquest of the Eastern European countries. Since the Western Powers did not refuse recognition for these Soviet conquests, but established ties with the Communist Eastern European governments, also permitting them to join the U.N., the Soviet Union was able to create a bloc from these Eastern European nations in which the votes and the stand taken by all of these countries is naturally dictated by Moscow.

Without the countries of Eastern Europe the Soviet Union would stand alone and would share the Communist world empire only with China. If the Soviet Union had not been able to consolidate Communism in this area, we would not today have Communism in any single small country of Asia.

I would like to believe that had the Western Powers realized after the Second World War that the Eastern European conquests would result in the creation of a worldwide Communist system, the rivalry between great powers, the beginning of the cold war, that this would be the starting point of the armaments race—they would have, through their military and armaments superiority, forced the Soviet Union to cooperate with the various international agreements and withdraw her troops and influence from Eastern Europe.

Truly the present world situation, the uncertainty of the balance of power, the general world tension and armaments race was begun by the conquest of Eastern Europe by the Soviet Union and the toleration of these conquests by the West.

The halting of Communist expansion, the insuring superiority of power, and the safety of the free world is creating a grave problem for the West. There are pessimists who are now talking not of the victory of the free world, but of the survival of the free world.

The problem of Eastern Europe in international politics stands at an undeservedly low level. It seems as if the free world does not realize, even today, that changing the direction of international politics to benefit the free world, the lessening of world tension, and the safety of the free world depends primarily on whether the Soviet Union can solidify her conquests in Eastern Europe or whether she can be forced by the West to honor the great international agreements concluded during the war and after the war, resulting in the restoration of the right to self-determination for the peoples of Eastern Europe.

The broad political plans of the free world do not embrace the necessity of solving the problems of the Eastern European area with the intensity and dynamism so clearly necessary.

We cannot be particularly surprised if the political planning of the new Asian and African nations does not include ideas for solving the question of

Eastern Europe. But the Western Powers who are responsible for the direction of international politics should not omit such concrete plans for solving this burning and important issue.

Let us first examine the ideas dealing with the strengthening and unity of Western Europe. After the outstanding and unprecedented success of the Common Market, the European powers are now striving to achieve political unity.

While we Eastern Europeans are sincerely happy on the one hand to see the new renaissance of Europe and the slowly but surely emerging unity of the European peoples, we sadly observe, on the other hand, that while the architects of European unity are incessantly talking about the unity of Western Europe, the problem of reannexing the subjugated countries of Eastern Europe is not given any discernible attention.

Let us examine the slowly crystallizing policies of America often referred to as "the great design." Although America is striving to serve the strengthening of the free world in a positive direction, the problem of Eastern Europe remains but a hazy goal of the political programs planned by America. The lofty ideas of Atlantic partnership and the Alliance for Progress serve hemispheric solidarity.

This policy, through its great sacrifices, serves the economic strengthening of the newly liberated colonies of the free world, but Eastern Europe is not included in any of these future plans in a way which is really hoped would draw the peoples of Eastern Europe toward the Western World.

We Eastern Europeans agree with the wide-scale, long-range plans of American politics: The idea of the Atlantic partnership, the creation of hemispheric unity in America, the economic strengthening of the underdeveloped peoples; we even agree with those purposes which hope to achieve an improvement in the relations with the Soviet Union. But we cannot understand why an incessant demand for self-determination for the Eastern European peoples would be counter to or hinder the carrying out of these lofty ideals.

Since the end of the Second World War a total of 45 Asian, African, and European countries have gained national sovereignty and the right to self-determination. These peoples, without exception, lived under colonial rule until the time they regained their rights to self-determination.

During the same period, since the end of the Second World War, not one of the countries subjugated by the Soviet Union has regained similar rights. While the Soviet Union is unceasingly fighting for the restoration of the right to self-determination for the still colonial peoples, the West has taken no action to liberate even a single country from the colonial rule of the Soviet.

The most vociferous champion in the fight against colonialism is the Soviet Union, which, while carrying on this fight, continues, with all the power at her command, to consolidate her colonial rule in Europe. . . .

The opinion is widespread in American political and diplomatic circles that the aspiration of the Eastern European peoples for freedom and their hopes regarding a change must not be supported by political action, but through economic aid.

When the Senate voted upon the question of granting economic aid to the Communist countries, the President of the United States stated, at his press conference which followed, that granting aid to the countries under Communist leadership is important, because it strengthened hope in these peoples for the future.

Speaking frankly, I am afraid that this concept is erroneous, arising from not being fully informed about the prevailing situation. The hope placed by the peoples of Eastern Europe in the future must not be nurtured by lending economic aid to their governments, but through positive political statements and political action designed to insure the right to self-determination for these peoples. I am not opposed to the granting of such economic aid to Eastern European countries. I would be happy if I would see that owing to such aid from America there would be a rise in the level of the living standards of the peoples of Eastern Europe.

But economic aid granted to these peoples by America will serve this purpose only if this aid is given directly to the people and not to the Communist governments which are trying to correct their economic mistakes by utilizing such aid, and if this economic aid will be accompanied by decisive statements in which America and the other Western Powers will demand the restoration of the right to self-determination for these people.

The confidence of the peoples of Eastern Europe is unceasingly directed toward America. Naturally, these subjugated nations will never deny their allegiance to Europe even though they have, during the course of history, suffered many Western European decisions which have been unfavorable to them.

But these people, despite their European background, first of all rely on America, that great power which can, more than any other Western European power, make its voice heard on any question concerning the settlement in the European sphere.

The great aspiration of the Eastern European peoples, therefore, cannot be satisfied simply with economic aid. These people expect to achieve their freedom through assistance from the West—chiefly America—and only after that do they want economic aid.

Let us recall the Hungarian revolution. Hungary was plundered by the Nazis, destroyed by the war, devastated by the Soviet Union, and still at the time of the revolt she did not ask for bread or economic aid from the West—she asked for political support in her effort to regain freedom.

This is characteristic of all the Eastern European nations. Any kind of American aid can be effective and appealing to the people of eastern Europe only if this aid is tied to a demand for self-determination on the part of the Western Powers. Such a demand would not be a provocative stand on the part of America or the West. The right to self-determination is accepted as one of the most productive and lofty ideals of our times.

For this reason, supporting the idea of the right to self-determination for the peoples of Eastern Europe at all forthcoming international conferences and including such demands in the various political programs of the West would be completely understandable not only from the standpoint of mankind in general, such a demand will be understood even by the Soviet Union.

The State Department View*

W. Averell Harriman

I want to say quite bluntly that Eastern Europe is no longer the monolithic structure it was under Stalin. The forces of nationalism and self-interest, the desire for freedom and a better life have worked fundamental changes. There are changes within the Soviet Union, but not like those in the satellites and particularly the loosening of the bonds that held Eastern Europe so tightly under the Soviet Union and Stalin.

These Eastern European countries face both serious economic problems and an increasing need to cope with the basic human demands of their people for more freedom, better living conditions, and recognition of national interests. The rising tide of nationalism is becoming increasingly a factor in all these countries. The right kind of nationalism is a good ally of freedom if it isn't carried to the wrong kind of nationalism which interferes with other people's freedom.

Under the pressure of these forces, and in the context of world Communist disunity and diminished authority on the part of Moscow, there is more inclination among the Eastern European governments to consider alternative ways of coping with the problems of their countries. In varying degrees they are taking a more independent line, including more practical approaches to dealing with the interests of their own people.

As a result, there has been a significant trend away from the rigid pattern and the uniformity that Moscow imposed on this region after the war. It is clear that this important evolution beginning with Stalin's death continues.

It has a gradual but considerable effect upon the life of the Eastern European people and on their relations with both East and West. They are becoming less isolated from the West. It is true that they remain within the

* "Recent Developments in the Soviet Bloc." Hearings before the Subcommittee on Europe, Committee on Foreign Affairs, House of Representatives, March 10, 1964 (Washington, D.C.: Government Printing Office, 1964), pp. 348–352. Mr. Harriman is Under Secretary of State for Political Affairs.

sphere of Soviet military domination which was imposed upon them by the advance of the Red army after the war. Their governments remain allied with the Soviet Union and are supported by Moscow.

But this alliance and support has not been able to prevent the natural and national diversity of these countries from asserting itself increasingly.

An exceptional case was that of Yugoslavia. In 1948, Tito broke with Stalin. I want to say if it hadn't been for our help to Yugoslavia there would have been a serious question whether Yugoslavia could have remained independent from Moscow. I was there in 1951, and at that time Tito was extremely concerned over whether there would be an invasion ordered by Stalin of the satellite countries, and he wanted to get in a position where he could defend himself. Since that time Khrushchev has changed the policies and Yugoslavia has established improved relationships with Moscow, but I think it is correct to say Yugoslavia has retained its independence in political, military, economic, sociological, and ideological affairs.

Among the other Eastern European countries, the trend toward independence was seen first 8 years ago in Poland. That country has maintained its departure from orthodox Communist programs and from complete subordination to Moscow, which national feeling and economic problems forced upon the rulers in 1956. On religion and church-state relations, the government has had to accept the role of the church as a major element in the life of the people, even though the church suffers from administrative controls and other restraints which we abhor. I might say one of the interesting examples of a difference between Poland and the Soviet Union is that 85 percent of Poland's agricultural lands are owned and farmed by the peasants themselves or private owners.

Rumania has recently demonstrated that it pursues an economic development program of its own choosing involving greater industrial expansion and increased trade with the West in place of the program proposed by the economic organization of the bloc, known as CEMA [COMECON].

In Hungary reforms in a moderate direction and efforts at national conciliation have made for some solid improvements for the people. There was an amnesty last year. The farmers and perhaps some of the industrial operations are given a little more freedom. One of the interesting facts about Hungary is that last year some 80,000 Hungarians were permitted to leave the country to go to Austria. They are allowed to travel in a way that has been unknown to bloc countries before.

Several bloc states have taken steps to relax the rules of collective farming so as to encourage output from private plots. In Poland, for example, 85 percent of the farmland is privately owned. There are other, similar signs of a more pragmatic approach by the regimes, aimed at eliciting badly needed cooperation from the working population where the old dictatorial methods and harsh police controls have notoriously failed.

Though these governments have a long way to go to create adequate incentives in their economic systems, here and there the problem at least seems to be recognized and certain initial and tentative steps are being taken in an effort to cope with it.

In their external relations, a sign of the times is the effort of all the Eastern European states to increase their already substantial trade with other Western countries and to open up commercial channels with us. . . .

As far as our policy is concerned, our Government's basic aim with regard to Eastern Europe is to see its peoples fully independent, prosperous, and restored to their natural relationship with the rest of Europe and the free world. This policy reflects a strong and enduring American interest.

For one thing, bonds of blood and friendship have long existed between the United States and the peoples of Eastern Europe. Of even more importance is our American conviction that the unqualified achievement of self-determination in Eastern Europe, as everywhere, is essential to a just and secure world order.

We hope to see, and are trying to encourage, a progressive loosening of external authority over Eastern European countries and the continuing reassertion of national autonomy and diversity. We believe such evolution is a slow but sure way toward freedom and national independence.

We want the Eastern European peoples to be able freely to determine their own forms of government and achieve an independence that can bring a stable, natural relationship with all their neighbors, including the Soviet Union. Such a healthy relationship would contribute to the peace and security of Europe and of the whole world.

From the standpoint of accomplishing this long-range objective of U.S. policy, the most significant aspect of the situation in Eastern Europe is its increasing fluidity and change. This reflects the increasing tendency among Eastern European governments to take more account of the national interests and human needs of their peoples.

In dealing with these trends, the United States is maintaining the greatest possible flexibility of means for exerting our influence to promote developments favorable to the goal of independent self-government and an open society for the peoples of Eastern Europe. We shall steadily persist in this endeavor and use our influence in every practicable way toward that end.

In this effort we shall keep in mind that no two of these countries are alike in the tempo or manner in which they are breaking away from the Stalinist past. We plan to shape our policies to the different needs and opportunities that each of them presents.

In this connection U.S. policy will not remain passive. Our policy is to encourage the evolution now in progress by using every kind of peaceful contact available. There are increasing opportunities for doing this as Eastern European governments turn more and more to the West for trade and other exchanges, and at the same time start lowering more of the barriers toward the West.

The people of Eastern Europe for their part welcome anything that breaks down their isolation and brings them into touch with our part of the world. From this increasing knowledge of and association with the West, they are stimulated further to assert their national identity and their desire for improvements at home.

There are many ways in which U.S. policy can encourage and assist this evolutionary process. Our material aid to the Polish and Yugoslav peoples over a period of years has promoted independence and change in those countries and kindled hopes for similar developments elsewhere in Eastern Europe.

As the bloc governments have begun to improve their relations with us and to settle claims and other outstanding problems, we find opportunities gradually opening wider to many-sided approaches that bring their peoples and ours into significant contact. An increasing stream of American tourists directly acquaints the Eastern Europeans with our interest in and regard for them, as well as with the Western ideas and events they are interested in knowing.

We now exhibit at fairs in Poland, Czechoslovakia, and Bulgaria, and send other exhibits to these countries as well as to Rumania. We encourage artists, writers, scholars, scientists, and athletes to take part in exchanges, and we want to expand this trend wherever it is feasible.

The Voice of America provides all of Eastern Europe with a steady flow of information on United States and world developments. Some of these countries have stopped jamming the Voice of America. The magazine *Ameryka* is distributed in Poland and cultural bulletins in some of the countries.

Trade is of advantage to both sides and will play a part in these developments. In trading with us, the Eastern European countries involve themselves with our free economy and further expose their representatives and their people to the dynamism and practical effectiveness of our system. The Western European countries are way ahead of us in trade. . . .

While we shall maintain our controls on strategic commodities going to Eastern Europe, we think expanding trade in peaceful goods is a useful and desirable means of drawing these nations into practical contact with the free world.

A part of our many-sided approach to the changes now accelerating in Eastern Europe is to improve and extend our relations with Eastern European governments wherever feasible. Our purpose in this extension of relations is to broaden our access to their people, to communicate more effectively with the bloc governments and to influence their views and conduct.

We believe that Europe cannot enjoy a full measure of security and prosperity until the Eastern European countries are drawn back into their historical relationship with the rest of Europe. We share with our friends in Western Europe the desire to see this inevitable transformation.

They are in a position to influence the Eastern European countries at close range toward that goal by their policies. It is essential, therefore, for the United States to work with them in facilitating this process. . . .

part two

Africa

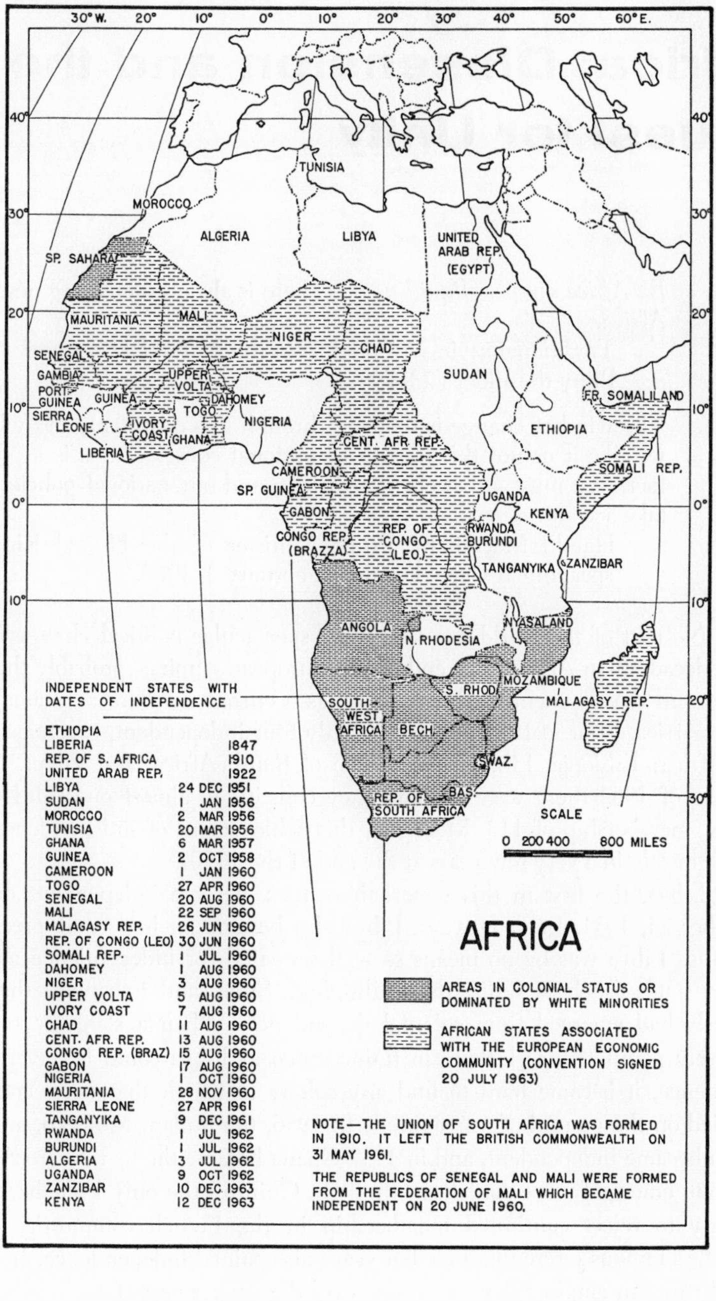
30° W.
20°
10°
0°
10°
20°
30°
40°
50°
60° E.
40°
30°
20°
10°
0°
10°
20°
30°
TUNISIA
MOROCCO
ALGERIA
LIBYA
UNITED ARAB REP. (EGYPT)
SP. SAHARA
MAURITANIA
MALI
NIGER
CHAD
SUDAN
SENEGAL
GAMBIA
PORT. GUINEA
GUINEA
UPPER VOLTA
DAHOMEY
TOGO
SIERRA LEONE
IVORY COAST
GHANA
NIGERIA
LIBERIA
FR. SOMALILAND
ETHIOPIA
CENT. AFR. REP.
CAMEROON
SOMALI REP.
SP. GUINEA
GABON
UGANDA
KENYA
CONGO REP. (BRAZZA)
REP. OF CONGO (LEO.)
RWANDA BURUNDI
TANGANYIKA
ZANZIBAR
ANGOLA
NYASALAND
N. RHODESIA
MOZAMBIQUE
S. RHOD.
MALAGASY REP.
SOUTH-WEST AFRICA
BECH.
SWAZ.
BAS.
REP. OF SOUTH AFRICA
SCALE
0 200 400 800 MILES
INDEPENDENT STATES WITH DATES OF INDEPENDENCE
ETHIOPIA
LIBERIA 1847
REP. OF S. AFRICA 1910
UNITED ARAB REP. 1922
LIBYA 24 DEC 1951
SUDAN 1 JAN 1956
MOROCCO 2 MAR 1956
TUNISIA 20 MAR 1956
GHANA 6 MAR 1957
GUINEA 2 OCT 1958
CAMEROON 1 JAN 1960
TOGO 27 APR 1960
SENEGAL 20 AUG 1960
MALI 22 SEP 1960
MALAGASY REP. 26 JUN 1960
REP. OF CONGO (LEO) 30 JUN 1960
SOMALI REP. 1 JUL 1960
DAHOMEY 1 AUG 1960
NIGER 3 AUG 1960
UPPER VOLTA 5 AUG 1960
IVORY COAST 7 AUG 1960
CHAD 11 AUG 1960
CENT. AFR. REP. 13 AUG 1960
CONGO REP. (BRAZ) 15 AUG 1960
GABON 17 AUG 1960
NIGERIA 1 OCT 1960
MAURITANIA 28 NOV 1960
SIERRA LEONE 27 APR 1961
TANGANYIKA 9 DEC 1961
RWANDA 1 JUL 1962
BURUNDI 1 JUL 1962
ALGERIA 3 JUL 1962
UGANDA 9 OCT 1962
ZANZIBAR 10 DEC 1963
KENYA 12 DEC 1963
AFRICA
AREAS IN COLONIAL STATUS OR DOMINATED BY WHITE MINORITIES
AFRICAN STATES ASSOCIATED WITH THE EUROPEAN ECONOMIC COMMUNITY (CONVENTION SIGNED 20 JULY 1963)
NOTE—THE UNION OF SOUTH AFRICA WAS FORMED IN 1910. IT LEFT THE BRITISH COMMONWEALTH ON 31 MAY 1961.
THE REPUBLICS OF SENEGAL AND MALI WERE FORMED FROM THE FEDERATION OF MALI WHICH BECAME INDEPENDENT ON 20 JUNE 1960.

6

Africa: Dissension and the Quest for Unity

> *Ex Africa semper aliquid novi.*—There is always something new from Africa.
>
> Traditional saying adapted from the *Natural History* of Pliny the Elder (23–79).

> The wind of change is blowing through this continent, and whether we like it or not this growth of national consciousness is a political fact. We must all accept it as a fact, and our national policies must take account of it.
>
> Harold Macmillan, Prime Minister of the United Kingdom, speaking at Cape Town on February 3, 1960.

No part of the world has seen more spectacular political change in the past decade than Africa. The end of the European empires, probably the most important development of this period, has occurred nowhere so dramatically as in Africa. Prior to 1951, there were only four independent, sovereign states in Africa: Ethiopia, Liberia, the Union of South Africa, and Egypt. In the spring of 1964 there were 35, and they constituted almost one third of the U.N. membership of 113. Moreover, this achievement of independence took place mostly in a very few years at the end of the 1950s.

Libya, the first in this remarkable series, became independent on December 24, 1951. In some ways, Libya also became an important precedent, because Libya was by no means so well prepared for independence as were other states (such as India, the Philippines, Syria, and Lebanon) that previously had emerged from colonial dependence. When a state so poor,[1] so sparsely populated, so lacking in trained men as Libya could be given independence, it became hard to find any colony to which that boon could be denied on the ground of unreadiness. In 1956, the Sudan, Morocco, and Tunisia became independent, and in 1957 Ghana became the first Negro African state to emerge from colonialism. In 1958, Guinea (the only French African colony to reject continued membership in the French community in de Gaulle's famous referendum of that year) also gained independence. In 1960, the European empires came to an end over the greater part of the continent as seventeen new sovereign African states emerged. In 1961, there followed two

[1] As a result of large oil discoveries in the early 1960s, Libya is no longer poor; but this event was not foreseen at the time of independence in the 1950s.

(Sierra Leone and Tanganyika); in 1962, four (Rwanda, Burundi, Algeria, and Uganda); and in 1963, two more (Zanzibar and Kenya).

Africa is extremely large—one and a quarter times the size of all North America, fourteen times the size of Greenland. Because of Africa's size, it is necessary to distinguish between the different main areas of the continent. The Mediterranean littoral has a character quite different from the rest. Egypt, in particular, has a unique role. In population, language, and culture, it is more Middle Eastern than African; and its leader, President Nasser, has ambitions to be, and in some measure already is, an international leader in both regions. The other states of the north shore of Africa—Libya, Tunisia, Algeria, and Morocco—comprise the region known as the Maghrib (in Arabic, *the West*); although they are Islamic, these states have a certain sense of standing apart from the rest of Islam. Because they front the Mediterranean, they have never been isolated from Europe, as has the rest of Africa. The North African states and Europe have had a mutual influence, and there has been considerable European settlement in the Maghrib, particularly in Algeria and Morocco.

South of the Sahara Desert, which divides Africa horizontally and north of the Zambesi River lies the essential Africa—Negro Africa.

One state in this area provided for several years one of the world's most intractable problems—the Belgian Congo. After Belgium's precipitate withdrawal in 1960, the Congo became a kind of ward of the world as the United Nations attempted to establish order within it so that it could begin to function on its own. It is a moot point whether the troubles of the Congo are over, but they seemed for the moment to be well enough in hand to justify the withdrawal of the U.N. forces as of June 30, 1964. In January 1963, U.N. military action ended the possibility of secession in the mineral-rich province of Katanga, and Moise Tshombe, Katanga's Jefferson Davis, flitted off into exile for eighteen months.

East Africa, in its regions of higher altitude, and Africa south of the Zambesi provide, along with the Mediterranean littoral, the only parts of the continent where climatic conditions are suitable for European settlement. These portions, likewise, are areas where the end of empire creates tangled problems, and where any solution that can properly be called "just" is hard to come by and perhaps even inconceivable.

A survey of the problems and the prospects of the African countries is provided here in the article by Waldemar A. Nielsen. As Nielsen points out, the southern part of the continent contains the most explosive problem areas of contemporary Africa: (1) the two large Portuguese colonies of Angola and Mozambique, which Portugal is determined to retain; (2) Southern Rhodesia, which has a white population between 7 and 8 per cent of the total and has been internally self-governing since 1924 (so that it is difficult for the British Government to do an "Algeria" and force the white minority to accept an end to its privileged position); and (3) the Afrikaner-dominated Republic of South Africa. South Africa, virtually ousted from the British Commonwealth when it adopted republican status in 1961, has a white population of over 3 million in a total of approximately 18 million. Its native policy of *Apartheid* (separate development)—which has been progressively applied by the nationalist governments of South Africa since 1948 and which represents essentially the views of the Afrikaner majority (about 60 per cent) of the white part of the population—has been the object of worldwide criticism and attack. The report of the U.N. Special Committee on *Apartheid* excerpted here provides a vigorous example of that criticism. Eric H. Louw voices the South African government's intransigent response to the attacks.

In their hostility to South Africa's racial policy, all of the new African states are united. However, the continent is still fragmented into numerous political units. For several years it was possible to distinguish two important rival groupings. The Casablanca group (Ghana, Guinea, Mali, Morocco, and Egypt) was the less friendly toward the Western powers. The Brazzaville group consisted of twelve states, all former French colonies.[2] It had, therefore, a natural basis for cohesion. The Brazzaville group has been quite friendly toward the West, and particularly toward France, which has successfully maintained cooperative relations with its former colonies. The Brazzaville group attended the Monrovia Conference of May 1961, as did nearly all other independent African states except the Casablanca states—which had, however, been invited. The Monrovia group thus has sometimes been regarded as an enlarged Brazzaville group. The largest and most successful pan-African conference so far was held at Addis Ababa, Ethiopia, May 22–25, 1964. The conference created a new continent-wide body, the Organization of African Unity (OAU), with a constitution and a permanent seat and secretariat. Selections from the Organization's charter included in this chapter indicate some of the pan-African objectives. It is easy to exaggerate the achievements of OAU; nevertheless, to set up a permanent international organization within Africa so few years after most states achieved independence is itself a noteworthy feat.

However, many causes of dissension persist among the African states. The ambitions of Nasser or Kwame Nkrumah, both of whom have tried to make the pan-African movement an instrument for personal aggrandizement, alarm the other states. Nkrumah's militant approach to African unity is apparent in the selection from one of his speeches; a more cautious approach is presented by Nigeria's Prime Minister, Sir Abubakar Tafawa Balewa. Frontier disputes are endemic: Somalia has claims against all her neighbors; Morocco and Algeria fought a small border war early in 1964; Ghana wishes to annex Togo; Rwanda and Burundi, administered jointly under Belgian rule, have set up mutually harmful trade barriers; Morocco considers Mauritania a part of *Morocco irredenta*. Unfortunately, there is something to be said in favor of almost every one of such claims. African frontiers are the old borders of colonies. They were not drawn to coincide with ethnic, tribal, or geo-

[2] Cameroun, Central African Republic, Chad, Congo (Brazzaville), Dahomey, Gabon, Ivory Coast, Malagasy Republic, Mauritania, Niger, Senegal, and Upper Volta.

graphic divisions, but for European convenience. Julius Nyerere, President of Tanganyika, has rightly said that the only way to keep peace in Africa is to accept the existing frontiers, however anomalous. Meanwhile, the creation of OAU has led to the dissolution of some lesser groups.

Within each African state are numerous acute problems. The article by Balewa mentions the problem of poverty. Political fragmentation exacerbates this problem. Approximately twenty of the African states have populations of less than 5 million, and some are barely viable as economic units. Economic difficulties are often compounded by governmental corruption and high living on the part of politicians and officials.

In the face of internal problems and threats of disintegration, it is natural that one-party systems are becoming the rule in Africa. Frequently, the leader of the one party achieves an astonishing concentration of power, as Nkrumah has in Ghana. The states where multi-party systems on a Western model still prevail—such as Morocco, Madagascar, Nigeria, or the Congo—can almost be numbered on one hand. This may be deplorable from the point of view of Washington—or of Westminster—but the problems of Africa are *African* problems; and—profound though the influence of the West continues to be in Africa—if solutions are achieved, they will be *African* solutions.

Africa Is Poised on the Razor's Edge*

Waldemar A. Nielsen

In one of the most ironic episodes of recent history, the leaders of three new nations of East Africa—all of them former colonies of Great Britain—appealed for British troops to put down mutinies in their armies. Through prompt and effective British response, order seems now to have been restored.

The lightning chain of events illuminated for a vivid and frightening moment the utter frailty of civilian, constitutional government in these new-born nations. Seen in the context of mounting signs of stress in every part of Africa in recent months, the disorders arouse an urgent question: Are these "growing pains" or the beginning of a collapse of stability in Africa?

The first thing to be said is that in one sense the troubles occurring in Africa have for the most part been quite ordinary and not unexpected. Push aside the fly-whisks, the beaded hats, the feathered dancers, the Watusi war-

* From *The New York Times Magazine*, February 9, 1964, pp. 11, 61–62. © 1964 by the New York Times Company. Reprinted by permission. Mr. Nielsen is President of the African-American Institute.

riors 7 feet tall and the unfamiliar names and places and it becomes clear that the new African states are going through the process—and the mistakes—which new states, especially those conceived in revolution, have normally gone through.

Even the oldest of the newly independent nations of Africa is but seven years old; and 25 of the 35 have yet to celebrate their fourth birthday. Thus, in terms of parallels with American history, Africa is in the 1790's. That was the period when we physically drove out of the country and into Canada a good portion of our opposition, tarred-and-feathered some who remained and expropriated (legally and illegally) the property of not a few. We oppressed the native tribes, saw corruption flourish in our new officialdom and denounced the idea of foreign military bases on our soil.

We took large quantities of foreign aid and credits, while simultaneously denouncing the greed of those who offered it. We applauded every revolution anywhere, declared our firm intention to remain neutral and aloof from the struggles among the then Great Powers, and issued holier-than-thou statements on the political and international troubles of other nations.

We passed the Alien and Sedition Acts, which made it a criminal offense to organize to oppose measures of the Government or to speak ill of the Congress or the President. The Jeffersonians complained bitterly that the Federalists had created a one-party state and were resorting to illegal measures to smash all political freedom.

In the end, the United States found its way back to democracy and the fulfillment of the ideals of its revolution. Africa, too, in the end must find its own best means of governing itself. However, there are at least three debits which may make the achievement of unity and stability even more difficult for the new nations of Africa than it was for the United States.

The first debit, internal military problems, did not immediately arise to plague our new Union. It was 70 years before civil war put the durability of our constitutional system to the crucial test; and our military has honored the principle of civilian control from the start. But the Congo had Katanga in its first year; Algeria and Morocco began a border war on the heels of independence; and military revolts, including those recently in East Africa, have already occurred in more than half a dozen of the new African states.

In weak and unstable nations, military elements are often the single strong, organized and disciplined factor. In situations of instability, they move toward power. That has been a marked tendency in Africa—and may become increasingly so.

A second problem of special difficulty for the new African states is a hangover from the era of colonialism—namely, a network of borders and boundaries which makes no sense at all. Africa's political map was essentially drawn in the late 19th century by European statesmen sitting in European conference rooms—totally without reference to African realities. Natural geographical boundaries were ignored; and old, well-established and often proud language and ethnic groups were split up by arbitrary and artificial lines. The present rash of border disputes—notably between Ethiopia and Somalia, between Somalia and Kenya, between Togo and Ghana, between Morocco and Mauritania—is one obvious and inevitable result.

Regrettably, frontiers are more easily traced than erased and it will require miraculous statesmanship and forbearance on the part of the African nations if these fateful markings are rationalized without the fighting of hundreds of battles and the death of thousands of men.

The third factor working against the unity and progress of the new states is also a leftover from the past: tribalism.

To a large degree the tribe is still the social, psychological, economic and even governmental reality in much of Africa. It is the embodiment and the fortress of primitivism and the past. To modernize and stabilize the new states, means will have to be found to reconcile tradition and change, to shift loyalties from the tribe to the nation, and to convert the tribes into building blocks rather than roadblocks to progress.

But this is especially difficult because tribalism, which might have been greatly weakened by the influences of modernism over the past century, was preserved and fortified by the policy of "indirect rule"—of governing through the traditional chiefs—which was followed by the colonial powers. Useful as it was as an efficient means of controlling subject peoples, the policy had the effect of entrenching and reinforcing ignorance, superstition, stagnation and separatism.

If one is inclined to be pessimistic, one can catalogue quite a long list of other difficulties. Poverty, though not so bad as in some parts of Asia, is still serious and widespread. Population, as in all of the underdeveloped areas, is increasing rapidly, too rapidly. Sickness and disease are particularly common in the tropical areas and availability of medical care is as limited as anywhere in the world. Illiteracy is perhaps greater in Africa than in any other major region.

On the economic side, Africa is caught in the same vast downward spiral of prices for the commodities which it sells to the world as are Latin America and Asia. Foreign private investment understandably is not venturing into Africa in any substantial quantity at present and Africa is at the bottom of the list of continents receiving American foreign aid. Increasingly great numbers of hopeful young people from the countryside gather around the mushrooming cities in quest of jobs—jobs which are not there. Their discontent and disillusionment is just beginning to be felt.

But the key problem, and the key danger for Africa, lies in the possibility of outside intervention in such a destructive way—as in the eras of slave-trading and colonialism—that the continent will be left prostrate. To a very considerable degree, whether this occurs could turn on either of two factors: the role of Soviet and Chinese policy with respect to the area, or—the ugliest specter of all—the possibility of a major race war in South Africa.

The surprising fact, up to now, is that Soviet programs on the whole have had little success in Africa. Ideologically, although "African Socialism" is a phrase in great currency, Marxism has had little attraction for Africans. With the exception of Ghana, there is hardly an African country which can seriously be called Marxist in its thinking or its avowed objectives.

Operationally, the Soviets' efforts on the whole and up to very recently have been a fiasco. In the Congo, after a most vigorous attempt to establish their influence, they were thrown out, body, pamphlet and checkbook. Guinea, Mali and other countries were receptive to offers of Soviet help after they won independence. But Russian efforts to provide economic aid produced rapid disenchantment on the part of the Africans, followed by a turning back to Western aid and relationships.

Soviet efforts to undermine and paralyze the United Nations have aroused strong and general resentment on the part of the Africans. The Chinese attack on India in 1963 similarly produced sharp and critical reactions from many areas, especially East Africa. More recently, incidents involving African students in Bulgaria and Moscow have made Africans in all parts of the continent fully aware of the existence of racism in the Communist bloc countries.

Despite these setbacks, however, the Soviets have not given up. The recent arms agreement with Somalia has dangerously altered the strategic balance in East Africa. The meaning of the recent coup in Zanzibar is not yet fully clear, but there is evidence of serious Chinese and Soviet involvement. In the Congo the current disorders in Kwilu province again clearly show a red thread in the pattern. In South Africa, Communist penetration of the protest organizations, already deep, grows deeper.

The Chinese, too, independently of the Russians, have been active. The Angolan and Mozambique liberation movements have, in recent weeks, decided to accept aid from Peking after failing to get encouragement from the United States. The recent tour of Chou En-lai through Africa has laid a basis of relationships upon which further activity will undoubtedly be built.

Figures recently gathered in a careful private survey of the movement of young political refugees through Dar-es-Salaam, Tanganyika, the principal exit of the underground railway for refugees from southern Africa, reveal that about 1,000 such refugees have passed through in the past two years. Of these, some 900 have gone on for training to Cuba, China and the Soviet bloc. Only one-tenth have come for education and training to the United States or elsewhere in the West. Recent outbreaks in various parts of Africa appear to have been led by Soviet-trained Africans. As Africans trained in Communist-style agitation and propaganda begin to return to their home countries in coming months and years, their presence could mean severe problems for the newly independent governments.

The other great danger is the brewing trouble in southern Africa, where the last act of the drama of independence is about to be played. In Angola and Mozambique, rebellion is already under way and active fighting can be expected to spread rapidly.

In Southern Rhodesia, it is still not impossible that some evolutionary means of increasing African political control will be found. But it is just as likely that major violence could occur within the next few years.

It is in South Africa, however, that the great danger both for Africa and for the world simmers. As matters now stand, it seems inevitable that a massive and hate-laden race war will rip that country to shreds. When it does, the emotions of all Africa will be electrically engaged. In a predictable sequence, as the killings and atrocities mount, great waves of feeling will be stirred throughout the underdeveloped areas of the world, among colored people everywhere and among the Western countries, particularly the United States.

In such circumstances it is difficult to imagine that the great powers will not be drawn in. If they should become involved, the United Nations, hobbled as it is by financial stringency, may not be able to mount a peacekeeping operation adequate to head off a direct confrontation.

Despite this ominous outlook, there are some basic facts about Africa that give reason for hope. Indeed, in the view of many knowledgeable observers, Africa, of all the underdeveloped areas of the world, is theoretically the one in which real economic, social and political progress is the most likely.

It is inherently a rich continent and has natural resources sufficient to support substantial economic growth. And, unlike the Indian subcontinent, for example, population pressure is not yet a matter of desperate and immediate concern.

A great new energy has been released by the independence movement in Africa. There is a mood of determination to overcome the servitude of the past and to modernize every aspect of society. Unlike some of the other impoverished regions of the world, Africa is not characterized by cynicism, fatalism or lassitude. There is excitement and a freshness of spirit. In time, it could, of course, be wilted by frustration; but at present it constitutes a vast potential for progress.

There is also an almost universal hunger and demand for education. Africans in rapidly increasing numbers are going to school, and more and more at the higher levels are going abroad for training. Those who have come to the United States have been both capable and hard working. Despite shifting to a very different educational system and despite personal and social adjustments, they have made remarkable academic records. On the whole, even in our best colleges and universities, their grades are as good as or better than those of American students at the same institutions. . . . Nations that were launched into independence, sometimes with only a handful of college graduates in the entire country, will shortly have dozens—and before long hundreds—of qualified people whose presence in the management of affairs will make itself immediately and constructively felt.

Particularly important for the future of Africa is the caliber and outlook of the new leaders who have come to the fore since independence. Nyerere of Tanganyika, Kaunda of Northern Rhodesia, Mboya of Kenya, Azikiwe of Nigeria and Touré of Guinea are among the most impressive personalities to have appeared on the world scene since World War II. They began as vigorous natural leaders of independence movements, leading those struggles with courage and flair. And following independence, they have settled down capably and earnestly to the long, hard task of nation building.

Despite a meager educational background in some cases, their natural talents have enabled them to become not only effective national leaders but increasingly effective figures in international affairs. To a remarkable and reassuring degree they have moved from revolution to responsibility. In Africa the more radical leaders have steadily been losing ground and influence to the more moderate figures.

The Addis Ababa Conference of African States last year was an exceptional demonstration of the maturity and world outlook of the participants. It would be hard to name another international meeting of recent years whose results were as positive and productive.

Indeed, the practicality, the flexibility of mind, the openness to new ideas and the basic common sense of African leaders are their distinctive marks. Compared with the other emerging continents, Africa carried into the modern age a less burdensome baggage of history, of self-pride, of destructive ideology and of encrusted social structure to impede progress.

Thus, if determined, hopeful and hard-working human beings can transform the poverty and disorder of a potentially rich continent, then there is good cause to feel optimistic about the longer future of affairs in Africa—if the Africans are permitted the time and the tranquility to accomplish their task.

But, taking into account all the current difficulties as well as the many small beginnings of constructive development, it would appear that in the short run the prospects for stability and advancement are disquieting, though not bleak. There is no likelihood that parliamentary democracy will soon become rampant on the political scene, and indeed all but five of the 35 independent African states have already abandoned all pretense of it. But if means are found to maintain discipline and control of national military forces, the chances for internal order and, in turn, for some general progress are moderately good.

However, if it is difficult to see clearly even the short-run prospects for peace and progress in Africa, it is utterly futile to undertake prognostication over the long run.

The whole vast continent is tremblingly poised on the razor's edge between peace and calamity—between one of the most inspiring possibilities of human liberation and progress in all history and one of the ugliest eventualities of chaos and international danger.

Apartheid in South Africa: Defiance of the United Nations*

U.N. Special Committee

On November 6, 1962, the General Assembly again deplored the refusal by the Government of the Republic of South Africa to abandon its racial policies, and strongly deprecated its continued and total disregard of its obligations under the United Nations Charter and its determined aggravation of racial issues by enforcing measures of increasing ruthlessness involving violence and bloodshed. Reaffirming that the continuance of these policies seriously endangers international peace and security, the Assembly requested Member States to take various measures to dissuade the South African Government from pursuing its policies of *apartheid*.

The South African Government, however, has shown no inclination to comply with the demand for the abandonment of the policies of *apartheid*, but has manifested open hostility toward the United Nations and its decisions. It claimed that the resolution need not cause panic, as South Africa's major trading partners did not support the recommendations, and announced that South Africa would accept limited isolation, if necessary, to preserve its "White civilization."

On August 7, 1963, the Security Council adopted a resolution strongly deprecating South Africa's perpetuation of racial discrimination as inconsistent with the principles of the United Nations Charter and contrary to its obligations as a Member State and calling upon the South African Government to abandon the policies of *apartheid* and discrimination, and to liberate all persons imprisoned, interned or subjected to other restrictions for having opposed the policy of *apartheid*.

During the past year, the Republic of South Africa has enacted new discriminatory and repressive laws such as the Transkei Constitution Act, the Bantu Laws Amendment Act and the General Law Amendment Act. It has uprooted thousands of families from their homes in the urban areas and expelled many thousands of Africans to distant reserves. It has arrested and

* From the Report of the U.N. Special Committee on the Policies of *Apartheid* of the Government of the Republic of South Africa, September 1963, issued as Document A/5497. (New York: U.N. Office of Public Information, 1963), pp. 13–29. Officers and membership of the committee included: Diallo Telli (Guinea), Chairman; Fernando Volio Jiménez (Costa Rica), Vice-Chairman; Matrika Prasad Koirala (Nepal), Rapporteur. Members: Algeria, Costa Rica, Ghana, Guinea, Haiti, Hungary, Malaysia, Nepal, Nigeria, Philippines, and Somalia.

convicted hundreds of thousands of persons under pass laws and other racially discriminatory measures. It has excluded non-Whites from new categories of employment. It has instituted a reign of terror against opponents of *apartheid:* the leaders of the non-Whites have been jailed or restricted, and thousands of persons have been thrown in jail for opposition to *apartheid,* with no certainty of ever being set free. Harsh penalties have been imposed on members of the major non-White organizations. . . .

Government leaders admit that the non-Whites cannot be treated forever as inferior, nor would they accept concessions which do not provide for equal rights. They claim that the move towards self-determination of both the major groups is the only solution which will preserve the nationhood and the vital interests of the Whites. Hence the development of "Bantustans" in the African reserves is given great emphasis in Government policy.

Under the Government's plans, the African reserves will be progressively granted the rights of self-government. The Africans will exercise their political rights only in the reserves and the Whites only in the rest of the country, described as the "White" area.

This ingenious formula represents, in fact, a serious attack on the rights of a great majority of inhabitants. It means that Africans will lose all existing rights, and all hope of equal rights, in 87 per cent of the territory of the country in return for self-government in the reserves which constitute only 13 per cent of the territory. . . .

Moreover, the steps towards self-government are misleading. They are not the fulfilment of the aspirations of the African people, but political moves to resuscitate the tribal chiefs, provide limited opportunities for some Africans and deceive public opinion.

The Government could implement its policies only by the institution of an ever more severe repressive regime to stifle the growing opposition from the non-Whites and all who believe in racial equality. The result has been increased tension, the massive expansion of security forces and a vicious circle of greater discontent among the majority of the people and a growing fear among the privileged, with the almost universal expectation of a dangerous conflict. . . .

One of the main developments during [1963] was the promulgation of the Transkei Constitution Act providing a degree of self-government for the African reserve of Transkei.[1] The Government has indicated that this is a step toward the creation of a series of "Bantustans" in the African reserves.

In justification of their plans, South African Government spokesmen claim that the Europeans arrived in the country before or at about the same time as the Bantu and that there was a traditional geographical separation between the White and Black areas. The theory that the Europeans were the first settlers, which applies only to a small part of the country around the Cape Peninsula, has been disputed by many historians and is of little rele-

[1] The Transkei, situated on the coast in the northeastern part of the Cape Province, has an area of 16,350 square miles and a population of over two million.

vance at the present time, as the right of the people of European origin to live in South Africa has not been disputed.

It is true that, as a result of a number of wars in the eighteenth and nineteenth centuries, Africans were progressively confined to limited areas of land. Moreover, African landownership rights were restricted by legislative measures in order to force Africans to work in mines, factories, and White farms. . . .

The traditional geographical separation is mainly a restriction on landownership imposed by the Government in which the Africans had no voice and which the African leaders had protested strongly. The reserves contain only 38 percent of the African population of the country, and even a Government commission found that they can decently support only half of their present population. The majority of Africans live outside the reserves. The Africans outnumber the Whites in the urban areas. The number of Africans is about four times the number of Whites in the "White" rural area.

The National Party came to power in 1948 after a campaign in which it stressed the alleged dangers of increasing African population outside the reserves, and the trend towards economic integration. It embarked on a series of laws to outlaw all social intercourse between the racial groups, to restrict the rights of Africans outside the reserves and to reinforce tribalism.

The Bantu Authorities Act of 1951 abolished the Native Representative Council and authorized the Governor-General to establish Bantu "tribal authorities." The establishment of these authorities was opposed by the Africans, and the Government had to impose them by threats, deportation and arrest of African leaders and severe police action. African resistance had been ruthlessly quelled in Tembuland and East Pondoland between 1957 and 1960. . . .

The Transkei Constitution Bill was introduced in the Parliament on January 28, 1963 and promulgated on May 24, 1963. The Act confers self-government on the Territory of Transkei and vests executive functions in a Cabinet consisting of a Chief Minister and five ministers. The Cabinet is made responsible for the administration of six departments, namely: finance, justice, education, interior, agriculture and forestry and public works.

The Legislative Assembly will consist of 109 members: the four paramount chiefs and the 60 chiefs of the Transkei, and 45 members elected by Transkei "citizens" resident in the territory or in the rest of the country.

The Assembly may make laws in regard to taxation, Bantu education, agricultural improvements, inferior courts, wills, registration of deeds, public works, Bantu authorities, traffic, certain labor matters, welfare services, vital statistics, elections, liquor, markets, game preservation and licensing of trading and business. All its bills, however, are subject to the assent of the State President of the Republic.

The Assembly cannot legislate on: (a) the establishment of military forces; (b) the manufacture of arms and ammunition; (c) the appointment and recognition of diplomatic and consular representatives and the conclusion of international treaties and agreements; and (d) the control over the entry and presence of any police force of the Republic sent to the Transkei for the maintenance of law and order and for the preservation of internal security. (The territory will, however, have control of any police force stationed in the Transkei and transferred to it by the Republic's Minister of Justice.)

The Government of the Republic will also retain control of the post office, railway and harbors, national roads, civil aviation, the entry of aliens into the territory, currency and public loans, and customs and excise. . . .

A number of comments may be made on these moves towards "the creation of Bantustans."

First, these moves are engineered by a Government in which the African people have no voice and are aimed at the separation of the races and the denial of rights to the African population in six-sevenths of the country.

Second, the "Bantustans" were not demanded by Africans but are being imposed against their wishes. The leaders of the African people are imprisoned or silenced, entry into reserves by Whites is controlled by permit, and, under Proclamation 400, the Transkeians are denied freedom of assembly and speech.

Third, the self-government granted to Transkei at present is limited in many ways. . . .

Fourth, the scheme aims at strengthening tribalism and utilizing the tribal system against African aspirations for equality.

Fifth, the "national units," made up of scattered reserves, are not economically viable. They do not provide a minimum standard of living even for the existing population of less than four million. They have few known mineral resources and are almost devoid of industries. Their economies depend largely on the export of labor to the "White" areas at the rate of over half a million migrant laborers a year.

The creation of "Bantustans" may, therefore, be regarded as designed to reinforce White supremacy in the country by strengthening the position of tribal chiefs, dividing the African people through the offer of opportunities for a limited number of Africans, and deceiving public opinion.

The policy of the Government of the Republic of South Africa, as indicated earlier, is to keep most, if not all, of South Africa under White control by treating Africans outside the reserves as transient aliens allowed to remain only to minister to the needs of the Whites. The movement of Africans to the "White areas" is strictly regulated and African family life is restricted. Any African who is unemployed or becomes a "problem" is expelled. Some of the disabilities imposed on the Africans and other non-Whites are briefly reviewed below.

The Group Areas Act of 1950, which provides for the forcible separation of racial groups, continues to be implemented actively though the General Assembly has repeatedly called upon South Africa to refrain from enforcing its provisions. "Black spots," where Africans hold freehold rights, are being rapidly cleared.

Between November 6, 1962, and the end of August 1963, "group areas" were proclaimed in about 40 cities and towns. Tens of thousands of families, mostly of non-Whites, are forced to move from areas in some of which they have resided for generations.

In Nelspruit, Transvaal, 400 families of Indian and Pakistani origin have to move, though Indians had pioneered in that fever-infested area and had arrived there in 1921. Five thousand Indians and a number of Malays, Coloreds[2] and Chinese have to move from Pageview, one of the main Indian trading areas in Johannesburg which had been set aside for non-Whites in 1902. More than 6,500 non-Whites, mostly of Indian and Pakistani origin, have to vacate South End, Port Elizabeth.

In the Alexandra Township, Johannesburg, where Africans have held freehold rights from the beginning of this century, all family accommodations are to be eliminated and the population reduced from 50,000 to 30,000. The Colored population of the township, which numbers over 6,000, has been told that it would have to leave the area.

This uprooting of settled communities has created serious hardship for the families which are obliged to move to distant new locations. It has caused great insecurity and bitterness.

In line with its policy of territorial separation, the Government is proceeding with plans to replace and remove the African population of 250,000 in the Western Cape and reserve the area for the Whites and the Coloreds. Thousands of Africans are being expelled to the reserves.

The scheme has been opposed by many industrialists, farmers and political leaders. The United Party leader, Sir de Villiers Graaff, speaking in the House of Assembly on May 28, 1963, said that the National Party seemed to see the Western Cape as "the stronghold of White civilization" where the Whites in a kind of siege could make a last stand while there was trouble elsewhere.

Under the Bantu Laws Amendment Act of 1963, popularly known as the Servants Act, the residence of African domestic workers on the premises of their White employers is severely restricted. . . .

The pass system has often been described as perhaps the most serious grievance of the African people, as it restricts their freedom of movement at every turn. Over the years, the African people have staged numerous protests against the passes, regarded by them as "badges of slavery," including the demonstrations at Sharpville and other areas in 1960.

Under the Natives (abolition of Passes and Coordination of Documents) Act of 1952, the National Party Government replaced the passes of the Africans by "reference books." The rest of the population has been issued identity cards. While non-Africans rarely suffer penalties for non-possession of identity cards, the Africans are subjected to severe punishments for even accidental misplacing of reference books.

[2] The term "Colored" is used in South Africa to denote mainly people of mixed racial origin.

The reference books contain permits to remain in an urban area, tax receipts and other particulars. Africans found outside the reserves without permits are taken to courts, for fine or imprisonment, and expelled. Juvenile offenders may be sentenced to whipping.

The regulations have been strengthened during the past year, particularly by the requirement that all African women must carry "reference books" from February 1, 1963. The extension of the pass system to African women has always been strongly resented by Africans, as the subjection of women to the procedures may lead to serious consequences for their families. Mothers of small children may be suddenly arrested. Husbands and wives may be arrested separately and expelled to their respective "homelands" which may be hundreds of miles apart. A mother may be "endorsed out" even though her child was born in the city: if she takes the child with her, the child loses the right to return to the city without special permission. . . .

An integral part of the *apartheid* policy is the preservation of the skilled and higher-paid professions to the Whites and the limitation of African workers to unskilled and low-paid occupations. Through the implementation of this policy, the Republic has provided for its White inhabitants one of the highest standards of living in the world, while the non-Whites receive only a fraction of White earnings.

The National Party Government has greatly extended the "color bar" in employment. The Industrial Conciliation Act of 1956 provides for the reservation of occupations for particular racial groups. As the Whites monopolize political power, their interests are paramount when there is competition among racial groups. The non-Whites can never be certain of being able to utilize the skills they have acquired or seek to acquire. . . .

One of the most significant aspects of the policy of *apartheid* is the determined effort to bring education under Government control, segregate the educational system on the basis of race and tribe, and train the non-Whites for the inferior position assigned to them by Government policies.

A major step in this direction was taken in 1953 with the promulgation of the Bantu Education Act, transferring responsibility for African education (except higher education) from the provincial governments to the Central Government, and granting wide powers to the Minister over both Government and private schools.

Religious missions were obliged to transfer control over their schools to the Government or lose state subsidies if they chose to remain as private schools. Only a small number could survive without subsidies.

A separate account was established for grants-in-aid to non-Government schools. The Government's contribution was pegged at 13 million Rand, with the result that the Africans were obliged to pay for educational expansion through increased taxes and contributions by communities.

The Government then proceeded to extend *apartheid* into higher education by dividing the higher institutions on a racial and tribal basis, and locating African colleges outside urban areas. Dr. Verwoerd, as Minister of Native Affairs, announced the Government's policy in June 1954:

> My Department's policy is that education should stand with both feet in the reserves and have its roots in the spirit and being of Bantu Society.
>
> The Bantu must be guided to serve his own community in all aspects. There is no place for him in the European community above the level of certain forms of labour. Within his own community, however, all doors are open.

In 1959, legislation was adopted to take over control of the Fort Hare University College and to establish separate university colleges for non-White persons. No White person may attend any of the colleges for non-Whites, and, after a transition period (during which students already enrolled in one of the "open" universities were to be allowed to finish their courses subject to the annual approval of the Minister), non-Whites are restricted to their colleges. . . .

The iniquities suffered by the non-Whites under individual laws or aspects of policy provide but a partial picture of the varied effects of the *apartheid* policy in terms of poverty, malnutrition, disease, breakdown of family life, humiliation and racial tension.

Because of racial discrimination, the White population of the Republic of South Africa has been able to enjoy one of the highest standards of living, while the non-Whites are denied an equitable share of the national income. A few facts from a recent report to the Economic Commission for Africa are illustrative:

> (a) The ratio between the average wage earnings of Whites and Africans in the mining industry is approximately 15:1; in secondary industry it is 5:1.
>
> (b) In 1960, the Whites who constituted 19.3 per cent of the population accounted for 67 per cent of the national income; the Africans who constituted 68.4 per cent of the population received 26.5 per cent; and the Coloreds and Asians, who constituted 12.4 per cent of the population, received 6.5 per cent.
>
> (c) In 1959, the Whites had a *per capita* income of £425 a year; Africans £39; and Asians and Coloreds £54.

. . . The South African Government has enacted a mass of repressive legislation in recent years to silence and suppress all opposition to the policies of *apartheid*. Such legislation has been further strengthened during the past year.

The General Law Amendment Act of 1963, promulgated in May, provides *inter alia* for the detention of persons for 90 days at a time without trial on suspicion of having committed a crime or of possessing information on the commission of a crime. This legislation evoked widespread criticism in South Africa and abroad as ending the rule of law and creating a police state.

The Minister of Justice is now empowered to ban political organizations and public meetings. He is authorized to prohibit persons from public activities, restrict their movements, banish them, place them under "house arrest" or detain them for recurring periods of ninety days each. He may prohibit publications or require deposits of 20,000 Rand for registration of newspapers. In many cases, the Minister is not required to give grounds for action or may only have to charge the victim with furthering the aims of communism, defined so widely as to cover all active opposition to the policies of *apartheid*. The powers of the courts to review his actions are extremely circumscribed. . . .

Acting contrary to the Security Council resolution of August 7, [1963,] which called for the liberation of "all persons imprisoned, interned or subjected to other restrictions for having opposed the policy of *apartheid*, the South African Government continued detentions without trial. The Minister of Justice, Mr. B. J. Vorster, announced on August 23 that more than 300 persons were under detention under this Act. He stated that 165 detainees would be charged in the coming weeks with sabotage and related activities and that similar charges against 85 other detainees were being investigated.

Sabotage, it may be noted, is defined very broadly and carries the maximum penalty of death.

One result of this series of repressive actions was the growing conviction among the opponents of *apartheid*, including all the major non-White organizations, that there was no legal means of fighting the policy and that violent resistance was essential to secure equal rights for all the people of the country. . . .

The Government has consistently refused to recognize that the demand by non-Whites for a share of political power in the country is legitimate, and has put down all such demands as mortal dangers to the social order.

This has created increasing frustration and increasing disillusionment in the methods of non-violence. A recent survey of attitudes of middle class Africans, published by the South African Institute of Race Relations, indicated that most of them were prepared to accept violence as a method of political action and that nearly half held that force had become inevitable.

A wave of sabotage and violence has been reported since the middle of December 1961 when bombs were exploded in a Johannesburg post office and an attempt was made to destroy an electric power station in Port Elizabeth. . . .

Incidents of sabotage continue to be repeated. On August 17, [1963,] the offices of the Bantu Affairs Commissioner at Wynberg, which contained vital statistics covering the African population of Alexandra and Johannesburg North, were completely destroyed by fire. At the same moment, the largest Dutch Reformed Church in Alexandra was completely destroyed by fire.

On September 3, 1963, signal cables were dynamited at five different places on a suburban railway near Cape Town. This was described as the boldest action by saboteurs in recent months.

To cope with the increasing tension in the country, the Government has undertaken a tremendous expansion of all branches of the armed forces, the setting up of air commando units, the establishment of police reserves and home guards, the training of civilians in the use of arms, the development of the radio network to link all of the nearly one thousand police stations, the import of vast quantities of modern arms, and the great increase in the defence and police budgets. . . .

The problem in South Africa is not merely the perpetuation of inequalities arising from historical developments or the continued existence of such inequities as the denial of franchise to a majority of the population and the separation of peoples by race or the discrimination in the sharing of the fruits of labor. Such terms as segregation and discrimination can hardly describe the humiliation and oppression to which millions of people, who constitute a large majority of the population of the country, have been subjected by the policies of its Government.

The problem, moreover, is not one of a peculiar political or social system which democratic-minded peoples find objectionable, nor one of color or race, but the consequence of a racialist ideology enshrined as State policy, and implemented by force against the majority of the people of the country, in violation of the obligations of the South African Government under the United Nations Charter. The racist creed that the policies of *apartheid* are based on is the very antithesis of the concept of international cooperation which is at the root of the existence of the United Nations.

The Special Committee rejects as unfounded the claim of the Government of South Africa that the choice in South Africa is between White domination and the end of the White community in the country. It feels that the White community cannot ensure its survival by seeking perpetual domination over the non-Whites, and that efforts to that end can only lead to catastrophic consequences. . . .

In the context of the historic developments in Asia and Africa since the establishment of the United Nations, the policies and actions of the Republic of South Africa have increasingly serious international repercussions. They have become a constant provocation to peoples beyond the borders of the Republic who feel an affinity with the oppressed people of South Africa, and to all opponents of racism everywhere. They have obliged many States to break relations with the Republic of South Africa or to refrain from establishing relations. They have caused friction between African and other States on the one hand, and Governments which, these States feel, have not taken adequate measures to dissuade the South African Government from its present policies. Finally, they constitute a serious threat to the maintenance of international peace and security.

The Special Committee rejects the claims of the Government of the Republic of South Africa that it is, by its policy, defending the Western or Christian civilization in its territory or that it is the victim of attacks led by one of the protagonists of the cold war. The racial policies of the Republic of South Africa are a matter of concern to all States and to all peoples. It is the responsibility of all Member States, irrespective of other differences, to cooperate in an endeavor to put an end to the dangerous situation in the Republic of South Africa, in the interests solely of the people of South Africa and the maintenance of international peace and security. . . .

With regard to the request to the Member States by the General Assembly that they refrain from exporting all arms and ammunition to South Africa, and by the Security Council that they cease forthwith the sale and shipment of arms, ammunition of all types and military vehicles to South Africa, the Special Committee submits the following supplementary recommendations: (a) Member States should be requested not to provide any assistance, directly or indirectly, in the manufacture of arms, ammunition and military vehicles in South Africa, including the supply of strategic materials, provision of technical assistance, or the granting of licenses; (b) Member States should be requested to refrain from providing training for South African military personnel; and (c) Member States should be requested to refrain from any form of cooperation with South African military and police forces.

. . . the Special Committee suggests that the General Assembly and the Security Council give consideration to additional measures, including the following, to dissuade the Government of the Republic of South Africa from its racial policies: (a) recommendation to all international agencies to take all necessary steps to deny economic or technical assistance to the Government of the Republic of South Africa, without precluding, however, humanitarian assistance to the victims of the policies of *apartheid;* (b) recommendation to Member States to take steps to prohibit or discourage foreign investments in South Africa and loans to the South African Government or South African companies; (c) recommendation to Member States to consider denial of facilities for all ships and planes destined to or returning from the Republic of South Africa; (d) recommendation to Member States to take measures to prohibit, or at least discourage, emigration of their nationals to the Republic of South Africa, as immigrants are sought by it to reinforce its policies of *apartheid;* and (e) study of means to ensure an effective embargo on the supply of arms and ammunition, as well as petroleum, to the Republic of South Africa, including a blockade, if necessary, under the aegis of the United Nations. . . .

Considering the extreme gravity of the situation in the Republic of South Africa, and its serious international repercussions, the Special Committee deems it essential that the General Assembly and the Security Council should keep the matter under active consideration in order to take timely and effective measures to ensure the fulfilment of the Purposes of the Charter. The Special Committee feels that they should consider, with no further delay, possible new measures in accordance with the Charter, which provide for stronger political, diplomatic and economic sanctions, suspension of rights and privileges of the Republic of South Africa as a Member State, and expulsion from the United Nations and its Specialized Agencies. The Special Committee will actively pursue its task of assisting the General Assembly and the Security Council in connection with this problem, and, to this end, invites the continued cooperation of the Member States and the Specialized Agencies, as well as all organizations and individuals devoted to the principles of the Charter.

The Truth That Hurts*

Eric H. Louw

As the representative of an African State, I naturally would like to review the African scene. What is happening on this vast continent which occupies the strategic position of being situated between the West and the East?

The outstanding feature of events in Africa has been the large number of African territories that have attained independence during the past two or three years. . . .

While the attainment of full national independence by a country or people is a matter for congratulation, the question must inevitably arise whether such a country is able, and ready, to assume the responsibilities of independent statehood. That question has arisen, and will again arise, in connection with the Soviet item on the agenda calling for a timetable for independence for all dependent countries except in their own occupied territories.

In August of last year, no less a person than Sir Abubakar Balewa, the Prime Minister of Nigeria, stated in a television interview at New York: "I do not believe that Africa's non-self-governing territories will benefit from the immediate granting of independence. I don't think there are enough trained people to man the civil service."

Sir Abubakar speaks from experience. Under the system of "colonial oppression," as it is so often termed, the British not only prepared his country for independence but were good enough on their departure to leave a large number of trained civil servants and technicians to assist Nigeria during the first years of independence.

In view of his statement, one wonders whether the Prime Minister of Nigeria approves of the high-handed action of the United Nations in arresting and also deporting European civil advisers of President Tshombe of Katanga, who was anxious (as were the Governments of Ghana and Nigeria) to

* From a speech delivered before the United Nations General Assembly on October 11, 1961. Issued by the Information Service of South Africa, New York, pp. 9–47. Mr. Louw is Minister of Foreign Affairs of the Republic of South Africa. Mr. Louw's speech evoked an unprecedented vote of censure from the U.N. General Assembly.

retain the services of trained advisers for the purpose of ensuring the continuation of the stable economic conditions which have prevailed almost since the United Nations General Assembly decided to take action in the Congo.

Mr. Iain Macleod, new Leader of the British House of Commons, who certainly cannot be described as being antagonistic to the aspirations of the Africans, is filled with similar misgivings. He recently stated: "There is considerable anxiety about the pace of events in Africa . . . I share these anxieties. I think that the pace of events in Africa, and elsewhere in the Colonial Territories, is dangerously fast."

The leaders of the anti-colonial campaign in the United States, in Europe, and also in the United Nations Assembly, laboured under the mistaken impression that the parliamentary system of government, born in Britain and adopted by other Western countries, including the United States of America, could be grafted on to the traditional customs and practices of the African peoples—or shall I say, transplanted to the alien soil of age-old African tradition. It simply does not work that way. One reason is that the masses in many African countries are illiterate, and in some cases are told to vote for a symbol, e.g., an animal, printed on the voting paper. In any case, even the educated Africans do not appear to be interested in or enamoured of the Western system of political parties that compete with each other for governing the country. It is a foreign plant that will not thrive on African soil. . . .

Mr. John Tettegah, the Secretary-General of the Ghana Trade Union Congress, . . . told an Accra gathering in December last: "Africa does not need a Westminster-type parliamentary system in which two or more political parties compete with each other for authority . . . Africa cannot afford to accept foreign systems which are incompatible with the African way of life, thought and practice."

In speaking thus, Mr. Tettegah was echoing the sentiments of his leader Dr. Nkrumah, who, soon after achieving independence, rid himself of an effective Parliamentary Opposition, and further threw overboard the democratic principles which had been preached in Ghana by a succession of British administrators and Governors. Only ten days ago, further steps were taken to convert Ghana into an authoritarian State. The ruler of Ghana is flirting with Moscow and Peking. Guinea, soon after being given its independence, promptly became a disciple of Moscow. Mali appears to be going the same way, and others are likely to follow. The Congo (Leopoldville) may well be the next. In past years, when the United States and other Western delegations were taking the lead in attacking colonialism and urging the African States to become independent, they little thought that they were securing future recruits for Moscow and Peking.

As I shall show later in my address, South Africa has profited by the mistakes made by some of the Colonial Powers, and in its Bantu legislation is building up a system of self-government for the different Bantu ethnic groups, which, while observing democratic principles, takes account of Bantu tradition and custom.

Let us take a look at my country.

The first thing that strikes one, is that while there has been unrest and turmoil in several other African countries—from the U.A.R. and Ethiopia in the North and Ghana in the West to Northern Rhodesia in the middle-South—quiet conditions prevail in South Africa in spite of strenuous efforts by subversive elements in London, New York, Accra and Cairo, acting in concert with Bantu subversive organisations, to stir up trouble in the Republic. The activities of these organisations and of expatriate Bantu agitators has had little influence on the South African Bantu who prefer satisfactory social conditions and economic progress. . . .

According to United Nations statistics, the annual per capita income of the South African *Bantu only* has, during the five years from 1953 to 1958, increased by more than 64 per cent. This increase is progressively being maintained. He is living in a well laid-out Bantu township, in a neat home, provided with the necessary amenities, electric light, drinking water, satisfactory sanitary arrangements. His children receive both primary and secondary education, and the elders of his community draw old age pensions at the end of each month.

Medical and social services are provided for the physically unfit. In respect of social and medical services, housing and education, South Africa per capita of its nonwhite population spends considerably more than any other State on the whole of the continent of Africa—about 5 or 6 times more.

This particularly applies to health services. The Baragwanath Hospital, which serves the Bantu and coloured population only of Johannesburg and its environs, is the largest and best equipped on the continent of Africa, and in fact ranks among the best in the world. There are 46 wards and 10 operating theatres. Beds are available for 2,500 patients. The hospital is served by 182 *full-time* medical doctors, of whom about half are specialists. At present 15 of these are Bantu doctors, and this number will be progressively increased. There are 1,000 Bantu nurses, and all the ward-sisters are Bantu.

Six hundred thousand out-patients receive medical attention annually. No African country can boast of anything nearly approaching a hospital of this size which serves nonwhites of only one of South Africa's large cities. There are large hospitals for nonwhites also in many other centres, particularly the huge King Edward VIII Hospital at Durban.

These facts are of course never disclosed by South Africa's enemies and critics. The totally false impression is given again in the course of this general debate that the nonwhites of South Africa are ill-treated and oppressed, and that they have to be "saved" by the United Nations.

I have said that the nonwhites in South Africa share in the growth and prosperity of the country. I have indicated the extent to which the needs of the Bantu are being attended to by way of housing, social and medical services.

But South Africa's growth and the advanced state of its industrialisation could be of great benefit also to the emergent African States. . . . The new

States of Africa could look to South Africa for substantial aid and for guidance in regard to industrial, scientific and other matters—provided, of course, that the African States wish to make use of that aid. . . .

On many occasions, and again this year, we have willingly acceded to requests from African States and territories to supply vaccines and other remedies for animal diseases from the world-famous Onderstepoort Veterinary Institute. We have done so also in cases where the African country concerned has taken up an actively hostile attitude towards South Africa.

South Africa has played a leading part in the work of the C.C.T.A., and yet, at the Abidjan Conference earlier this year, several African delegates demanded South Africa's expulsion from that body. One of the delegations even walked out whenever the South African delegate participated in the discussions. Similar hostility to the South African delegation was shown at the E.C.A. Conference at Addis Ababa.

On the other hand, where certain African countries have taken measures to boycott imports from South Africa, we have not retaliated, and their exports are still freely admitted to South Africa. . . .

African leaders who, I am sure, keep in touch with happenings in other parts of the world are, of course, aware of the fact that colour and racial discrimination is practised in certain Western and also in certain Eastern countries that are members of this Organisation.

The reply generally is: "Ah! but in those countries discrimination and segregation are not sanctioned by law, as in the case of South Africa." Leaving aside for the moment the question whether South Africa's policy of differentiation and separate development is the same as the discrimination and segregation practised in other countries, that reply offers cold comfort to the nonwhites in those countries who are victims of racial discrimination. Does it help them in any way if the central Government of a particular country frowns upon racial discrimination, while it is sanctioned and certainly not prohibited by municipal, provincial or state authorities of that country? Have leaders of African delegations in this Assembly taken note of this "unofficial" type of racial discrimination? And what about the almost criminal neglect of the needs of small nonwhite communities in certain Western countries? Why pick on South Africa? Are there perhaps political and particularly economic and financial considerations which induce the leaders of the African States to close their eyes to the actual practice of colour discrimination as well as religious, caste and other forms of discrimination in certain countries, while threatening sanctions against South Africa? In the history of the Union (now the Republic) of South Africa, there has never yet been a single instance of organised attacks by whites on nonwhite members of our population. Again I ask: "Why pick on South Africa?"

What actually is the basis of the charges made against South Africa, inside and outside of this Assembly?

The main complaint is that the huge nonwhite majority does not share full political equality with the whites—that the principle of "one man, one vote" is not applied. It is not seriously contended by our critics and enemies that the nonwhites in South Africa are oppressed, and that their material needs—housing, social services and education—are not attended to. On the contrary, as I have pointed out, in these respects far more is done for South Africa's Bantu and other nonwhites than in any state or territory on the continent of Africa.

In order to appreciate the position in South Africa, the following basic facts must be borne in mind:

(a) The white population of South Africa is a permanent one whose ancestors came to the country more than 300 years ago. We are not "colonists," as is often erroneously alleged. We cannot return to the countries of our forebears. We are strangers in those countries, just as the Roosevelts, the Eisenhowers, the Diefenbakers and Vanderbilts are today strangers in the countries of their forebears.

(b) The Bantu, or black, peoples of South Africa are *not* the original inhabitants of the country. Their ancestors moved southwards from East and Central Africa and crossed the Limpopo River at about the same time that the original Dutch settlers arrived at Table Bay. At that time the only inhabitants of South Africa were nomadic groups of Hottentots and Bushmen. The Bantu living in South Africa, therefore, have no greater claim to the southern end of the African continent than the white population.

(c) As was correctly stated by Mr. Tom Mboya, South Africa is today the most highly developed and industrialised country in the continent of Africa. This was accomplished against tremendous odds with considerable sacrifices, and by the initiative of South Africans of European descent. By providing the necessary labour, nonwhites contributed their share to the development of the country.

(d) And now the white population of South Africa is being told by the Afro-Asian countries, and also by the delegations of certain Western countries, that what has been built up over three centuries by their forebears and by successive generations of white South Africans, must be placed under the control of the nonwhite majority. That will be the logical consequence of the demand for full political equality in the same State. (There can, of course, be political equality if each of the races in the State is able to have a separate political development.)

Would the United States of America, Canada and the Latin American States—all countries whose respective early histories of colonisation are similar to that of South Africa—would they, if their relative proportions of white to nonwhite populations were the same as in South Africa, be prepared to hand over the control of their countries to Negro or to "Indian" majorities?

Why is it that certain Western countries with large white populations are taking steps to limit quotas for nonwhite immigrants? Is it because in those countries racial friction has already manifested itself, and that they are taking timely precautions to prevent the extension of such friction? Are they perhaps worried about the formation of racial political "blocs" or pressure groups in years to come, particularly in the larger centres? I do not for a moment criticise those countries for taking timely precautions. But then they—and particularly their press and some of their clerics—should not criticise or attack South Africa for taking similar precautions, and for more valid and more urgent reasons.

Let me remind our critics and enemies that if the system of differentiation practised in South Africa is to be regarded as discrimination, then it is practised also against the whites. Whites are not allowed to enter urban Bantu residential areas without permits, and they enjoy no trading rights in Bantu townships. Similarly, whites are debarred from land-ownership in the Bantu Homelands, and are not permitted to participate in Bantu Authorities. Eventually, whites will be barred from trading in the vast Bantu Homelands.

What exactly is South Africa's policy of "apartheid," which has become almost a swear-word in many countries? How many of those who attack South Africa, and who actually are threatening to apply sanctions, have any conception of what our policy is? Few know that the word "apartheid" is in fact an abbreviated term for the policy of "aparte ontwikkeling," which means "separate development"—with the emphasis on the word "development." . . .

South Africa's policy of separate development is not, as is generally supposed, the creation of the present Government. . . .

The policy of separate development, also known as apartheid, is . . . the traditional policy of South Africa, and is not, as is generally alleged, the evil conception of the present Government, and more particularly of the present Prime Minister, Dr. Verwoerd. It is a policy which is equally in the interests of the white and of the Bantu population. It is intended to safeguard what has been built up over three centuries by the whites, but at the same time it takes account of the political aspirations, as well as of the traditions, cultures and also the material needs of the Bantu peoples.

The Bantu Self-Government Act provides for progressively increased legislative, judicial and administrative powers for the Bantu authorities in their own territories. These territories, mostly situated in some of the most fertile areas of South Africa, were voluntarily occupied by the Bantu tribes, which, at the time of the arrival of the first Dutch immigrants, were themselves migrating from Central and East Africa. The territories were subsequently reserved for the Bantu only. Not only are the laws excluding white occupation strictly applied, but huge tracts of adjacent land have subsequently been acquired by expropriating white owners. The Bantu Self-Government Act avoids the mistakes made in other parts of Africa, of over-hasty growth and of creating independent territories which are not yet "ripe" for self-government.

By this legislation, eight Bantu National Units are established on an ethnic basis, and provision is made for the corresponding Territorial Authorities.

Experience in South Africa and elsewhere in Africa has shown that the splitting or the mixing of ethnic groups leads to clashes and internecine warfare.

Under this system of self-government, the Bantu have since 1951 increased their governing councils from about 60, with about 300 individual members, to 445 councils with no less than 6,550 individual members in 1961. This shows that the system is not only democratic, but that it has been well received by the Bantu, in spite of attempts by subversive organisations and white agitators to discredit this policy and to create unrest.

South Africa's policy is not, as is sometimes alleged, one of "back to the tribe," or "back to the bush." The object is to start with a system of government which is based on Bantu custom and tradition, but which will be further developed by the progressive introduction of fully representative government.

The undermentioned leaders of Bantu Territorial Authorities have in public statements signified their unqualified acceptance of the Government's policy of separate development, and have also expressed their appreciation of what is being done to develop self-government in the different Bantu ethnic areas. They are Chief Botha Sigcau, Presiding Territorial Chief of the Transkeian Territorial Authority; Chief M. C. Chuene, Chairman of the Pietersburg Regional Authority; Regent P. M. Shilubane of the Banuna Tribal Authority; Cyprian Bhekuzulu, Paramount Chief of the Zulus; Paramount Chief Victor Poto of Western Pondoland.

Among the most interesting of these testimonies is that which came from the leader of the Bantu in Ovamboland, South West Africa, who stated in August of last year: "The Ukuanyama have never been betrayed by the Union Government and have retained their country intact. This applies to the whole of Ovamboland and after forty years under Union administration the vast majority of the people are content that it should continue, despite agitation for changes from small and unrepresentative sections at home and abroad."

This statement, coming from the outstanding leader of Ovamboland in South West Africa, is an effective reply to Mr. Fabregat and his fellow members of the South West Africa Committee, who have been grievously misled by a small group of agitators from South West Africa.

Earlier in my address I quoted from statements by African leaders to show that the Western system of parliamentary government cannot simply be transplanted to the African territories. This is further proved by the testimony of Bantu leaders to which I have referred. We in South Africa, with our experience and knowledge of Bantu life and traditions, extending over a period of more than 200 years, have always realised this fact, which is the basis of the policy we have evolved which will eventually give to our Bantu fellow-citizens in their respective homelands full self-government, in accord with their own customs and traditions, and which is best suited to their own outlook, culture and temperament.

A Bantu Industrial Development Corporation has been created for the establishment of industries in those areas. The Government of the Republic is providing the initial capital and will continue to assist financially. These industries will ultimately be owned and controlled by the Bantu themselves. I wish to emphasise that they will *not,* as in some of the African territories, be controlled by financial interests operating from other countries that pocket the profits and at the same time detract from the political independence of those States.

Industries are also being established near the borders of these Bantu Authority Territories, thus providing employment for Bantu across the border, where they are living in their own country with their families, and in their own homes, under their own form of government.

The Government of the Republic is meanwhile undertaking the task and the expense of developing the Bantu territories; e.g., irrigation projects, fencing and soil erosion. The younger men are being instructed in the latest agricultural methods, and the Bantu are being provided with stud cattle to improve their herds. I would add that the Bantu areas are in no way inferior to corresponding areas occupied by whites, and in fact in some cases they are superior and able to support a larger population per acre than in most other parts of South Africa.

A Commissioner-General for each of the ethnic groups serves as a link between the Government of the Republic and the relative Territorial Authority. He must reside at the headquarters of the Territorial Authority and it is his duty to bring to the attention of the Central Government the political, economic and social needs of the ethnic group to which he has been assigned. It should be emphasized that the Commissioner-General is not an Administrator, but that his post is analogous to that of an Ambassador to a particular country.

I would add here that, in order to accelerate the transfer of administrative and judicial functions to the recognised leaders of the Bantu, special schools have been and are in the process of being established in the different ethnic areas for the training of young men who are likely to be leaders of their people in modern methods of administration and also in economic and business principles.

There are 2½ million Bantu who work and live in the European urban areas. Another 3 million are scattered in other European areas. It has been urged here, and elsewhere, that they should receive full political equality with the whites. I have already explained that the Bantu who live in the white areas will retain their voting rights in the self-governing areas from which they come and can return there for that purpose, as is done by many of the 400,000 Bantu from the neighbouring British Protectorate of Basutoland, who are working in the Republic. There are altogether about 1⅓ million Bantu who are not of South African origin. Our policy aims at maintaining the unity of each of the Bantu ethnic groups. It regards the Bantu living in the European area as part of his particular ethnic community in the Bantu Homelands. This policy is appreciated by the Bantu themselves, and leads to a greater measure of co-operation with the Government in the European area.

It is, however, recognised that provision must be made for Bantu living in cities and in the large towns to have a voice in municipal and other local affairs which affect their living conditions. The system of Advisory Boards, which has been in practice for decades, was recently extended so that the Bantu in urban residential areas will now be able to form Urban Councils to which are entrusted specified duties and responsibilities.

While on the subject of urban Bantu, it is interesting to note that 1⅓ million Bantu from neighbouring territories who have come to live in South Africa evidently do not mind the alleged oppression. On the contrary, they share in the many benefits, e.g., social and medical services, housing and education, provided by the Government and by municipal authorities of South Africa for their own nonwhite citizens.

One hears and reads much of illiteracy. This is not only an African problem. It is found also in leading Western countries and is rife in the Middle East and in Asian countries. I need hardly remind the Assembly of conditions in many of the independent African states. Having had experience of the way in which false information is spread about my own country, I do not unreservedly accept what I read about other countries. It is, however, interesting to find that more than one book dealing with conditions in two of the oldest independent African states, Liberia and Ethiopia, tells of the appalling state of living conditions and also of illiteracy among the masses in those states. Even more interesting is the fact that it is those two states that have taken proceedings against South Africa in the International Court in which, *inter alia,* the Republic is charged with not having promoted to the utmost the welfare of the inhabitants of South West Africa.

In fairness, I must point out that illiteracy is a feature not only of Liberia and Ethiopia. According to a literacy map of the world only a few of the African states or territories show an illiteracy rate below 80 per cent. I may add that the South African Bantu *only* is well below this figure, viz. 65 per cent.

The great progress made in Bantu education in South Africa is considerably in advance of that made by most other African countries.

The success obtained is due to the fact that an educational system has been evolved which recognises that educational methods designed for European or American children with a different background, habits and behaviour patterns cannot simply be grafted on to the methods used for children that have grown up under entirely different circumstances. In most cases, these children are acquainted only with values, interests and behaviour patterns learned from a Bantu mother, and who more often than not are living in surroundings still in an early stage of civilisation. Too often, missionaries from Europe or America have tried to transplant their systems of education to African countries, with unsatisfactory results. That mistake has been avoided in the system employed in South Africa, with the result that about 80 per cent of Bantu children up to the age of 14 years are attending 7,412 primary schools. Eight years ago the percentage was only 58.

But similar progress has also been made in the secondary or higher schools, which are providing higher education to 49,000 pupils. There are 48 institutions for the training of 4,500 teachers, and also 30 technical schools where at present 1,850 young Bantu are being trained. There are 27,800 teachers in Bantu schools, of which only about 1 per cent are whites. This year at least 10,500 Bantu students will be writing the standard VIII (Junior Certificate) examination, and 2,000 will take the matriculation examination, which is necessary for entrance to a university.

But also in the field of higher education considerable progress has been made. There are three Bantu University Colleges where at present 1,580 students are enrolled.

In accordance with South Africa's policy of separate development, the primary and secondary schools are controlled by Bantu parents who serve on 500 School Boards and 4,500 School Committees.

Finally, there are also Bantu Agricultural Schools where training is provided to enable the Bantu to improve their agricultural methods.

I suggest that the progress made in South Africa in the field of Bantu primary, secondary and university education far exceeds that of any other African state or territory. And yet the leaders of those states accuse the South African Government of neglecting, and even of oppressing the Bantu people!

I have referred to political and economic conditions prevailing in most of the states and territories of Central and North Africa—conditions of political unrest and of economic instability. By contrast, there is peace, prosperity and economic stability in South Africa, in spite of attempts by agitators and subversive elements, inside and outside of South Africa, to stir up trouble among the nonwhites, and to harm South Africa's economy. Inside South Africa there are subversive Bantu organisations, aided and abetted by overseas ultra-Liberalistic organisations, such as the American Committee on Africa in New York, and Christian Action in London, and by certain sections of the press in those countries.

They are further actively encouraged by the leaders of certain African states. An interesting feature of this latter type of encouragement is that it is an important element in the keen competition among certain leaders to assume the leadership of the African states. In bidding for that honour, the idea is that the one that hits South Africa the hardest is likely to gain the favour of the smaller African states. The leaders are of course not really worried about the Bantu in South Africa, because they know that they are far better cared for than the masses in their own countries.

We firmly believe that the course upon which we have embarked in South Africa will ultimately solve the problem of relations between white and nonwhite races in our country. It is a policy which aims at progressively giving to the Bantu the complete control of his own Homelands, and which by means of Urban Councils will provide the urban Bantu with the means to promote their material welfare and social needs. Similar steps have been taken and will be further developed also in the cases of the Coloured and

Indian population. At the same time, this policy will ensure to South Africans of European descent control of their homeland, which over the past three centuries has been opened up and developed by their forebears and by succeeding generations of South Africans.

We believe that this policy of peaceful but separate co-existence will provide the solution of our racial problems, and ensure the happiness and prosperity of all South Africans—white, black, Coloured and Indian.

All that we ask is that we be permitted to carry out our policy of looking after the interests of our Bantu and other nonwhite peoples, without interference from outside, be it from Western, Eastern or African countries.

Toward African Unity*

Organization of African Unity Charter

We, the Heads of African States and Governments assembled in the city of Addis Ababa, Ethiopia;

CONVINCED that it is the inalienable right of all people to control their own destiny;

CONSCIOUS of the fact that freedom, equality, justice, and dignity are essential objectives for the achievement of the legitimate aspirations of the African peoples;

CONSCIOUS of our responsibility to harness the natural and human resources of our continent for the total advancement of our peoples in spheres of human endeavor;

INSPIRED by a common determination to strengthen understanding and cooperation among our states in response to the aspirations of our peoples for brotherhood and solidarity, in a large unity transcending ethnic and national differences;

CONVINCED that, in order to translate this determination into a dynamic force in the cause of human progress, conditions for peace and security must be established and maintained;

DETERMINED to safeguard and consolidate the hard-won independence as well as the sovereignty and territorial integrity of our states, and to fight against neo-colonialism in all its forms;

DEDICATED to the general progress of Africa;

PERSUADED that the Charter of the United Nations and the Uni-

* From the Charter establishing the Organization of African Unity, the Summit Conference of Independent African States meeting in Addis Ababa, Ethiopia, May 22–25, 1963. As printed in *Africa Report,* June 1963, pp. 11–12.

versal Declaration of Human Rights, to the principles of which we reaffirm our adherence, provide a solid foundation for peaceful and positive cooperation among states;

DESIROUS that all African states should henceforth unite so that the welfare and well-being of their peoples can be assured;

RESOLVED to reinforce the links between our states by establishing and strengthening common institutions;

HAVE agreed to the present Charter.

Establishment

Article I. (1) The High Contracting Parties do by the present Charter establish an organization to be known as the "Organization of African Unity."

(2) The organization shall include the continental African states, Madagascar, and all the islands surrounding Africa.

Purposes

Article II. (1) The organization shall have the following purposes: (a) to promote the unity and solidarity of the African states: (b) to coordinate and intensify their cooperation and efforts to achieve a better life for the peoples of Africa; (c) to defend their sovereignty, their territorial integrity, and independence; (d) to eradicate all forms of colonialism from Africa; and (e) to promote international cooperation, having due regard to the Charter of the United Nations and the Universal Declaration of Human Rights.

(2) To these ends, the member states shall coordinate and harmonize their general policies, especially in the following fields: (a) political and diplomatic cooperation; (b) economic cooperation, including transport and communications; (c) educational and cultural cooperation; (d) health, sanitation, and nutritional cooperation; (e) scientific and technical cooperation; and (f) cooperation for defence and security.

Principles

Article III. The member states, in pursuit of the purposes stated in Article II, solemnly affirm and declare their adherence to the following principles:

(1) the sovereign equality of all member states;

(2) non-interference in the internal affairs of states;

(3) respect for the sovereignty and territorial integrity of each member state and for its inalienable right to independent existence;

(4) peaceful settlement of disputes by negotiation, mediation, conciliation or arbitration;

(5) unreserved condemnation, in all its forms, of political assas-

sination as well as of subversive activities on the part of neighboring states or any other states;

(6) absolute dedication to the total emancipation of the African territories which are still dependent;

(7) affirmation of a policy of non-alignment with regard to all blocs. . . .

The Assembly of Heads of State and Government

Article VIII. The Assembly of Heads of State and Government shall be the supreme organ of the organization. It shall, subject to the provisions of this Charter, discuss matters of common concern to Africa with a view to coordinating and harmonizing the general policy of the organization. . . .

Article IX. The Assembly shall be composed of the Heads of State, Government, or their duly accredited representatives and it shall meet at least *once a year*. . . .

Article X. (1) Each member state shall have one vote.

(2) All resolutions shall be determined by a two-thirds majority of the members of the organization. . . .

Needed: A Central Authority*

Kwame Nkrumah

Mr. Speaker, and Members of the National Assembly, it is of great consequence that the States of the organisation of African Unity have, in article three of the Charter, solemnly affirmed and declared their adherence to the principle of a non-aligned policy.

Non-alignment is now a world factor and moral force in international relations. The contribution of Africa as a continent united in its observance of a truly non-aligned policy will give tremendous weight to that force. It will also give a great fillip to the search for permanent world peace.

Nothing has stood so firmly in the way of African Freedom or hindered African Unity as the existence of foreign bases on African soil and African involvement through military alliances and pacts with powers outside the African continent. If we are to combine our forces and create a common strategy both in support of Africa's freedom fighters and in the defence and protection

* From a speech to the National Assembly on the Ratification of the Charter of the Organization of African Unity at Accra, Ghana, June 20, 1963. Press Release No. 17/63, June 20, 1963. Information Section, Embassy of Ghana, pp. 6–7, 10–12. Kwame Nkrumah is President of Ghana.

of our established independence, then it goes without saying that all such bases and all such pacts need to be annulled. Unless this is done, we stand exposed, and our charter will remain nothing but a mere scrap of paper.

In saying this, I am not unmindful of the grave difficulties which face some of us. Lack of capital, economic weakness and political instability are conditions that have been responsible for the acceptance of economic and military dependence upon former colonial powers. In some instances, such as is obtained not only for development, but even for meeting normal recurrent budgetary expenses. It is an act of high courage on the part of Sister States thus boldly to have set their hand to a policy of non-alignment which can hardly be in keeping with the policy of those on whom, unhappily, they find themselves dependent.

Yet it is these states, particularly, that should find the greatest advantage in developing our African Unity into a firmly welded concert of nations as a real political force with political direction under a central authority within which they can shed their economic and military dependence and regain their dignity. Proposals of aid need to be examined with care. Most of all, we must beware of any kind of military help, for it can so easily place us in the hands of foreign powers and make them, in effect, the arbiters of our fate. Apart from drawing us into their orbit, they become intimately familiar with details of our defence structure and its strength. They can even become the designers of our defence structure and place us completely at their mercy. Aid of this kind, even where ostensibly free, can be most dangerous, and costly in its consequences, for it creates pockets of cold-war presence on the African continent and lets in the neo-colonialists, with danger not only to the harbouring country but to its neighbours, to whom it poses an open threat. Above all, it creates frictions and disputes that will disturb the unity upon which we have embarked and to which, I am convinced, all of us are sincerely dedicated. That is why it is so urgent for us to get together within a centralised framework that will give shape and purpose to the agreements which we made at Addis Ababa.

Co-ordination of our political and diplomatic policies, harmonisation of our economic, educational and cultural activities, collaboration in health, sanitation and nutritional matters, co-ordination in scientific and technical fields, co-operation for defence and security will go their dilatory pace unless the organisation of African Unity is pivoted upon a centralised authority capable of giving effective political direction to these aims.

Political and diplomatic co-operation cannot function in a void. It needs some sort of a political constitution to direct it. Economic development in separate states is ineffective, but with our combined resources, governed by an overall plan, we can make Africa great, prosperous and progressive.

Above all, the full development of all our countries needs the most economic exploitation and husbanding of our natural and human resources. This is possible only on a continental scale, if we are to extract the greatest advantage from the latest industrial and administrative techniques as applied to our extensive land mass and population. . . .

Mr. Speaker, Members of the National Assembly, we can safeguard our independence and economic interests in Africa only if we speak with one voice. Only a united Africa can obtain capital on a large scale and technical aid from the industrially advanced countries without undue pressures and restrictive conditions. The only alternative I can see to this is confusion in our ranks, economic retrogression and pitiful sell-out of our patrimony to the colonialists and imperialists. Did we fight to secure sovereignty and independence only to exchange these precious attributes for a state of despair and despondency? We have proved at Addis Ababa that we are ready to build a united Africa, united in our conception of its importance and in our common desire to move forward together in a triumphant march to the great kingdom of the African personality, where although we may be Ghanaians, Nigerians, Ethiopians, Algerians, Egyptians or Sierra Leoneans, we shall have a common purpose and a common objective in working for the destiny of our continent as Africans. Until Africa achieves total independence and national unification, the African revolution will not have completed its destined task. When we talk of African Unity, we are thinking of a political arrangement which will enable us collectively to provide solutions for our problems in Africa.

Time is everything in our march. We must in Africa crowd into a generation that experience and achievement attained through centuries of trial and error by the older nations of the world. We do not wish to see Africa set on a course in which her nations grow in different, separate and competing directions until they develop into a confused and disorderly economic tangle of "sixes and sevens." Because Europe has become the victim of such economic circumstances that is surely no reason why Africa should follow a similar course. Those who set the example of Europe as an illustration for the need to develop step by step in Africa do not seem to appreciate that Africa need not begin by imitating the mistakes of Europe. After all, what use is the experience of human progress if we who study its course fail to learn from its errors and muddles. As I said at Addis Ababa, this world is no longer moving on camels and donkeys. Speed has become a new, potent factor in the progress of the world. The progress of the modern man, like the agile kangaroo, leaps and jumps.

More than that, we have to remove the gap between those nations and ourselves if we are to emerge from the grip of the economic imperialism that will retard us, the longer it remains a master, or even a part, of our economy. We have to keep in mind, however, that the gap is not a static one, but that it grows as modern technology improves and its productive capacities and output potentials increase. Thus the gap can widen seriously, and new dangers threaten us, unless we hasten forward at a much accelerated speed. Consciousness of the time element among the leaders of Independent Africa was clearly revealed in the course of our deliberations at Addis Ababa. This awareness enabled us to examine our problems with a striking sense of urgency. It was responsible for the speed with which we were able to adopt a charter of unity for Africa. Why, then, cannot we observe the same consciousness of time and the same sense of urgency, in pushing forward our unity into a form that will give it direction and authority, so that we can speed up our common development and advancement? In the horizon of Africa's future I see clearly the bright dawn of a union Government, the birth of a great nation which is no longer the dream of a new utopia. Africa, the sleeping giant, is now awake and is coming into her very own.

We Must Be Realists about African Unity*

Sir Abubakar Tafawa Balewa

I will try to explain the views and the stand of Nigeria as far as African unity is concerned. I feel that the mere presence of all the Heads of African States and Governments here shows the success of the Conference, and I have no doubt that all of us will leave Addis Ababa satisfied that we have done something. . . .

There have been quite a lot of views on what we mean by African unity. Some of us have suggested that African unity should be achieved by political fusion of the different states in Africa; some of us feel that African unity could be achieved by taking practical steps in economic, educational, scientific and cultural co-operation and by trying first to get the Africans to understand themselves before embarking on the more complicated and more difficult arrangement of political union. My country stands for the practical approach to the unity of the African continent. We feel that, if this unity is to last, we must start from the beginning. Nigeria's stand is that if we want this unity in Africa we must first agree to certain essential things: The first is that African States must respect one another. There must be acceptance of equality by all the States. No matter whether they are big or small, they are all sovereign and their sovereignty is sovereignty. The size of a state, its population or its wealth should not be the criterion. It has been pointed out many times that the smaller states in Africa have no right to exist because they are too small. We in Nigeria do not agree with this view. It was unfortunate that the African States have been broken up into different groups by the Colonial powers. In some cases, a single tribe has been broken up into four different States.

* From a speech to the African Summit Conference at Addis Ababa, Ethiopia, May 24, 1963. Reprinted in *Vital Speeches of the Day*, August 1, 1963, pp. 620–622. Sir Abubakar Tafawa Balewa is Prime Minister of the Federation of Nigeria.

You might find a section in Guinea, a section in Mali, a section in Sierra Leone and perhaps a section in Liberia. That was not our fault because, for over 60 years, these different units have been existing, and any attempt, on the part of any African country, to disregard this fact might bring trouble to this continent. This is the thing we want to avoid and, for this reason, Nigeria recognises all the existing boundaries in Africa, and recognises the existence of all the countries in Africa. This, I think, is the basis of the unity which we in Nigeria pray for on our continent.

As I have said, we have to start from the beginning. I have listened to speeches in this conference, and there have been only a very few members who spoke on the desirability of having a political union. Almost all the speeches indicate that a more practical approach is much preferred by the majority of the delegation. I am glad to say that the stand we have taken right from the beginning is the stand of nearly almost all the countries in this conference. It appears from the speeches as if we were just sitting idle and doing nothing towards the achievement of this unity. For our part, in Nigeria, we are already co-operating with some of our neighbours. For example, the other day, my friend the President of Malagasy said he could not contact Lagos by telephone from Cotonou. This is no longer the case. Now he can speak direct. What we are trying to do is to link up with all our neighbours by means of telecommunications and by exchanging more postal facilities; and we are already entering into bilateral agreements with many of our neighbours. We are discussing this matter with the Republic of the Cameroun, discussing our common problems with Tchad, Congo Leopoldville, with Dahomey, and also we have a direct link with Togo. We hope to continue in this work because we feel that, if we are to unite, it is important that our communications system should be excellent and transport facilities should be such that it would enable us to move freely around, to move not only ourselves but to move our goods to different parts of the continent. Also, we have been trying in Nigeria to join other states in trying to discuss common problems—educational and scientific problems. . . .

Now, the Hon. President of the Sudan, I think, when he spoke, told us that we should be frank. I think it was the President of Malagasy who said that we in Africa do not want to speak the truth. We have a saying in Nigeria, which is that "Truth is bitter." I want to be frank; I want to tell the bitter truth. To my mind, we cannot achieve this African unity as long as some African countries continue to carry on subversive activities in other African countries.

Many of the members have spoken very strongly on the decolonization of the continent. I want to say that we in Nigeria are prepared to do anything to secure the freedom of the continent of Africa. There has been a suggestion that we should pull our resources together, that we should make arrangements, if necessary, to help the nationalists in different countries in Africa, which are still dependent, to fight their way to independence. We in Nigeria are prepared to do anything towards the liberation of all African countries. I have observed that when we give assistance to another country which is fighting for its independence, some of us are in the habit of imposing obligations on those States. That is wrong. If we give assistance to African people in any dependent territory, we should not ask for any obligation on their part; because that would come almost to the same point that many of the speakers have made that they would only accept foreign aid without any strings attached. I do not believe that any aid, no matter from where it comes, is without strings attached to it. Let us not fall into the same trap. If we assist any dependent territory in Africa, we must see to it that we do not attach conditions to our assistance. This is very, very important if we want to establish the solidarity of the continent of Africa, to make sure that any form of assistance we give is free. . . .

Now, I come to a very vital matter, which is the development of the continent. The African continent is very rich in resources but, unfortunately, these resources are not developed yet. We are born at a very difficult time: we have not the necessary capital, the necessary equipment, or the necessary know-how for the development of our continent. Therefore, we find it absolutely necessary to rely on outsiders for the development of the African territories. I would like to tell the conference that we must take every care to know whom we invite to assist in the development of our resources, because there is a fear, which is my personal fear, that, if we are not careful, we may have colonialism in a different form. Colonialism can take many different forms. Our countries can be colonialised economically, if we are not careful. Just as we have fought political domination, it is important that we fight against economic domination by other countries.

Let us not forget that we in Africa are part of the world. We have our international obligations as well. Whatever we do, we cannot isolate ourselves from the rest of the world. Therefore, in all that we do, and in all that we say, we should be careful because we belong to one human society. I always tell people that I do not believe in African personality, but in human personality. The African is a human being and, therefore, we have to see to the development of human personality in Africa. I think any talk of African personality is based on inferiority complex. I do not regard any human being—red, white, brown, yellow or green—as superior to me. I regard myself as equal to anybody. I am a human being.

Now, some people have suggested, and this is a thing which is already underway, the establishment of an African Development Bank. I hope that, when the Ministers of Finance of different countries of Africa meet in Khartoum, they will be able to produce something which should be of benefit to all of us. Also a suggestion has been made for the establishment of an African Common Market. This is a very good idea; but I must say that we in Nigeria feel that it is a very complicated matter. We want an African Common Market. But can we do it by taking the continent as a whole? Or can we do it by certain groupings in Africa? What appears to us to be more practical is that we should have an African Common Market based on certain groupings. We are thinking of a North African grouping which will include the Sudan; a West African grouping which will extend to the River Congo; an East African grouping which will include almost all the Central African countries. If we base our examination on these groupings, I think we will arrive at a very successful establishment of an African Common Market, because I think it is good for the trade of Africa. For example, the inter-State trade in Africa is 10 per cent, and 90 per cent is done with countries outside Africa. There is no reason why we should not increase the inter-State trade on this Continent. I think that if we are able to establish an African Common Market, we shall overcome many difficulties and we shall be in a position to stand on our own in relation to the other parts of the world. My fear of our being colonised will disappear if we are able to establish this African Common Market.

The question of disarmament was raised by several speakers. I think all of us feel strongly about this question. . . .

The mere fact that Africa has been declared a nuclear-free zone will not make Africa free in the event of a world war. If there is war, we in Africa will be directly involved. It is our concern that there should be peace in the world, and that there should be understanding among the great powers. Some people have suggested that we should organise ourselves into a Defence Bloc. Well, all of us have been talking about the bad nature of the armament race. It has been suggested that we should embark on an arms race in Africa. All of us know very well that we are at present incapable of joining in such a race. Our idea is that we should not be talking about an arms race. All we should talk about is how to stop it, and I would not suggest that we should join in that race at all.

A suggestion was also made that we should come together as a bloc in the United Nations. Well, that is a very good idea; but I must tell the conference that we in Nigeria hate the idea of blocs, and we do not like it. If we can find some kind of name for it, such as African Committee or an African "something," it will be much better, because the whole idea of blocs is revolting. I think we should try to find better names for these different groupings. I think that we have been working for some time now in the United Nations where our different representatives meet and discuss matters of common interest. May I suggest to the conference that it is time now that we find a permanent small secretariat for such an African Committee in New York? That does not mean, of course, that we will instruct our delegates to close their eyes to the wider issues of world problems. But, as a Continent which has suffered for so long and also as a people who have suffered for so long, I think we have to do everything to get our proper position in the United Nations Organisation. Some of us have suggested that we should seek greater representation in the Security Council and also in all the bodies of the United Nations Organisation. . . .

That world organisation, I have always maintained, is a sure guarantee of our African states. . . .

part three
The Middle East

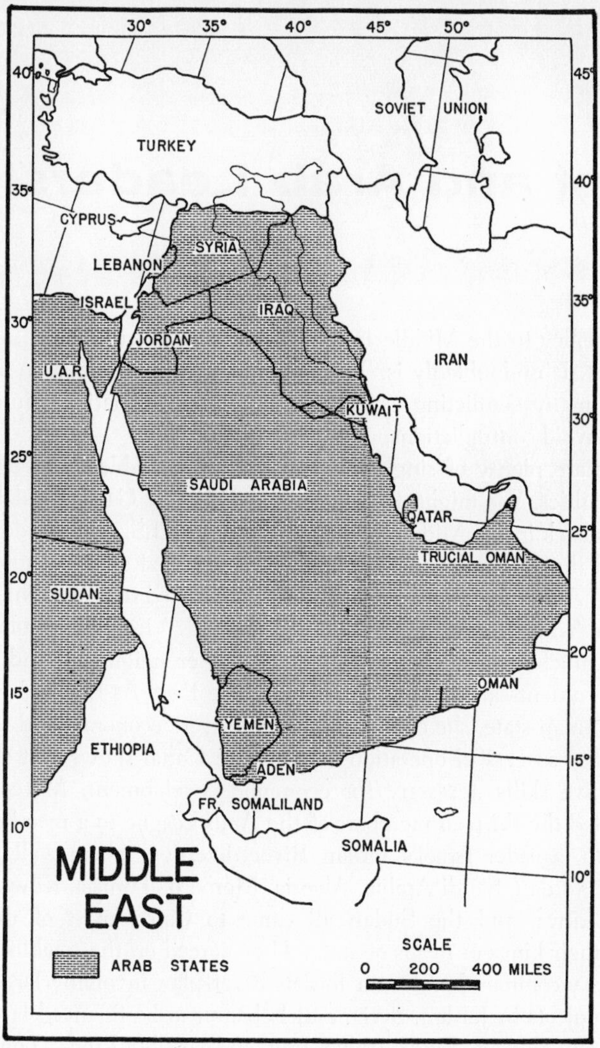
MIDDLE EAST
ARAB STATES
SCALE
0 200 400 MILES
TURKEY
SOVIET UNION
CYPRUS
SYRIA
LEBANON
ISRAEL
IRAQ
JORDAN
IRAN
U.A.R.
KUWAIT
SAUDI ARABIA
QATAR
TRUCIAL OMAN
SUDAN
OMAN
YEMEN
ETHIOPIA
ADEN
FR. SOMALILAND
SOMALIA
30°
35°
40°
45°
50°
10°
15°
20°
25°

7

Egypt and Arab Leadership

U.S. policy in the Middle East[1] is sometimes described as confused and inconsistent. It undoubtedly is. The only question is whether, in an area involving so many conflicting aspects of the American national interest, it is possible to avoid contradictions.

There are plenty of single-minded policies available, but each contains grave difficulties. We might, for example, decide that Gamal Abdel Nasser is the man to back in the Middle East. John Badeau, U.S. Ambassador in Cairo, has argued that Nasser's Egypt "has rapidly emerged as the dominant influence in the Arab world, and its revolution has spilled over the Nile Valley to become the 'wave of the future' in adjacent lands." Egypt's population of 27 million is much greater than that of any of her neighbors, and she has a stable government—an exception in the Middle East. As Leonard Binder and Alfred Sherman state, she continues to have severe economic and social problems; but her successful operation of the Suez Canal shows that she has the administrative skills necessary for economic development. Moreover, when Nasser called the thirteen members of the Arab League to a meeting in January 1964 to consider Israel's Jordan River diversion scheme, all responded. Iraq, Syria, Jordan, Saudi Arabia, Algeria, Morocco, Tunisia, Kuwait, Yemen, Lebanon, Libya, and the Sudan all came to Cairo, most of them represented by their kings or heads of state. They agreed on the establishment of a joint military command and on a Jordan River plan involving large-scale reclamation projects in Jordan, Syria, and Lebanon to be financed largely by oil revenues from Kuwait, Saudi Arabia, Iraq, and possibly Libya. The new Arab military command would back this venture. In addition, they made various moves toward amity on issues that had long divided members of the Arab League.

Yet to assume that we should therefore unequivocally support Nasser ignores other obstinate elements in the situation. First, Nasser's claim to be the natural and inevitable leader of a united Arab world was not established

[1] This chapter makes no attempt to deal with the non-Arab countries of the Middle East (Turkey, Iran, Afghanistan, and Pakistan). The Arab states are the core of the Middle East geographically as well as culturally. It is, however, in the "Northern Tier" non-Arab countries that the West has been able to find Middle Eastern allies. The Baghdad Pact, uniting Turkey, Iraq, Iran, and Afghanistan with the United Kingdom, was created in 1955. After the 1958 revolution, Iraq, the only Arab member-state, withdrew; in 1959 the pact was renamed the Central Treaty Organization and its headquarters were transferred to Ankara. In 1959, the United States made bilateral defense agreements with Turkey, Iran, and Pakistan although it has never accepted more than observer status in CENTO.

beyond dispute at the Arab League meeting of January 1964. This meeting, together with the December 1963 coup in Iraq, suggests that Nasser's prospects have improved since Alfred Sherman's analysis, but Sherman's point that the United Arab Republic (U.A.R.) consists of Egypt alone remains uncontroverted. And since coup and countercoup have followed in rapid succession in Iraq and Syria, it would be difficult to build a United States policy on any assumption that Arab unity is an immediate prospect. As for the kings and sheikhs who rule other Arab countries, the cordial discussions in Cairo will hardly lead them to a revolutionary nationalism led by Nasser, though in various degrees they are engaged in programs of modernization.

Second, U.S. companies have extensive Middle Eastern oil holdings, and so do the British—and the British are also concerned with keeping open their lifelines to the East. But, despite the fact that the British are our allies, we were compelled to move against them in the Suez crisis. We also took an opposing position in the Yemen dispute between the U.A.R. and Saudi Arabia. (We recognized the insurgent republican government in Yemen against the wishes of Saudi Arabia, Jordan, and Britain; yet we tried—fruitlessly—to get Nasser to withdraw his pro-republican troops from Yemen, so that our policy irritated almost all of the countries involved.)

Third, there is Nasser's neutralism. Charles D. Cremeans argues that we can live with this kind of neutralism—U.S. policy does not insist that we work only with those countries that support our positions with unflagging zeal. Still, one major objective of U.S. policy in the Middle East is to keep the Russians out; and Nasser's friendship with the Soviet (though not with Egyptian Communists) is bound to concern the State Department.

Finally, there is Israel. Nasser has argued that U.S. policy in the Middle East is determined primarily by domestic politics. But, even if there were no Jewish population in the United States, America would still not necessarily back the Arabs in all of their differences with the Israelis. Gamal Abdel Nasser and David Ben Gurion present opposing positions here on some of the issues concerning the two nations.

Essentially, the Arabs have not reconciled themselves to the existence of the state of Israel. On occasion, they have contended that they are not against the idea of a delimited Jewish as well as an Arab state in Palestine. Israelis, however, are convinced that the Arabs want to destroy Israel. Furthermore, Israel sees itself as a state with a special relationship to all the Jews of the world, and will do its best to encourage further immigration. The Arabs refuse to accept this role, and all the other issues stem from this essential difference. Inevitably, boundary differences lead to border tensions and hostilities; U.N. forces have managed to keep disturbances in check recently, but they cannot dispose of the underlying causes of hostility. The Arabs justify their political and economic boycott of Israel, including denial of transit through the Suez Canal, on the grounds that the Arab-Israeli war has never ended. There is, also, a continuing problem of Arab refugees—more than a million in Jordan, Syria, Lebanon, and the Egyptian-controlled Gaza strip, many in

U.N. camps. (Israel asserts that a half million of these are not really refugees, but people who claim to be in order to get U.N. ration cards.) Arab leaders contend that the only just solution to the refugee problem is to give these people the choice between compensation or return to their former homes. Israelis reply that they cannot absorb so many people, that the refugees should instead be settled permanently in the Arab countries, and that resettlement would have been accomplished by now but for the fact that the Arab leaders want to keep the issue alive for political purposes.

Another major source of contention, the immediate cause of the Arab leaders' meeting in January 1964, is the development of the Jordan River basin. In 1955, the U.S. tried unsuccessfully to get Arab and Israeli agreement on the Johnston plan for joint development of the basin. Since then, Israel has gone ahead with her own project, which she claims will take only the amount of Jordan water allocated to her under the Johnston plan—about 39 per cent of the total flow. The first stages of this project will move water 100 miles from Lake Tiberias (wholly within Israeli territory) to irrigate the Negev plain. Israel is not entirely happy with this plan, since Tiberias water has an even higher saline content than the Jordan River. The Arabs are totally opposed to it, for it means the settlement of more Israelis on the land and an improved military position in the Negev for Israel. (Estimates of the possible settlers have ranged into the millions; however, the population in the Negev will probably not increase by more than 50,000 in the forseeable future.)

The Arab conference in January 1964 proposed a joint Arab plan for Jordan River development. This proposal might portend a military confrontation with Israel, or it could be a face-saving formula designed to discourage—at least temporarily—a direct attack on the Israeli project by Syria, whose border disputes with Israel have been the bitterest of any of the Arab states. Even if the latter is the case, which would suggest a moderate, more cautious approach by Nasser toward Israel, harmony between the Arabs and the Israelis cannot yet be expected. Israel is still an issue on which all of the Arab countries can get together. Arabs and Israelis continue to suspect each other of planning war, and each side has purchased arms.

Alfred Sherman raises the specter of a nuclear arms race in the Middle East. Missiles must seem tempting to the Arabs in the light of their past defeats. Israel, with less than two and a half million people, would feel less vulnerable if she had nuclear weapons. Although immediate prospects of a nuclear arms race in the Middle East have probably been exaggerated, they are sufficient to cause apprehension among the great powers. Moreover, if the U.S. were to adopt an unequivocally pro-Nasser position, the Israelis might well decide that only a nuclear stockpile could enable them to survive.

All of these factors point up the difficulty of developing a consistent policy in the Middle East. The U.S. is thus unlikely to declare for Nasser without reservation. Yet Nasser, for all the ebbs and flows of his strength in the

Arab world, remains by far the most impressive and important leader in the region. The prospects are that we shall continue a series of policies that will be described by critics as muddled and self-contradictory and by proponents as pragmatic and flexible.

Nasser's Decade*

Alfred Sherman

Gamal Abdel Nasser has now held absolute power in Egypt for over a decade. During that time his regime has settled into a regular and recognizable—if not altogether stable—pattern. It has, moreover, developed along lines broadly similar in many of the newly created nationalist states—Ghana and Indonesia, for example—and has served as an inspiration if not actually a model, to some. And while it has proved to be neither a full-blown political or ideological system, Nasserism can no longer be viewed—as many of Nasser's critics, both in the Arab world and in the West, prefer to view it—as merely the particular reflection of a personal dictatorship.

What, then, is Nasserism and what are likely to be its long-range effects on Arab society? The now-certain failure of Nasser to realize his ambition for a centrally organized Eastern Arab federation under Egyptian hegemony, combined with the virtual disintegration of his hoped for "Casablanca bloc," provide what is perhaps the most convenient point for assessing both the phenomenon and its future. For these failures of his ambitions in foreign policy are no more fortuitous than his fantastic success in consolidating his position inside Egypt. And, though Western observers have usually paid more attention to the pan-Arab aspects of Nasserism than to its domestic political content, Nasser's policies for Egypt, unlike his aims for the Arab world as a whole—which are elusive and changeable, and by no means special to him—have undergone a clear and necessary evolution and tell us a good deal about "emerging" revolutionary society.

Nasser's regime of "Arab socialism," while diverging very considerably on the theoretical plane from Communism, nevertheless bears an enormous likeness in practice to Sino-Soviet society. Thus, for example, Nasser explicitly rejects the theory of class struggle, but he has still done away with private ownership and individual enterprise in one sphere of economic and cultural activity after another. His expropriations began with foreign-owned enter-

* Reprinted from *Commentary*, August 1963, pp. 151–157, by permission. Copyright 1963 by the American Jewish Committee. Mr. Sherman is a former correspondent for the BBC and the *London Observer*, and is a freelance writer in London.

prises and the large Egyptian-owned estates, moved on to indigenous non-Moslem businesses (Jewish, Christian, Greek, Syrian), and finally were extended to group after group of Moslem or Coptic Egyptians.

The purpose of these expropriations has not been to foster economic progress or efficiency (as many of Nasser's American and British apologists insist), but rather to consolidate and centralize his power—which has been further consolidated by his assumption of direct control over the communications media, culture and education, the armed forces, and religious life. Such enterprises as *Bank Misr,* for example, or the industrial empire of the Abboud brothers—spread through textiles, transport, chemicals, food packaging, engineering, and insurance—were, as Egyptian businesses, perfectly willing to co-operate with Nasser in speeding up the country's development and independence from foreign capital. But they, too, were in due course expropriated, along with publishing houses, newspapers, merchants, schools, contractors, and banks. In short, the distinctions between political and economic, civil and military, private and public—which are a prime feature of Western society—have eroded under Nasser in much the same way as they have in Soviet society.

The country's new ruling elite consists of its military leaders. Its second echelon of leadership is made up of junior army officers, former revolutionaries, journalists, civil servants, and those intellectuals who threw in their lot with Nasser in his early days. Next in line are schoolteachers, social workers, propagandists, land-reform administrators, and other minor officials and executives. The rest of the middle class and the intelligentsia—many of them people who had once hoped that the overthrow of Farouk would bring democracy to Egypt—co-exist with the regime as best they can. But these groups still account for only a tiny percentage of the population, the bulk of which is made up of peasants and the urban poor: workers, stall-keepers, unemployed, and hangers-on of all sorts without visible means of support. The new regime, to be sure, has involved itself far more than its predecessor in the problems of the villages and the peasantry—but with little effect. The peasants remain illiterate and as poor as they were, and local affairs are run in much the same manner as they have always been. The reforms of which the regime and its friends among the Western journalists are so proud—land-redistribution, resettlement, housing, rural cooperatives—have, according even to official statistics, affected only a small part of the population.

Part of Nasser's difficulty, not in maintaining his power—which seems assured beyond any question—but in establishing a real channel of communication between himself and the public, has been his inability to create a viable political party to represent the regime. His opposition, both actual and potential, has been thoroughly atomized; but on the other side, there is no organizational structure to rouse or mobilize grass-roots support: no party, that is, like the Republican party in Turkey before 1946, the Algerian F.L.N., Bourghiba's Constitutional party in Tunisia, or Nkhrumah's NCPP.

So far three attempts have been made to create a "Nasserist" party. The first was in 1953, when in cooperation with a group of former radical nationalist politicians, Nasser established the "Liberation Rally." Liberation Rally boasted a large membership and branches throughout the country, but it never gained its own momentum, and it had long since ceased to carry public weight by the time it was officially dissolved in 1958. Meanwhile, the "constitution" of 1956 had endorsed the formation of a "National Union" to realize the objectives for which the Revolution was started, and to concentrate efforts to build a sound political, social, and economic foundation for the country. But the N.U., too, was slow in getting started—and then short-lived. Early in 1958, Nasser set up its Supreme Committee, and in mid-1959—after Syria's accession to the U.A.R.—elections were held in both the Northern (Syrian) and Southern (Egyptian) regions. Finally, in 1961, following the break-up with Syria, Nasser dissolved the N.U. on the ground that it had been infiltrated by selfish people and other unsocialist elements.

The most recent attempt to create a Nasserist party was made in 1962, with the formation of a new organization, the "National Congress of Popular Forces," which was to take over the functions of the defunct Liberation Rally plus some supervisory duties in the economy and a role in the surrounding Arab world. What the actual relation of the Congress to the state bureaucracy is, however, does not yet seem to have been worked out in detail, and there is no evidence that it is any more vital or active than its two predecessors.

The ever increasing concentration of economic, political, and cultural power in the hands of the central government has served to intensify the traditional helplessness of the individual *vis-à-vis* the state—that helplessness which has always been the curse of Egyptian life. So long as the presence of Nasser himself can protect the over-all social and political structure from any really serious shock, therefore, Egyptian stability can be taken for granted. The fact that there is no political machinery for determining the succession does not in itself constitute an immediate problem. On the other hand, the regime's economic shakiness and its dependence on foreign aid do make it vulnerable. Nasser has failed to expand production of food and consumer goods. Not only is the *fellah* as badly off as ever, but the country's textile industry—so basic to the economy—must depend on American aid for its supplies of raw cotton, since nearly the whole of the local cotton crop is mortgaged to the Soviet bloc in payment for arms and other imports. If American aid, now approaching $500 million a year, were for any reason to be cut off suddenly, the result would be mass unemployment and a serious shortage of food. Under circumstances like these, the absence of a loyal party to back up the regime's military and administrative operations could become a very grave matter—if not, indeed, a decisive one.

Nasser's failure to surround his own power with an effective party also contributes to his inability to realize the dream of a united Arab world. This question, the problem of pan-Arabism, is for the most part improperly understood in the West. It is neither true that the only obstacles to Arab unity are retrograde feudal rulers and foreign interference, nor that the whole business is merely a political gimmick of Nasser's. Pan-Arabism—the belief that all Arab-speaking communities constitute a single nation—is, to be sure, of recent origin. It came to birth in the Levant at the turn of the century but did not take hold in Egypt until the late 1930's. Before then, Egyptian sympathies and aspirations had tended to run North-to-South (from Europe and the Mediterranean, and toward the upper Nile valley) while longings for an East-to-West Arab axis were suspected of being the expression of a reactionary clerical medievalism. The pioneer pan-Arabist in Egypt was none other than King Farouk, who dreamed of a restored Arab Caliphate—with himself as the first incumbent. Farouk was not devout, nor was his proposal ever precisely worked out; it was generally assumed, therefore, that he was chiefly interested in enhancing his prestige among traditionally minded Egyptians and counteracting the mass political appeal of the nationalists. Farouk's tactics were largely those used subsequently by Nasser: namely, to aggravate both anti-Western feelings and dissatisfaction with local dynasties in countries like the Sudan, Libya, Trans-Jordan, and Iraq through the agency of Egyptian teachers sent into other Arab countries, local nationalists, or students in Egypt returning home. It was Farouk's men who financed Col. Tal's assassination of Jordan's King Abdulla in 1951. And it was under Farouk, too, that Cairo's inflammatory broadcasts to the rest of the Arab world were initiated.

Yet Farouk's pan-Arabism misfired. His attempt to play a larger part than Egypt could manage in the Palestine War of 1948 brought about, or at least hastened, his overthrow. At first, the new revolutionary regime shunned pan-Arabism, returning to modern Egypt's traditional North-South preoccupations, and it was not until Nasser's original hopes for the quick reform and rehabilitation of Egyptian society had been crushed that he took up pan-Arabism seriously.

Pan-Arabism had much to offer Nasser. For one thing, it made an exciting slogan for the Egyptians; for another, it held out the promise of new political and military strength. Arab unification could help solve Egypt's economic problems, both by providing additional resources and by increasing Nasser's international nuisance value. And it could also bring him within striking distance of a second round against Israel, thereby buttressing his claim to be the true successor to Saladin. Yet despite the high prestige Egypt has always enjoyed in the Arab world, despite the instability of some of the existing regimes in that world, and despite the universal popularity of the notion of Arab-Moslem unity and solidarity, Nasser has hardly come any closer to realizing this ambition than Farouk did. Time and time again he has seemed to be on the point of success, only to fail in the end. Apart from a none too secure foothold in the Yemen, he is faced with an Arab world whose members are either avowedly hostile or pay lip service to solidarity while keeping him well at arm's length.

There are a number of good reasons for Nasser's failure here. First, though Arab societies have much in common with one another, many things besides their separate political histories divide them. Ethnic and linguistic differences, for instance, are very real (in Iraq, the Kurdish minority fears being completely swamped by a pan-Arab state, as does the Christian majority in Lebanon). In some Arab countries, too, dynastic and theocratic traditions remain vital. The fact is, the very term "Arab unity" means different things in different countries, and rarely does it carry Nasser's radical connotation. Even those of his Arab neighbors who admire Nasser are chary of becoming mere provinces of the Cairene metropolis and of sharing their countries' resources with twenty-seven million Egyptians, most of whom have a lower standard of living than is generally prevalent in the Arab world. Moreover, many people who favor unity in theory are opposed to the totalitarianism of Nasser's regime.

A case in point is the history of Nasser's relations with the Baath (Arab Socialist Resurrection Party). Like Nasser, the Baath is anti-imperialist and supports unity, socialism, and Afro-Asian solidarity. At one time or another the party has been highly influential in Syria, the Lebanon, Jordan, and Iraq. Yet within a year of Syrian-Egyptian unification in 1958—and despite the fact that its members were being persecuted by Kassem in Iraq and Hussein in Jordan for being pro-Nasser—Baath was ousted from power and eventually banned. Today in Syria and Iraq it constitutes the single most important obstacle to effective union with Egypt, although its leaders still wish to collaborate with Nasser against Israel (the Baath is strongly in favor of armed invasion), Communist infiltration, and Western influence. The reason for the head-on clash between Nasser and the Baath is quite simply that he can neither agree to its separate existence nor allow it the special position in the Arab world that it claims for itself.

It would appear that Nasser's passion for unifying the Arabs has intensified as the possibility of his doing so has receded. In the early '50's he enjoyed the advantage of being the first Arab ruler to make use of the paraphernalia of a dynamic modern dictatorship, combining revolutionary nationalism with Moslem xenophobia, playing on a cult of personality, and employing such devices as radio propaganda and underground activity. He was the only Arab leader with any real standing outside his own country, accepted by like-minded Afro-Asians, approved of by the Communist world, feared by the West. But by 1960, many other Arab leaders had caught up: Kassem, King Muhammed of Morocco (and later his son Hassan), Bourguiba. The Sudan had its own military dictatorship modeled on Nasser's, but with the primary purpose of keeping the country out of Egyptian hands. And every Arab state now had powerful new transmitters and teams of radio-warriors.

In addition to all this, the dissolution of the union with Syria in 1961 was (and remains) an enormous setback for Nasser. Yet defeat has only made him all the more intransigent. During the months following the Syrian secession he enunciated his theses on "Arab Socialism," which proposed Egypt as the "nucleus of liberty, unity and socialism of the whole Arab Nation." Egypt's duty, his argument ran, was to act as the spearhead of the Arab drive for unity, and as such, she was not obligated to "recognize outworn arguments about interference in the affairs of other Arab governments."

In the early '50's, too, it seemed that the "Palestine question"—that is, the question of how to overrun Israel and replace it with an Arab Palestine—would by itself aid enormously in unifying the Arabs, while also serving Nasser as a magical stick with which to beat all opponents. But even here things have failed to work out as expected. To be sure, Nasser has no difficulty whatever in whipping up the denizens of the refugee camps in Jordan, Lebanon, and Syria; and he can always count on the support of former Palestinians now living in Jordan. But this agitation has only resulted in determination by the Jordanian government to "integrate" the refugees into the national life as soon as possible in order to pacify them (the word "re-settlement" is taboo). Nasser's propagandists accuse his rivals of being "soft on Zionism"—but by now they have learned to pay him back in the same coin and to attack him in turn for allowing the United Nations Emergency Force to remain along his borders with Israel and for not closing the Straits of Tiran to Israeli shipping (which he could not do without risking an armed clash). Nasser's plan to create a "Palestine Entity" in Western Jordan, whose army would be under his control and which could serve as the springboard for an eventual attack on Israel, has been successfully resisted by Jordan, with the backing of the other Arab states. An attack on Israel must, for purely strategic reasons, await the achievement of a high degree of Arab unity, which would make it possible to set up a joint command and to deploy troops where they are most needed (i.e., Iraqui and Egyptian troops in Jordan, Syria, and Lebanon along Israel's exposed borders).

Since such a high degree of unity is at the moment politically unattainable, Nasser has been forced back to the idea of using an Egyptian attack on Israel as a lever for dominating the Eastern Arab world. But, given the present state of the Egyptian economy, the level of health and education, and the psychology of the people, Nasser would have to wait a long time before he could create a land army to match Israel's. His only hope against Israel, therefore, lies in some sort of technical breakthrough—missiles, or bacteriological, chemical, or atomic weapons—that would enable him to launch a sudden and unanswerable attack. This is what accounts for his recent employment of German and Austrian scientists.

Most of the experts agree that even with the aid of these scientists it will take a fairly long time for Nasser to develop weapons of mass destruction. But if and when he should acquire even something so modest as ground-to-ground missiles with conventional warheads, Israel will be faced with the necessity for an agonizing strategic reappraisal. So long as Nasser threatens only with land forces, backed by naval and air support, Israel can depend on her capacity for defense and counterattack. But at present there is still no defense against missile warfare, only a choice between deterrence and a pre-emptive strike. And, considering Nasser's previously demonstrated attitude toward the cost of military adventures, the Israelis cannot be expected to place too much faith in deterrence. It stands to reason, therefore, that if Nasser's first-strike capacity, in whatever form, comes near to being operational, the Israelis will be obliged to weigh the pros and cons of a pre-emptive attack. This decision, however, may not have to be made for several years, and in the meantime Nasser's main entanglements are likely to be with his Arab neighbors. So far as Israel is concerned, these entanglements are both an advantage and a curse, for while inter-Arab feuding mitigates the danger to her from Arab hostility, it also prevents the working out of an accommodation with Nasser.

Where Farouk tried to call in the Arab world to redress the political balance inside Egypt, Nasser has gone further by trying to build and lead an effective Afro-Asian bloc to enhance his prestige at home and in the Arab world and to increase his bargaining power with both East and West. Thus far, the attempt has been no more successful than his efforts toward Arab unity. The "Casablanca group," originally meant to be an all-African organization, never grew beyond its original six members (Egypt, the then provisional Algerian government, Morocco, Mali, Ghana, Guinea), and has largely disintegrated. Whenever he engaged in a direct conflict with the West, Nasser could be sure of solid Afro-Asian support—as, indeed, any Afro-Asian nationalist government could. But this solidarity has dissolved whenever he has tried to exploit it for the purpose of extending Egyptian hegemony, or of furthering the interests of the Soviet bloc as part of his bargains with Moscow. . . .

Nor has Nasser fared any better in mustering Afro-Asian support for use in his inter-Arab disputes or in his quarrel with Israel. Groups in which Communist or extreme "positive neutralist" influence is dominant, like the Casablanca group in its heyday, will back him, but wherever he has been involved with a broader spectrum of countries—such as he was at the 1961 Belgrade Conference or the recent African Conference in Addis Ababa—his campaigns against Israel and his Arab rivals have invariably been stopped short.

Nasser's relations with the West on one side and the Communist bloc on the other are marked by similar complications. His periodic assertions that he regards the Communist world as essentially friendly, and the Western world as unreliable if not hostile, are perfectly sincere. He and his generation grew up in a time and place dominated by the British and French empires; their political thinking still centers on a simple anti-colonialism—that is to say, anti-Europeanism. Added to this is the age-old hostility of the Moslem for the Christian West, which Nasser has been able to exploit in the interests of his own popularity. The West, moreover, seems likely to continue with a more or less benevolent attitude toward Israel, whereas the Soviet bloc follows a line of pure expediency on this question. The result is that for the past decade Egyptian and Soviet policies have moved in broadly parallel directions and any friction that has chanced to arise has been fairly easily ironed out.

As far as ideology per se is concerned, however, Western influence is still far greater among the Arabs than is that of Communism—thanks to all those decades of Western-controlled education, to the attraction of Western universities, the influx of Western publications, and the special role of the French and English languages. The Arab Communist parties, by contrast, have not made a very impressive showing. The prominence of the Communists in Iraq, where they managed to batten on the Kassem-Nasser feud for a while, seems to have been a flash in the pan, and Kassem had broken their back long before he himself was overthrown. Moscow has come to understand this apparent paradox and to accept with equanimity the persecution of Arab Communists by governments with which the Soviet regime wishes to remain on good terms, including Nasser's. There is, to be sure, a sharp contradiction between Moscow's claim to universal leadership of progressive mankind and its de facto cooperation with "national-bourgeois" regimes, but we have no reason to doubt Nasser's repeated assurances that this contradiction casts no present shadow over Soviet-Egyptian relations.

Khrushchev, however, has carefully abstained from anything that might be interpreted as approval of pan-Arabism in general or of Nasser's own striving for hegemony in particular. Even in the case of regimes which are anathema to Moscow, like the Jordanian, Libyan, and Saudi Arabian, Soviet propaganda pointedly refrains from questioning their right to separate statehood. This question could conceivably become an Egyptian-Soviet bargaining counter, but since there is little if anything that Russia could effectually do to help Nasser in his drive for hegemony over the Arab world, neither side has raised the issue. At one time Nasser, like Tito, made great play in his propaganda of being able to lead sections of the Arab and Afro-Asian world in the Soviet direction. In practice, though, this has come to mean little. The real motive for Soviet aid and comfort to Nasser is, as it has always been, his role as a major threat to the West's position in the Middle East, and not the hope that he will become an ideological ally.

American policy toward Nasser is much less straightforward; indeed, from the point of view of logic, it seems to make no sense, swinging back and forth as it has from extremes of generosity to extremes of hostility. In 1956, for example, within the space of one year, Dulles suddenly withdrew the promise of American aid for the Aswan Dam, then vigorously supported Egypt against the Anglo-French-Israeli attack, and then once again embarrassed Nasser by enunciating the "Eisenhower Doctrine." State Department policy nowadays is predicated on the idea that by massive aid Nasser can be weaned away from his dependence on the Soviet bloc and brought to concentrate on the economic and social development of his country. In answer to any marshaling of evidence that this policy has not changed Nasser's behavior in the least, Washington offers the assurance that though Nasser has his faults like everyone else, he will come around if enough patience is shown.

Summing up, then, we can see that after ten years of rule Nasser has at least one thing in common with Farouk: he too has chosen to stake his political appeal primarily on pan-Arabism and has met with a series of crushing setbacks. Nor have his domestic achievements been of an order to compensate for such defeats—particularly the critical recent breakdowns in negotiations over federation with Iraq and Syria. The economy, overstrained with development projects—some legitimate, others not—record military expenditures, and the vast administrative overhead inevitable in a regime like Nasser's, annually becomes more dependent on foreign aid. The only thing to prevent the Western powers from applying the economic sanctions that would necessarily bring Nasser to heel is their fear that his downfall would open the way for a Communist takeover. Yet if there is today a real danger of Communism in Egypt—whereas such a danger was negligible in 1952—Nasser himself bears the largest burden of blame: it was he who made modern totalitarianism fashionable in the Middle East and who in large measure abetted the Soviet political breakthrough into Africa.

Nasser's Foreign Policy*

Charles D. Cremeans

Nasser has given his foreign policy the label "positive neutralism." Like the doctrines which bear the label of Arab nationalism, the foreign-policy doctrines which bear this name are essentially pragmatic and leave plenty of room for modification and adjustment to individual situations. The essential idea behind "positive neutralism," like that behind Arab nationalism, is independence. "Positive neutralism," Nasser has said, "means independence. In other words I do not yield to one bloc, nor to the influence of any power, and I avoid zones of influence." Nasser's neutralism means action; it is not passive. He has said ". . . our policy is decided in accordance with our interests and in accordance with our conscience. This is the difference between positive and passive neutrality. The latter does not care about what is going on in other parts of the world, but positive neutrality means that our policy is based on our interests." His brand of neutralism does not preclude self-defense: "Our call for neutrality is one thing and our right to self-defense against any aggression is another," he said in an interview in 1958.

Nasser has repeatedly asserted that his policies reflect Egyptian and Arab interests which are independent of the interests and ideologies of the great-power blocs. The criticism most commonly leveled against him in the West, however, is that his neutralism—if it is neutral at all—leans toward the Communist bloc, and in fact, on major international issues he has stood with the

* From *The Arabs and the World: Nasser's Arab Nationalist Policy,* by Charles D. Cremeans, pp. 278–286, 301–304. Published by Frederick A. Praeger, Inc., for the Council on Foreign Relations, 1963. Reprinted by permission. Mr. Cremeans is a consultant on Middle Eastern affairs to the U.S. Government.

Communist bloc more often than with the West. This seems to prejudice his claim to a neutral and nonaligned position.

The five principal objectives of Nasser's foreign policy are: (a) independence and security from external domination for the entire Arab area; (b) arms with which to build military strength; (c) the economic development of Egypt; (d) regional political and economic development and unity; (e) the end of "colonialism" in Asia and Africa and the development of Afro-Asian solidarity in international politics independent of the two great-power blocs.

The realization of these objectives would be acceptable, and probably advantageous to the West. To the Communist bloc they are in the long run unacceptable. Yet Nasser's efforts to achieve them more often than not are carried on in an atmosphere of Sino-Soviet approval and Western disapproval. The circumstances that explain this paradox are significant.

The Objective of Independence

. . . To the Westerner, it is likely to appear that the issue of Arab independence has been resolved, or nearly so, since the remaining areas of special Western influence are insignificant and are likely soon to gain their freedom. From this point of view, all Nasser's screaming about imperialism appears to be bad manners or chicanery, or both. To the Arab nationalist, however, it does not seem that independence is entirely won. Furthermore, renewed Western intervention by force seems entirely possible. Arab independence and security from great-power interference is an objective with which the West has every reason to agree, but the Soviets usually manage to appear to be supporting the Arabs on this point, although independence is the last thing they want for the Arabs over the long run.

The Objective of Military Strength

The objective of obtaining arms has been important to Nasser for a number of reasons. A strong and loyal army has been both a political necessity and, potentially at least, a support to his policies in the Arab area.

American and British policy has been to provide arms in substantial quantities to Arab states only on the basis of an explicit or implied political alliance, as in the case of Jordan and formerly of Iraq, and also to maintain some kind of balance between Arab and Israeli military power. Convinced as he has been of the reality of the Israeli military threat and of the existence of a considerable body of opinion in the Western governments that his downfall would be in the interest of the West, Nasser found irresistible the Soviet offer to supply him with arms at reasonable prices and in generous quantities in exchange for cotton which he had in good supply, no questions being asked about the ability of his armed forces to absorb them.

Furthermore, the Soviet arms have been made available in such a way as to meet the conditions which he had insisted were necessary for the protection of Arab sovereignty. Arms agreements have been made between the Soviet bloc and Egypt and the U.A.R. without stated political conditions, without the requirement of an alliance, express or implied, without inspection of their disposition and use, generally with abundant spare parts, and with technicians provided only on Egyptian and Syrian request and only for such periods as they were wanted. There have been exceptions to the general pattern: arrogant Soviet officers, technicians who tried to preach communism, periods when spare parts or certain kinds of additional equipment were especially difficult to obtain, and a few occasions when Nasser's anti-Communist policies were brought up when he made requests for more arms.

When asked if the mere fact of dependence upon Soviet arms supplies does not involve a commitment, Nasser has always insisted that he accepted Soviet arms only so long as there was no commitment involved and that he was ready to take the risks involved in breaking off the relationship if necessary. . . .

Nasser has consistently demonstrated his determination to oppose local Communist activity in the Arab world and on occasion has shown that he means what he says about risking the breakup of his relationship with the Soviets if he feels his independence threatened. He knows as well as anyone that the Soviet willingness to supply him with arms is not disinterested. He certainly understands that the Soviets consider that they receive adequate compensation for their arms by the fact that they thereby thwart Western designs in the Arab area and win the Arabs' favor by providing them with the means to defend themselves against a threat that they believe is Western in origin. He also knows that the worse relations are between the Arabs and the West the better the Soviets like it. The question is whether he feels, consciously or unconsciously, that in order to keep the arms channel open it is sometimes useful to provide the Soviets with a *quid pro quo* by attacking the West more vigorously than he otherwise might.

The Objective of Economic Development

Nasser is aware that the economic development of Egypt cannot take place successfully without extensive assistance from outside. Fearing dependence upon one of the two protagonists in the cold war he has hoped to benefit from their rivalry and, on balance, he has succeeded. The United States has granted substantial aid and, under Public Law 480, has sold him wheat for Egyptian pounds, half of which are loaned back to him. From the Soviet bloc he has obtained substantial low-interest loans and cotton barter deals which have enabled him to purchase arms, industrial equipment, and some manufactured goods. There has been a rough balance in the over-all quantity of assistance from American and Soviet sources.

The impression given, however, by Nasser himself and by the Egyptian press and radio is usually that the United Arab Republic has considerably more reason for gratitude to the Soviet bloc than to the United States. The reasons for this are extremely complex, but probably boil down, as do so many other matters in Nasser's and the Arab posture, to . . . basic psychological factors. . . . One is the more spectacular and dramatic character of Soviet aid projects. There are also aspects of the general American approach to the provision of foreign aid, irritating to its recipients almost everywhere, which have been particularly aggravating to the sensitive Arab temperament. The complexity of American aid agreements, the great length of time required to complete the administrative procedures before aid which has been promised is actually allocated and delivered, the elaborate machinery for checking and inspecting its use, and the important consideration that American aid has been available only on a year-by-year basis, making long-term projects difficult and risky—all these have adversely affected the Arab evaluation of American assistance, especially in Egypt and Syria. In the field of technical assistance, the American system of sending technicians under the control of the American aid mission for set periods of time has contrasted unfavorably with the Soviet system of making technicians available at the request of and under the authority of the U.A.R. government and of keeping them in the country only so long as the local authorities wanted them.

On numerous occasions some minor irritation has caused an outburst against American aid. Nasser attacked the United States in April and early May of 1960, when U.S. congressmen questioned the continuation of U.S. aid to Egypt while it denied to Israel freedom of transit through the canal. He said: "We tell these people, brethren, and we also tell these Senators, that if Israel and Zionism dominate the U.S. Senate and if the American people bow to and are dominated by Zionism it is because Zionism, through bribery and corruption, exercises domination over the lives and livelihood of many leading Americans." He explained to the senators "who threaten to starve us by ceasing to provide us with wheat" that the American wheat shipments to Egypt were simple commercial transactions supported by loans at 4 per cent interest. He failed to point out that grain purchases under PL 480 are quite different from the normal commercial transaction.

Opening a spinning mill at Damietta built with funds from a Soviet loan, the Egyptian leader said: "In spite of the clouds that have, at times, loomed over our relations, the economic agreement (signed in January 1958) was never affected. At no time did the Soviet Union utter one single word threatening to boycott us economically and on no occasion did the Soviet reproachfully remind us of the economic aid they extended to us or the loans they provided for our industrialization schemes."

It is hard to believe that President Nasser does not understand that the American system permits, and in fact encourages, discussion of every aspect of government activity and that, given the size and outlook of the American Jewish population, discussion of any aid given to him, including a lot of adverse comment, is inevitable. Soviet aid, however, appears to be more graciously and generously given, partly as the result of circumstances and partly owing to careful contrivance.

Nasser's specialists who handle the development program often appear in private to understand the differences in Soviet and American aid better than the President's public statements would indicate that he does. They understand that low interest rates on Soviet credits are usually canceled out by high prices, and that the quality of Soviet equipment is often much below the Western standard. Bloc technicians, though they may lack some of the irritating qualities of the Americans, often are arrogant and difficult to deal with. The Egyptians, despite their commitment to a planned socialist economy, are eager for the advice of American and other Western economic planners.

In the early years of Nasser's regime the phrase "no strings attached" was in common use. In military assistance agreements, it referred to provisions granting rights of inspection and control to the Western donors, making them, in the eyes of the Egyptians, the senior, controlling partners. In economic aid agreements, it meant the attachment of political conditions such as the Egyptians apparently believed the United States and the World Bank wanted to attach to the High Dam agreement. The continuation of assistance, they believed, would have been contingent upon their satisfying the other parties to the agreement that Egyptian affairs were properly conducted. In the agreement for building the second stage of the Aswan High Dam, the critical issue was not political conditions but rather the choice between two alternatives. If Nasser was really interested in balancing the amount of aid he received from the East and from the West, he might have preferred to obtain aid for the second stage of the project from the West. However, the West offered a combination of separate agreements, some on an annual basis, with several countries and institutions, while the Soviet offered the whole thing in one package. Western leaders also showed a certain lack of enthusiasm for the project, which would certainly have been the subject of debates in Congress and in the American press. Hence, on balance, Nasser's acceptance of the Soviet offer seems to have been logical and practical.

The Objective of Regional Development and Unity

The U.S. government has indicated that it has nothing against Arab unity so long as it is accomplished in accordance with the popular will freely expressed. The Soviet Union has reiterated its support for Arab unity. Nasser probably believes, however, that neither of the two great powers would like to see the Arab states united, and particularly not under his leadership. The U.S. point of view is affected by the belief that unity under Nasser would bring unwelcome changes; the end of the friendly and cooperative regime of King Hussein of Jordan and a transformation in the present role of Lebanon as a kind of entrepôt for Western ideas in the Arab East. There is also the question of the oil concessions granted by Arab rulers with whom the West has established relatively satisfactory relations. Moreover, Nasser has been so often intransigent in his attitude toward the United States that, if he were to gain control of the entire Arab East, there is every reason to expect he would prove even more difficult to deal with. He might even mobilize the resources of the area for a showdown with Israel.

Nasser surely knows that the leaders of the Soviet bloc would be equally opposed to Arab unity under his leadership. It suits their purpose to support him when such support erodes the Western position and encourages anti-Western activity. But having a "bourgeois dictator" like Nasser in a position to consolidate the resources of the Middle East behind an independent and anti-Communist policy would be quite another thing.

Though the Soviets do not look with favor on Arab unity, they support every sort of opposition to the conservative Arab regimes which for the most part object to Nasser's revolutionary nationalism. Nasser, for his part, naturally does not repudiate such support and therefore often appears to be in league with the Soviets on an issue on which both he and they know they cannot agree.

Nasser undoubtedly believes that U.S. activities at the time of the Syrian crisis in 1957 and the U.S. landings in Lebanon in 1958 were designed to prevent his gaining the upper hand in those countries. Also he must regard the frequent mention of the likelihood that Israel would intervene militarily if a pro-Nasser coup were to take place in Jordan as warning that the West will not tolerate steps toward Arab unity under his banner. But he must also recognize that Soviet maneuvers in Syria in the summer of 1957 and 1958 and in Iraq in 1959 had the same objective in view. Thus, on balance, his interest in Arab unity does not put him on the side of either of the great-power groupings.

The Objective of Ending Colonialism through Afro-Asian Solidarity

On this issue the Soviets have all the advantages and the United States most of the possible disadvantages. Imperialism, as stated by Nasser and many Afro-Asians, links the United States and the West with the evils of the past and the present and puts on them the burden of reform. This means, first, giving up all authority and control and then providing economic assistance "with no strings attached" to the emerging nationalist states. Steps taken by the Western nations to promote independence are often ascribed, not just by Nasser but by a substantial proportion of the Afro-Asian community, to weakness and response to pressure.

On these issues Nasser has had no hesitation in repeatedly voting with the Soviet bloc in the U.N. His point is that the Soviets, being on the right side, are voting with him and the other Afro-Asians rather than the other way around. The United States, by contrast, abstained from voting on the resolution put forward at the end of the Fifteenth Session of the General Assembly calling for an end to colonialism. When the American press criticized him on his voting record, Nasser answered in anger:

Positive neutrality means that we are the enemy of our enemies and the friend of our friends. NATO is our enemy in Algeria. NATO is showing us enmity by helping and arming Israel. NATO, the Western states and Western imperialism are showing us enmity and fighting our principles, yet we insist on principles.

What do the Americans say? They say that we are not neutral because we voted 14 times with the Russians and did not vote once with them. We tell them they should understand we do not sell our votes. Our votes are not for sale to them or to the Russians or others. We vote in accordance with our principles.

Take the case of the resolution submitted by the Afro-Asians against imperialism. How could we vote with them so long as they did not vote in support of the resolution which denounced imperialism and recommended the liquidation of imperialism. We vote in accordance with principles. If the Americans see that we do not vote with them, it is because they vote against the principles of freedom which they announced after the Second World War and the Atlantic Charter, which Roosevelt announced, yet on which they later turned their backs.

Nasser and the U.S.

. . . Over the years Nasser has become more and more plaintive on the subject of American attitudes. He points out repeatedly that "every Israeli point of view meets with great attention from you, and every Arab point of view only meets with neglect." "The New York newspapers," he has said, "are always writing about the rights of Israel but they never mention the rights of the Palestine Arabs to return to their land. . . ." Zionist control of the American press, Zionist influence in the American government, Zionist influence in American intellectual circles, Zionist influence in American business and finance—in Nasser's opinion and in that of most of his advisers, this all-pervasive and all-powerful influence explains the unfavorable attitude of the United States toward the Arab cause.

Nasser and his advisers seem to believe that the United States never does anything about the Arab situation, except when the pressure of events forces it to take action. In their view, it seems logical that they can get action from the United States only by building fires under the American people and government and that they can make us reconsider our position only by heaping abuse on us. The United States can save itself, they believe, only if it heeds the warnings of the neutralist nations. Because of the importance of the Arab and Afro-Asian peoples in international affairs, the United States must eventually take heed of them and grant them their due.

The difference in Nasser's treatment of the Soviet Union and the United States is explained in part by Nasser's belief that, whereas the leaders of the Soviet Union have calculated the international situation precisely and are working with great skill to take advantage of the inevitable trends of the times, the Americans are unaware of those trends or are being misled by special interest groups to take a course contrary to their own national interest and to the interests of the neutral nations. The Russians do not need to be waked up; there is no point in jeopardizing by unnecessary attacks the arms supplies and other assistance he gets from them. The Americans, on the other hand, he believes, are so preoccupied with irrational fears of communism that they cannot understand the most important fact of our time: that a world revolution bringing a third force of Afro-Asian nations into being is changing the whole pattern of world affairs. They are being betrayed by the Zionists and by the European imperialists who are still interested in exploitation of Asia and Africa. The United States must be waked up to the realities of the world situation; its power is needed to balance that of the Soviet bloc, but it should be exerted in favor of the independence of small peoples, not against it.

From the point of view of the West, the important questions about Nasser and his policies are not whether they are pro-Western or Communist. The evidence seems clear that they are neither. The important questions are whether they represent major historical forces at work in the Arab world, forces which must be seriously dealt with in one way or another; and, if this is so and Western policy takes account of it, whether Nasser and the people to whom he turns for advice and support have the honesty and the capability necessary to bridge the gulf that now separates the West from the majority of the Arabs, as well as much of the rest of the ex-colonial world.

. . . Nasser's Arab nationalist foreign policies represent valid historical forces. Nasser's has been the strongest and the most dramatic voice speaking for those forces, although it is not the only one. Arab nationalism speaks through many voices. He has captured the mood of the moment and seen the demands of the times.

The authoritarian practices characteristic of Nasser's government, and particularly his management and control of the press and public opinion, are often cited as fundamental weaknesses. But these practices do not differ substantially from those employed in most Arab countries, or in other developing countries in Africa and Asia. They must be related to the stage of political and social development in which the Arabs find themselves, and to the outside interference to which they are subjected. A real question, of course, is whether Nasser and his regime can adapt to changing conditions, whether they have the will and the strength eventually to permit the gradual relaxation of restrictions on public discussion and popular participation in the political process.

One can choose from a wide range of opinion on Nasser the man and on other Arab nationalist leaders and potential leaders throughout the Arab world. In the end any judgment on their honesty, sincerity, and on their dedication to the welfare of their people must be highly subjective. In the opinion of the present writer, Nasser and nationalists of similar stripe throughout the Arab world are honest and trustworthy in their dedication to national goals. What is more important, some of them are marked by a sincerity and commitment to the future of their people that is unusual. Their conduct is less influenced by self-interest than is that of the holders of power in the traditional governments in that part of the world. Their greatest weaknesses . . . are the consequences of the situation out of which they come. Their capacity for growth and development, and for setting aside the suspiciousness, toughness, and lack of restraint which have marked their early years in power, will determine their future and the future of the Arab world.

With all their shortcomings and human weaknesses the Arab nationalists are a real factor in their part of the world today. The United States cannot leave them out of account. It cannot deal with them only to the extent that they meet our standards of respectability. We must deal with them because they are there, because they or men like them will continue to hold political power and determine foreign policy in the Arab world.

Arab Socialism*

Leonard Binder

For many observers, the true nature of the political phenomenon known as "Nasserism" is to be understood in terms of the social change taking place in the Arab countries. Although the full explication of this view is extremely difficult, due to the absence of relevant empirical data and our limited understanding of the operative mechanism which relates social change to political protest and political protest to declared policy, it is nevertheless possible to elaborate on the idea itself. In its simplest form, the social change thesis holds that as a result of Western European pressures—economic, political, and military—on the Ottoman Empire, the traditional structure of Islamic society grew weaker, and new classes, rival elites, were created which challenged the existing distribution of social, economic, and political values. Although this social movement was at first moderate in its demands, its radicalism increased with the increase in the ranks of the new classes and with the increasing awareness of the weakness and economic and technical backwardness of the Islamic countries. From seeking military and bureaucratic reform it moved to demanding a constitutional form of government, then to opposition to foreign influence, to popular sovereignty, to secularism, to land reform, and more recently to socialism. In the Arab countries under the Ottoman Empire, the constitutional phase was followed by demands for independence. These political demands with implications of opposition to the traditional military,

* "Nasserism: The Protest Movement in the Middle East," in Morton A. Kaplan (ed.), *The Revolution in World Politics* (New York: John Wiley & Sons, Inc., 1962), pp. 163–171. Reprinted by permission of the author. Mr. Binder is Professor of Political Science at The University of Chicago.

the bureaucratic aristocracy, the ulama, the landowners, and to foreign and minority groups were justified by a nationalist ideology.

The hard facts at our disposal are few, but what there are of them indicate that the dominant ideology among the new classes, and especially among the Sunni Arabs of these classes, is pan-Arabism—probably under the leadership of President Nasser. If we proceed further for non-evaluative data to help us understand these things, we may attempt to assess the interests of these classes and compare those interests with the policies of social reform being carried out in the UAR. As we may now expect, these policies have been formed in the crucible of events, having been but vaguely fixed in the minds of the leadership before the revolution. The general direction was there, as part of the explanation of pre-revolutionary reality, but the method of achieving these goals was not at all clear, as Nasser himself has said. When once we have been able to compare these interests and policies, should we find some hiatus between the two, we shall then have some idea of the nature and strength of the ideological residuum.

The two most important of the groups bearing the new nationalist ideology are the military and the bureaucracy. These are not the only ones to have been affected by the changes of the last century and a half. The peasantry has been disturbed by the sometimes amazing growth of its numbers, by changes in tax-farming procedures, by new title-settlement procedures, by the change to cash crops in many places, by new irrigation systems which have relieved the peasant of ownership or control over his water requirements, and by extension of the network of modern transport and mass media to some rural areas. Tribes have been settled, decimated, moved to new areas, have had their traditional leaders removed, and have had their products replaced in the markets. Small merchants and artisans have been weakened by the competition of standardized manufactures and a new class of importers and wholesale dealers; their guilds have been dissolved, the activities of their semi-religious organizations have been restricted, their sources of credit have dwindled, and their dependence upon the bureaucracy has increased. The ulama have lost their independence of government and their financial independence, and have lost much influence and prestige at the same time. Whole new classes have come into being in the cities. There is a new and growing industrial labor group; a very large group in the lower services category: hawkers, porters, car-watchers, sweepers, doormen, garbage collectors, and domestics; a much smaller group engaged in finance, foreign trade, and industry; a new group of professionals: doctors, lawyers, accountants, engineers, professors, and economists and, at much lower levels, journalists, teachers, nurses, technicians, and artists.

But the earliest changes, deliberately instituted, were in the military and then in the bureaucracy, as a means of coping with the military pressures exerted from Europe. Efforts to modernize the military are a century and a half old, but the armies of the Middle East still reflect the characteristic dichotomy of modernity and often squalid traditionality which renders every Middle Eastern city incomprehensible to foreigners and an irritant to its middle-class inhabitants. The officer corps, but not the ranks, belongs to the modern middle class, though whenever imperialism held sway, or whenever there were important minorities, the officer corps was not "nationalized" until recent times; and then it was nationalized only where patriarchal forms of government had all but disappeared. (Until 1936, for example, the Egyptian army officer corps was predominantly Turkish, Circassian, or otherwise aristocratic in social origin.) These armies have been expanded, yet not so much as to account for their great influence. Their influence in recent times is not due to their size, but to their modern weapons, to the political impotence of the bulk of the urban classes, to the gradual loss of religious legitimacy by traditional rulers, and to the lack of cohesiveness among middle-class urban groups.

Students are still largely embryonic civil servants, and civil servants of the lower ranks are vestigial students. In these two groups we find the largest part of the urban middle class, especially in the politically dominant capital city. These, together with the far fewer professionals, high and low, create the climate of nationalist opinion; they read, listen, discuss political events, applaud or denounce government policy, and belong to political parties; but rarely do they create a government or bring one down. These are the ones described as educated, cultured, or as belonging to the intelligentsia, and it is the climate of their opinion which has provided the military with an ideology, even though the military was the first to be exposed to Western learning.

Nevertheless revolutionary governments dominated by the military, even when they have learned the extent of their dependence upon the bureaucracy, are not the exponents of bureaucratic interests, but more nearly the exponents of the middle-class ideology which was created to justify those interests. The distinction is important because the justification is made in general nationalist and often socialist terms, in the interest of the inarticulate peasantry and the relatively small class of workers. More emphasis is given to the interests which must be curbed rather than to those which must be benefited. The military, however, does not hesitate to include itself in this conception of the national interest. The six goals of the Egyptian revolution include the creation of a strong national army, along with statements of opposition to imperialism, feudalism, and monopoly capitalism. The other goals of establishing social justice and a truly democratic system are extremely vague in meaning, and . . . the Free Officers were at a loss as to how to achieve these ends when they came into power.

It is by no means easy to reconstruct the desires of the urban middle classes at the time of the revolution, but we may hazard a few generalizations. There can be little doubt that most would as soon have had Farouk go, and no doubt that all except some in the Canal cities wanted the British army to leave Egypt. If we bear in mind that many of the professionals are actually government employees, we may easily conclude that there was a broad consensus that salaries and allowances had to be raised, the cost of living lowered, inflation stopped, the rules for the protection of civil servants expanded and adhered to closely, promotions given regularly according to the book, and political victimization stopped. Low-cost housing was needed, bribery and corruption in the bureaucracy were sources of complaint, and the extension of urban amenities to outlying quarters was demanded. The great influence of the landowning class was felt by many to be the reason for the failure to realize these objectives and for the corruption of parliamentary democracy.

Another general aspiration existed, expressed as the need for industrialization or economic development, but perhaps just as often sensed in the discomfort or insecurity of life in an environment of immense social, economic, and cultural contrast. Doubtless, many feel that they will benefit directly from economic development and the spread of literacy and education; but many benefit at present from the easy availability of cheap menial services. More, however, fall into neither category but are ashamed of the squalor of the metropolis and feel that the economic and social conditions now prevailing do not afford the environment in which a respectable civil servant can live a moderately ostentatious bourgeois existence.

If the foregoing is a fair representation of the demands of the nationalist classes in Cairo, it is not unreasonable to suppose that the Free Officers were well aware of them. They are, after all, sprung from the same classes; their families were spread throughout many occupations, not excluding agriculture. Nor is it true that they had no objectives whatsoever when they took power. The objectives they had were mainly those which had been adumbrated, but not realized, under the monarchy. In many ways the revolution is a more vigorous continuation of pre-revolutionary tendencies.

Not only in international questions and in the issue of British occupation was the position of the Revolutionary Command Council similar to that of the Wafd, but the proposal for the High Dam at Aswan already existed. There had been a number of efforts to restrict landownership and regulate tenancy, most of which had failed. Cooperatives had been established but did not work too well. Various community-development projects for agricultural areas had been started but were not really off the ground. Food subsidies were granted on certain staples to ease the lot of the urban lower classes. Industrialization plans were being worked on. Expenditure on education was increasing yearly, and the right of labor to organize was recognized.

These facts have led some to argue that the revolution was "unnecessary," but a great many more feel that landowner domination of parliament and the king constituted formidable roadblocks to progress. The Free Officers swept them out of the way and proceeded as vigorously as they might to realize those projects which were already on the order of the day. The army was, of course, a direct beneficiary of the new regime, and large landowners were hurt, but it is difficult to single out any other group as having been particularly favored or marked for penalization. As the government's domestic policy developed, however, the position of some improved while that of others declined. And, it should be borne in mind, domestic, social, and economic policy is still not fixed. . . .

Not only have all banks and insurance companies been nationalized, but most large industrial establishments are government controlled and managed through three organizations: the Economic Development Organization, the Nasr Organization, and the Misr Organization. Eighty-two per cent of all non-agricultural investment is currently being made by the "Public Sector." The national income of Egypt was about 1267 million pounds during 1960–61, while the government planned to spend over 700 million pounds in the regular development budgets. Indirect taxes still account for much more than any other source of revenue for the regular budget, while profits from the Suez Canal and from government-owned companies, especially the nationalized British, French, and now Belgian concerns, contribute to the development budget. As a consequence, development policy is almost entirely a government affair; private investment, except through the purchase of shares of government companies, is no longer encouraged in fact. Even new enterprises requiring as little as 1000 pounds capital must receive the approval of the Ministry of Industries, and all obvious loopholes are stopped up by the usual austerity regulations on imports, building, currency, rents, foreign travel, and prices.

About 10 per cent of Egypt's agricultural land has been redistributed, and paternalistic cooperatives have been established in the villages of these areas, though it is hoped to expand the system to include all agricultural areas. Education and health, community development, agricultural extension, and labor exchange services have all been increased, some more and some less. New labor legislation has given some additional protection to industrial workers. Adequate supplies of staple foods have been assured, and fixed prices generally prevail in the markets.

Still, Egypt's problems are very great. Rural destitution remains the rule. Migration to the big city is unabated. The population continues to increase at a rate sufficient to counterbalance development. The universities turn out more graduates, B.A.'s, M.D.'s, social workers, and lawyers than can find employment. The regular service is overstaffed yet granted to specialized organizations working under their own regulations and hiring the graduates of special institutes, the Faculty of Commerce, or retired Army officers. The professional classes feel the squeeze as austerity is tightened and their clients become more circumspect about fees.

It is clear that the UAR is engaged in a difficult race against time and the birth rate. It has set itself a plan to double the national income in ten years, a plan which is heavily dependent on foreign currency to pay for capital goods, and it hopes to avoid all inflation during that period.

From the foregoing it would appear that the nationalist classes are not much better off economically than they were before. Some peasants are better off, as are some workers, some merchants, small industrialists, contractors, army officers, technical experts, economists, engineers, and apparently a small class of rural dignitaries of moderate land holdings and some of the higher ulama.

The variety of these groups indicates that the benefits they have derived are not the result of a fixed policy of redistribution. The peasants who are better off are those who have received land and who have had their rents reduced. Agricultural policy was one of the major foundations of the legitimization of the revolutionary regime until recently. Labor groups remain closely controlled, but the modest benefits they have received are the direct result of their assistance to Nasser during the crisis of March 1954. The other groups, all of whom are small, have benefited because of the importance of their contribution to the policies of the UAR or because development funds, jobs, or concessions aiming at administrative rationalization have been channelled in their direction.

If the conclusions of our analysis and our method are accepted, it follows that (1) there is a substantial gap between the interests of the nationalist classes and government policies, which is in a small part explained by alienation and in a much larger part explained by interpretations of the government's purposes and expectations, that is, their ideology; and that (2) if government policy has been oriented to the ideology of the nationalist classes, it has not responded in its development to the demands of these classes except in making some minor concessions.

Despite this gap between the expectations of the nationalist classes and the performance of the government, they support the present regime even if not with rabid enthusiasm. In general, the urban lower class believes that the revolution has benefited them by giving them greater dignity and protection, legal and otherwise, against the wealthier classes, the minorities, and foreigners. The government frequently resorts to organizing student and worker demonstrations which do not appear to be taken seriously by the urban middle class; but the latter, in turn, supports Nasser and his foreign policy especially. The nationalist classes, as earlier described, range in their views from complete support of the government and belief in its ability to raise standards of living and to achieve equality to the view that the government's preference for nation-building policies is ruining the country by ruining its educated elite.

The more usual attitude, however, is that the squeeze on the middle classes is justified in order to benefit the less fortunate, but that it is rather unpleasant medicine. Toward internal policy there is much complaining, but usually in a spirit of patriotic sacrifice, resignation, or of good-natured and self-directed laughter. Some are fairly optimistic about the future. Many would like greater political freedom. Surprisingly few, however, draw any conclusions from domestic problems to foreign policy.

These attitudes are no more than evidence of a largely unexpressed ideology. . . . One of the central problems of pan-Arabism, according to its literary exponents, is its lack of an agreed theory. Some, like Aflaq, argue that no theory is necessary, others, like Rimawi, argue that the theory is to be found in the evolving policies of the UAR; but it is likely that many more, like Nusaibeh, believe that the theory is somewhere out there waiting to be discovered. It is further evident that there is no ideology of social reform separate from Arab nationalism. That is to say, nearly all writers and speech-makers insist that the reform of Arab society is one integral part of the nationalist idea, that social reform is a necessary prelude to the full realization of Arab nationalism, and that (or but) Arab nationalism itself defines the nature of the required social reform or the nature of the genuine Arab society.

The details of this problem are complex, and the literature extensive, so that here we can give only a summary impression of the diffuse idea of the ideal society which apparently prevails among the nationalist classes. Four types of theory come to explain this ideology, and we assume that the authors, in this case, do reflect the sentiments of their public. All four types are concerned with what is called Arab Socialism. The adherents of the first of these we shall call the scientific socialists, the second are the humanists, the third are the Labor Party socialists, and the fourth the pragmatic etatistes.

The scientific socialists use Marxist terminology, are obviously well versed in Communist literature, and are mostly concerned to prove that Marxism does not apply to the Arabs. Most of these writers are Lebanese or Syrians. A good example of one of them is Afif al-Bahansi's *Introduction to Arab Socialism.*

The humanists are not economists but more likely belletrists who find in socialism a reflection of the goodness and charity of the simple human being. As yet I have found only Egyptians writing in this tone, and it would appear that there is a good deal of non-political literature expressed in the same nostalgic, almost banal and romantic manner. 'Abd al-Mon'im al-Sawi's *The Socialism of Our Country* illustrates the point only too well, and the same viewpoint has been expressed by Ihsan 'Abd al-Quddus in various articles in *Rose al-Yusuf*.

The Labor Party socialists are followers of Laski and sometimes graduates of the London School of Economics. The most prominent of this small group is Hatim, who has written only one pamphlet but has sponsored many others and has had translations made of Laski's, G. D. H. Cole's, and Rostow's works. The leading pragmatic etatist is, of course, President Nasser. The Ba'this fall somewhere between the scientific socialists and the humanists.

On the basis of a preliminary examination of this literature, certain important common features can be found. Because they appear to reflect popular opinion, we shall concentrate our attention upon them to the exclusion of the interesting differences among the exponents of Arab Socialism. All of these tendencies reject the Marxist idea of the class struggle. If there is any conflict among classes, it is subordinate to the national struggle against imperialism and foreign capitalism. The Arab socialist ideal is that of cooperation among all classes, or binding the classes together, or reducing the distance between them, or encouraging their mutually responsible interaction. . . .

As near as can be judged from our preliminary survey, Arab socialism is a kind of emotional extension of the nationalist idea to the problems resulting from the loosening of traditional social ties. As Nasser put it in a recent speech at Damascus University, Arabs must now think of the whole nation as their family and they should enjoy the same privileges and owe the same obligations as they do to their families. The Arab nation is one great *gemeinschaft,* and evidence for this assertion is found in the various traditional *gemeinschaftlich* customs prevalent within families or in village society. Class harmony and mutual responsibility are part of the distinctive Arab character and Arab philosophy.

If Arab Socialism is essentially an atavism, that did not prevent various writers from putting forward specific suggestions for its achievement. Hatim and Bahansi both do this, but the most remarkably portentous suggestions appeared in the Ba'th constitution. In its broad outlines, the government of the UAR has followed the Ba'thi line. To fully grasp the paradox here we must note again that the Ba'this are under a cloud in the UAR, that there is not a shred of evidence that the Ba'th has influenced economic policy in Egypt (as opposed to Syria), and that ex-Ba'thi Rimawi has developed a theory which looks to the pragmatic solutions of the Egyptian government for its inspiration.

The government of the UAR followed the Ba'thi suggestions not because they were Ba'thi suggestions, nor because they represented the most plausible operative interpretation of the national-social ideal, but because, after failing for a long while to find a way out of its economic difficulties, a number of circumstances made them seem the most plausible response to the existing situation and the great pressure for development. Practical difficulties prevented further time-consuming study. The next step was to rationalize the new policy in terms of the prevalent ideology of social reform, and the result is the aim of establishing a Socialist-Cooperative-Democracy. . . .

On Peace, Neutrality, and Israel*

Gamal Abdel Nasser

Question from the British and Ceylonese delegations:

It is said that there are West German scientists building atomic rockets for the U.A.R. How does this conform with the policy of positive neutrality and peaceful coexistence?

President Nasser:

Concerning this subject, we are not building atomic rockets, neither have we any atomic rockets. We build rockets in the U.A.R., but they are not atomic rockets. We find it our duty in this age of scientific development to

* From a press conference at the Third International Journalists' Conference in Cairo, October 1, 1963. Published by the Information Department, Cairo, U.A.R. Gamal Abdel Nasser is President of the United Arab Republic.

keep abreast of it in the world. Some countries have built rockets, and we find it our duty to keep pace with this scientific development. For there should not be a monopoly over science by certain countries. Besides the scientific purpose of making rockets, there is a defence purpose. In 1956 we faced an Anglo-French-Israeli aggression and before that we faced many aggressions from Israel, which declared continuously its intention to impose by force the de facto state as well as peace. We must possess the necessary force to repel any aggression. Towards this end we build rockets and at the same time we raise the standard of the people. And, since we are working for the development of our people, we have to protect our frontiers. We have to build a strong Army and get strong weapons. In fact, we spend 13 per cent of our budget on the Army and its development.

Then I shift to the question of peaceful coexistence. Peaceful coexistence is that nobody should stage aggression against us. We should repel any aggression against us. Peaceful coexistence is our purpose; but if Britain launches an aggression against us, how can we stand motionless and say that we want peaceful coexistence? In order to live in peace, it should be peace based on justice.

As for the policy of positive neutrality, it is based on our respect of our neutrality. If we are attacked by any bloc we have to repel the attack and use our legal right to defend our country.

We call for the policy of peaceful coexistence on condition that we should not be the target of any aggression. There is no peaceful coexistence between us and any country that attacks us.

Concerning the Ceylonese question, why we use the Nazi scientists for this purpose . . .

I cannot understand what is meant by the Nazi scientists? Are all the Germans Nazis? Before the war all the scientists worked in Germany. Are the scientists who work today in the big countries also Nazis? The word Nazi is used today only for intrigue. I have met the scientists working here and did not observe any fanaticism among them. I do not know whether they are Nazis or not, all I know is that they are scientists and that they talk only about their work.

The word Nazi was used in the Israeli propaganda and influenced many people, but to employ a German does not mean employing a Nazi. . . .

Question from the Bulgarian delegation and a Polish delegate:

What is your opinion of the Soviet proposal for clearing this area of nuclear weapons and the possibility of banning atomic tests in various parts of the world?

President Nasser:

Our general policy is based on banning nuclear tests, destroying atomic weapons and proceeding towards disarmament. We are one of the countries of the Geneva Disarmament Conference and we have defined our attitude, which is that we support the Soviet proposal for clearing the Mediterranean area of nuclear weapons.

We support every attempt to lessen the areas of atomic weapons because the less they become, the less are the chances of atomic destruction. . . .

Question from the Ceylonese, British and American delegations:

How do you hope finally to settle your dispute with Israel—will it be by throwing Israel in the sea or will you accept the de facto state of affairs? By negotiations or is war the only solution?

President Nasser:

Concerning these questions, we have first to understand the question of Israel. We should not be affected by the Israeli propaganda with which it tries to deceive the world. The problem of Israel is without parallel in history. It must be understood in an atmosphere far removed from Israel's deceptive propaganda.

When Britain held mandatory power over Palestine, the Palestinian people were 90 per cent or more of the population and the Jews were only 10 per cent.

Colonialism and Zionism allied together and evicted the people of Palestine from the country which was given to Israel to make a state based on religion. How can the *fait accompli* be recognised when over a million Arabs were driven out of their land, their property in Palestine looted, and their women and children massacred in 1948 under the yoke of Israeli terrorism?

The 1948 and 1949 U.N. resolutions on the repatriation of the Palestinians and compensation for the land that had been taken from them were ignored.

Moreover, the U.N. in 1949 passed a resolution for the formation of a Conciliation Commission of the U.S.A., France and Turkey at Lausanne. After the first meeting, Israel refused to attend the Commission and declared that no Palestinian would be allowed to return home.

In Israel now there are 2.5 million Israelis and 200,000 Arabs who are regarded as second class citizens living in closed areas, subject to martial law. There is also racial segregation against the Arabs who can hardly move from place to place. Is it fair to accept this *fait accompli* and to give up their rights? Is this justice? Suppose that the English were expelled from the South of Britain and that this area was occupied by strangers; would the British give up their rights to this area? Would Americans agree if the Israelis drove the American citizens out of California?

We believe that peace has to be based on justice. The Palestinians were driven out of their country by Israel backed by colonialism, and Britain then did not do its duty, Palestine being a British protectorate. Rather it helped Zionism to acquire arms and slaughter the unarmed Arabs of Palestine.

This problem, to my mind, will never end unless justice is realized. The Arabs will never succumb. The Arabs of this area fought the Crusaders in the 12th and 13th centuries. Palestine, Lebanon, Egypt and Syria were occupied, but the Arabs fought for 70 years till they completely managed to throw off this colonialism. And I am quite certain that the Arabs would, by no means, accept that the Palestinians will be thus sent away from their land and deprived of their rights and country. On the contrary, they are determined that the Palestinian people should return to their homeland.

I cannot say how; but the Arabs in this part of the world settled there thousands of years ago and are determined that the Palestinian people should go back to their land.

Question by the Cuban delegation:

Do you believe that there is a scope or a possibility for eventual unity of the Arab world?

President Nasser:

We believe that there is considerable scope for unity of the Arab world, which is an indispensable necessity. As a matter of fact, the Arab world was actually unified in the 13th century, but foreign conquerors and colonialists succeeded in dividing the Arab world, and creating artificial frontiers. The events taking place in the Arab world today are but the result of past colonialist domination and of social clashes as a sequel to reactionary and feudal factors. However, faith in Arab unity is bound to result in the attainment of this goal, as unity is an inevitable historical objective.

Question by the Mexican delegation:

What are the causes of dispute in the Middle East? Is there a possibility of a war breaking out in the region?

President Nasser:

The main reason behind the disputes in the Middle East is the creation of Israel, which has stolen a vital part of the Arab fatherland, forcibly driving its inhabitants out of their homes. Israel, moreover, is not content with the present area occupied by it, but proclaims its intention to extend its domination over a region from the Nile to the Euphrates. It has also repeatedly declared that it aims at making peace with the Arabs by force, that is to say, by means of war. These facts should induce us to be ever ready to check any attack or invasion by Israel.

The struggle against imperialism allied with reactionism is also one of the reasons of the dispute. . . .

Israel's Security*

David Ben Gurion

In a pamphlet called *The Philosophy of the Revolution,* [Nasser] gave a frank and open account of his arrogant ambitions. He laid down three objectives: (1) to gain power over all the Arab countries; (2) to become the head of all the Moslem peoples; (3) to become the leader of the entire African Continent.

The internal reforms needed by the Egyptian people, afflicted by disease and illiteracy, with its low material and spiritual standards, and the positive aims in the name of which the revolution was made—the improvement of the nation's health and education, the raising of the standards of the *fellah,* the development of the country—all these were apparently deferred to the distant future, and replaced by external political ambitions. Constructive reforms to improve the conditions of the people require patience, perseverance, prolonged effort, opposition to the great landowners, making demands on the people itself; but it is in the nature of dictatorships that they are eager for easy and rapid victories, and the new rulers of Egypt believed that it would be easier to achieve intoxicating victories in the field of foreign policy than to rectify the wretched and shameful situation at home. . . .

On June 7, 1955, Cairo radio declared: "Those responsible in the Arab countries must know that if they do not fight Israel, Israel will fight them. If they do not put an end to Israel, Israel will put an end to them. We cannot help being in a state of war with Israel, and this obliges us to mobilize all the Arab potential for its final liquidation."

On October 16, 1955, Nasser himself told the editor of the *New York Post,* in the style that we remember from Hitler's days, "I am not fighting against Israel alone, but also against international Jewry and Jewish capital!" Abdullah Ta'imah, secretary of the Egyptian Liberation Organization, which was established by Nasser as the Government party in case elections were held in Egypt, told a deputation of El-Azhar teachers in Cairo: "We are today engaged in a military dispute with the enemy. The enemy is Israel and Zionism; this is the first enemy which has to be liquidated."

These arrogant threats might have been dismissed with a smile, had not the copious flow of Soviet arms streaming into Egypt given them a real and dangerous significance. Egypt received from the Soviets jet fighters and

* "Israel's Security and Her International Position," excerpts from the *Israeli Government Year Book,* 1959/60. Mr. Ben Gurion is former Prime Minister of Israel.

bombers, tanks and artillery, in a quantity and quality far superior to those in Israel's possession. It was clear that these armaments were not supplied to Egypt for decorative purposes or for the improvement of the wretched state of the Egyptian masses, but to serve a definite military aim, which the Egyptian dictator did not find it at all necessary to conceal from public opinion in his own country and the world at large: *war against Israel.*

. . . it should not be forgotten even for a moment that Israel's security problem is quite unlike that of any other country. This is no problem of borders or sovereignty, but a problem of physical survival, in the literal meaning of the term. And it is a question of the survival not only of the people of Israel but of the Jewish people the world over. The one-third of Diaspora Jewry that lives in the Soviet bloc is imprisoned, silenced and forcibly cut off from the rest of the Jewish people and condemned by the Communist regime to forced assimilation; its only hope is immigration to Israel. About 10 per cent of Diaspora Jewry live in the Arab countries—in conditions of economic, political and spiritual oppression. As for the over 6 million Jews who live in the free and prosperous lands, their Jewish consciousness and the Jewish content of their lives are nourished mainly by the inspiration and creative achievements of the State of Israel. It is no exaggeration to say that the survival of World Jewry depends on and is maintained by the survival of the State of Israel, and that the problem of Israel's security is therefore equivalent to the problem of the survival of the entire Jewish people. . . .

Since the foundation of the State (and even before), the achievement of a Jewish-Arab alliance, and political, economic and cultural cooperation between the Jews and the Arab peoples, has been the primary, principal and supreme goal of Israel's foreign policy. This alliance is a historic and vital necessity for both sides. The greatest and truest need of the Arab peoples is not light and heavy armaments—a large part of which would fall into the hands of our Defence Forces in any war with Israel, as happened during the Sinai Campaign—but development, education, sanitation and the elevation of the Arab worker and peasant from his present degraded position. Israel can make a greater contribution to this process of regeneration than perhaps any other external factor in the East or the West. Israel's great and historic need is a constructive struggle with nature: the conquest of the desert, the exploitation of the latent natural resources of land and sea for the absorption and integration of further immigrants, and the establishment of a new society founded on cooperation and fraternity between men. For this purpose she needs peace and mutual assistance with her neighbours. But in our day almost every Arab country—with the possible exceptions of Lebanon and Tunis—is under the totalitarian rule of a military dictator or a medieval dynasty which still maintains the traffic in slaves, and these rulers aim not at meeting the needs of the masses but at consolidating their power and competing with each other for the expansion of their spheres of influence and domination. This competition is nourished to no small extent by the competition between the two world blocs—the Communist one and the democratic one—but its root lies in the internal situation among the Arab peoples, a heritage of many generations of servitude, poverty, indignity and backwardness, both spiritual and material.

This wretched and degrading heritage will not last for ever; it must inevitably give place one day to the aspiration, which is growing throughout the human race, for cultural and economic progress, more freedom and independence, and the enhancement of human honour and genius. But this change, however necessary and inevitable, is a slow and prolonged process, and in the meantime Israel is subjected to siege, pressure and ever growing threats from all her neighbours. And this pressure is fortified by the hostility of the Communist world, which will also disappear one day, though Israel cannot say when that day will come.

. . . History has not indulged our people with rich natural resources or large numbers, but in spiritual capacity we are not inferior to any country or people, and in the short period of our renewed independence we have already succeeded in arousing respect and sympathy both in Europe and America, and also in Asia and Africa. Israel is a democratic country, and it cannot survive without a democratic regime. Without respect for the individual and his freedom, his responsibility and his consciousness of his mission, without his free pioneering initiative, the Land of Israel would not have been built and the State would not have been able to arise or to survive. . . .

But Israel does not regard political democracy as the be-all and end-all. Even before the establishment of the State, we created in this country new and original forms of life and social patterns to which there is no parallel anywhere else: our labour settlements of all types (collective, cooperative, etc.), the variegated cooperative enterprises in all branches of the economy—in building, roadmaking, credit, commerce and housing; mutual assistance institutions like the Workers' Sick Fund, the Mish'an social welfare fund, etc. The institutions of higher education and research that were established in Jerusalem, Haifa and Rehovot even before the rise of the State have been improved and expanded during the last decade, and can bear comparison with educational and research institutions in the wealthiest and most progressive countries. In a short space of time Israel has succeeded in training new immigrants from lands of poverty and servitude to form a creative and defensive force no less valuable and efficient than the immigrants from the most civilized countries. Extraordinary energy and initiative have been shown in the establishment of a wide range of new economic undertakings in agriculture and industry, in land, sea and air transport; gigantic housing schemes are being erected for hundreds of thousands of newcomers and veterans; and the language which almost the whole world regarded half a century ago as a dead tongue, embalmed in the Scriptures and prayer book, has become a living language of speech, study and literature, which brings together exiles from afar, separated by time and space, and merges them into a single nation. . . .

The Arab rulers have established two principles to govern their relations with Israel, and even when they quarrel among themselves, they all act in accordance with these principles: (1) Refusal to make peace with Israel and the maintenance of a state of belligerency. For this purpose they boycott Israel, blockade her by land and sea, and blacken her name to other nations in order to isolate her. (2) Constant military preparations with a view to making it possible one day to defeat the Israel Defence Forces, annihilate Israel and wipe her off the face of the earth.

Though this hostile and negative policy has yet to bring the Arabs any advantage or any positive results from the point of their own interests, and though there may be individual statesmen here and there who recognize deep down in their hearts that this is a barren policy, harmful to the Arabs themselves, there is no reason to suppose that the Arab rulers—even those who have ceased to believe in its effectiveness—will change this policy of their own free will in the near future.

For this reason Israel must devote her energies to two efforts that will frustrate the hostile policy of the Arab rulers: (1) The maintenance of a military force endowed with sufficient equipment and skill to deter the Arab rulers from initiating any aggression against Israel. Deterrence and the prevention of war are more important and desirable than military victory, since no war can solve historical problems (unless the goal is to completely destroy the rival nation—which may be the aim of the Arab rulers, but cannot in any circumstances or under any conditions be Israel's aim). Moreover, a heavy price has to be paid for any war, even a victorious one. The primary consideration is not the financial and economic loss (though even this is by no means unimportant), but the loss of human life, whose importance is immeasurable, even if the casualties are few—and it will not be possible to minimize the losses in every battle, as we did in the Sinai Campaign.

(2) To establish friendly relations with as many nations and States as possible, in every continent, both in Europe and America, and in Africa and Asia. This friendship is important and necessary in itself because of its effect on Israel's international position, but it can also bring about the weakening and the collapse of the Arab wall of hatred, and finally pave the way for a pact of peace and cooperation between Israel and the Arabs.

part four

Asia

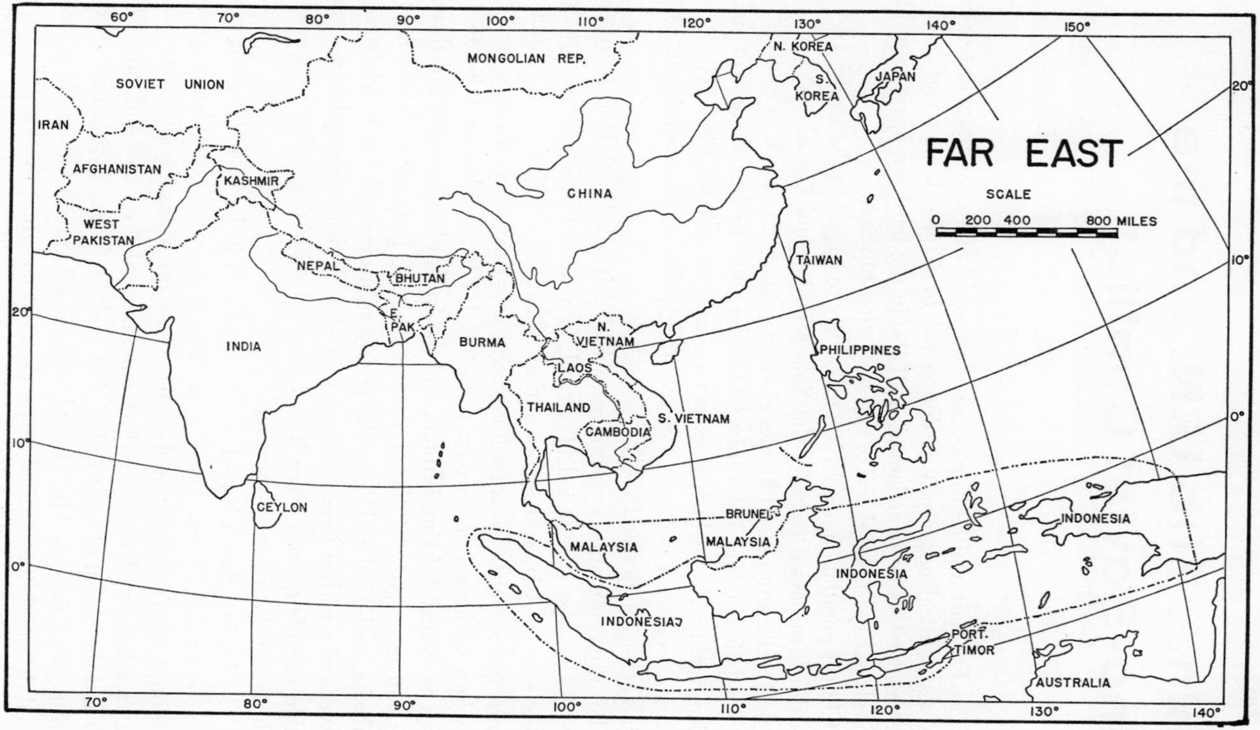
FAR EAST
SCALE
0 200 400 800 MILES
SOVIET UNION
MONGOLIAN REP.
IRAN
AFGHANISTAN
KASHMIR
WEST
PAKISTAN
CHINA
N. KOREA
S.
KOREA
JAPAN
TAIWAN
NEPAL
BHUTAN
E.
PAK
INDIA
BURMA
N.
VIETNAM
LAOS
THAILAND
CAMBODIA
S. VIETNAM
PHILIPPINES
CEYLON
BRUNEI
MALAYSIA
MALAYSIA
INDONESIA
INDONESIA
INDONESIA
PORT.
TIMOR
AUSTRALIA

8

China: The U.N. and the Sino-Soviet Conflict

The Far East, unlike Europe, does not consist of many more or less equal states; its political geography is dominated by China. China was anciently known as the Middle Kingdom, and all else in the Far East, apart from India, still tends to have a peripheral or radial relationship to it.

China's population, over 700 million, is the largest in the world. Her area ranks third, surpassed only by the Soviet Union and Canada. When President de Gaulle announced his decision on January 31, 1964, to establish diplomatic relations with Communist China, he said, "In fact, there is in Asia no political reality . . . which does not concern or affect China. There is, in particular, neither a war nor a peace imaginable on that continent without China's being implicated in it."

For the communist government, which has ruled mainland China since 1949, the present is a period of revival, of renewed insistence on her great historic role in Asia, and of reassertion of her imperial mission. China now reasserts her ancient claims to direct control or suzerainty of every peripheral area where Chinese influence once prevailed. China took over Tibet in 1950; presses on Nepal, Sikkim, Bhutan, and the Indian borderlands; and threatens more and more gravely the whole peninsula of Indochina (Vietnam, Laos, Cambodia, and Thailand)—besides posing an ultimate threat to Malaysia and every country with a large Chinese minority. Such a state makes an uncomfortable neighbor, even were it not inspired with the desire to spread the revolutionary doctrines of Marxism.

The United States is profoundly interested in both of the great current issues concerning China. The first problem is the whole complex of questions regarding China's international status. These questions are all loose ends that have been hanging loose since the Communist takeover of mainland China in 1949 and the retreat of Chiang Kai-shek and the former government of China to Formosa (Taiwan). The United States is allied with Chiang in a treaty of mutual defense.[1] The United States does not recognize the People's Republic of China and has no official diplomatic relations with it,[2] although a number of

[1] That is, the United States is pledged to defend Chiang. What aid Chiang is likely to be to the United States is not entirely clear.

[2] However, sheer necessity has led to an intermittent (and largely fruitless) series of negotiations between the United States and this government that it does not recognize. These rendezvous have been held in Warsaw.

her allies have. Britain and Pakistan recognized it almost immediately. France did so in 1964. The present government of China is not a member of the United Nations—or, more precisely, it is not regarded as entitled to the Chinese membership and does not enjoy the Chinese permanent seat on the Security Council. The policy of the United States, which opposes Communist Chinese membership and is voiced in this chapter by Adlai E. Stevenson, has been unchanging since 1949.

There are some indications, however, that the ice has possibly begun to thaw, and that the United States may consider recognizing Red China in some future circumstances if it seems expedient in the national interest to do so. Recognition of Bolshevik Russia took 16 years, from 1917 to 1933; but in the Russian situation there was no equivalent of the basic complication of Chiang's government and the commitments of the United States to it.

The speech of Roger Hilsman, Jr., reproduced here was generally taken as an indication of a possible coming shift in U.S. policy; however, the matter was thrown in doubt again by Hilsman's resignation in Februrary 1964. Eustace Seligman suggests that—since we cannot now in honor jettison Chiang, however ill-considered our original unqualified commitment to him might have been—the sensible long-term objective of U.S. policy should be some version of the "Two-Chinas Solution." This solution, however, happens to be anathema to the governments in both Peiping and Taiwan.

In his celebrated Senate speech of March 25, 1964, in which he pled for bringing U.S. foreign policy "reasonably close to objective reality," to end what he considers a dangerous "chasm" between the two, Senator Fulbright had an interesting passage on China policy:

> The Far East is another area of the world in which American policy is handicapped by the divergence of old myths and new realities. Particularly with respect to China, an elaborate vocabulary of make-believe has become compulsory in both official and public discussion. . . .
>
> I do not think that the United States can or should recognize Communist China or acquiesce in its admission to the United Nations under present circumstances. It would be unwise to do so because there is nothing to be gained by it so long as the Peking regime maintains its attitude of implacable hostility toward the United States.
>
> I do not believe, however, that this state of affairs is necessarily permanent. As we have seen in our relations with Germany and Japan, hostility can give way in an astonishingly short time to close friendship; and as we have seen in our relations with China, the reverse can occur with equal speed. It is not impossible that in time our relations with China will change again, if not to friendship then perhaps to "competitive coexistence."
>
> For a start we must jar open our minds to certain realities about China, of which the foremost is that there are not really "two Chinas" but only one, mainland China, and that it is ruled by Com-

> munists and likely to remain so for the indefinite future. Once we accept this fact, it becomes possible to reflect on the conditions under which it might be possible for us to enter into relatively normal relations with mainland China. One condition, of course, must be the abandonment by the Chinese Communists, tacitly if not explicitly, of their intention to conquer and incorporate Taiwan. This seems unlikely now, but far more surprising changes have occurred in politics, and it is possible that a new generation of leaders in Peking and Taipei may put a quiet end to the Chinese civil war, opening the possibility of entirely new patterns of international relations in the Far East.

The second main topic regards China's relations with the Soviet Union. The two excerpts here from the lengthy doctrinal missives that the rival Communist parties fired at each other in July 1963 show how serious the cleavage between them has become in regard to the basic issue of possible war with the West. The Russians, unlike the Chinese, argue that it may be possible to avoid war, and that it would be better avoided. Hugh Seton-Watson's essay expounds the historic origins of the present divergence. The possibility of a break between the two greatest communist states had clearly existed since the middle 1950's, but not until the middle of 1963 did the conflict appear irreconcilable. It has several roots. One is clearly doctrinal—yet the doctrinal conflict is at bottom sociological: Communist China's revolution is young, and her revolutionary ardor is at a more primitive and dangerous stage. A second is the natural restiveness of a strong, centralized (and, in its own terms, successful) Chinese government under the tutelage of *any* foreign government; even the immense prestige of Soviet Russia among all Communists could not persuade China to accept Russian leadership and direction indefinitely. Third, antagonisms arise from territorial questions in the Sino-Russian borderlands, particularly in Mongolia.

The implications for the United States, and for its allies, of this split in world communism are equivocal. It cannot be doubted, however, that we are observing a convulsion that will affect the course of world politics significantly throughout the rest of this century. It may further the *détente,* or even rapprochement, between the Soviet Union and the West that is already apparent, and of which the first fruit was the limited nuclear-test-ban treaty of July 1963. The Soviet Union has not been willing to assist the Chinese to achieve their own nuclear weapons and has no desire for them to do so.

On the other hand, with Russia's influence—which has recently been a restraining influence—removed as a factor, Chinese policy may become even more adventurous than it has been in the past. Yet, this prediction may be too gloomy. There have been some indications—trivial as yet, but possibly significant as straws in the wind—that the Peiping government is not altogether as indifferent to the perils of war as it has sometimes indicated in the past. There may be new openings in dealing with China that, if exploited wisely, may alter the Far East situation beyond recognition. In such developments the United States will have, inescapably, a major role to play. For she is tied by alliances to Taiwan, Japan, Korea, and a number of other states along or near China's borders.

United States Rejects Soviet Proposal to Seat Communist China*

Adlai E. Stevenson

Is the Soviet Union to be taken seriously when it argues that Peiping is "peace-loving"; that for more than 13 years it has been the rightful claimant to the seat of China in the United Nations; and that therefore the United Nations must reject its charter, even as it observes the anniversary of its adoption? The Soviet Union demands, in fact, that the majority of the Assembly wipe out its previous decisions, including the solemn condemnation of the Chinese Communists for their aggression in Korea, and expel a loyal member state in the hope that this will entice Peiping to send representatives to sit among us.

Does the Soviet delegate really believe his argument is valid?

Does the Soviet Government really think so highly of this regime?

I agree with the contention of the Soviet Union which has termed this agenda item a matter that is "important and urgent." Its importance and its urgency, however, are not in the Soviet demand for the expulsion of the representative of a charter member, the Republic of China, one of our founding states, but in the members of this body recognizing, as they have time and time again these past 13 years, that force is not a passport for membership in the United Nations.

But what of the 600 million people of the mainland? Do we forget them? Do we relegate them to the wings of the stage of history? No, we do not. It is their rulers that do. This body, by admitting the so-called People's Republic of China, would not be admitting 600 million Chinese. We would be admitting a small handful of tyrants who care little about the people and more, much more, about power. Is this representation? Is this giving recognition and representation to 600 million voiceless human beings?

* From a statement made at the United Nations on October 22, 1962 (Washington, D.C.: Government Printing Office, 1962), pp. 786–790. Mr. Stevenson is the U.S. Representative to the U.N. General Assembly.

I submit that the teeming millions of the mainland are today subjugated by a regime that cares less about their rights—fundamental human rights reaffirmed by the charter—than any regime in modern history, perhaps all history. Do we need the counsel of this regime? Is this a government that would support with a pure heart and clean hands the Charter of the United Nations?

This is a new imperialism, a new colonialism that seeks to carve out a new empire—not only in Asia—and dash the hopes of liberty the world over.

The world knows well what is going on even today in that huge arc which ranges from Manchuria through the Himalayas. Let us consider as examples only those events in the year since our last debate on this subject.

India. The Indian subcontinent, today, is also the victim of increasing military aggression along its borders. Chinese Communist military forces persistently cross the borders of India and press by force deeper and deeper into Indian territory. These are not undisciplined troops who have lost their way. These are regular units of the Chinese Communist armed forces acting under precise orders. By their actions the Chinese Communists again show their scorn for the charter of this organization.

I am appalled that we should even be asked to consider as one of our peers a government that expresses such disdain for all that this United Nations represents.

Korea. The Chinese Communists stand condemned by the United Nations as aggressors in Korea. They refuse to recognize either their own wrongdoing or the righteousness of the United Nations in defending a victim of aggression and in seeking to restore peace to this troubled land. They assert the United Nations had no business in Korea. Having mounted aggression, having thrown massive armed force against the U.N.'s efforts to restore peace in Korea, and having ravaged the country, they now insist that the blame was all Korea's. They even characterize the United Nations Command, which is in Korea on the peaceful mission of defending the armistice, as an agent of imperialism. This is a shopworn technique of calling white black and black white. The Chinese Communist Foreign Minister on August 15 of this year declared that "the Chinese people resolutely support" the efforts of the North Korean regime to "compel" the withdrawal of the U.N. Command from Korea; that is, the Chinese Communists proclaim the dismantling of the United Nations peacekeeping mission, a mission taken in solemn duty to the principles of the charter, as an objective of their national policy.

Taiwan. On December 22, 1961, the Peiping People's Daily, official organ of the Chinese Communist regime, declared: "However the United Nations may vote and whatever resolutions it may adopt, the Chinese people's determination to liberate Taiwan will never be shaken." On August 1 of this year General Lo Jwiching, Vice Premier of the Chinese Communist regime and Chief of the General Staff, speaking at a ceremony commemorating the 35th anniversary of the founding of the Communist army, stated: "Taiwan is

China's sacred territory. The Chinese people have the sacred right to liberate Taiwan at any time and by any means. . . ."

Consider the source of this statement and the occasion on which it was made. Clearly what they have in mind is something even more deadly than so-called "peaceful liberation," the fate which befell Tibet.

Southeast Asia, an area where the Chinese Communists even at this very moment are trying to export their revolutionary tactics and subversion against established authority.

Take the example of South Vietnam. Sun Hsiao-tsun, chairman of the China-Vietnam Friendship Association, at a rally in Peiping on August 31, 1962, declared, according to New China News Agency, that "the Chinese people would staunchly support the patriotic, just, anti-U.S. struggle of the Vietnamese people and that 650 million Chinese people would forever unite closely and fight side by side with the heroic Vietnamese people." What is meant, of course, is that they would support the undeclared war which the Communists of North Vietnam are waging to take over South Vietnam by force without regard for what the will of the people of South Vietnam may be.

Tibet. In the past years this Assembly has debated the tragedy of Tibet. It has repeatedly expressed its grave concern at the systematic violation of human rights by Chinese Communist armed forces which entered Tibet under the banner of "peaceful liberations." Last year this Assembly solemnly renewed "its call for the cessation of practices which deprive the Tibetan people of their fundamental human rights and freedoms, including their right to self-determination."

Fifty-six members of the General Assembly supported the resolution on Tibet last year, while it was opposed by only 11.

Peiping's specific reaction to this resolution was voiced in the official statement by its Ministry of Foreign Affairs on December 21, 1961, that "no foreign countries or international organization, the United Nations included, have any right to meddle" in Tibet.

But it is not only Communist China's neighbors who suffer aggression under the cloak of "peaceful coexistence." Chinese Communist leadership has repeatedly professed its belief in revolutions and subversion, it has shown its ability to export revolution, it has even boasted of doing so.

In his general debate statement on October 8 this year, the distinguished Minister for Foreign Affairs of the Cameroon offered proof of the Chinese Communists' longstanding policy of aggression toward his country, the training and arming—on the Chinese mainland—of terrorists promoting violent revolution thousands of miles away from China in the heart of Africa.

The official Chinese Communist organ People's Daily not only has failed to deny this infamous plot; on the contrary its editorials have boasted about the wide circulation in Africa, in Latin America, and throughout Asia of pamphlets on guerrilla warfare and on Chinese Communist revolutionary theories. People's Daily expressed the conviction that these pamphlets will gain favor among these far-distant peoples because "sooner or later they will rise in revolution." People's Daily ignores the fact that most of these peoples have had their revolution and are now free and independent nations.

Speaking before this General Assembly on the 1st of December last year I touched on this affinity for aggressive violence which characterizes the rulers of Peiping. I quoted a statement by the supreme leader of Chinese Communism, Mao Tse-tung, who summed up his world outlook in the words "Everything can be made to grow out of the barrel of a gun." Ten days later the same official organ, People's Daily, commenting on my remarks, declared: "All revolutionary people can never abandon the truth that 'all political power grows out of the barrel of a gun.' "

Let there be no mistake about it. Those who speak in support of the admission of the Chinese Communists into the United Nations inevitably lend support and encouragement to the aggressive concepts which today govern the actions and policies of this regime, thereby endangering the principles of the United Nations Charter.

The Republic of China is a loyal and dedicated member of the United Nations. It has been so since the founding of our organization. It participates fully in the economic and technical assistance programs of the United Nations and its specialized agencies. The Soviet Union cannot, of course, seriously expect this Assembly to expel the representatives of the Republic of China.

Though faced with a constant threat to its very existence, the Republic of China, despite the demand for vigilance and constant effort in its defense which this threat imposes upon it, has sought to preserve and foster those cultural values and traditions which have for centuries been the unique attributes of Chinese civilization. The family is respected as a fundamental social unit whose welfare is the concern of the community. Harmony among men is the goal of society. To each individual is due recognition of his identity as a human being whose wants, desires, and happiness cannot be ignored nor infringed upon.

The Republic of China has demonstrated that these values may be harnessed with great effect for the progress of society. More than 11 million people on Taiwan today enjoy political well-being and unprecedented economic growth under the rule of these social principles. Taiwan's industries have expanded and become steadily more diversified, and its commerce carries the products of its many factories to ever more distant parts of the globe. The farmers of Taiwan, working for themselves on their own land, have steadily pushed agricultural production to new levels and this spring reaped another record harvest. Meanwhile, the sons of these good farmers have gone abroad under the Republic of China's technical assistance program to share with farmers of other lands the skills they have developed, and representatives of some of the nations of Africa who sit in this hall can testify to the success of these efforts and to the good will these young men have created.

The mainland brothers of the people living on Taiwan have not been so fortunate either socially or economically.

The mismanagement of their economic affairs by the Chinese Communists has led to widespread suffering; since our debate here last year we have learned of many disturbances and disorders, particularly in South China, of the serious riots of the Canton railway station in early June of this year.

The Chinese Communist rulers have failed because they have concentrated not on building up their own country but in tearing down others.

We hear much about self-determination and the right of every nation to determine its own form of government. My government fervently believes in this principle. Indeed, we fought a war nearly 200 years ago to win that right for ourselves. Our own Declaration of Independence states clearly and unequivocally our belief that "Governments are instituted among Men, deriving their just powers from the consent of the governed." Have the Chinese Communist rulers, Mr. President, derived their power from the consent of 600 million Chinese? Or have they grasped it by the force of arms?

In our own Declaration of Independence, too, we emphasize our belief in "a decent respect to the opinions of mankind," and for nearly 200 years this respect has guided our actions. What opinions, other than their own, do the Chinese Communist rulers respect? (I daresay, incidentally, there are those in the Soviet Union who may well be asking the same question.) The answer is clear. The Chinese Communists today lack respect not only for the opinions of others but even for those held by 600 million of their countrymen. It would, I fear, be too much to hope, therefore, that some useful purpose can be served by our debate this year. Or to voice the hope that the rulers in Peiping will hear what we say and pay heed to the views we express. If they do not, however, it is hard to foresee how much more suffering the people of the mainland must endure.

A Two-Chinas Proposal*

Eustace Seligman

In the General Assembly last week the Chinese Minister of Foreign Affairs reaffirmed in emphatic terms his government's opposition to the admission of Communist China to the U.N. Within the month in all probability, a vote will have been taken on this question. What position should the U.S. take, and will it be supported or outvoted? Should we continue to op-

* From "A Two-Chinas Policy," *The New Republic,* October 16, 1961, pp. 11–14. Copyright © 1961 by *The New Republic.* Reprinted by permission. Mr. Seligman is a lawyer, a member of the firm of Sullivan and Cromwell, and Chairman of the Board of Directors of the Foreign Policy Association.

pose, or should we accept Communist China's membership [in The United Nations] as inevitable; and if so, in what form?

Many Americans—probably a large majority—believe passionately that we should stand firm; that if voted down, we should use our veto; and that if Communist China is admitted notwithstanding, we should withdraw from the United Nations, or at the very least give serious consideration to pulling out.

At the other extreme is a small minority which is of the opinion that the U.S. should support admission of Communist China to the U.N. *in place of* the present Republic of China, even though this would mean handing over Taiwan—or Formosa—to the Communists. An exponent of this view is Felix Greene, a British citizen residing in California who has recently visited Communist China. In his book *Awakened China,* he states:

"Our China policy—or more accurately, our lack of policy—will, it seems certain to me, involve us in ever-increasing difficulty and embarrassment. We are out of phase with our closest allies. But one day, perhaps by persuasion of our allies, the United States may find it to her best interest no longer to oppose China's entry into the United Nations. Whether this happens tomorrow or in ten years' time, such a change will necessarily appear as an American diplomatic defeat, for it will require abandonment of that guardianship of Chiang which we have so frequently justified on grounds of 'moral obligation.' The easing of the present tension between the United States and China is surely essential if the peace of our world is to be preserved. I do not believe that this tragically bitter enmity is likely to be resolved by any sudden 'bright' solution; and still less will it disappear as a result of clever maneuvers aimed at putting the other side to disadvantage in debate. And least of all are we likely to find a solution through the much-discussed 'Two-Chinas' policy, which would attempt to make Taiwan an independent country. For the Chinese consider (and with compelling historical reason) that Taiwan is part of China and any such 'solution' would only further embitter the Chinese people and would only consolidate and in no way ease the tensions that exist at present.". . .

Now, the chief argument that is advanced for our continuing to oppose the admission of Communist China to the U.N. is that Communist rule on the mainland is temporary, that it will some day be overthrown by internal revolt, and that the Nationalist Government will then be able to return. That this belief is firmly held by the Nationalists can be testified to by the writer as a result of a visit not long ago to Taiwan. The evidence adduced to support it is the steadily increasing popular discontent with the Communist regime resulting from growing economic distress and the dictatorial repression of individual rights. When asked whether this might be wishful thinking, a prominent official answered: "When de Gaulle arrived in England in June, 1940, what did you think were his chances of ever returning with his government to France? And yet he did some four years later and so shall we!"

Admiration for courage in clinging to a forlorn hope must be readily accorded. Yet the cold fact is that there is no present possibility of the Communist regime in China being overthrown unless the United States is prepared to go to war to assist the Nationalists to recover the mainland—a proposal which very few Americans advocate. The situation is therefore not analogous to that of de Gaulle, who was returned to France by British and American arms, but comparable to the White Russians who escaped after the Communist revolution of 1917 and who for a long time expected to return when the counter-revolution would be victorious.

Thus, the U.S. must determine whether there is any reasonable chance of the Communist government in China being overthrown in the foreseeable future. Unless there is, it is certain that the most populous nation in the world will, sooner or later, be admitted to the U.N. While obviously the question cannot be answered with mathematical certainty, it is submitted that we are going to have to accept the permanence of Communist China, just as after a period of years we accepted that of Communist Russia, and fashion our policies accordingly.

If this viewpoint were adopted by our government, what effect would it have in Asia?

Many of those in our foreign service in Asia—but not all—believe that the effect would be disastrous. They say that all of the other countries in Asia are acutely sensitive to shifts in power; that the prestige of Communist China would be immeasurably enhanced and that of the United States correspondingly decreased; that as a consequence, the idea of freedom which we have been seeking to spread would find fewer and fewer supporters; that Communism would spread over all of Asia; and that possibly some of the countries with whom we are allied, and certainly those still uncommitted, would team up with our enemies.

Other competent observers, however, reject this forecast. They say that the Asian appraisal of Communist power will not be changed by the admission of Peking to the U.N., since the actualities of Communist China's strength are already fully realized and will not thereby be increased. They say further that admission would lessen the sympathy for Peking now widely felt in Asia by those who believe it is being improperly excluded. Several visits to the Orient have persuaded the writer that this latter analysis is correct.

Let us now turn to the second view: Since Communist China will ultimately be admitted to the U.N. in place of the Republic of China (so the thesis runs), and since this will necessarily lead to the United Nations accepting Communist China as the lawful government not only on the mainland but also on Taiwan, the U.S. would be wise to abandon Taiwan.

The proponents of this position argue that there has been a civil war in China, that the preexisting government has been overthrown, and that a new government is in control. Since Taiwan is a part of China, the new government's legal rights extend to that island, even though a pocket of resistance may remain because of U.S. interference in a domestic Chinese fight.

This analysis can be met on purely legal grounds: First, it is not true that Taiwan is a part of China; it was taken from Japan after World War II and not given back to China and is still legally owned jointly by the nations which signed the peace treaty. Furthermore, just as the Communists revolted and overthrew the Nationalist government on the mainland, so the Nationalist government on Taiwan can use force to effect its independence of the Communist government. A revolution if unsuccessful is a treasonable act, but if successful sets up a new regime which is recognized as lawful.

Finally, quite apart from legal niceties, the United States defeated Japan and compelled its surrender and took possession of Taiwan and still is in a position where it can determine who should hold Taiwan.

What should that determination be? In my judgment, it should be to prevent Communist China from taking control of Taiwan, and instead to set Taiwan up as an independent nation.

To begin with, there is not the slightest question that the vast majority of the inhabitants of the island—Taiwanese as well as Chinese from the mainland—are opposed to subjecting Taiwan to the rule of Communist China. Accordingly, if the principle of self-determination of nations—which is so widely invoked in behalf of all colonial countries—should be applied here, Taiwan is entitled to be recognized as a country independent of Communist China and to have its own government. If any serious doubt were raised in the General Assembly as to whether it is true that the inhabitants of Taiwan would prefer independence, the U.S. could safely agree to a U.N.-conducted plebiscite.

A second reason for not surrendering Taiwan to the Communists is that it would be an ignoble abandonment of partners-in-arms. There is surely a moral obligation upon us to do what we can to prevent those who have been our allies—soldiers, officers, government officials and civilians—from being handed over to an enemy which would presumably not hesitate at wholesale liquidation.

Finally, Taiwan is almost equidistant from the Chinese mainland and the Philippines, and only a little further from Okinawa—a part of Japan. The Philippines and Japan rely upon us to come to their defense in the event of war. Such defense would be greatly weakened and perhaps in the case of the Philippines rendered impossible if Taiwan were in enemy hands.

For these reasons, it is submitted, the U.S. should continue to oppose any action by the U.N. which would permit Communist China to take over Taiwan.

Let me say here, parenthetically, that although criticism of the Nationalist regime in Taiwan is often heard, a brief sojourn in the island is sufficient to convince an objective observer that the government as far as its economic and social aspects are concerned, is progressive. A land reform program has been put into effect that is an example that many other countries could well follow; the accomplishments in popular education and public health are tremendous. Likewise in the field of local self-government there has been a great advance along democratic lines. Only in matters affecting foreign policy is the government completely in the hands of Chiang—and the justification given for it is that in every country which is at war democratic procedures must for the time being be violated and dictatorial powers accorded to the chief of state. If the war between Peking and Taiwan could be ended, there is every reason to believe that the Nationalist government would extend the Taiwanese the right of full representation (already granted them in local self-government) in the national government.

What is needed, therefore, is a U.S. policy aimed at securing the admission of Communist China to the U.N. in such a form as not to bring Taiwan under Communist control. This would involve two steps: one, continuing Nationalist China as a member of the United Nations; and two, admitting Communist China *as a new member*. The reasoning in support of this procedure is that, as a result of civil war, the mainland of China has revolted and set up its own independent government, and the territory over which the Nationalist government continues to rule has been reduced to Taiwan. Notwithstanding the fact that the territory of Taiwan is much smaller than that of mainland China, its government is actually the continuing, existing one; Communist China is therefore the one to be admitted as a new member.

Obviously, such a policy will not satisfy either side—Communist or Nationalist China. Furthermore, like all compromises it is opposed by both sides as a yielding to the dictates of expediency. The Communist Chinese claim that it involves a surrender of territory rightfully theirs; the Nationalists claim it means abandoning the U.N. Charter's requirement that applicants for membership be "peace loving." However, the fact that various Soviet satellites *have* been admitted amounts to a tacit repudiation of any membership qualifications and the recognition, instead, of the desirability of including all nations.

But could such a compromise be effected? The first step would be to obtain the necessary votes in the General Assembly to elect Communist China as a new member, entitled to a seat in the Assembly. This requires a two-thirds vote. Whether such consent can be obtained is a matter of conjecture. However, it is reasonable to believe that if the solution suggested above is not proposed at the pending General Assembly, an alternative proposal will be made to seat the delegates of Communist China *in place of* the delegates of Nationalist China, relying on the theory that Communist China has in fact and in law succeeded to Nationalist China and *is* the Republic of China named in the Charter as a member of the Security Council. One of the grave dangers from the standpoint of our government is that such a proposal could be adopted by majority vote, unless we can persuade the majority that this is a question of such importance that it should be decided only by two-thirds. Also, if such a proposal were to be adopted (either by majority or two-thirds vote) it is probable that it would not be subject to veto by the U.S.—at least as far as Communist China's right to be seated in the General Assembly. Conceivably it might result in one China being recognized by the General Assembly and the other by the Security Council, which would be a highly anomalous situation.

To block any such moves to bring Communist China in by the back door—on the issue of credentials—it would be desirable for the U.S. to take the initiative and propose the admission of Communist China to the United Nations, and to hope that we could get the necessary two-thirds to support us.

The second step—prior in time but assuming favorable action by the General Assembly—would be to obtain the approval of the Security Council. This can be blocked by either Nationalist China or the U.S.S.R.

With respect to a veto by Nationalist China, if the U.S. were to insist on this Two-Chinas solution, the Chiang government would have no choice but to accept. American naval forces are Taiwan's only protection at present from invasion by Communist China. We are justified in imposing reasonable conditions upon the continuance of this protection. This may appear drastic, but in a matter so vital to the U.S. as well as to Taiwan itself, strong measures are proper.

Much more serious, however, is the possibility that Communist China, and therefore the U.S.S.R., would never agree to such a compromise. Peking has consistently taken the position that Taiwan was a part of China until seized by Japan, and should again become a part of China. It has refused to renounce the use of force to recover Taiwan. This would seem to doom any program for an independent Taiwan to failure. But does such a pessimistic supposition mean that no attempt should be made to win acceptance by Communist China? Surely nothing would be lost in the attempt, even though it should prove unsuccessful.

One further question must be considered.

Under the proposal made above, Nationalist China would continue to hold its seat in the Security Council as well as its membership in the United Nations. This may lead some nations to vote against it who otherwise would support it. If this proves to be the case, it is suggested that we then add to the proposal an additional element, namely that the U.N. Charter be amended under Article 108 so as to eliminate China's seat as a permanent member of the Security Council, and to provide that in place thereof one additional seat on the Security Council shall be filled by election.

This suggestion has the merit of ending the indefensible situation whereby a government having actual control over only 12 million people is one of the five permanent members of the Security Council and has the right of veto. At the same time the suggestion avoids substituting Communist China for Nationalist China on the Security Council—a move which would be strongly opposed by all of the countries which are anti-Communist. And finally, it has the merit of reducing by one the number of nations which have the paralyzing right of veto.

However, here again under the Charter, Nationalist China would have a veto and would undoubtedly desire to exercise that veto over an amendment to the Charter. To prevent this, it will be necessary, as indicated above, for the U.S. to persuade, and as a last resort compel, Nationalist China to act in accordance with our judgment as to what is necessary in order to maintain the independence of Taiwan.

The U.S.S.R. also would have the right to veto this addition to the proposal, but it presumably would do so only if it decided to veto the whole proposal of admitting Communist China as a new member, and the addition does not therefore create a further obstacle.

This suggested Charter amendment would not only increase the likelihood of the U.S. being able to get a two-thirds vote for the compromise, but would also face Russia and Communist China with the choice of accepting the proposal or themselves being the ones who, through exercise of the Soviet veto, are responsible for keeping Communist China out of the United Nations.

In conclusion, one fundamental criticism of the program outlined here must be considered: namely, that it is wholly unrealistic because Communist China will not give up its claim to Taiwan or to a seat on the Security Council, and the proposal therefore is nothing more than another gambit in the propaganda game. The answer to this is clear. Even if it should prove true that Peking will not accept the proposal, the fact that the U.S. is willing to make it and that Nationalist China, much against its desires, is willing to accept it should be sufficient to prevent the General Assembly's seating Communist China *in place of* Nationalist China.

Keep the Door Open to the Possibility of Change*

Roger Hilsman, Jr.

Let me begin by disposing of a myth. It is frequently charged that the United States Government is ignoring China and its 700 million people. This is simply untrue. We do not ignore our ally, the Government of the Republic of China. We do not ignore the 12 million people in Taiwan. Nor, in fact, do we ignore the people on the mainland. We are very much aware of them and we have a deep friendship for them.

Nor, finally, do we ignore the Communist leadership which has established itself on the mainland. We meet with them from time to time, as at the periodic talks between our ambassadors in Warsaw. We should like to be less ignorant of them and for them to be less ignorant of us. To this end, we

* From an address to the Commonwealth Club in San Francisco, California, December 13, 1963. Printed in *The New York Times,* December 14, 1963, p. 2. Mr. Hilsman is former Assistant Secretary of State for Far Eastern Affairs.

have been striving for years to arrange an exchange of correspondents; but we have been put off with the assertion that, so long as the principal issue—which they define in terms of their absurd charge that we are "occupying" Taiwan—is unresolved, there can be no progress on "secondary issues."

If we have not persuaded the Chinese Communists to allow an exchange of correspondents and to lower the wall of secrecy with which they surround themselves, we have nevertheless spent considerable effort in trying to understand what manner of men the Chinese Communists are, what are their ambitions, and what are the problems which stand in their way. We have tried to be objective, and to see to it that dislike of Communism does not becloud our ability to see the facts.

We shall be in danger if we let our policies be guided by emotionalism, or our thought processes by clichés. First and foremost, the Chinese Communist leaders have shown themselves to be dangerously overconfident and wedded to outdated theories, but pragmatic when their existence is threatened.

Take the example of the so-called Great Leap Forward of 1958–1960. You have undoubtedly heard that it was a catastrophe, and so it was. The Chinese Communist leaders did not understand the laws of the economically possible, and they undertook to do what could not be done. The collapse was extraordinary. Agriculture has barely regained its 1957 level, but there may be 70 million more mouths to feed. Industrial production fell by perhaps one-half between 1959 and 1962. The Chinese Communists first blamed the weather, then blamed the Russians. But, as their educated men must know, they have above all else to blame their own attempt to rewrite economics.

Failure of the Great Leap is not the only lesson which we may learn from this period of internal crisis. Though the economy collapsed, the regime did not. Nor was its authority effectively challenged. Equally important, the leaders have learned, and publicly admit, that it will take generations before China becomes a modern industrial power. They have finally shown an ability to temper their grandiose slogans and frenetic schemes.

To be sure, Communism has yet to prove that it can make agriculture work. The Communists have swallowed their Marxism and allowed the return of small private plots, but they have not abandoned collectivized agriculture. This dogmatic contrariness in a land which is still overwhelmingly agricultural may yet bring them even greater troubles. Moreover, recent failures have eroded the morale and discipline of the movement. Nevertheless, the Communists did correct the most dangerous mistakes of the Great Leap Forward. When their survival depended upon it, they showed flexibility in meeting the threat, and we have no reason to believe that there is a present likelihood that the Communist regime will be overthrown.

A second major fact about Communist China's leaders is their parochialism: They have seen extraordinarily little of the outside world, and their world view is further constricted by their ideology.

Thirty to 40 years ago, they took over certain Marxist economic assumptions and Lenin's technique for organizing a disciplined party. To these, Mao Tse-tung added certain tactical innovations. Such methods worked in their struggle for power, and they expect them to work in their struggle for modernization.

I believe, however, that there are men at the second echelon who know that the Great Leap Forward reflected a stubborn addiction to theories which do not work in a modern world. Yet I wonder whether the leadership has absorbed the same lessons. These are the "Marxist puritans." They see all the world as a conflict between unblemished good and unredeemable evil. Few people consider themselves wrong and evil, but there are very few people on earth who are so sublimely confident as are the Chinese Communist leaders that they are always right and good. They have arrogated to themselves the right to represent the "revolution." Those who disagree are automatically wrong and evil. This attitude is displayed in their quarrel with the Russians.

Perhaps I am too optimistic, but there is some evidence of evolutionary forces at work in mainland China. As I have said, the present leaders have seen remarkably little of the outside world. They have conquered mainland China. They may believe that, with concepts unchanged, they can go on to conquer the world.

These leaders, however, were deep in rural China when the rest of the world was debating Keynes and sharpening the tools of economic analysis. They may not yet have absorbed all the lessons of the Great Leap Forward; but the more sophisticated second echelon of leadership undoubtedly knows that it was simple ignorance of the techniques of administering a complex economy which led to many of the mistakes of 1958 . . .

As these ideas seep upward or as the present leaders retire, this awareness may eventually profoundly erode the present simple view with which the leadership regards the world.

Furthermore, an economy becomes geometrically more complex as it modernizes, as the stages of production multiply, and as wants become more diverse. Rule by command becomes progressively less effective than encouraging the exercise of personal initiative in running such a society. The Chinese Communists have shown that they see the problem; but they have not shown themselves willing to sacrifice their doctrinal orthodoxy, as will be required if they are to deal with the problem . . .

What about the appeal of the Chinese Communists to the new nations of the world? They have scored some successes with extremists everywhere in identifying themselves as the radical end of the Communist movement.

Peking has been alert to the worldwide opportunities for playing on nationalistic differences and prejudices and gaining toeholds within the so-called national liberation movements or among the dissatisfied and disgruntled. We may expect this process to continue. These successes, however, may be more apparent than real. As extremists approach power, they may become less radical and may weigh more heavily the questions as to who can offer them more support and more protection.

The Chinese Communists have set themselves up as a model for the less developed nations. But, like the king in the fairy tale, they seem unaware that they have no clothes. Others see, though the Chinese Communists have not, that the failure of the Great Leap Forward has shown the model to be gravely deficient.

The tragedy of the closed and stagnant society on the mainland is dramatized by the robust survival of an alternative model for Chinese development: The record of the Government of the Republic of China on Taiwan.

Stereotypes die hard, and Communist China by its sheer size exercises a fascination; but if the economic techniques used by the Republic of China over the next few years yield the great gains in economic and social welfare that we have reason to expect, the impact on other developing nations will be considerable.

There has perhaps been more emotion about our China policy than about our policy toward any single country since World War II. Yet our nation must look squarely at China, pursuing policies which will protect the interests of our country, of the free world, and of men of goodwill everywhere.

Our prime objective concerning Communist China is that it not subvert or commit aggression against its free world neighbors. It must not be allowed to accomplish for Communism through force of arms that success which it has rarely achieved at the ballot box. President Kennedy called our purposes in the Far East "peaceful and defensive." And so they remain.

There is one other area in which questions have been raised about American policy, and in which a clarification of this Government's position is timely: I refer to the apparent differences in the policies which we are adopting toward the Soviet Union and toward Communist China. We maintain a policy of nonrecognition and a trade embargo of Communist China—at a time when we are willing to broaden contact with the Soviet Union.

The Soviet Union and Communist China do share the goal of Communizing the world. But we see important differences in the thinking and tactics of the two. In the U.S.S.R., the Communists were developing a modern industrial society precisely when in China they were conducting a guerrilla war from rural bases.

The Soviet leadership seems to have absorbed certain lessons from its more extended development—as to the values and priorities which one may safely pursue on a small planet, and as to the price of miscalculating the nature of the outside world. We believe that the policies which have proved their worth with Moscow are equally valid for our long-term relations with Peking. But we also believe that our approach should be adapted to the differences in behavior between the two, as they relate to our own national objectives.

First and foremost, we fully honor our close and friendly ties with the people of the Republic of China on Taiwan, and with their Government . . .

Our differing policies toward the Soviet Union and Communist China derive, secondly, from their differing attitudes toward negotiations, as such, even in limited areas. Faced with the realities of the nuclear age, the Soviet Union appears to recognize that certain interests—notably survival—are shared by all mankind.

Peking, however, remains wedded to a fundamentalist form of Communism which emphasizes violent revolution, even if it threatens the physical ruin of the civilized world . . .

United States policy is influenced by Chinese Communism's obsessive suspicion of the outside world, far exceeding even that of the Soviet Union . . .

Fourth are the differing circumstances and opportunities on the peripheries of the Soviet Union and Communist China. The Soviet Union and European members of its bloc border on long-established, relatively stable states defended by powerful, locally based—as well as more distant—deterrent and defensive forces.

Communist China's neighbors, on the other hand, include newly established states struggling to maintain their independence with very limited defense forces. There is a wider range of opportunities for aggression and subversion available to Peking, which renders it even more important that in dealing with Peking we not permit that regime to underestimate free-world firmness and determination.

Much speculation has been made of possible commercial relations between private American firms and Communist China, especially in view of the declining trade between Communist China and its Soviet bloc partners. Peking's own policies, however, seem crystal-clear on this point. Peking apparently wants none of it . . .

In sum, while respecting the right of others to view the matter otherwise, we find important differences in the willingness and ability of the Soviet Union and Communist China, at the present stage of their respective development, to reach limited agreements which can bring some reduction of the terrible dangers and tensions of our present-day world.

We believe that policies of strength and firmness, accompanied by a constant readiness to negotiate—policies long and effectively pursued with the Soviet Union—will best promote the changes which must take place on the China mainland before we can hope to achieve long-sought conditions of peace, security and progress in this half of the globe.

We do not know what changes may occur in the attitudes of future Chinese leaders. But, if I may paraphrase a classic canon of our past, we pursue today toward Communist China a policy of the open door: we are determined to keep the door open to the possibility of change, and not to slam it shut against any developments which might advance our national good, serve the free world, and benefit the people of China.

Patience is not unique to the Chinese. We too can maintain our positions without being provoked to unseemly action of despairing of what the future may hold. We will not sow the dragon's seed of hate which may bear bitter fruit in future generations of China's millions. But neither will we betray our interests and those of our allies to appease the ambitions of Communist China's leaders.

We hope that, confronted with firmness which will make foreign adventure unprofitable, and yet offered the prospect that the way back into the community of man is not closed to it, the Chinese Communist regime will eventually forsake its present venomous hatreds which spring from a rigid class view of society.

We hope that they will rediscover the Chinese virtue of tolerance for a multitude of beliefs and faiths; and that they will accept again a world of diversity, in place of the gray monolith which seems to be Communism's goal for human society.

Wars of National Liberation Are Not Dangerous*

Central Committee, Chinese Communist Party

Certain persons say that revolutions are entirely possible without war. Now which type of war are they referring to—is it a war of national liberation, or a revolutionary civil war, or is it a world war?

If they are referring to a war of national liberation or a revolutionary civil war, then this formulation is, in effect, opposed to revolutionary wars and to revolution.

If they are referring to a world war, then they are shooting at a nonexistent target. Although Marxist-Leninists have pointed out, on the basis of the history of the two world wars, that world wars inevitably lead to revolution, no Marxist-Leninist ever has held or ever will hold that revolution must be made through world war.

Marxist-Leninists take the abolition of war as their ideal and believe that war can be abolished.

But how can war be abolished?

This is how Lenin viewed it:

> Our object is to achieve the Socialist system of society, which, by abolishing the division of mankind into classes, by abolishing all exploitation of man by man, and of one nation by other nations, will inevitably abolish all possibility of war.

* From a letter of the Central Committee of the Chinese Communist Party to the Central Committee of the Soviet Communist Party, June 14, 1963.

The statement of 1960 also puts it very clearly:

> The victory of Socialism all over the world will completely remove the social and national causes of all wars.

However, certain persons now actually hold that it is possible to bring about "a world without weapons, without armed forces and without wars" through "general and complete disarmament" while the system of imperialism and of the exploitation of man by man still exists. This is sheer illusion.

An elementary knowledge of Marxism-Leninism tells us that the armed forces are the principal part of the state machine and that a so-called world without weapons and without armed forces can only be a world without states. Lenin said:

> Only after the proletariat has disarmed the bourgeoisie will it be able, without betraying its world-historical mission, to throw all armaments on the scrap heap; and the proletariat will undoubtedly do this, but only when this condition has been fulfilled, certainly not before.

What are the facts in the world today? Is there a shadow of evidence that the imperialist countries headed by the United States are ready to carry out general and complete disarmament? Are they not each and all engaged in general and complete arms expansion?

We have always maintained that, in order to expose and combat the imperialists' arms expansion and war preparations, it is necessary to put forward the proposal for general disarmament through the combined struggle of the Socialist countries and the people of the whole world.

If one regards general and complete disarmament as the fundamental road to world peace, spreads the illusion that imperialism will automatically lay down its arms, and tries to liquidate the revolutionary struggle of the oppressed peoples and nations on the pretext of disarmament, then this is deliberately to deceive the people of the world and help the imperialists in their policies of aggression and war.

In order to overcome the present ideological confusion in the international working-class movement on the question of war and peace, we consider that Lenin's thesis, which has been discarded by the modern revisionists, must be restored in the interest of combating the imperialist policies of aggression and war and defending world peace.

The people of the world universally demand the prevention of a new world war. And it is possible to prevent a new world war.

The question then is, what is the way to secure world peace? According to the Leninist viewpoint, world peace can be won only by the struggles of the people in all countries and not by begging the imperialists for it. World peace can only be effectively defended by relying on the development of the forces of the Socialist camp, on the revolutionary struggles of the proletariat and working people of all countries, on the liberation struggles of the oppressed nations and on the struggles of all peace-loving people and countries.

Such is the Leninist policy. Any policy to the contrary definitely will not lead to world peace but will only encourage the ambitions of the imperialists and increase the danger of world war.

In recent years, certain persons have been spreading the argument that a single spark from a war of national liberation or from a revolutionary people's war will lead to a world conflagration destroying the whole of mankind. What are the facts? Contrary to what these persons say, the wars of national liberation and the revolutionary people's wars that have occurred since World War II have not led to world war. The victory of these revolutionary wars has directly weakened the forces of imperialism and greatly strengthened the forces which prevent the imperialists from launching a world war and which defend world peace. Do not the facts demonstrate the absurdity of this argument?

The complete banning and destruction of nuclear weapons is an important task in the struggle to defend world peace. We must do our utmost to this end.

Nuclear weapons are unprecedently destructive, which is why for more than a decade now the United States imperialists have been pursuing their policy of nuclear blackmail in order to realize their ambition of enslaving the people of all countries and dominating the world.

But when the imperialists threaten other countries with nuclear weapons, they subject the people in their own country to the same threat, thus arming them against nuclear weapons and against the imperialist policies of aggression and war. At the same time, in their vain hope of destroying their opponents with nuclear weapons, the imperialists are in fact subjecting themselves to the danger of being destroyed.

The possibility of banning nuclear weapons does indeed exist. However, if the imperialists are forced to accept an agreement to ban nuclear weapons, it decidedly will not be because of their "love for humanity" but because of the pressure of the people of all countries and for the sake of their own vital interests.

In contrast to the imperialists, Socialist countries rely upon the righteous strength of the people and on their own correct policies, and have no need whatever to gamble with nuclear weapons in the world arena. Socialist countries have nuclear weapons solely in order to defend themselves and to prevent imperialism from launching a nuclear war.

In the view of Marxist-Leninists, the people are the makers of history. In the present, as in the past, man is the decisive factor. Marxist-Leninists attach importance to the role of technological change, but it is wrong to belittle the role of man and exaggerate the role of technology.

The emergence of nuclear weapons can neither arrest the progress of human history nor save the imperialist system from its doom, any more than the emergence of new techniques could save the old systems from their doom in the past. . . .

World War Can Be Averted*

Central Committee, Soviet Communist Party

What is the gist of the differences between the C.P.C., on the one hand, and the C.P.S.U., the international Communist movement, on the other hand? This question is undoubtedly asked by anyone who familiarizes himself with the letter of the C.P.C. Central Committee of June 14.

At first glance, many theses of the letter may seem puzzling: Whom are the Chinese comrades actually arguing with? Are there Communists who object, for instance, to Socialist revolution or who do not regard it as their duty to fight against imperialism, to support the national-liberation movement? Why does the C.P.C. leadership set forth such theses so obtrusively?

This question may also arise: Why is it impossible to agree with the positions of the Chinese comrades set forth in their letter on many important problems? Take, for instance, such cardinal problems as war and peace. In its letter, the C.P.C. Central Committee speaks of peace and peaceful coexistence.

The essence of the matter is that having started an offensive against the positions of the Marxist-Leninist parties on cardinal problems of today, the Chinese comrades firstly ascribe to the C.P.S.U. and other Marxist-Leninist parties views which they have never expressed and which are alien to them; secondly they try, by verbal recognition of the formula and positions borrowed from the documents of the Communist movement, to camouflage their erroneous views and incorrect positions. To come out openly against the people's struggle for peace and peaceful coexistence of states with different social systems, against disarmament, etc., would mean to lay bare their positions in the eyes of the Communists of the whole world and peace-loving peoples, and to repel them.

Therefore the further the polemics develop and the clearer becomes the weakness of the positions of the C.P.C. leadership, the more zealously it resorts to such camouflage.

If this method of the Chinese comrades is not taken into consideration, it may even seem from outside that the dispute has acquired a scholastic nature, that separate formulas far removed from vital problems are the points at issue.

In point of fact, questions that bear on vital interests of the peoples are in the center of the dispute.

These are the questions of war and peace, the question of the role and

* Central Committee of the Soviet Communist Party to all party organizers and Communists of the Soviet Union, July 15, 1963.

development of the world Socialist system; these are the questions of the struggle against the ideology and practice of the "personality cult"; these are the questions of strategy and tactics of the world labor movement and the national liberation struggle.

These questions have been advanced by life itself, by the deep-going changes that have occurred in the Socialist countries throughout the world, the changes in the balance of forces in the recent years between Socialism and imperialism, the new possibilities for our movement.

The Communist movement had to give, and gave, answers to these questions by outlining the general course applicable to the conditions and the demands of the present stage of world development.

The unanimous opinion of the Communist parties is that a tremendous role in this respect was played by the 20th Congress of the C.P.S.U., which ushered in a new stage in the development of the entire Communist movement. This appraisal was recorded in the 1957 declaration and in the 1960 statement—documents of the Communist parties worked out collectively and formulating the general political course of the Communist movement in our epoch.

But the C.P.C. leaders have now advanced a different course as a counterbalance to it; their positions diverge more and more from the joint line of the Communist movement on basic issues.

This, first of all, refers to the question of war and peace.

In the appraisal of problems of war and peace, in the approach to their solution, there can be no uncertainties or reservations, for this involves the destinies of peoples, the future of all mankind.

The C.P.S.U. Central Committee believes its duty is to tell the party and the people, with all frankness, that in questions of war and peace the C.P.C. leadership has cardinal, based-on-principle differences with us, with the world Communist movement.

The essence of these differences lies in the diametrically opposite approach to problems so vital as the possibility of averting world thermonuclear war, peaceful coexistence of states with different social systems, interconnection between the struggle for peace and the development of the world revolutionary movement.

Our party in the decisions of the 20th and 22d Congresses, the world Communist movement in the declaration and the statement, set before Communists as a task of extreme importance the task of struggling for peace, for averting a world thermonuclear catastrophe. We realistically appraise the balance of forces in the world and, from this, draw conclusions that though the nature of imperialism has not changed, and the danger of the outbreak of war has not been averted, in modern conditions the forces of peace, of which the mighty community of Socialist states is the main bulwark, can, by their joint efforts, avert a new world war.

We also soberly appraise the radical, qualitative change in the means of waging war and, consequently, its possible aftermaths. The nuclear rocket weapons that were created in the middle of our century changed the old notions about war. These weapons possess an unheard-of devastating force.

Suffice it to say that the explosion of only one powerful thermonuclear bomb surpasses the explosive force of all ammunition used during all previous wars, including World Wars I and II. And many thousands of such bombs have been accumulated!

Do Communists have the right to ignore this danger? Do we have to tell the people all the truth about the consequences of thermonuclear war? We believe that undoubtedly we must. This cannot have a "paralyzing" effect on the masses, as the Chinese comrades assert. On the contrary: truth about modern war will mobilize the will and the energy of the masses to the struggle for peace, against imperialism—this source of military danger.

The historic task of Communists is to organize and head the struggle of the peoples for averting a world thermonuclear war.

To prevent a new world war is quite a real and feasible task. The 20th Congress of our party formed the extremely important conclusion that in our times there is no fatal inevitability of war between states.

This conclusion is not a fruit of good intentions but the result of a realistic, strictly scientific analysis of the balance of class forces in the world arena; it is based on the gigantic might of world Socialism. Our views on this question are shared by the entire world Communist movement.

World war can be averted; a real possibility to exclude world war from the life of society will appear yet before the complete victory of Socialism on earth, while capitalism still remains in a part of the world. . . .

The Great Schism: On Sino-Soviet Conflicts*

Hugh Seton-Watson

No problem of world politics today is likely to have greater effects on the fate of the human race in the rest of this century than the relationship between Russia and China. Plenty of mystery still surrounds this subject, and it is hardly surprising that the leaders of the two countries are unwilling to speak plainly about it to citizens of hostile states. But this does not mean that nothing is known of it. On the contrary, not only are Chinese official materials available in some quantity in English, in addition to a steadily improving coverage of Chinese news in the Anglo-Saxon press, but the secondary literature

* From *Encounter*, May 1963, pp. 61–70. Reprinted by permission. Mr. Seton-Watson is Professor of Russian History at the University of London.

of the subject in Western languages is already large, and includes some works of high quality. This literature certainly makes it possible for persons who are not Old China Hands, know no Chinese, but are politically literate and possess critical powers, to get a reasonable idea of the issues involved.

It is convenient to distinguish three periods: the background before Communist victory in China, the first eight years of the Communist regime, and the period of acute Sino-Soviet conflict since 1958. In the first two periods an attempt will be made to separate the relations between the Governments from the relations between the Communist Parties, but in the more recent period these have to be taken together. The survey of the course of the conflict will lead to some observations about future prospects.

First among the historical factors is Chinese pride, the survival of the belief that China is "the Middle Kingdom" and that the rest of the earth consists of outer barbarians, placed around the periphery of the civilised world, and destined to pay tribute to it. China, we are repeatedly assured by the Sinologues, is not a nation or an empire but a civilisation. The non-Sinologue gets the impression, from reading or conversing with Sinologues, that there is some unique quality in Chinese arrogance, and something with which very often Westerners who have lived in China consciously identify themselves. This special essence, if it exists, is something which those of us who do not know China cannot grasp. But at least it is not difficult to understand that the educated class of a country which for millennia was either the greatest or one of the greatest Powers, and whose civilisation, if not the oldest, was perhaps the most uninterruptedly maintained for the longest consecutive period in human history, should have passionately resented the humiliations of the last two hundred years at the hands of Europeans. Among the Europeans, perhaps even outstanding among them, were the Russians.

Second in importance are the territorial problems that have caused conflict between China and Russia since the mid-19th century. The Russian government exploited China's involvement in war with Britain and France to seize the land between the Amur, the Ussuri, and the Pacific, and to found there a naval base with the arrogant name of "Ruler of the East" (*Vladivostok*). Russia did its best to seize Korea, a tributary state of China, and its plans were defeated not by China but by Japan. In Manchuria the Russians were more successful, and even after their defeat by the Japanese in 1905 they kept their Chinese Eastern Railway, a fortress of political and military as well as economic value. When the Bolsheviks took the place of the Tsar, they first talked of handing the railway back to China, but they did not repeat the promise when they were in a position to implement it. (They kept the railway until 1935, and then sold it to the Japanese.) In Mongolia the Russians in 1911 appeared as protectors of the Mongols against the Chinese, and though Mongolia was nominally autonomous under Chinese suzerainty it became a vassal of Russia. In 1919 the Bolsheviks repudiated the privileges held by the Imperial government in Mongolia, but in 1921 they invaded it, and since then the Mongolian People's Republic has been a vassal of the Soviet

Union. Chinese Turkestan (Sinkiang) was also an object of contention between Imperial Russia and China. Here, too, in the 1930s, Soviet influence was strong, at the expense of the Chinese government.

The story of relations between the Communist Parties of the Soviet Union and China is not one of happy comradeship. Soviet advice to the Chinese Communists in the 1920s was close alliance with the Kuomintang. This continued long after Chiang Kai-shek had shown himself an enemy. Insistence by the Comintern (which meant Stalin) that the Chinese Communists should take no action against Chiang led to the massacre of Communist workers in Shanghai in April, 1927, and to further humiliations and repression by the Kuomintang later in the year. These disasters have never been forgotten by Mao Tse-tung, who saved a remnant of Communist forces in the wilderness, and built up his nucleus of power in the following ten years, despite Stalin's preference for his rivals within the party. Factional disputes were connected with the question whether greater reliance should be placed on urban workers or peasants. But essentially this was a dispute not about social analysis but about power. Mao used peasants because they were the only people available to be used by any Chinese revolutionary movement, whether Marxist or not. Mao showed later that he was no romantic "peasant-loving Populist." But his struggle against the Moscow leadership did not teach him to love Stalin.

The Chinese Communists are often called "Stalinists." This is only true in the very vague sense that they are men who use "hard" rather than "soft" methods. It would be better to drop the adjective "Stalinist." The striking thing about them, when they emerged into the public view at the end of World War II, was how little they conformed to the universal Communist practice of fawning on Stalin. In his speech to the 7th Congress of his party, on May 14th, 1945 (published in 1951 under the title *On the Party*), Liu Shao-chi at one point referred to Mao as "a disciple of Marx, Engels, Lenin, and Stalin." But this homage is dwarfed by the endless references to "the Thought of Mao Tse-tung," repeatedly described as that which "unites the theories of Marxism-Leninism with the actual practice of the Chinese revolution." . . .

After the Communists had conquered China in 1949, it seemed at first that their relations with the Soviet Union were friendly. But behind the façade things were not so good. Stalin had given little help to the Communists in the civil war. He admitted to the Yugoslavs in 1948 that he had "underestimated their chances." In 1945 he had secured the interests of the Soviet Union by a treaty with their enemy Chiang Kai-shek which had given him control of the Manchurian railways, Port Arthur and Dairen. These were not given back to the Communists until well after their victory—the railways in 1952 and Port Arthur in 1955. The Soviet government continued to insist on the independence of Mongolia, which Communists and Kuomintang alike regarded as part of China. Perhaps most important, the Soviet government showed itself far from generous with economic aid. In 1945 the industrial equipment of the factories built in Manchuria by the Japanese since 1931 was removed to Russia. It was not until the mid-1950s that it was replaced. The new equipment was of higher quality than that which had been removed, but the Chinese had to pay for it. It is true that in the post-war years the Soviet Union, painfully recovering from wartime devastation, was not in a position to give much help to anyone. But it remained a fact that the total aid given by the Russians to the Chinese was negligible in relation to China's needs for economic development. . . .

The relations between the Soviet Union and China during the Korean War (and the effect of Chinese military intervention on the relative strength of Soviet and Chinese influence within the Korean Communist party) are still obscure. But one important consequence of the war is clear. The Chinese learned that the newly independent states of Asia, and especially India, were not—as Soviet propaganda since 1947 had said they were—puppet creations of the Western imperialists who continued to rule them by other means. The Chinese learned that India was an independent state, and that it was both desirable and possible to have friendly relations with her. The Chinese led the way in adopting a new Communist policy towards "Asian neutralists," which received its most striking expression at the Bandung conference of 1955. In the Soviet Union the death of Stalin did not bring a change, perhaps because the new Soviet leaders were exclusively concerned with Lenin's old problem of "Who-whom?" They lagged behind China, and it was not until the Khrushchev-Bulganin visit to India in November, 1955, that courtship of neutralists began to be a priority of Soviet foreign policy.

The twentieth congress of the CPSU seems to have been received with mixed feelings in Peking. As we have seen, Mao had little love for Stalin, but Khrushchev's impetuous launching of "de-Stalinisation" was hardly to his taste. In the summer of 1956 the Chinese began to take a hand in the affairs of Eastern Europe. In September, 1956, a Polish delegation to the Ninth Congress of the Chinese Communist Party, led by Edward Ochab, found much encouragement for the Polish party's independent attitude (including its opposition to the Soviet view of the Poznan rising of July). For months after this, the "liberal" elements in the Polish party were convinced that China was on their side. In reality, the Chinese were interested not in "liberalism" but in equality between parties, that is, in reducing the predominance of the Soviet party. This became clear when they came out strongly in defence of the Soviet action in Hungary. In an emergency all Communists must stand together. However, this did not mean perpetual deferment to the Soviet comrades, nor did the Chinese patronage of the Poles improve Sino-Soviet relations.

During 1957 the Chinese made their curious experiment with the "Hundred Flowers" campaign. Strongly urged by Mao himself to express their opinions freely, the intellectuals fiercely attacked the regime. The party replied with brutal repression, and a general change of course, in economic and political affairs, from a "right" to a "left" policy. The other event of 1957 which most impressed the Chinese was the launching of the first *sputnik*. This seems to have convinced Mao that the balance of world power had decisively changed, and that a much bolder foreign policy was possible for "the socialist camp." At the conference of Communist parties in Moscow in November, 1957, Mao declared:

> I think the characteristic of the situation today is the East wind prevailing over the West wind. That is to say, the socialist forces are overwhelmingly superior to the imperialist forces.

At the end of the year, with the definite restoration of Soviet superiority in Eastern Europe, with Khrushchev's victory over the "anti-Party group" of Molotov and the failure of the Army's challenge represented by Marshal Zhukov, and with the publication of the militant Manifesto of the twelve ruling Communist parties, Sino-Soviet relations seemed once more to be on a sound basis.

However, the year 1958 brought the worst conflict yet seen between the two regimes.

The adoption of a "left" course in China led to a rush forward into extreme policies and fantastic ideological claims. A Resolution of August 29th, 1958, announced the introduction of "People's Communes." This decision must no doubt mainly be explained by economic factors. China's economic backwardness was being made more intolerable every year by steadily mounting population pressure. The only line of advance seemed to be the ruthless exploitation of the country's main resource, manpower. The Communes were designed to mobilise manpower still more ruthlessly and systematically than had been the case in Russia at the beginning of the First Five Year Plan. Public hardships could have been reduced only if substantial aid were forthcoming from an advanced industrial country. The only possible source was the Soviet Union, and it seems reasonable to assume that an important reason for the decision to embark on People's Communes was the knowledge that the Soviet Union would not give large-scale aid. But if economic necessity was the motive, the opportunity was taken to claim ideological virtue. The Chinese asserted that through their Communes they had discovered a short-cut to *Communism*. They clearly implied that they might reach Communism ahead of the Soviet Union, whose Revolution had preceded theirs by thirty years. This monstrous affront was greeted in Russia with public silence (though there was plenty of indirect evidence that it was repudiated). What arguments or recriminations were conducted in secret, is not known. But in December the Chinese publicly retreated. A Resolution of the Central Committee of December 10th admitted that even the completion of *socialism* in China would still require "ten, fifteen, twenty, or more years. . . ." There was no more talk of achieving Communism in the near future. But it would take more than a party Resolution to remove the ideological rage caused on both sides by the earlier claim.

In July, 1958, the revolution in Iraq and the civil war in Lebanon caused an international crisis. Khrushchev suggested a summit meeting. At first he agreed that this should take place at the Security Council of the United Nations—of which the government of China was not a member but the Formosan government was. A few days later he rejected this idea, but still favoured a summit meeting at which India was to be present, but not China. Thus, he was placing the "non-socialist" India above his "socialist" ally China, and also according India a higher status as a Great Power than the 600-million Power China. It is hardly surprising that when Khrushchev arrived in Peking on July 31st, 1958, he received a cold reception.

There was a further reason for this. Acting on the assumption that, with the launching of *sputnik* and of a Soviet ICBM, "the East wind prevailed over the West wind," Mao Tse-tung decided that the time had come to "liberate" Formosa. He expected his Soviet ally to go to the brink of war to support him. But Khrushchev would do nothing more than promise that if the United States attacked mainland China with nuclear weapons he would retaliate on the United States. This, of course, was not enough. The Chinese alone could not take Formosa, or even the off-shore island of Quemoy. Nor would the Soviet Union give them nuclear weapons to use on their own behalf. The shelling of the off-shore islands from mid-August to the end of September, 1958, ended in a Chinese retreat.

The importance of the Formosa issue in Sino-Soviet hostility cannot be overrated. . . .

At the beginning of 1959 there was a lull in Sino-Soviet relations. The doctrine expounded by Khrushchev at the 21st Congress of the CPSU in February, that all socialist states would enter Communism "at about the same time," was intended to smooth over the difficulties. But Chinese resentment at Soviet failure to support China in Formosa, and at its attitude to India and to the new states generally, remained bitter. The bitterness was greatly increased by two factors which continued to operate for the next three years. One was the growing economic chaos in China, largely resulting from the People's Communes policy and the fantastic projects for small-scale heavy industry associated with it. The other was the growing economic aid offered by the Soviet Union to "non-socialist" countries of Asia, Africa, and Latin America. Every year the plight of the Chinese people became more desperate, and every year the discrepancy between massive Soviet aid outside the bloc (or to European countries of the bloc) and Soviet indifference to China's needs became more shocking. . . .

The next major event in the Sino-Soviet controversy was the publication on April 22nd, 1960, the ninetieth anniversary of Lenin's birth, of an article in *Red Flag* entitled *"Long Live Leninism!"* This boldly stated the Chinese doctrine in what was to become the main ideological issue in the Sino-Soviet conflict, the issue of "the inevitability of war." It insisted on the incurably bellicose and predatory nature of the imperialists, and dismissed the argument that nuclear war was an unacceptable disaster for the human race. Should the imperialists resort to nuclear war, the sacrifices endured by the human race would be worth paying.

> On the débris of a dead imperialism, the victorious people would create very swiftly a civilisation thousands of times higher than the capitalist system and a truly beautiful future for themselves. . . .

In November–December, 1960, a conference of the Communist Parties of the world wrestled for more than a month with the Sino-Soviet conflict. It ended with the publication of the Manifesto of the 81 parties, which solved nothing. The document indicated a victory for the Soviet point of view, though there were some phrases which appeared designed to placate the Chinese. But in fact the Chinese abandoned none of their positions. They were strongly supported only by the Albanians. . . .

Apart from Albania, the Chinese had some support from the Indonesian and Vietnamese parties, and possibly enjoyed more sympathy in some Asian and Latin American parties than their official leaders would admit. But overwhelmingly the Communists of the world supported Moscow against Peking. . . .

During the first half of 1961 there was at least less open hostility between Moscow and Peking, but there was no reconciliation. In China economic failure reached the point of famine, and Soviet help was negligible.

At the 22nd Congress of the CPSU the Sino-Soviet conflict once more became public, with Chou En-lai's ostentatious homage at Stalin's mausoleum, the Congress decision to remove Stalin's body from it, and the denunciations of Albania. Thereafter the conflict took the form of polemics between Moscow and Tirana, with the Chinese press giving greater publicity to the Albanian than to the Soviet point of view. . . .

The Cuban crisis and the Chinese attack on India coincided, and during the Cuban crisis the Soviet government appeared for a few days to be backing the Chinese. But when the crisis was over, it became clear that Khrushchev was not going to commit himself. The Chinese, speaking through the Albanians, denounced the Soviet government for failing in Cuba and for refusing to condemn India. . . .

A series of articles in *People's Daily* at the beginning of March carried on the ideological polemic against the modern revisionists. It denounced those who "claim to possess the totality of Marxist-Leninist truth," but are "cowardly as mice." The Chinese proudly declared that they had published the articles hostile to themselves, together with their replies, but that the press of their opponents would not do likewise.

> You fear the truth. The spectre of "dogmatism," the spectre of genuine Marxism-Leninism, is haunting the world, and it threatens you.

Hardly less alarming for the Soviet leaders than this echo of the Communist Manifesto was another argument, raised in *People's Daily* on March

7th. Some time earlier, reacting to Chinese criticism of his retreat in Cuba, Khrushchev had taunted the Chinese with their failure to liquidate the imperialist outposts of Hongkong and Macao. *People's Daily,* replying ostensibly to a similar taunt from the American Communist Party, pointed out that there were nine unequal treaties formerly signed by China with imperialist Powers which had annexed Chinese territory in north, south, east, and west, and held leased territories on the seaboard and in the hinterland of China. These nine clearly included those by which Imperial Russia had acquired the Maritime Province with Vladivostok, and some territories in Central Asia over which China had once had sovereignty. *People's Daily* now asked:

> By raising questions of this category, do you aim at re-opening all the unequal treaty questions in order to have a general settlement? Has it ever entered your head what the consequences would be?

On March 10th it was announced in Peking that there had been an exchange of letters between the Soviet and Chinese Communist parties which had "affirmed the necessity of holding talks between the two parties on important questions affecting the international Communist movement at present." The Chinese stated that they would be glad to see Khrushchev or some other leading Soviet comrade in Peking.

Whether this was a genuinely friendly move, or merely another manœuvre in the political warfare, was not clear. It seemed, however, highly improbable that a conference could now remove the most important sources of conflict between the Soviet Union and China. These are: (1) Soviet refusal of brinkmanship on behalf of Formosa; (2) Soviet refusal of economic aid to China on a scale remotely approaching China's needs; (3) jealousy of India and resentment of Soviet aid to India; (4) the ideological claims of Mao as a prophet of Marxism; and (5) latent territorial disputes of which the most important is probably Mongolia, but which may now include also the future of the Far Eastern Province of the Soviet Union. It is impossible to assign an order of priority to these, but together they constitute a formidable body of disagreement.

What are the possible consequences of the Sino-Soviet conflict? I can offer no more than a few working hypotheses which may be worth keeping in mind.

The most important of the unknown factors is the development of the economy. The pressure of population on resources relentlessly increases. It is sometimes argued that because Stalin was able to achieve economic progress in the 1930s by ruthless mobilisation of manpower, the Chinese will be able to do the same, even if at greater cost in human suffering. But it is arguable that the problems facing China are different in kind from those which faced Russia in the 1930s. Far too little comparative study has been made of the two economies, and perhaps even in Peking too little is known. Superficial comparisons are not enlightening. China's economic problems may be substantially increased if it becomes necessary to fight a long war with India. In March, 1963, it seems possible that the Indian-Chinese quarrel may be allowed to smoulder quietly for a time, but this is by no means certain. China was able to achieve successes on the north-east frontier in October and November, 1962, because her immediately available striking force was larger and better armed than the Indian; but in a long war India, with substantial help from the West, could put up a resistance which before long would place a severe additional strain on China. Moreover, China has other military opponents of which at least some account must be taken: the Tibetan guerrillas and the Formosa army. Thus a second unknown factor, the strength of India's will to resist, will be of great importance.

In March, 1963, it appears that economic conditions in China have somewhat improved in recent months. However, in the longer term it is difficult to see how China can stand up to its economic and military tasks unless its whole economic policy is reversed and unless it receives substantial Soviet aid. But it is most unlikely that the Soviet government will do anything to help the present Chinese leadership. It is even arguable that Moscow would rather see Indian victories, the loss of Tibet, economic chaos, and occupation of part of the mainland by Chiang Kai-shek, than see the Mao Tse-tung–Liu Shao-chi leadership strengthened. However this may be, it seems a reasonable hypothesis that a restoration of Sino-Soviet friendship, and a large increase of Soviet aid to China, will require a drastic purge of the Peking leadership. Whether this is likely to occur, I am quite unqualified to predict. Yet even if there were a purge in China, we may doubt whether the Soviet government would show much enthusiasm for helping China. It may well feel that *any* government in China is likely to frustrate the aims of Soviet policy in regard to Japan, India, and South-East Asia, and to interfere with Soviet-American relations in unpredictable and dangerous ways. It will almost certainly feel that the economic demands of *any* Chinese government would far exceed the resources which *any* Soviet government can spare, at a time when the demands of the Soviet people for a higher standard of living can no longer be ignored.

Meanwhile, Chinese action against India has affected Soviet policy both in the *tiers monde* and in Eastern Europe.

Soviet strategy towards the under-developed countries has been based for some years on wooing the "national bourgeoisie." Countries allied with the West (in CENTO or SEATO) have not been regarded as independent states. But non-aligned countries are considered politically, but not yet economically, independent. The goal held out to them by Soviet propaganda has been "economic independence," and the bogey which they have been urged to avoid has been "neo-colonialism." As long as any foreign private business firms control any important branches of the economy of a new state, neo-colonialism is said to be present. Economic independence can be achieved only when all major foreign business is expropriated, when Western aid is for the most part replaced by the "unselfish, disinterested aid of the socialist camp," and when trade with the Soviet bloc is more important than trade with the West. Meanwhile the "state sector" of the economy in such countries as India and Egypt is regarded as "objectively progressive," and is felt to deserve Soviet support, even if it is controlled by the "national bourgeoisie," and not by "the working class" (a euphemism for the Communist Party), and though the claims of such men as Nehru, Nasser, or Nkrumah to be "socialists" are consequently fraudulent.

This policy brought considerable successes to the Soviet government in the years 1957–62. The "neo-colonialist" charge is particularly effective in tropical Africa, in many of whose new states it must be admitted that it is more than a bogey. But the show-piece of Soviet policy was certainly India. The Chinese attack appears to have wrecked Soviet policy in India. Even if the fighting is not revived, it seems improbable that India will for a long time revert to the Nehru-Menon "double standard" which gave such satisfaction in Moscow. In the perhaps improbable event that the talk about Indian-Pakistan reconciliation were translated into action, the Soviet loss would be still greater. On the other hand it is not certain that India's changed position need damage Soviet interests in Africa. It may be that the Arab states will be worried by India's troubles—but in tropical Africa the Indians are not loved. It is by no means clear that the Indian-Chinese fighting will diminish the attraction of the radical African nationalists towards the Communist world. Nor is there much reason to believe that Latin American revolutionaries will prefer a Chinese to a Soviet orientation. The Soviet Union is in a position to give them far more help than is China. No doubt Castro prefers Mao to Khrushchev, but what can Mao do for him? No doubt those Communists who wish to make greater use of the peasant guerrillas in Colombia and in north-east Brazil will look to Peking for inspiration, but the existence of "left-wing sectarianism" within some Latin American Communist parties is not likely to create much alarm in Moscow. In fact, the harm done to Soviet policy in the *tiers monde* by Chinese action may be confined to the Indian subcontinent. Even so, this is a serious loss.

An important effect of the conflict with China has been that Khrushchev has felt an increasing need for the support of other Communist parties, and has had to pay the price of granting them greater freedom from Soviet control.

Two East European Communist parties which have very little genuine support among their peoples—the Hungarian and Rumanian—have used this situation to court greater popularity by giving their subjects better material conditions and somewhat more liberty. . . .

In non-bloc Communist parties in Europe the trend has certainly been towards less subservience to Moscow and less doctrinal rigidity—in short, towards a "right-wing" course. This has been most marked in the Italian party, which has incurred the bitterest insults of the Albanians. It seems also likely that if the French party thinks there are good prospects of a Popular Front in France, it too will adopt a more "moderate" posture.

In general, Western observers may be pleased that Soviet policy in

India has suffered a reverse, and that Hungarians, Rumanians, and perhaps now even Bulgarians are enjoying a more agreeable existence. For both these changes they may thank the Chinese. If there should arise a rival Communist international, Trotskyism with a territorial base, under Chinese leadership, with its agents intriguing within existing Communist parties or creating rival parties, this too would help the West. But extravagant speculations about an alliance "between the West and Russia against China" would seem to me to have no justification for the predictable future. It is also important not to fall into the error of regarding Khrushchev as "a liberal" because the Chinese dislike him, or of interpreting the Soviet double-talk "peaceful coexistence" as equivalent to the Western concept of "peace." Before the Cuban crisis, Khrushchev appeared to believe that the incurable decadence of "the capitalist world" and the weak will of its leaders, would give him victory on a world scale without war and—in contrast to the Chinese view—without even having "to go to the brink." In Cuba he tried his hand at brinkmanship, thus coming closer to the action recommended by the Chinese (though there are no grounds for believing that he was influenced by Chinese pressure). Having approached the brink, he drew back, incurring Chinese abuse. But this does not mean that his world-wide aims have been abandoned.

A realistic Western policy will bear all this in mind. It will avoid all dogmatism, either a doctrinaire belief in negotiation, or a doctrinaire belief in toughness for toughness' sake. It will recognise that both Khrushchev and Mao are enemies of the West and enemies of each other.

9

India: The Prospects for Democracy

India, though it cannot be classed as a Great Power, is one of the most important states of the world. With a population of about 440 million, it is the second most populous country of Asia and the world. Among the "new countries" that have emerged from colonial status since World War II, India enjoys a clear primacy because of her size and population, and because she is the largest democracy in existence. Her form of government sets an example of success and stability to other newly independent states. In foreign policy, also, India is a leader in the "Third World"; for, being among the first to gain independence, she set the pattern of emphatic nonalignment and nonparticipation in the Cold War that has been the typical foreign-policy attitude of the ex-colonial countries.

Although India has a fairly large area and a very large population, China so greatly exceeds India in both respects that India cannot possibly overtake or surpass the Chinese giant. Indeed, if China enjoys any considerable measure of success at all in her efforts at economic development and particularly industrialization—as it is clear she is already beginning to do—it is inevitable that she will far surpass India in gross national product and other measures of economic success, just as she already clearly surpasses India in military might. The states of Southeast Asia are not very likely to decide between communism and democracy on the grounds of an abstract consideration of the merits of the two systems, as exemplified respectively in China and India. Nevertheless, it is a matter of some moment whether India can demonstrate to all the underdeveloped, non-Western states that there is a democratic path to rapid economic development.

India's written constitution provides for a Union (federal) government and governments for each of the sixteen states; there are also nine Union territories. It was adopted on January 26, 1950, and bears a strong basic resemblance to the Government of India Act of 1935, which was India's constitution until 1950. The constitution is one of the many features of contemporary India that are British endowments or at least show British influence; also profoundly important are India's possession of an extensive and efficient railway system and the excellent tradition of her civil service.

As Clinton Rossiter points out, India's government has functioned with a high degree of competence and stability since she achieved her independence on August 15, 1947. India has maintained internal stability, has solved some difficult internal problems (perhaps that of the Communist government of Kerala state was the most acute), and has played a leading role on the international stage—even if it has not always been a role that the Western world has enjoyed watching. The question is how far one can expect this success to continue. For India, the difficulties of the near future are likely to increase. Many of the benefits of British rule are diminishing, especially in regard to Indian unity, which was in some sense a British creation. Whatever political unity had been achieved in the past had been a transitory and exceptional achievement. Britain was not able to transmit to the new, independent India an undivided inheritance; for the moment of independence was also the moment of partition, as Pakistan formed a separate nation.

Unity in India is bedeviled by separatisms of many kinds: state and regional loyalties; linguistic differences; communalism (the separatist influence of the Hindu, Islamic, Sikh, or other religious communities); and caste differences within the Hindu majority. Among the most important is the absence of a national language. Hindi or Urdu is spoken by about 45 per cent of the population, but neither is much spoken in South India, where cultural and even racial differences from the North are considerable. The desire of linguistic groups in particular areas to possess their own states poses one of the gravest threats to national unity, inasmuch as it reflects a disintegrating series of subnationalisms. In several instances, the government of India has had to give way to pressures of this kind, as in the creation of Andhra state (1953), the partition of Bombay state (1960) into Gujarat and Maharashtra, and the decision to create a Naga state (1960–62).

From all these divisive forces, Selig S. Harrison draws pessimistic conclusions about the prospects for democracy in India. Certainly, the stability of Indian government since 1947 is likely to be regarded as exceptional. It has rested primarily on the control of the country by the Congress party, the political group that led the movement for independence, and secondly on the leadership of Jawaharlal Nehru, who was Prime Minister of India from its independence until his death in May 1964, and who in effect held that office even before independence. Continuity and stability largely rested on a single personality. With Nehru gone from the scene, they could become much more fragile. The Nehru regime was probably a transition. In an interview on the BBC, Michael Edwardes asked Mrs. Pandit, "Is it wrong to say that Mr. Nehru is the last Viceroy . . . ?"[1] The Indian Prime Minister's sister replied, "The new type of leader who will come forward after my brother . . . will have to be probably more Indian than our group is now, or my brother is now." She also pointed out accurately that someone who was "completely a product of Hinduism or Islam or Buddhism" would not be able to play the role on the international stage that Nehru had. There, his English education and his superb command of the language were of immense benefit to him. Mr. Shastri, his successor, lacks most of these advantages.

In matters of foreign policy (which Nehru directed himself), India has

[1] *The Listener,* March 10, 1960, p. 438.

operated in an outer and an inner orbit. The country has championed such general causes as the United Nations, the attack on the relics of colonialism, nonalignment between the great power blocs, and peaceful coexistence. In the inner orbit, a more cold-blooded, nationalistic approach has prevailed. The contrast between India's preachments and India's conduct in her own arena has often been pointed out. The annexation of Hyderabad, Junagadh, and Goa do not show any high degree of abstinence from the use of force. The steadfast refusal, decade after decade, to hold a plebiscite in Kashmir—a plebiscite once promised—can hardly be called the upholding of moral standards in the field of foreign policy.

The two orbits have intersected in the matter of Indian relations with China. India was among the first to recognize Communist China, has urged since 1950 that it be admitted to the United Nations, and has even argued for returning possession of Formosa to the mainland. Nehru and Chou En-lai exchanged several visits, and promulgated in 1954 the too-celebrated, platitudinous *Pancha Sila,* or "Five Principles of Co-existence." But all this amity has not prevented the eruption of frontier disputes between the two countries. China has made claims for frontier revision at both the extreme western end of the frontier (in Ladakh) and at the eastern end ("the McMahon Line"). In August and in October 1959 sporadic fighting was begun by China; and in the fall of 1962 continuous hostilities began. But toward the end of November China announced that it was making a unilateral withdrawal from its advanced positions, whereupon the fighting stopped.

Brief and inexplicable as the Indian-Chinese border war was, it compelled a revision of the Indian determination to view Chinese policies through rose-colored glasses. It caused India to call with desperation for military aid from the United States, Britain—and Russia; and the requested aid was promptly made available. Finally, it caused realignment within the triangular relations of India, China, and Pakistan.

Pakistan and India are, perhaps necessarily, more obsessed with their relations with each other than with any other foreign-policy issue. The bulk of their armed forces are massed along their common borders. Pakistan came into being in 1947 in response to the refusal of the Moslem populations of the Indian Empire of Britain to be governed as a part of a Hindu-dominated independent India. For India, Pakistan is an unnecessary invention.

Pakistan and India have had serious differences from the beginning, the worst of which is Kashmir. Chanakya Sen presents an Indian view of these problems in his discussion of the impact of the Indian-Chinese border war. A contrasting position is presented in President Mohammed Ayub Khan's article on the current stresses and strains in the Pakistan-American alliance; Pakistan, at any rate, has taken the bull by the horns in a very successful manner in coming to terms with Communist China. At his press conference at Rawalpindi on February 21, 1964, President Khan criticized the intransigent Indian attitude on the border questions, and said of his own discussions with Chou En-lai, "One thing has emerged clearly, and that is that the Chinese are prepared to be reasonable with anybody who is prepared to be reasonable with them."

Thus, on the Indian subcontinent, as in other parts of the globe, old alignments are undergoing fundamental reconsideration; "the sticks break, the stones crumble, the eternal altars tilt and tumble." In foreign policy, there are *no* eternal altars, and it is hardly surprising that Pakistan is pursuing its national interest by re-evaluating and modifying its foreign policy in the light of changing circumstances.

A Splendid Exception to All Our Generalizations*

Clinton Rossiter

A standard lecture in the introductory course in political science at many American colleges is called "The Prerequisites of Democracy." Solemnly and even didactically—I know, because I have given this lecture more times than I want to count—the professor ticks off the social, economic, cultural and spiritual conditions under which popular, representative, constitutional democracy has flourished at different times in different parts of the world.

After pointing to the existence of all these conditions in the United States, Great Britain, Canada, Sweden, Switzerland and Israel and to the absence of most of them in China, Spain, Guinea, Paraguay, Bulgaria and Afghanistan, he then finishes off by framing the general rule: only in societies where conditions are favorable can men even hope that democracy will arise and flourish.

Having recently spent some weeks on a lecture-study tour of India, I have returned home a chastened political scientist and an exhilarated democrat. Reluctantly but firmly I have decided never to give that standard lecture again, or at least to throw away my old notes and start in afresh on this fascinating and indeed fateful subject of the prerequisites of democracy. India has taught me a lesson I am not likely to forget: that to this rule, as to all the great rules we have tried to abstract from our studies of political history, there can be astounding exceptions.

If I have not been totally misled by the evidence presented for my consideration, India may well be the most astounding exception of all time. The truth is that one who goes in search of the real and the possible in modern

* "The Paradox of India's Democracy," *The New York Times Magazine,* June 3, 1962, pp. 15, 70–71. © 1962 by The New York Times Company. Reprinted by permission. Mr. Rossiter is Professor of Government at Cornell University.

India comes away impressed by two overpowering and apparently contradictory facts about its political life: first, that almost none of the alleged prerequisites of democracy exists to any marked degree in that country; second, that democracy itself does exist, and shows remarkably few signs of giving way to any other form of government.

Political scientists, an independent breed, disagree warmly over the weight to be assigned to each of the prerequisites of democracy, yet few would deny the primary importance of these six:

A productive economy that raises the mass of men above the level of exhausted privation; a progressive society that offers these men both the satisfactions of security and the delights of opportunity; a literate citizenry that has been given the tools of learning and taught how to use them in passing judgment on the issues of the day; the will and means to perpetuate this literacy from generation to generation in the form of a well-supported scheme of universal education; a system of values that gives primacy to notions of opportunity, equality, self-reliance, morality and personal liberty; and a deep-rooted consensus about this system of values and about the institutions that embody them.

Only in soil that is fertile, we have been telling ourselves for years, can democracy grow from a delicate shoot to a tough-fibered plant.

The visitor to India learns in short order—principally from Indians who know their country intimately and fondly—that the social and economic soil is anything but fertile, that most of the prerequisites simply do not exist, and that India is therefore about the last place in which one would expect democracy to flourish.

An economy in which the average annual wage is something like $70, a society upon which the phenomenon of caste has barely loosened its immemorial grip, a citizenry only 25 per cent of which can be classed as literate, a system of education that has performed miracles and yet leaves millions of children untouched, a venerable tradition that makes room for many splendid values but most certainly not for political liberty and social equality—these are not exactly the foundations of a great experiment in democratic government.

Three harsh realities of contemporary India strike the hopeful visitor with particular force, and about all of them I found most of my hosts to be both knowledgeable and despairing.

The first is the familiar fact of overpopulation, a fact that one senses crudely by walking through any village or city and understands perhaps more sharply by digesting this simple statistic: there are today within the boundaries of India perhaps 100 million more persons than there were at the time of independence fifteen years ago. The problems that these persons—or would it be more dramatic to say these children?—represent in terms of food, housing, health, education and jobs would stagger even the most efficient of democracies or hard-fisted of dictatorships.

The second is the existence of vast areas of discontent and despair among the people. Paul Grimes, New York Times correspondent in India, has described the poverty of the majority of Indians as "suffocating," and one can read three or four meanings, all of them unfavorable to the prospects of democracy, into this well-chosen word. I found no one in India who could be certain of the number of the unemployed; I found dozens of men who were certain that a majority of Indians were underemployed—and also, in the biting words of one of them, "underfed, underclothed, undereducated and underhoused."

And the third is the existence of at least five mighty forces of disunity—language, caste, class, regional loyalty, religion—that threaten relentlessly to tear India apart. To those who love to boast, as I once did, of the "wondrous diversity" of American life, I can say only: Go to India and discover a nation whose diversity is so wondrous as to be stupefying—a nation of men divided into 3,000 sub-castes, a nation that recognizes fourteen regional languages in its constitution, a nation whose very consciousness of nationhood is still at best a surface phenomenon. India, is, as W. H. Morris-Jones, has written, "a fragmented society, a society with an absence of basic consensus."

Here, then is a country from which the committed democrat, overpowered by evidence of poverty and illiteracy and dissension, should return to his own country in a mood of despair. And so he would return if he had not also been overpowered by evidence of the second great fact of Indian political life: democracy ought not exist, yet it does; it ought not survive, yet it may.

In a part of the world where every other country is governed under some form of dictatorship, ranging from the benevolent to the malevolent by way of the merely feckless, India is governed as a recognizable form of democracy.

It has a responsible Prime Minister and Cabinet, a freely elected and by no means docile Parliament, an independent and learned judiciary, a civil service that is the envy of Asia, and a collection of state governments that are at least as faithful imitations of the Government in New Delhi as ours are of the Government in Washington. Elections are largely unrigged, parties sprout like weeds (although one party remains ascendant) and the press is uncontrolled and of infinite variety.

Two overt signs of the health of Indian democracy, struck me with particular force: the jails are virtually free (as are the jails of very few countries these days) of political prisoners; the Army takes orders from, rather than gives them to, the elected leaders of the people.

In hundreds of thousands of villages, to be sure, life goes on just as slowly and unimaginatively as it has for centuries, which is evidence enough to support the generalization that political democracy is something imposed upon Indian society from the top down—and not too far down at that. Yet from these villages, as from the bustling cities, come the votes—more than 130 million in the elections of 1962—that give legitimacy to the most broadly based parliament in the history of the world.

India is an imperfect democracy, as Indians are the first to admit, but a democracy nevertheless, and who are we to smile or sneer over the imperfect results of this great experiment? We should, rather, remember our own imperfections, contrast the successes of democracy in India with its failures in the half-dozen countries grouped around it, and give thanks that at least one people in that part of the world has made the democratic gamble in good faith and with high hopes.

We are left with a jumble of questions about the nature, extent, condition and prospects of Indian democracy, and in particular with the leading question: how does India manage to defy the rules and govern itself democratically in circumstances that are supposed to be fatal to democracy?

This is a question to which even professionals in Indian studies have returned only tentative answers, and mine, the answers of an amateur, must be so very tentative as to be little better than hunches. Here, in any case, would be my list of the elements or influences in Indian society that have helped so far to redress and maintain the balance of social forces in favor of democracy:

Faith in democracy. Anyone who doubts that ideas are important, and can often be determining, in the destiny of a nation, should go to India and talk to some of the men who govern it, who teach its children and who are helping to build its future. I have heard experts on India—Britons, Americans and Indians themselves—argue all day about the sources of this faith, yet I have never heard one deny its power and tenacity.

While India has its full share of cynics, skeptics and "practical men who care not for doctrine," it also has men at every level of responsibility—and for the time being enough such men—to whom concepts of stern dictatorship or benevolent autocracy or even "guided democracy" are wholly foreign.

A leader who has kept this faith, Nehru is, by any standard, a rather difficult man for Americans to understand and deal with. He is cranky, preachy and imperious; he looks at the world too often with the eyes of an arrested Socialist of the Nineteen Twenties; he has failed as badly as Franklin Roosevelt to encourage the development of men in his party who can take over the burdens of national leadership.

Yet, he is, also by any standard, a very great man—and a man who, however unsettling his manner and moods, is committed deeply to parliamentary democracy. It is, surely, a fact of immense importance that this living demonstration of the influence of "the hero in history," whose hold upon the mass of men is powerful beyond belief, would not dream of giving up on democracy and taking command as a dictator.

"We have definitely accepted the democratic process," Nehru said to his colleagues in 1957, "because we think that in the final analysis it promotes the growth of human beings and of society."

A party that embodies this faith. It is easy to poke fun at the ruling Congress party or, when one wearies of poking, to rake it with caustic fire. Like its charismatic leader, it is cranky and imperious; and to go further with this comparison of man and movement, it is torn by internal stresses and is something less than immortal. Yet one is bound to grant three points in its favor: it was the driving force in the struggle for independence; it never drove so hard that it abandoned permanently either the ideals or practices of democracy; it has given India a special kind of political stability in these critical years.

Whatever else it has been, the Congress party has been as democratic as a party of revolution and national liberation could ever be, and thus quite different in organization and procedure and spirit from those movements organized by such as Castro, Nasser and Nkrumah.

The British influence. The visitor from the West is doubtless more likely than Indians themselves to be impressed by the good effects of British rule, which he can see without straining, and to overlook the bad effects, about which he has to be instructed. Yet almost every Indian I met was quick to acknowledge that his masters had left behind a goodly heritage: schools, universities, factories, cities, railroads, ports, a famous civil service and a crack Army led by men who respect civilian authority.

More than that, they left behind a language in which educated Indians could talk to one another, the machinery with which they could govern themselves democratically, and even some splendid buildings in which to do the talking and governing.

The elites. The most important of all legacies inherited by the new India, in part a gift from its masters but in even larger part a consequence of its own struggle for dignity and independence, is the pool of trained and competent men in politics and public administration, commerce and industry, the professions and the armed forces. The contrast between India and, let us say, Indonesia in this respect goes far to explain the different political paths they are traveling.

India was almost uniquely privileged among the emergent nations of the postwar era to begin its new life under the guidance, not merely of what Paul Appleby has rightly described as an "extraordinary national leadership," but, at the next level down, of thousands of men who knew their jobs. It is especially encouraging for the visitor to learn that new men are pushing their way up into these levels of responsibility in respectable numbers, and that most of the new men, like most of the old, are democrats by nature as well as by nurture.

The policy of neutrality. While Americans cannot be expected to be entirely happy about Nehru's foreign policy, especially when he makes use of a double standard that is harder on us than it is on the Communists, we ought to recognize that, were India to move decidedly closer to the West or to the East, the consequence would be a severe strain on national unity. We, who so wisely took refuge in a policy of nonalignment in our early years should be able to understand better than most peoples how much tension India is spared by pursuing a similar policy.

The mixed economy. India is pre-eminently the underdeveloped country in which public control and private initiative coexist peacefully in a rather judicious balance. There is enough activity going on in what Indians call "the public sector" to give men a rough sense of economic and social justice; there is enough room for the operations of private enterprise to give a real lift to the rate of economic growth in the area of consumer goods.

The secular state. Nehru's flat insistence, in the words of Norman Palmer, that "free India should be a noncommunal, secular state" has also served to reduce tensions that could easily tear India apart. The integration into Indian democracy, I heard another wise man answer, should not be expected to do for a people what it has no will to do for itself; whereupon I recalled for their edification the sobering fact that the processes of American democracy had failed utterly to produce a solution to the two greatest problems of our first century as a free people: the preservation of the Union and the elimination of slavery.

We, the lucky Americans, were able to solve these problems on the field of battle without doing permanent damage to the processes of our democracy. India, however, can hardly expect history to be as tolerant of her departures from constitutional propriety as it was of ours.

Democracy, I feel, will be given only one throw of the dice in India, and that throw is being chanced at this very moment. To mix the metaphor, it must now be proved whether this graft called democracy can be made a permanent and integral part of the living body of Indian society.

In the end, of course, it will be for the Indians themselves—especially for those great masses of village-bound men and women who have thus far been heard from only faintly—to decide whether their legitimate economic and social goals should be pursued through more autocratic methods than those now being employed. For the time being, however, we ought to look with more admiration than we have hitherto expressed at the miraculous existence of Indian democracy, and perhaps convert some of that admiration into the hard coin of increased economic and technical assistance.

We, after all, can have something to say about the ultimate decision of life or death for Indian democracy, and it strikes me as a tough-minded rather than soft-minded policy for America to extend all the help that India can absorb in its historic effort to create the prerequisites of democracy *after* the fact.

India is a splendidly defiant exception to all our generalizations about these prerequisites, a country that has endured for fifteen years, and will certainly endure for some years to come, as an example of the power of faith in democracy to overcome the most adverse environment.

But it will not endure forever, not without the support that comes from improving social and economic conditions. Since either a transition to dictatorship or, as seems more likely, a dismemberment of the nation itself would be a tragedy for our cause, indeed for all mankind, we must do what we can to help Indian democracy to survive and prosper. It remains to be decided whether modern India will appear as a sad footnote or a rousing chapter in the history of democracy.

The Most Dangerous Decades*

Selig S. Harrison

Once, recalls Nehru, when a crowd of villagers shouted the inevitable Bharat Mata Ki Jai—Victory to Mother India—he conducted an unpremeditated experiment in the semantics of nationalism. "Who," he asked, "is this Mata you salute?" Dharti—the earth—responded the villagers. "Whose earth? Your village earth? Your province? India? The world?" The villagers were, of course, struck dumb, a fact of little consequence in itself but all too symbolic of the larger inability of India as a whole to discover a coherent nationalism. The Indian who shouted anti-British slogans during the movement for Independence and who now shouts to the victory of "Bharat Mata" senses that change is in the air, that change for the better is possible, and that to shout for it, to claim it, is a prerequisite for getting it. But who is this Mata in whose name he joins the revolution of rising expectations?

"Bharat Mata" (Mother India) is the standard of a nationalism that is subcontinental in its horizons. The horizons of those summoned to the standard, however, are in most cases still the limited ones of a caste unit or a linguistic region. Thus Mata is in practice the name for whatever horizon the manipulator chooses to fix upon in a particular political circumstance. It is the responsiveness of the new nationalism to contradictory political invitations which above all guarantees that the decades ahead will be turbulent ones for India. Political invitations will multiply with each year that change penetrates more deeply into Indian society, churning up new desires and claims at a rate that will outdistance the capacity of any central government to deliver. The bravest attempts to keep pace with rising demands will require a political foundation of national unity. Yet the central authority in India is caught in a vicious circle: unity depends on rapid development as much as development presupposes unity.

Although, on the one hand, development demands central direction, the economic upheaval set in motion by planning on a subcontinental scale carries its own endemic challenge to national unity. The central authority in making planned economic expansion possible gives rise to new and perhaps self-defeating forces. . . . As the social unity of village life is destroyed by the

* Reprinted from *India: The Most Dangerous Decades* by Selig S. Harrison by permission of Princeton University Press, pp. 319–339. Copyright 1960 by Princeton University Press. Mr. Harrison, formerly a member of the editorial staff of *The New Republic,* is now the South Asia correspondent of the *Washington Post.*

new competition between castes, as more and more villagers leave their folk culture for towns and cities, men grope accordingly for new allegiances. Millions disengaged from their native ground wander through uncharted social realms. The man who once talked only to a bullock in a field now communicates with a progressively broadening circle. Language circumscribes the outer limits of this new, wider world, and so it is his regional caste and language groups which are the natural foci of his new allegiances, which provide social alliances equal in breadth and power to the new competitive challenge surrounding him. . . . Thus the psychological underpinnings of the subcontinental state are eroded as rapidly as the state succeeds in economic development.

The period now beginning in India presents striking similarities to the rise of nationalism in nineteenth century Europe, especially the nationalist upsurge in the Balkans which culminated in the collapse of the Austro-Hungarian Empire. "Will India succeed in carrying out this experiment," pondered Toynbee at the time of the reorganization of states, "without bringing on herself eastern Europe's tragic fate?" . . . The scramble to see who gets the biggest slice of the economic cake in India is an unregulated scramble of regions and regional caste lobbies with none of the common overriding loyalty to a national feudal hierarchy and an emperor—and hence to a national state—which gave Japan the social control for its rapid modernization. . . .

The intensity of the inter-regional competition in India gains with each year that the unity achieved in opposition to the British ruler slips away. When opportunities for development were denied equally to all of India, all regions blamed the outside oppressor for their plight. But now that India is independent, as the States Reorganization Commission has observed, "consciousness of the lack of a community of interests between different language groups tends to become deeper and deeper with the progressive realization of their divergent economic and other needs." If Nehru can to some extent hold down the claims of regional self-interest it is because he embodies a link with the Independence movement and its spirit of a common cause. Even Nehru's lieutenants in Assam protested for months on end when the central government sought for economic reasons to locate an oil refinery drawing on Assam oil outside the state. But this was restrained protest, warned one of them, compared to what could be expected in years hence. "Now, so long as our tall leaders, our all-India leaders, are there," he said, "perhaps people will be submitting to their advice. But this cannot be stretched too long."

To the extent that all regions can look to New Delhi for the wherewithal of progress, the financing and know-how that build dams, irrigation canals, and industries, the Indian Union gains in strength. Conversely, the exercise of economic development power demands statesmanlike care. For to the extent that regions believe the central authority discriminates in the allocation of capital, the Union is weakened.

The central government calls on the regions to trust in an ephemeral national unity, but the regions demand down payments before they will trust to an uncertain future. On the one hand they demand their down payments in development expenditure. At the same time they watch to see that they are not surrendering more tax money than they can see returning to their own home ground. "You want us to make a fetish of Indian unity," exclaims the propagandist for a sovereign Mithila republic in northern Bihar. "But the unity of India is a mere means to an end, which is our social well-being, a higher standard of living. If this unity, this Leviathan of an Indian State, is a bar to our progress, a weapon in the hands of our opponents, we should frankly go against it." . . .

With all parties equally ready to use New Delhi as a whipping boy, the central government is placed on the defensive and must constantly justify every planning decision, not only in economic terms but in political terms as well. The Second Five Year Plan pledged that "in the location of new enterprises, whether public or private . . . every effort should be made to provide for balanced development in different parts of the country." Nehru has on repeated occasions reassured India's own underdeveloped areas that they would be helped to catch up with the rest of the country. Indian leaders must steer a narrow passage between "this Scylla and Charibdis"—too much care, on the one hand, and not enough, on the other, that each region gets its fair share of development expenditure. As Maurice Zinkin points out, the planner cannot decide where he will build new railway lines simply on the basis of traffic offering—or where he will put new dams simply on the basis of the acres irrigated per million spent—if that means some states will get a great many railway lines or dams and others none at all. Yet at the same time, if he goes too far in appeasing regional leaders, "though there may be more equality, or greater regional fairness, or possibly, fewer revolutions, there is also less development."

. . . The man who leaves his native region to find greater economic opportunity seldom does so without misgivings. To stay too long away from home, away from the group observance of marriage and eating restrictions, of religious and social strictures, is to endanger his position should he ever return. Therefore, since he normally migrates as a member of a group of his kinsmen or caste-fellows, he tends to settle with them in his new environment. As a result, observes a UNESCO report, Indian cities are little more than "an agglomeration of what are in effect villages within the urban framework. Not only do primary groups of kinsmen and caste-fellows fail to dissolve into an urban mass. Instead, they formalize their organization and accentuate their distinctiveness." It is a commonplace in Indian cities to find enclaves within which linguistic minorities, far from becoming assimilated into new patterns of life, maintain their own schools and cultural institutions. Unlike the immigrant in New York or Chicago, who pulls away from group discipline in the second or third generation, the Tamil in Calcutta or the Gujarati in Trivandrum holds tenaciously to his mother tongue and social ties. The industrial suburbs of Calcutta are in reality a chain of small cities in which linguistic minorities dispersed during working hours return after-hours to their own separate social and political unity. . . .

Urbanization in Asia now runs ahead of industrialization. Migration to the cities is more often impelled by the "push" of underemployment and overpopulation in the countryside than by the "pull" of assured employment in the city. Even the present urban populations in India cannot be kept employed under the Second Five Year Plan. Yet urban centers continue to grow. Mere density of population by itself increases the risk of irresponsible political action, and in the case of Indian cities, density aggravates tension between easily manipulated social groups. The fact that these groups are often away from home explains to some extent the militant tenor of discontent in the new multilingual centers. Absence has indeed been found to make the heart grow fonder: students of nationalism cite numerous cases to show that native allegiances are accentuated in alien surroundings. But this reawakened sense of identity only serves to channel a more fundamental Indian psychological urge to find a group commitment, any group commitment, for its own sake. The dissolution of the individual into an endless unknown in both Hinduism and Buddhism—the indifference to the "brute particular" in favor of the universal type in Indian philosophical systems—is the parallel of a political authoritarian personality. The militance of the search for new group allegiances does not necessarily correspond in intensity to economic misery; Henry Hart found at D.V.C. and Hirakud that the greatest discontent prevails not among the petty contractor's workers, living in hovels and paid at the caprice of a foreman, but among the drivers of the earth moving machines—"lords materially, but lonely psychically." The drivers were the men most fully disengaged from their old allegiances. They provided the leadership of discontent. At the same time their laborers—transplanted as a body in their "villages within the urban framework"—provided easily manipulated blocs of political manpower whenever there was a strike or a demonstration to be called. For both the drivers and the laborers it is the "changing of worlds" which guarantees a surcharged political atmosphere.

In this changing of worlds, this readiness to cross regional frontiers for new opportunity, India understandably looks for a ray of hope. In a society with a settled level of population, the promise of progress would gradually become a reality as increasing mobility coupled with increasing national wealth relieved the social tensions dividing men from each other. But the social upheaval that accompanies economic change in India becomes an increasing irritant to social tensions, rather than a source of relief, in a society which has yet to achieve a settled level of population. As population mounts, densely populated regions cry *lebensraum* at their neighbors. Bihari laborers flock to jobs in the mining and industrial towns bordering Bengal, and overcrowded Bengal protests in return that the towns should be the preserve of its own jobless. The tea plantations of Assam become a battleground between rival groups of Assamese and Bengali unemployed. Tamilnad demands the border plantation land of Malayalan-speaking Travancore-Cochin to protect

Tamil coolies from Malayalee competition. With each year that more and more people—made more and more group-conscious by scarcity—compete ever more feverishly for limited economic spoils, the hope for ultimate escape from India's vicious circle grows more remote.

On the assumption that the birth rate will not significantly decline, India's population will almost certainly reach 500 million by 1971. Demographers may estimate slightly more or slightly less, but all agree that this is no alarmist exaggeration. . . .

The strain that population growth will impose upon food resources is a grim preoccupation of responsible Indians. . . .

Population control is, to be sure, a nominal objective even now of public policy in India. But can population be controlled on a sufficiently grand scale to change the course of events? Can action be taken in time, before India passes what may be her demographic point of no return in 1966? Only, more and more Indians are answering, if the conditions and incentives for low fertility can be brought within practical control of a highly centralized authoritarian regime. A Union which gives to each state a legislature empowered to set policy in such important fields as education and agriculture will seem more and more intolerable as the population dilemma looms larger and larger. Population pressures will magnify and drive forward all the other pressures pushing India into authoritarian political adventures. Consider the sheer weight of numbers involved in the clashes of regional economic self-interest, in the competition for vantage between caste lobbies and regional elites. The nationalist in a hurry will be a prisoner of vast impersonal forces that will become stronger rather than weaker as population growth intensifies the conflict inherent in a Union of unevenly matched regional rivals.

In not too many years the nationalist ambition to confront the West as an equal must be reconciled with the fact that the political and economic order in India is in crucial respects dependent on outside capital and, as matters stand, will be progressively more so in the future. If there are indigenous resources adequate for development, these are the untaxed hoards of the upper ten percent of the peasantry. Yet the power to tax agriculture rests . . . predominantly in state hands. The dominant farmers, wholesalers and moneylenders who can most afford to pay for development—and who are so often one and the same person in the Indian village—are also the powers behind state machines not only of the Congress Party but of most existing Indian parties. This is why state governments are failing to raise the revenues demanded of them, while still demanding, on their part, that New Delhi find funds for their development. This is why the peasant proprietors who form the strongest of the new caste lobbies are so often on the side of regional autonomy. As sectionalists they can best keep their margin of prosperity beyond the reach of national power. The bureaucrat in New Delhi is uniquely situated to see through to the crux of the stalemate, but he acts on his insight, all too often, by systematically putting his own wealth and the wealth of his friends into the colossal tax haven that is the Indian countryside.

The nationalist in a hurry knows well that there are unexploited resources in India. Even if massive enough Western assistance were forthcoming—which it is not—to support the whole existing order indefinitely, nationalism, by its very nature, rules out prolonged acquiescence in any such state of affairs. In the long run, nationalism dictates the attempt to minimize reliance on support from abroad no matter what the cost in institutions at home. Who is to make this or that attempt and at what cost depends less on the politics of Right versus Left than on the politics of national survival. Residual political power in India in the decades ahead will rest in the regional capitals: the makers of any regime in New Delhi, Right- or Left-inclined, will face first and foremost the necessity for coming to terms with widely dispersed centers of power. The great imponderable in India's future is the possible rise of some charismatic national leader equal to this necessity; all that seems certain, in his absence, is that no one political force and no one elite group at the national level can hold a commanding position for long against the onslaught of so many divergent interests. No "final" outcome is in prospect, neither the enduring triumph of a strong central state nor irrevocable Balkanization. Instead India is likely to experience a succession of political shocks as centripetal and centrifugal forces alternately gain dominant strength. The shock might at some point be great enough to detach certain regional entities from the central power, but probably not for long.

Nationalism implies shifting coalitions in which the national political personality is impelled to share power with the strategically entrenched bureaucrat, and both align at one moment or another with the military. The Indian Army may not yet be in the strictest sense a "truly national Army." But it is, relatively speaking, insulated from regional pressures. The discipline of a military establishment properly permits a degree of linguistic indoctrination inappropriate to a university campus. Varying degrees of linguistic homogeneity of the enlisted ranks in Hindustani and of the officer corps in English reinforce all the other factors giving the Army its obvious magnetism as an instrument of national control.

An outside chance does exist for orderly progress through representative civil institutions, and this is the chance that scientific breakthroughs will come sooner than now seems probable. However, most of the technological short-cuts, such as solar and nuclear energy, that would give India her greatest opportunity—Nehru sees no other opportunity—to maintain a program of self-sustaining development, seem to imply, necessarily, the management of a very highly centralized state. The politics of national survival will clearly not conform to Western conceptions of "democracy" and will almost certainly, at one time or another, appear "totalitarian" according to the experience and definitions of the West.

What can the West do?

Not much, or not as much as is often supposed, limited as the West is by political realities within India. What the West does cannot, first of all, control the dynamic forces within India that seem so certain to overwhelm free institutions. Enough Western economic assistance, soon enough, can improve the chances that India will escape the uglier forms of totalitarianism. But a realistic Western approach to India must rest on a clear recognition that the odds are almost wholly against the survival of freedom and that in "the most dangerous decades" the issue is, in fact, whether any Indian state can survive at all.

Persistence in an approach to India that seems to condition friendship and assistance on the democratic commitment of a particular generation of political leaders progressively forecloses the possibility of Western friendship with a new generation embracing a new commitment. This, in a world alive with mounting racial xenophobia, is a most dangerous and shortsighted gamble. The passing of the present generation of Indian leadership makes it more, not less, necessary for the West to remain on cooperative terms with New Delhi and to assist India in her struggle for national survival.

The Challenge to India's Integrity*

Chanakya Sen

The Indian Union was born to a challenge of disintegration. Independence was accompanied by partition of the sub-continent into the two Dominions of India and Pakistan. Within the Indian Dominion 500 or so princely states were left with theoretical paramountcy. Before the process of integrating these states with the Indian Dominion was completed, there was fighting in Kashmir involving the two new States. There were mass communal and religious killings and a terrible uprooting of population. Even internal physical integration could not be achieved without "police action" against the Nizam of Hyderabad.

In many countries such grave internal and external threats might have given rise to an authoritarian State. But the democratic convictions of the Congress party leaders were so deep and the liberal democratic tradition of the Indian struggle for independence was so strong that the country deliberately, and with a full sense of responsibility, chose a parliamentary system of government. The Constituent Assembly met against an unsettled background, but the Constitution it framed guaranteed fundamental human rights, recognized the dignity of the individual and the sanctity of private property, and

* From *The World Today,* March 1963, pp. 116–124. Published by the Oxford University Press for the Royal Institute of International Affairs, London. Reprinted by permission. Mr. Sen is an Indian commentator on current affairs.

extended the right of universal suffrage to some 340 million people, 70 per cent of whom were unable to read or write. It worked out a viable compromise between a federal and a unitary form of government, gave the Provinces substantial local autonomy, and, at the same time, vested the Central Government with sufficient powers to maintain the integrity of the country at times of emergency.

As soon as the Central Government was able to settle down to its job, it began to work in terms of planned economic development under state initiative. It declared its objective to be an informed political democracy supported by an adequate economy and proclaimed as the ultimate goal a socialistic structure of society. Thus, even before administration of the country could be fully integrated and a modern economic infrastructure built up, the Indian leaders deliberately plunged the nation into a gigantic struggle for democratic equality. This struggle released diverse contradictory currents of hopes and aspirations, many of which threatened to erode the very unity and integrity of the Union. Yet they were the inevitable off-shoots of the democratic experiment upon which India had boldly embarked.

This experiment has attracted the attention of the whole world, and deservedly so, for nothing on so vast a scale, and with so many imponderables, has ever been attempted before. Democratic nations have undertaken a policy of industrialization with the minimum of government participation and direction. Relatively backward countries like Japan have leapt forward to progress under authoritarian rule. Communist countries like the Soviet Union have moved forward under government control and planning, but without democratic freedom. But the world has yet to see a country as big as India, with so vast and divided a population, with appalling poverty and a complex social system, make rapid strides towards industrialization, with government participation and under government direction and yet keeping intact its democratic set-up, the rule of law, and the liberty of the individual to dissent and differ. This is the Indian "miracle."

Not that it has been a miraculous success; the pace of economic progress has been far from rapid. But it has not been a failure either. The country has had three general elections in total freedom, and the illiterate electorate has shown remarkable political wisdom. Two five-year Plans have been completed, albeit with shortfalls in key sectors; the third has now been launched. If this Plan can be completed, even on the scale of the first two, India should be able to achieve an industrial base, and then make a bid for the much-coveted take-off stage.

Within the last few months, however, an entirely new situation has suddenly arisen. Neither the British rulers nor the Indian leaders had envisaged, at the time of independence, that within fifteen years India would have to face massive aggression from China (or from any other big Power). The hostility of Pakistan had been taken into account. But Pakistan was an infant State; she might harass and irritate India, but she could never be a menace to her freedom. Even when Pakistan embarked on a policy of accepting U.S.

military aid, and the Government of India lodged an indignant protest with Washington, she knew that the U.S. Government would not permit Pakistan to launch aggression against her.

The Government of India, therefore, did not consider that it was called upon to spend an unduly large amount on national defence. The army was maintained on an operational level which could enable it to repel any attack from Pakistan. But it was short of equipment. The purchase of equipment from abroad meant either spending valuable foreign exchange or paying a political price; the Indian Government was not ready or willing to undertake either. To ask for arms aid would have been a departure from its policy of non-alignment; and the home manufacture of sophisticated weapons of war required an industrial base which was still to be constructed. The armed forces, therefore, had to be kept relatively small for a country of India's size, with 3,500 miles of land frontiers and almost an equally long coastline—not more than 600,000 men, rather modestly equipped. Even to maintain this army the Central Government had to spend over a third of its annual revenue. Every Finance Minister, in presenting his Budget, bemoaned this "necessary evil," and stated that he would have preferred to be able to spend the money on much-needed development projects.

The recent Chinese attack has demolished many of the premises on which the "Indian miracle" was proceeding. During the past few years, India had worried a great deal about internal forces of disintegration (all of them resulting from her struggle for a democratic way of life); suddenly she has found her integrity threatened by foreign aggression. This situation has lent a new perspective to Indian thinking. All of a sudden she has been forced to realize that her integrity and independence depend upon her ability to defend herself from a powerful neighbour.

In face of the Chinese attack, the Indian people have stood more firmly united than ever before in their long and ancient history. The great emotional upsurge which has swept the country is all the more remarkable because it has risen from the grass-roots. The Chinese invasion found the national leadership in considerable emotional disarray, no less conspicuous than the country's military and diplomatic confusion. But the spontaneous rallying of the entire people behind the leadership of Mr. Nehru reinforced his strength at the weakest moment of his career. All divisive forces suddenly withdrew, all controversies were hushed. The state Governments placed their entire resources at the disposal of the Union; they even surrendered some of their fiscal prerogatives. Leaders of separatist parties affirmed the unity of the country; trade unions withdrew strike notices; employers called off lock-outs. And all this happened even before the emergency was proclaimed. Newspapers and party leaders did not hesitate to criticize the Government for its failures; but not one voice has been raised in doubt of the national integrity and unity of the Indian people.

Such emotional unity, however, valuable as it is, does not in itself protect a country from external aggression. The crux of the problem of India's national integrity is now a matter of arms and economics. The country must have adequate means to defend its frontiers against aggression from a big Power; it must, at the same time, carry forward its basic struggle for economic progress. Failure in either field will pose a real threat to India's integrity.

For some years to come the main national preoccupation will be with defence. But defence does not only mean a bigger army and better weapons; it also means physical development of the land frontiers which have leapt back into prominence after a spell of 200 years.

During the last fifty years of British rule, every care was taken to keep these frontiers "dead," against the threat from Czarist Russia (and possibly from Imperial Germany). Generations of Indians grew up in the lulled complacency that the north-west and north-east frontiers, guarded by the "impregnable" Himalayas, afforded the country priceless security. Now that security has collapsed. Not only have the traditional invasion routes from the north-west sprung back to life; the Chinese have shown that the north-eastern frontiers are even more vulnerable.

The map of Asia reveals at a glance how indefensible the Indian sub-continent is except taken as a whole. In no respect has the division of the sub-continent into two mutually hostile States been so grievous as in the matter of defence. The present situation, with East Pakistan lying athwart the Indian states of Assam, West Bengal, and Bihar, and the centrally administered areas of the North-East Frontier Agency, Manipur, Tripura, and Nagaland, makes any strategy of defence immediately ineffective. The easternmost states are linked with the rest of India by a narrow corridor in the north, connected by a metre-gauge railway system from Katihar in Bihar state. A rail journey from Calcutta to Tezpur, in Assam, takes the best part of four days. It is not even a direct rail link, and involves a ferry across the Brahmaputra. The strategic lines of communication with the eastern states are, thus, either by costly and cumbersome air routes over-flying East Pakistan or through the highly vulnerable northern corridor.

This is an extremely perilous situation. To the north of the narrow neck of West Bengal lie Sikkim and Bhutan, two principalities with which India has special relations. This narrow neck also touches a part of Tibet. To the south is East Pakistan, at points no more than thirty miles away. An Indian defensive force in this area would, therefore, have no room for development and regrouping. It is relatively easy for any powerful invading army to seal off the whole of Assam, NEFA, Manipur, Tripura, Nagaland, Sikkim, and Bhutan. It can easily approach the highway leading into Bihar. And once West Bengal and Bihar fall to an enemy, India loses her richest industrial and mineral areas as well as her most important city, Calcutta. The north-western flank is only slightly less vulnerable. Chinese planes concentrated in Ladakh are within 500 miles of Delhi.

The economics of defence for India is, therefore, mixed up with the geopolitical aspects of the defence of the sub-continent. Sooner or later, there must be a *rapprochement* with Pakistan, unless both countries are eventually to accept communist tutelage. For the present, however, it is difficult to see how such a *rapprochement* is to be brought about. There is not only the problem of Kashmir, which no Indian Government can hand over to Pakistan, and without which no Pakistani Government can come to an agreement with India. The basic problem is one of deep distrust between the two countries. The present generation of politicians in India and Pakistan have grown up against the background of Congress–Muslim League animosity. It is difficult for them to live down the past and to turn a new leaf of friendly collaboration. Moreover, Pakistan has been born of hatred for India, and her people have been fed on this hatred for the last fifteen years. Few Indians are satisfied that, given Kashmir, Pakistan will not ask for something more. Reports reaching New Delhi from reliable sources stated that, when the Chinese armies had almost reached the plains of Assam, the East Pakistan leaders, who have managed to occupy vantage positions in President Ayub Khan's Cabinet, were pressing him to march troops to the areas of southern Assam, where the majority of the population is Muslim. Whether this was true or not, it shows the serious psychological aspect of the Indo-Pakistani problem. Public opinion in India has been greatly dismayed by Pakistan's unconcealed attempts to make political, diplomatic, and even military capital out of the Sino-Indian conflict.

The problem is difficult. But it will have to be resolved sooner or later if the Indian sub-continent is to be physically protected from communist aggression. There is already a growing realization in India that the traditional pattern of thinking with regard to defence will no longer do. This is the durable impact of the Chinese invasion. The Chinese did not come to conquer India; but they have opened India's eyes to a new assessment of the situation.

Faced with these realities, India cannot afford to rely any longer on means which have so far paid only a modestly profitable dividend. Her approach to domestic as well as international questions is bound to undergo major changes, the most important of which are likely to be in the fields of defence and economics. On developments in these two fields will largely depend her future as a sovereign political entity.

The accumulation of sufficient defence strength will entail enormous expense. The Finance Minister, Mr. Morarji Desai, has hinted that the defence budget will have to be doubled. The Budget for 1962–3 allocated for defence about £280 million out of a total central revenue of something above £1,000 million. Doubling the defence budget for the coming financial year will mean spending on defence about half the central income at the existing rate of taxation. Since this normal budgetary defence allocation does not include most of the capital outlay on defence, which will now claim a much larger amount, overall military expenditure will probably be in the region of between £700 million and £800 million.

In contrast to pressure upon the Government from a powerful section of the press to seek massive assistance from the United States, the Government's line of thought at the present moment seems to be that, while essential help in the form of transport and fighting equipment must be accepted, India should continue to try to build up an industrial base in order to meet her own defence requirements. This was the plan devised by Mr. Krishna Menon with Mr. Nehru's full approval; and although Mr. Menon is no longer in the Government, his ideas on the production of defence equipment remain. It is generally recognized in India that too great a dependence on the United States for arms would jeopardize the country's independence in both its domestic policy of building a socialistic economy and its foreign policy of non-alignment. There is no inclination in New Delhi to abandon the prospect of Soviet assistance, nor to lose the political advantages which a policy of non-alignment seeks to obtain. Moreover, for the present the U.S. Government does not seem to want India to lose favour with Moscow; nor does the Soviet Government appear to object very strongly to India's acceptance of limited quantities of defensive weapons from the United States.

So long as the U.S. Government insists on a settlement of the Kashmir problem as a condition for large-scale and long-term military aid to India, the chances of military collaboration between India and the United States must necessarily remain limited. Equipment supplied by the United States and Britain at the time of the Chinese emergency, valuable as it is, will not make much difference from the point of view of a long-term arms build-up. And if joint Commonwealth–U.S. arms aid over an unspecified period is not to exceed $100 million, as reports from Washington suggest, the burden of building up a sufficient military "deterrent" to China (which seems to be Mr. Nehru's objective over the next five years) will fall squarely on India's own shoulders.

The agonizing question for India is whether she can carry this burden and still go ahead with her plans for economic development. If she can, there should be no danger to her integrity as a democratic nation. If she cannot, it is doubtful if she can function very long as a democratic republic.

A remarkable feature of India's economy over the last decade has been the conservatism which has gradually crept over her revolutionary zeal. When Indian leaders describe the economic revolution as "peaceful," they mean that it has been "painless." The agrarian reforms have stopped half-way; at present the landed class happens to be the most privileged economic class. Agricultural income is not taxed. Land revenue which comes within the bounds of state finance is among the lowest in the world. Neither the Planning Commission nor the Taxation Inquiry Commission has suggested an agricultural income-tax; a recent move in the state of Uttar Pradesh to raise the land revenue rate nearly brought down the Ministry. In spite of the "socialist" experiment, the disparity between rich and poor has increased rather than decreased. There is in present-day India more concentration of wealth than in any European country, including Western Germany. A handful of business houses control an extraordinarily large share of private industry; they also control the mass-circulation newspapers. No amount of persuasion has succeeded in bringing out hidden wealth; huge arrears of income-tax continue to remain unpaid; gold hoarded by moneyed people (apart from the large Hindu temples) is officially estimated to be worth £13,000 million, little of which has been invested in the emergency gold bonds. This control over internal money resources enables the wealthy class to exert considerable influence over economic planning or, rather, on the execution of Plan projects.

Even during the present emergency the richer classes have contributed relatively little to the National Defence Fund and the gold bonds. This has been the subject of criticism in newspapers (not controlled by the big commercial houses) as well as by political leaders, including Mr. Nehru and some members of the Congress party. What is significant is that even in devising emergency plans to meet the Chinese threat, the Government has so far attempted no structural changes of the economy, and it is doubtful if the leadership of the Congress party can do so, at this stage. A revolution which has spent itself is scarcely capable of gathering new momentum.

The economics of the third five-year Plan would seem to underline the painless nature of India's ambition of growth. The Plan calls for a total outlay of nearly £10,000 million—£4 per head per year. Of this, the Union and state Governments are to find £6,000 million; the rest must come from the private sector. The planners hope that 30 per cent of the finance from the public sector will be forthcoming in the form of external assistance. The Central Government and the states are required to raise £1,320 million by means of additional taxation (this will now have to be considerably increased if the defence bill is to be met and the essentials of the Plan carried out). Economists doubt whether the Indian people, already one of the most heavily taxed, can be made to yield this amount. The annual rate of increase in the income and corporation taxes does not exceed £10 million. An annual increase of 5 per cent in exports is considered quite satisfactory. (This modest rate was achieved in the last financial year, but during 1962 imports have fallen.) Industrial enterprises of the Central and state Governments, other than the railways, are expected to contribute over £340 million towards the resources of the Plan; but it is doubtful if this can be achieved.

This situation brings out the major contradiction of the Indian "miracle." The Indian cake is too small; but 440 million people are jostling with one another for the lion's share. The struggle for democracy is basically a struggle for an equal share of the cake. The struggle becomes more and more acute as the demands of the people increase without a comparable increase in the size of the cake, and the prospect becomes almost hopeless in view of the rapidly rising population rate.

These increasing demands from the mass of the people, who possess the ultimate political power, have brought to light during the past five years many disintegrating forces. If the pace of the Indian revolution were quicker, or if the country were under authoritarian rule, many of these divisive forces would not have raised their head. To complain that the Indian masses have not been fully involved in the national economic effort is to complain that

India is a democracy; in a democratic society, a citizen cannot be forced to participate in any project. Nor has the democratic Government of India been able to devise rural projects which would mobilize productively the country's biggest single source of strength, its manpower.

Major problems which threaten the unity of the country are inherent in the physical composition of the Indian Union. Nowhere is this more evident than in the linguistic field. India has at least fifteen "national" languages. Hindi is spoken by no more than 38 per cent of the population, and is less developed than at least four other Indian languages. It is not surprising, therefore, that the non-Hindi-speaking people should resent the official attempt to install Hindi as the "language of the Union," or the *de facto* national language. The linguistic controversy has an additional edge because the Hindi-speaking belt, and notably Uttar Pradesh, the second largest state, occupies a predominant position in Parliament as well as in the Council of Ministers. This political predominance is all the more envied by the non-Hindi regions because of the educational, cultural, and economic backwardness of the Hindi belt. The struggle for equality inevitably becomes a struggle for equality of all languages, economic groups, and regional interests. At the root of the linguistic conflict lie complex economic and social issues—clamour for jobs, for the location of industries, for a bigger share of development. In order to woo the illiterate voter, politicians find it convenient to appeal to caste and group loyalties, regional interests, linguistic patriotisms, religious associations. One or two political parties even try to blackmail the national leadership by threatening "separation."

These are issues of the old India that is passing. Indians are essentially men of compromise, and they generally have a shrewd sense of self-interest. There are built-in weaknesses in the Indian Constitution but there are also considerable hidden strengths. Over the past few years, the tendency has been towards strengthening the Central Government's authority. Now, in the face of external danger, this tendency is bound to gather further momentum. Under Article 351, a national emergency has been declared, suspending fundamental rights and enabling the Central Government to mobilize the entire resources of the country. An official measure is now before Parliament to amend Article 19, thereby making all separatist moves unconstitutional. There is little doubt that separatist forces will suffer a major set-back and the centre will emerge from the national emergency considerably stronger.

At the same time, the old leadership is fast dying out, and the era of Mr. Nehru is coming to an end. Within the Congress party, the centre of power has already shifted from the leaders in New Delhi to the more important of the Chief Ministers, especially of those states like Maharashtra, Madras, West Bengal, and Orissa where the party is better organized, less weakened by internal feuds, and where it gained considerable victories from the Communist party at the last election. The decline in power and influence of the Congress Working Committee and the Central Parliamentary Board has been counterbalanced by the growing command of the Congress party in Parliament, where the backbenchers are now more articulate than before. The base of the ruling party has been captured by the new landed gentry; traditionalist and conservative, they are more inclined to lean towards the Right than to the Left. There is, therefore, little prospect of a more openly Rightist party capturing power in the near future. The Leftist forces are divided between the scattered groups of Socialists and the Communist party, which, in spite of disciplined organization and a card-holding membership of 200,000, lacks an agrarian base and is at present passing through a deep ideological crisis. The army is without political ambition; its tradition, linguistic and caste composition, and leadership are guarantees against a military take-over unless there is widespread chaos and a collapse of political leadership.

The Indian Union is not likely to disintegrate unless it fails to carry forward its economic development and to meet the minimum demands of its teeming population, or unless it succumbs to external aggression. It is wrong to imagine that India's unity depends even largely on Mr. Nehru's leadership. His successors (the plural is deliberate) are expected to be more practical, realistic men, ready to take more drastic measures to suppress divisive forces. But they may very well decide to compromise on democracy.

The Pakistan-American Alliance: Stresses and Strains*

Mohammed Ayub Khan

It is nearly ten years since Pakistan became an ally of the West. . . .

Pakistan is associated with the United States through not one, but four mutual security arrangements. In this sense, it has been sometimes termed "America's most allied ally in Asia." It is the only Asian country which is a member both of SEATO and CENTO.

The strategic location of Pakistan is of some significance in this connection. West Pakistan borders on the Middle East, is close to Soviet Russia's southern frontier and shares a common border with China. It stands across the great mountain passes through which all land invasions of the Indian subcontinent have taken place in recorded history. East Pakistan, on the other hand, borders on Burma. Thus West Pakistan and East Pakistan flank India on her northwest and on her northeast. So situated, Pakistan virtually constitutes a defensive shield for India. It constitutes also the gateway to South

* From *Foreign Affairs,* January 1964, pp. 195–209. Copyright 1964, Council on Foreign Relations, Inc., New York. Reprinted by permission. Mohammed Ayub Khan is President of Pakistan.

Asia. It should therefore be in the interest of world peace, particularly of India's security, that Pakistan remain strong and stable.

Nevertheless, Pakistan came in for bitter criticism from India when she joined these purely defensive alliances. India charged that by so doing "Pakistan had brought the cold war to the sub-continent." The real purpose of this Indian outcry became clearer, however, as time advanced, and more particularly when in 1959 Pakistan signed the bilateral Agreement of Cooperation. According to this agreement, the United States would under certain circumstances assist Pakistan if she became the victim of aggression. India demanded and, according to Mr. Nehru, received a "specific assurance" from Washington that this pact "could not be used against India." Shorn of sophistry, this demand amounted to seeking an assurance that if India should commit aggression against Pakistan or threatened Pakistan's security, the United States would not come to the assistance of Pakistan under this pact. There could not be a more illuminating commentary on India's historic attitude toward Pakistan.

This attitude also explains why India has throughout opposed the grant of military aid to Pakistan. It is not that she feared that Pakistan—a fifth her size and with armed forces a quarter the size of hers—would, through the kind of military aid program the United States contemplated, become a serious military threat to India. In actual fact the military aid to Pakistan was designed to give it merely a deterrent force. Even with the aid, the armed forces of Pakistan were not to be more than one-third of India's strength before her border clashes with China. Therefore, Pakistan could not possibly pose any threat to India.

The real reason behind India's opposition to Pakistan's receiving military aid was a combination of several factors, including the bitter opposition of the Hindu community to the very creation of Pakistan, India's refusal to honor her solemn pledges in respect of Jammu and Kashmir, and India's desire to dominate what she considers to be her own sphere of influence in Asia.

. . . over the last decade, the policies of the United States have undergone a change which has operated progressively to the disadvantage of her ally, Pakistan, vis-à-vis neutral India.

When we first joined the alliance with the United States, neutralism—"non-alignment" as India prefers to call it—was suspect in American eyes. It was in fact regarded as "immoral." It was another name for "playing both sides of the street." Over the years, it has come to assume a mantle of respectability in American eyes. Indeed, some four years ago it gradually began to occupy, in American estimation, a privileged position. The favor of neutral countries began to be actively sought, in some cases in competition against the Soviet Union. In particular, influential American circles began to advocate "massive aid" to India.

At the same time, there grew a feeling among the allies of the United States—not in Pakistan only—that, in a variety of ways, they were being increasingly taken for granted. Gradually, as a result of this change in American thinking, neutral India became the largest recipient by far of American economic aid, while she continued freely to castigate the United States in the United Nations and outside whenever opportunity offered. Pakistan watched this transformation in American foreign policy with increasing perplexity and dismay.

India regards herself as a big power in Asia. Her eventual aim has been, and still is, to have her sphere of influence in Southeast Asia. The Indian leaders have often stated that their true border extends from the Hindu Kush mountains to the Mekong River, that is to say, wherever the influence of Hinduism has existed in the past. Their earlier friendly overtures to China were based on the hope that there would be an understanding between them and China over their respective spheres of influence in Asia, and that China would recognize and endorse India's claim. They moreover felt that as long as the American influence existed in Asia, the achievement of any such objective would not be possible. That was the reason why India, although accepting aid from the United States, made strenuous efforts to oppose the United States on every major issue in the world forum and elsewhere in order to belittle its prestige and influence. If America lost face before the whole world it did not matter so long as her influence was reduced, if not eliminated altogether, in Asia.

It follows that as soon as India arrives at some sort of settlement with China, she will revert to the traditional policy of eliminating United States influence from Asia. It is for this reason that India's façade of neutrality is still maintained in spite of massive arms aid from the West and close collaboration in the military field. She has retained sufficient flexibility and political freedom to revert to her traditional anti-American policy as soon as circumstances permit. The receipt of arms and economic aid now is not going to make any more difference than the previous supply of military and economic aid made in India's open hostility to the United States.

In the past, if the United States gave economic aid to India we were not against it as such. We were concerned rather over its massiveness and scale. It enabled India to divert her own resources very substantially to the strengthening of her armed forces; she was, in effect, receiving indirect military aid. Our concern arose from the fact that the Indian military build-up was aimed solely against Pakistan. The pronouncements of Indian leaders and the continued massing of India's army on Pakistan's borders clearly suggested this.

Until last fall, however, the policy of the United States continued to distinguish somewhat between a "non-aligned" India and the American ally, Pakistan. Although under a Mutual Defense Assistance Agreement signed in 1951 (reaffirmed in 1958), India also was receiving certain military aid from the United States—without accepting any of the obligations that devolve on an ally—American policy continued generally to maintain, in the matter of *direct* military aid, a substantial difference between an ally and a neutral. An ally was qualified to receive military assistance on a scale that the United States considered justified in the light of that country's obligations under the alliance; a neutral, by and large, was not entitled to receive military aid on any commensurate scale. However, this remaining distinction between Pakistan and "non-aligned" India also disappeared last fall when the border disputes between India and China flared up into an armed clash.

Despite the fact that over the decade the distinction in American eyes between an ally and a neutral had become increasingly blurred to a vanishing point, Pakistan continued steadily to stand by the alliance. Our view has been that, so long as we are in this alliance, we must continue honorably to discharge so far as we can whatever obligations devolve on us as a member.

Last fall, however, Pakistan received a new cause for disillusionment with American foreign policy. Following the India-China border clash, the United States proceeded to rush arms to India on a scale which to us seemed totally unjustified by the requirements of the situation. Since then, arms aid has been flowing into India continuously on a very substantial scale, not only from the United States but also in almost equal measure from Britain and, to a small extent, from some other members of the Commonwealth. We are profoundly concerned over this new development. We consider that this continued arming of India, in which the Soviet Union has also, for reasons of its own, joined, poses a serious threat to Pakistan's security.

. . . The unilateral declaration of a cease-fire by the Chinese forces at a time when not only the disputed territory but the whole of north-eastern India, including Assam, lay within their easy grasp, their withdrawal from the entire NEFA territory which they had overrun, and their offer to settle the dispute peacefully—none of this supports the thesis that the Chinese had planned to embark on a major attack on India. Since then, the Chinese military threat to India has, it is now generally recognized, receded. The Chinese have demonstrated their willingness to settle the dispute peacefully. The Indians, on their part, are anxious to avoid any further fighting with China and have been working steadily for a peaceful settlement. . . .

It is our belief that the Sino-Indian dispute can and will be resolved peacefully. In our view, therefore, the continuance of military aid to India is unjustified. Furthermore, it poses a grave threat to Pakistan's security. We apprehend that after India has settled her dispute with China, she will revert to her traditional policy of intimidation of Pakistan. And she may even turn her newly acquired might against Pakistan when a suitable opportunity occurs, particularly at a time when the Western countries are so preoccupied with their own internal and external problems that they cannot undertake military commitments in this subcontinent or they find it inadvisable to do so for fear of provoking a world conflict.

Even in the unlikely event of a recrudescence of border fighting between China and India, India could not, considering the mountain terrain, deploy more than 3 to 4 divisions against the Chinese. One may justifiably ask, then, why India is doubling the size of her standing army to 22 divisions. Even allowing for the necessary reserves, what are the remaining divisions aimed against? The fact of the matter is that, taking advantage of the favorable

Western response to her demands for arms, India is planning to raise two armies, one with which to face China and the other to use against Pakistan and her other smaller neighbors in pursuance of her expansionist objectives. It should also be noted that any army meant for China would by the nature of things be so positioned as to be able to wheel round swiftly to attack East Pakistan. Thus both the armies pose a grave threat to this country.

Having built up this enormous war machine, India's leadership would need to justify the great hardships it has imposed on the Indian people in that process. It might also want to regain face which India has lost in the fighting with China. It is possible, therefore, that India might decide to do so—as soon as a suitable opportunity offers itself—by throwing its massive armor against Pakistan, and possibly striking, in the first instance, against that part of Kashmir which is under Pakistan's control but which India claims to be "Indian territory." . . .

Until the outbreak of fighting with China, and even during most of that fighting, more than three-fourths of India's best-equipped forces remained massed on Pakistan's borders. In December 1962, Mr. Nehru himself admitted that Indian military preparedness had been directed primarily against Pakistan. This still remains India's basic position, and although there have been some changes in the disposition of the Indian forces, the collective strength of those massed on the borders of West Pakistan and East Pakistan remains formidable.

Nor, indeed, would an act of aggression by India be unusual. India has used force time and again to settle her territorial disputes. Let me recall some of these instances. Immediately after independence in 1947, Junagarh, a state with a Muslim ruler, acceded to Pakistan. India strongly protested when she learnt that the ruler contemplated this. In a telegram to the Pakistan Prime Minister, the Indian Prime Minister said that since the population of Junagarh was 80 per cent Hindu and was opposed to accession to Pakistan, the Government of India could not acquiesce in the ruler's decision to accede to Pakistan. They would, however, be willing to accept the verdict of the people of the state on this question, provided the plebiscite was held under the joint supervision of the Indian and Junagarh Governments. Since Pakistan would not agree to this proposition, Indian troops marched into Junagarh and seized it by force.

In the case of Kashmir, on the other hand, Indian logic was conveniently reversed. There, the Indian army marched into the state on the strength of an instrument of "accession" signed by the Hindu Maharaja against the known wishes of the 80 percent of the people of Kashmir who are Muslims. In fact, at the time the Maharaja signed this document his armies were in retreat against the popular forces and he himself had fled the state capital, Srinagar, and taken refuge in Jammu. . . . Thereafter, the Indian forces moved in, took possession of the major part of Kashmir and have held it ever since. A pledge repeatedly given by Mr. Nehru that India would let the people of Kashmir decide the question of accession to India or Pakistan in a free plebiscite still remains to be honored.

On September 11, 1948, Quaid-i-Azam Mohammed Ali Jinnah died. The nation was plunged into sorrow over the death of the Founder of Pakistan. India chose that particular moment to march her forces into Hyderabad, another state with a Muslim ruler, and forcibly seized it, not because Hyderabad had wanted to accede to Pakistan, but because it had hesitated somewhat to accede to India.

India again employed the same technique recently to settle her territorial dispute with Portugal over Goa. Within a few weeks of Mr. Nehru's visit to Washington in November 1961, in the course of which he declared that India had "a passion for peace," the Indian army invaded and forcibly annexed Goa. It is interesting also to recall in this connection that on several occasions in the past Mr. Nehru had strongly repudiated any suggestion that India take over Goa by force. . . .

It is because of this background of India's hostility toward Pakistan, her expansionist designs and her aggressive policies that Pakistanis view the continued flow of Western arms into India from their allies with deep dismay and alarm. Indian assurances to the effect that she will not use American arms against Pakistan fail to carry conviction with the people of Pakistan in the light of India's repeated repudiation of her solemn pledges regarding Kashmir and her record of aggression. . . .

Apart from the fact that continued Western arms assistance to India causes deep concern in Pakistan and subjects Pakistan's alliance with the West to increasing strain, it is unlikely that it will achieve the objective in view. For if the security and welfare of the Indian sub-continent are the objective, then what is needed is not the injection of massive doses of military aid into India but a rapprochement between India and Pakistan, such as would ensure a disengagement and could even open the way to a reduction of the Indian and Pakistan forces. Such a rapprochement can be brought about only through a just and honorable settlement of the Kashmir dispute. It can be achieved in no other way.

10

Vietnam: Military or Diplomatic Solution?

"The crisis in South Vietnam is rooted in the oppressively dictatorial character of the Ngo family government and its wide-spread unpopularity," *The New York Times* said on August 23, 1963. Little more than two months later the Ngo family (headed by President Ngo Dinh Diem, his brother Ngo Dinh Nhu, and Mme. Nhu) had fallen. Yet the crisis in South Vietnam continued, and less than three months after the military coup that overthrew Diem and the Nhus another coup had taken place.

Fear that the political situation in South Vietnam might be even worse without Diem—and that the country might then fall to the Communist Vietcong insurgents—had long restrained the U.S. from withdrawing its support of the Diem regime. But, in May 1963, conflict between the regime and the Buddhists brought about a sharp deterioration in the situation. In protest against alleged government persecution, several Buddhist monks of both sexes publicly burned themselves to death. In face of this popular unrest, Diem responded with mandarin hauteur; Nhu with rigorous repression; Mme. Nhu with her comment, "I would clap hands at seeing another monk barbecue show, for one cannot be responsible for the madness of others."

The U.S. still hesitated, but in August 1963 it replaced Ambassador Frederick E. Nolting (who was closely indentified with Diem) with Henry Cabot Lodge, Jr. For a time, Lodge tried unsuccessfully to bring about a fundamental change in the structure and policies of the Saigon government. At last, as a tour of the U.S. by Mme. Nhu was coming to an end, a military coup, approved if not supported by the U.S., overthrew the reign of the Ngo family.

In two respects, however, the results of the coup were still unfavorable to the U.S. First, government stability had not been secured. The junta that followed Diem was split within itself, and it failed to arouse popular enthusiasm for waging the war against the Vietcong. When it was removed by a bloodless coup, the U.S. feared that the same fate might befall the new regime.

Second, the strategy explained in the selection by George W. Ball has been in serious trouble since the beginning of 1964. The program of "strategic hamlets," which requires a major regrouping of the rural population into fortified centers defended largely by the inhabitants themselves, was not proving to be a key to military victory; and, because of its nature, it could hardly be popular. No matter what strategy and tactics the South Vietnamese forces and their U.S. advisers introduced, the Vietcong continued successfully to exemplify Mao Tse-tung's analogy of guerrillas that live like fish in an ocean of peasants. This situation has not improved, despite the fact that American expenditures in Vietnam since 1955 total over 2½ billion dollars. Yet no major change in policy has emerged from the repeated visits to South Vietnam by Secretary of Defense McNamara. U.S. policy-makers still assume that if South Vietnam were to fall, our entire position in Southeast Asia—and thus in the rest of Asia—would be undermined. So McNamara made assurances of increased U.S. economic and military aid, with the hope that there would be a reversal of fortunes under General Nguyen Khanh, the leader of the January coup.

If this does not happen, and if instead the situation gets much worse, other alternatives will have to be considered. In his selection here, Hans J. Morgenthau proposes one of these alternatives—a diplomatic rather than a military settlement.

This kind of proposal had little impetus, however, until late in 1963, when General de Gaulle raised the possibility of neutralizing Vietnam, Cambodia, and Laos—those countries that had formerly comprised French Indochina.

The military rulers of South Vietnam have reacted indignantly to de Gaulle's suggestions. However, de Gaulle received impressive support in the U.S. when Senator Mansfield, in a Senate speech in February 1964, argued in favor of "true neutralization—a status based on guarantees and not on words or promises or continued infiltration from the north." Senator Thomas Dodd replied to this speech on the floor of the Senate with the statement excerpted in this chapter. Dodd agreed that the war was not going well; but he argued that we must take the offensive, and that doing so required carrying military activity into North Vietnam. Bernard B. Fall examines here the Mansfield and Dodd alternatives, as well as the other options available to us in Vietnam today. His conclusions favor negotiation and settlement, but his article makes it clear that each of the alternatives contains grave hazards and dark uncertainties. As is the case with so many of the problems discussed in this book, the Vietnam dilemma offers no clear, clean, total solution. The choices open to us are merely among competing kinds of risk, cost, and confusion.

Vietnam: Free-World Challenge in Southeast Asia*

George W. Ball

The struggle in South Vietnam today is not a local civil war. It is a carefully planned and mounted campaign of subversion and insurgency—equipped and directed from Hanoi.

Consider, for example, what the Viet Cong is seeking to destroy. Its targets are the very symbols of economic progress—schools, hospitals, first aid stations, malaria eradication teams, and the transport system.

Tactics such as these are directed to the ends of a Communist takeover; they do not serve the people.

There is no doubt as to what we are observing in Vietnam. It is another attempt by the Communists to extend their control by fomenting disorder and revolt against established governments. We have seen this same pattern before—in Greece, Malaya, and the Philippines. As it was defeated there, so, with our support, the free Vietnamese will defeat it in South Vietnam.

The Communists in Vietnam have fitted their tactics to the conditions of the struggle. Given the present stage of weaponry and the difficulties of supply through the narrow bottleneck of Hanoi, they have avoided the kind of naked aggression that marked the war in Korea. Instead they have employed the tactics of guerrilla warfare, the techniques of terror and propaganda, in an effort to achieve the same end—the conquest of territory and people.

Since 1958 the Viet Cong terror campaign has increased sharply. Officials have been assassinated, teachers killed in their schoolrooms; anything and anyone that represented stability or order has served as a likely target. The control apparatus in the north has been vastly expanded. Political cadres and military replacements have been sent south in increasing numbers. Infiltration systems—by sea and by land—have been expanded. Local recruitment has become a priority assignment for all Communist units. Given the size of the country and the resources available, the Communist effort, directed from Hanoi, to penetrate, subvert, and conquer South Vietnam is one of the most extensive of its kind in history.

* From an address to the Economic Club of Detroit, April 30, 1962. Department of State Publication 7388, Far Eastern Series 113, released June 1962 (Washington, D.C.: Government Printing Office, 1962), pp. 1–19. Mr. Ball is Under Secretary of State of the United States.

But one can say: What does this mean to us? Granted the valiance of the Vietnamese people, the high quality of their fighting spirit, how does a guerrilla war 10,000 miles away in the fetid jungles of Southeast Asia concern America? How is it relevant to the larger interests of our policy? Is it worth the millions of dollars we have poured into Vietnam or the risk of American lives?

The answer to all of those questions must be affirmative. We have consistently given that answer for a number of years.

In 1955, with the overwhelming approval of the Senate, the United States joined its partners in the Southeast Asia Treaty Organization. Although, because of the provisions of the Geneva Accords, South Vietnam could not be a signatory to that treaty, the protective umbrella of the treaty was extended to cover Vietnam by means of a protocol agreed to by all the signatories.

President Eisenhower defined our obligation well when he stated in a message to the Vietnamese Government in 1960:

> Although the main responsibility for guarding independence will always, as it has in the past, belong to the Vietnamese people and their government, I want to assure you that for so long as our strength can be useful, the United States will continue to assist Vietnam in the difficult yet hopeful struggle ahead.

The protocol to the SEATO treaty is an expression of the signatories' vital interests in the preservation of the integrity and independence of Vietnam. Those interests derive both from geography and from the very nature of the power struggle now going on in the world between aggressive Communist power and freedom.

One does not have to accept fully the automatic operation of the so-called "domino" theory to recognize the strategic significance of South Vietnam. It forms one shore of the South China Sea, which is the gateway to Malaya and Indonesia. It controls the mouth of the Mekong River, which is the coronary artery of Southeast Asia. If the Vietnamese people were to lose the struggle to maintain a free and independent nation, it would be a loss of tragic significance to free-world interests in the whole of Asia and the South Pacific.

And more than that, if the United States were to neglect its responsibilities to the Vietnamese people, the consequences would not be limited even to those areas; they would be worldwide. For the free-world's security cannot be given away piecemeal; it is not divisible. When the going gets rough we cannot observe those responsibilities that are easy or near at hand and disregard the others.

What we do or fail to do in Vietnam will be felt both by our antagonists and our friends. How we act in Vietnam will have its impact on Communist actions in Europe, in Africa, and in Latin America.

Last December, in responding to President Diem's request for assistance, President Kennedy reaffirmed the American position clearly:

> . . . our primary purpose is to help your people maintain their independence. If the Communist authorities in North Vietnam will stop their campaign to destroy the Republic of Veitnam, the measures we are taking to assist your defense efforts will no longer be necessary.

The peace of Southeast Asia is not threatened from the south or from the west; the threat comes only from the north, from those who have declared their intention to force the rest of the world into their pattern—in spite of the fact that no people has yet chosen that pattern in a genuinely free election.

There *can* be peace overnight in Vietnam—provided the aggressors stop their campaign of terror, murder, and subversion and adopt a peaceful course. The situation is just as simple as that.

. . . under the best of circumstances the creation of a secure Vietnamese state will be a long, slow process. It will require not only the building of indigenous political support but the achievement of a rate of economic progress that alone can assure political stability—political stability that can in turn provide the base on which to build the military strength needed to create the climate of confidence and security in which economic and social progress are possible.

Inevitably the main burden of meeting and beating the Viet Cong threat must fall on the people of South Vietnam, on their Government, and on their armed forces. It is their country, their lives, their future that are most directly in danger.

But we can provide, we are providing, and we must continue to provide the means to help the Vietnamese help themselves. We are increasing our effort in training, in logistics, in the transport of the Vietnam forces.

Let there be no misunderstanding as to the shape and dimensions of the role we are playing. The United States has *no* combat units in Vietnam. We are *not* fighting the war, as some reports have suggested. We are *not* running the war, as the Communists have tried assiduously to argue.

What we are doing is to provide material and training personnel—all at the request of the Vietnamese Government. We are helping them in their struggle. Even this limited effort cannot be accomplished without some danger. A part of our men are necessarily exposed to combat situations as they work with their Vietnamese comrades. . . .

Can the Vietnamese win their battle against the Communists even with our help? Here again the answer is definitely yes. Systematic insurgency is not unbeatable if the proper methods are used to beat it.

The guerrillas whom the Vietnamese Army is fighting are under distinct handicaps. In many cases they are poorly trained and equipped and not motivated by deep conviction. Rather, they are merely unsophisticated villagers or peasants who have been conscripted by terror or treachery. In such a case they are likely to have had only rudimentary training in weapons handling and tactics. Their equipment may be makeshift, often just what they can capture or fabricate themselves.

Only the leaders and the hard core have a strong ideological commitment. The rank and file are their puppets—those whom they have bought, coerced, or intimidated.

The Viet Cong guerrillas are seeking, by a variety of means, to achieve psychological dominance over the Government forces. They are relying heavily on propaganda and psychological warfare techniques. But such techniques are vulnerable; they depend to a large extent on maintaining the *mystique* of success. They can, therefore, be undercut by a serious defeat or a succession of defeats that will destroy the aura of invincibility on which their effectiveness depends.

To counter the guerrilla attack, the guerrillas must be deprived of their source of support, which means that they must be denied access to the villages. In Vietnam the guerrillas do not have the support of the people. Yet so long as they have *access* to the people, they can undermine confidence, disrupt local government, and compel submission by terror and threat.

To deny this access the villages must be provided with security and protection. Strong ties must be developed between local communities and the central Government. The village people must be helped to acquire a sense of identity with the National state.

And at the same time the *mystique* of success must be dispelled. Military units must be trained and deployed to destroy or capture the insurgent forces. Effective action depends on the development of sound, dependable intelligence—quick knowledge of guerrilla movements and sufficient mobility to permit force to be brought to bear rapidly to repel guerrilla attacks.

Within the past few weeks the Vietnamese Government has embarked on a course of action patterned in part on the successful British antiguerrilla campaign in Malaya during the 1950's. This plan calls for subdividing areas of heavy guerrilla penetration into small districts. Key villages within these districts are then encircled with a protection of barbed wire and watchtowers. Entry is carefully scrutinized. Everyone over 12 years of age must have a special pass. Curfews are ordered by the civil authorities. Controls are being placed on food, clothing, and other supplies to make sure that none are diverted to the guerrillas.

To the greatest extent possible the villagers are being armed and trained and the villages provided with radios that will enable them to request aid when an attack occurs.

In the occasional situations where necessary—but only where necessary—scattered villages and areas heavily infested by marauding bands will be abandoned and their occupants moved into defended villages that will afford them protection.

As these actions are taken, the guerrillas are beginning to find themselves uncomfortably conspicuous. Without identification they find it difficult to intermingle. After the curfew they find it difficult to move.

The progressive insulation of the villages will deny the guerrillas their chief source of food and supply. As their supplies diminish, the guerrillas will be forced to take greater risks, even to attack the fortified villages. And when attacked, the villagers will not only be prepared to defend themselves but will be able, by radio, to call for immediate help. The helicopters we are supplying will make it possible for Government forces to respond immediately.

Through fear of reprisal the villagers, in the past, have provided intelligence to the guerrillas but little to the Government. With the elimination of that fear they should serve as equally diligent sources of information on guerrilla movements. Meanwhile, recruitment of new guerrillas within the villages should drop off sharply.

As each area is pacified and brought under effective protection the program will be extended to other areas of heavy infiltration. Finally, the entire nation should be once again under total Government control.

Yet all these aspects of a counterinsurgency campaign can only create the conditions in which social and economic progress is possible. Without that progress there can be no permanent success, for an unstable society is a fertile soil for insurgency.

The response to the Communist threat in Vietnam cannot, therefore, be limited to military measures, no matter how well conceived and conducted. The Government in Saigon is aware that, in the long run, victory will be won or lost in the villages and cities and in the minds and hearts of men.

While carrying on the struggle against externally supported forces, the Vietnamese authorities are tackling, as rapidly as conditions permit, the tasks all new nations face. With assistance from the United States and other friendly countries they are rebuilding road systems, training teachers, and erecting schools.

South Vietnam is potentially a rich agricultural area. Before enemy action increased in recent months, rice production had been stepped up so that exports were again possible. Research and experimentation in diversification of agriculture has had a high priority. New fiber crops are now grown in the highlands. Rural credit facilities have been established to aid small farmers.

United States loans and Vietnamese Government funds are being used to reequip the railroads, modernize the Saigon water system, and increase the power resources. French aid is helping to reestablish coal production and build a cement plant. German assistance has developed a technical training school. The Japanese are building a power dam.

Small industries are taking hold. In spite of the insecurity of the area, Vietnamese and foreign investors are taking the first steps toward creating industrial strength. The beginnings are there—a papermill, a glassworks, pharmaceutical plants, textile mills. American and British oil companies have just signed an agreement to build a refinery. The native ability of the Vietnamese people has been proven. Granted the possibility of peace, their destiny is assured.

The task that we have set for ourselves in Vietnam can thus be simply stated. It is to help a courageous people maintain and defend their independence in a strategic area where the free-world's interests are deeply committed.

This is a task that we must stay with until the Viet Minh stop their aggression. This task may not be concluded quickly. It took 8 years in Malaya. Since then much has been learned—but it will still take time.

The struggle in Vietnam requires the slow, relentless execution of a tried and proven plan of counterinsurgency. This is not a type of struggle congenial to the American temperament. We prefer dramatic victories, frontal attacks, the organization and mobilization of massive force and its effective employment.

What we can expect in Vietnam by contrast is the long, slow, arduous carrying out of a process. Results will not be apparent overnight, for the operation is, of necessity, the patient winning back of a land to freedom, village by village.

Yet it is important that we recognize the nature of the conflict underway in that remote corner of the globe, that we study it and that we comprehend its meaning, for the struggle in Vietnam represents a type of threat that we would be well advised not to underestimate.

Insurgency of this sort we have seen before in recent years. We are likely to see it again and again as the Communists seek, through the methods of stealth and terror, to disrupt the newer nations that are struggling toward the establishment of an independent national life and to frustrate the hopes of their peoples for peace and freedom.

It will take effort to defeat this insurgency in Vietnam. Most of all it will take the patient application of effort over a long period of time. But the Vietnamese people are sturdy and resilient and they have the will to win—and when they do win, the world can count one more victory on the side of freedom and justice and the hope for stable peace.

Vietnam—Another Korea?*

Hans J. Morgenthau

The involvement of the United States in the Vietnamese war poses acutely two fundamental issues with which American foreign policy has tried to come to terms elsewhere, and which it is likely to have to face in Vietnam and elsewhere in an even more acute form. These issues are: the unqualified support we are extending to regimes whose political weakness compels us in

* From *Commentary,* May 1962, pp. 369–374. Reprinted by permission. Mr. Morgenthau is Albert A. Michelson Distinguished Service Professor of Political Science and Modern History at the University of Chicago.

the end to commit ourselves militarily beyond what our national interest would require; and the peripheral containment of Communist China. In order to understand the nature of the issues as they pose themselves in Vietnam, it is first necessary to take a look at the history of our involvement in the affairs of Vietnam.

That history has been determined by a number of paradoxes. The war which France fought in Indochina until the Geneva agreement ended it in 1954 was for her essentially a colonial war, no different from the wars that France and Spain had fought in Africa in the 1920's. For the great majority of the Vietnamese, on the other hand, the war was a war for national liberation. However, for the two powers without whose intervention the Indochina war would have taken on a different character and might well have had a different outcome, the United States and Communist China, the war had nothing to do with national liberation or colonialism. As far as Communist China was concerned, the war was an attempt to extend the area of influence and domination of Communism. For the United States, too, the main issue of the war was the expansion of Communism. Certainly the United States did not support France for the purpose of maintaining French power in Indochina. The United States looked at the Indochina war as part and parcel of its over-all strategy of containing Communism throughout the world.

Yet while American interests were directly affected by the outcome of the Indochina war, the United States intervened only to the extent of supporting the French war effort; it did not intervene in the war itself nor did it participate actively in the Geneva settlement. On the one hand, the United States realized that the war was lost for the West, short of American intervention. On the other hand, it did not see fit, recovering as it was from the trauma of the Korean war just ended, to take over the military burden in Indochina which France had shouldered so long, with such enormous liabilities, and such lack of success. While the United States is committed to the containment of Communism everywhere in the world, this commitment is obviously subject to qualifications; the limited involvement of the United States in the Indochina war and its passivity during the Geneva negotiations are cases in point.

The Geneva Conference ratified the military defeat of France and the political bankruptcy of its policy in Indochina. This defeat and bankruptcy having been complete before the conference, one must ask why a conference was held in the first place. From a strictly military point of view, the Vietminh could have marched south and forced the French to evacuate. Why, then, did the Communists agree to hold a conference? Why did the Soviet Union even emphasize at the Berlin Conference of 1954 the necessity for such a conference? And why was it that at the conference itself the Communist powers, for the sake of agreement, made important concessions to the West? The Communists went into the conference proposing the fourteenth parallel as the dividing line between North and South Vietnam, and they retreated to the seventeenth parallel. They originally demanded that elections be held six months after the armistice, and they conceded two years.

We have heard much of negotiating from strength. Certainly at Geneva in 1954, the Communists had strength. Yet they conducted the negotiations in the spirit of compromise, and the political settlement to which they agreed was much more advantageous to the West than was warranted by the actual military situation. It would certainly be absurd to suggest that it was magnanimity which induced the Communists to make these concessions, or that it was simply for the sake of an agreement per se that they were made. It seems to me that a consideration of why those concessions were made, why there was a conference to begin with, with a compromise agreement to terminate it, will give us an inkling of the place that South Vietnam holds today in the over-all world situation, particularly from the point of view of the United States and its interests.

First of all, Communist China pursues in Asia an over-all military and political objective which parallels the objective of the Soviet Union in Europe. It is to remove the power of the United States from the continent of Asia; for American power on the continent of Asia, especially in the form of military strong points, constitutes a permanent challenge to the power of Communist China on that continent. A continuation of the Indochina war, ending foreseeably with a complete military disaster for France, might still have led to the active participation of the United States and established it as a military power within the traditional sphere of influence of China.

Secondly, what the Communists conceded at Geneva, both they and many Western observers viewed as only temporary concessions. It was then generally believed that South Vietnam was doomed; that Ngo Dinh Diem was the creation of the United States, pulled out of a hat by desperate American officials; that he would be unable to master the chaos then prevailing in South Vietnam; and that elections, whenever held, would give an overwhelming majority to the Communists. Thus the Communists expected, and in view of the facts then available had a right to expect, that sooner or later South Vietnam would fall to them.

Thirdly, the Vietminh wanted to take over the Red River delta intact rather than to have to conquer it.

Finally, and perhaps most importantly, the Soviet Union had just embarked upon its new policy of transforming the cold war of position into a cold war of maneuver, which was to be decided not in Southeast Asia but Europe. At that time, France occupied a key position in the over-all struggle for power in Europe. Its attitude was decisive for the success of the European Defense Community. By making a concession to France, by not humiliating France to the limit of its ability, the Soviet Union must have hoped to prevent France from ratifying EDC. For whatever reasons, France did not ratify EDC, and in that measure the expectations of the Soviet Union were justified.

However, the expectations of friend and foe alike, which anticipated the absorption of South Vietnam into the Communist orbit as inevitable, were belied by the vigor and success with which South Vietnam set about creating a new state from the ruins of a French colony. The vigor and at least temporary success of this seemingly hopeless experiment were due to three factors: American support, the qualities of the Vietnamese people, especially of the refugees from the north, and the personality of President Diem.

The United States, once the danger of getting involved in another Korean-type war had passed, recovered the ability to correlate its commitments to the objective of its foreign policy. That objective being the containment of Communism, the United States embarked upon a concerted policy of political, military, and economic assistance to President Diem's regime. Without that assistance, President Diem could not have achieved his initial successes.

Yet these successes owe a great deal also to the extraordinary qualities of the Vietnamese people. Anybody who has traveled in Asia with his eyes open, beholding the different degrees of decay and backwardness, must have been impressed with the vitality and intelligence of the Vietnamese people. The order, vigor, and productivity of the refugee camps were—to take only one example—monuments to these qualities.

But the qualities of the Vietnamese people and American aid would not have been enough by themselves; they needed the fulcrum of President Diem's extraordinary personality in order to become effective as raw material in the building of a temporary political order in South Vietnam. In little more than a year Diem managed to get rid of the Emperor and make himself President; to establish his control over the army; to purge the police of the gangster element; to push back, and in part eliminate, the independent power of the religious sects and of the Communists; and thus to establish something approaching efficient administration in a considerable part of the territory of Vietnam. All this was done entirely by totalitarian means—suppression of political opposition, muzzling of the press, arbitrary executions, and so on. Nor were the positive—puritanical and ideological—elements of totalitarianism missing. Diem embarked upon a successful "Anti-Loose Living" campaign which soon transformed Saigon, the former Paris of Southeast Asia, into the dullest of French colonial towns, and he also set up a most intricate and elaborate system of propaganda and control in the villages.

It was obvious to me when I visited Vietnam in 1955—and I told President Diem so to his evident displeasure—that these policies would inevitably lead to a bipolarization of politics in South Vietnam. Supported by an oligarchy whose interests were tied to the regime, he would have to govern a politically frustrated and hence indifferent population, while the Communist underground would provide the only organized opportunity for political opposition. By equating all opposition with Communism, he would force the popular aspirations for change into Communist channels. This is in fact what happened. Having to choose between President Diem's personal totalitarianism and the totalitarianism of Communism, which at least can justify itself by a forward-looking philosophy, the Vietnamese people at best have abstained from choosing and at worst have chosen Communism.

The extent of popular disaffection with the Diem regime is not known to American public opinion, which, following the example of the government, prefers to think of the problem of South Vietnam in terms of Communist aggression versus the defense of freedom. This disaffection is particularly widespread among those classes which are the natural supporters of a democratic regime or else its indispensable allies, such as business and professional men, university teachers and students, civil servants, and army officers. It is especially strong among the refugees from the North, who, after fleeing from Communist totalitarianism, are disappointed and embittered at the discovery that they have exchanged one totalitarianism for another. Their disaffection extends to the Kennedy administration from which they expected support for their aspirations. It is significant and bodes ill for the future of the regime, moreover, that the intensity of disaffection increases with the degree of education and political sophistication.

The attitude of the great mass of the peasants, on the other hand, is marked by indifference to the ideological positions of either side. They tend to look at Diem as a kind of American puppet, the successor to Bao Dai, the French puppet, and at the Americans as the successors to French colonial rule. Communism means nothing to them one way or the other. What interests them and determines their attitude are the benefits and disadvantages to be expected from either side. Thus they will submit to, and cooperate with, whoever happens to exercise authority at a particular time, and prisoners will join the other side almost as a matter of course, only to rejoin their former friends if the fortunes of guerrilla war should change.

How has American policy tried to cope with this situation? It has done so by two simple expedients, which have recommended themselves here as elsewhere exactly because of their simplicity: support for the domestic political status quo and military defense against the foreign enemy. Both policies are simple, as compared with the alternatives, in terms of the intellectual effort to be expended and the short-term political risks to be taken. But they also contradict each other in that the domestic political status quo is the greatest single impediment to successful military defense short of commitments in men and material on the part of the United States out of all proportion to the American interests at stake. Nothing could be simpler than to see in President Diem's regime the only viable anti-Communist government of South Vietnam, which therefore must be supported come what may, despite one's misgivings about its philosophy and policies. Nothing could be simpler than to reduce the political and military instability of South Vietnam to the result of Communist aggression from without, to be countered by military action. But the very simplicity of these conceptions distorts a complex reality, and in consequence, policies based upon them are bound to be unsuccessful or can be made successful only at disproportionate costs and at inordinate risks.

If it was obvious to a casual observer like myself in 1955, it could not have been lost upon the experts six years later that the main source of the political and military instability of South Vietnam must be sought in the very status quo which our policy is committed to maintain. If South Vietnam had a government which could count upon the loyalty of its civil service and armed forces and the support of the peasants, guerrillas would not be able to control whole provinces and penetrate to the very outskirts of the capital. Guerrilla warfare is a political problem before it is a military one. Both in Malaya and Greece, military action against the guerrillas remained ineffective until drastic political reforms removed the causes for popular indifference and hostility. The case of Greece is particularly instructive in this respect; for here the United States in the late 40's had to cope with a situation not dissimilar from that which confronts it today in South Vietnam. The United States was able to restore peace and order in Greece through a coordinated political, economic, and military campaign which required the commitment of limited American resources because it gave priority to political and economic reforms. The arguments advanced on behalf of the inevitability of the existing political and economic status quo were as specious in the case of Greece as they are now in the case of South Vietnam.

The idea that there is no alternative to Diem is in the nature of a self-fulfilling prophecy. There appears to be no alternative to Diem only because we have placed all our bets on him. Six years ago, I was impressed with both the number and quality of public figures who took a passionate and intelligent interest in establishing a free and decent political order in South Vietnam. It is of course impossible to say from a distance whether such men are still available today. But certainly the United States could, if it had a mind to, find a general who could take over the reins of government and through whom the necessary political, economic, and social reforms could be effected.

The United States has two alternative policies to choose from: political reforms as a precondition for the restoration of peace and order in South Vietnam, or purely military means. The former policy requires the elimination of Diem and demands of American officials in the field great manipulative skills and exposes them to considerable short-term political risks, while it is likely to require of the United States but a limited military commitment. On the highest level at least, the government of the United States seems to have recognized the need for such political reforms, but there is no indication that this intellectual recognition has been transformed into effective political action in Saigon. Thus we have been forced to choose, half-heartedly and almost by default, the other alternative of a purely military solution.

This policy is a legacy from the Dulles era. It was then widely held that the acquisition by a Communist power of any piece of territory, regardless of its size and location, was a calamity which signaled the beginning of the end for the free world. Vietnam, for instance, was considered to be the "cork in the bottle," the "first in a row of dominoes"; if it fell, all of Indochina would fall, too. In fact, of course, North Vietnam went Communist, but South Vietnam did not, nor did the other states of Indochina. This unexpectedly favorable outcome of the Indochina war provides empirical proof for the proposition that Communist territorial gains can be localized and affect the interests of the United States adversely in differing degrees.

The misconception that each Communist territorial gain constitutes for the United States a calamity of the first magnitude has as its corollary the proposition that the United States must commit its military power to the defense of any territory that might be threatened by Communist subversion or aggression. The indiscriminate policy of alliances, offering our military support to whatever nation was willing to accept it (i.e., SEATO and the Eisenhower Doctrine) reflects that conviction. However, when the chips were down we were fortunately capable of distinguishing among interests which did not require any American military commitment at all, those which required a limited military commitment, and those which might require an all-out military commitment. Thus we did not intervene in the Indochina war, risking thereby, and reconciling ourselves to, the loss of all of Vietnam to the Communists. We did not commit our military strength to the liberation of the countries of Eastern Europe, of Cuba, and of Tibet. We were very careful in limiting the Korean war, and it was Mr. Dulles himself, the most consistent proponent of a militarily oriented foreign policy, who liquidated the Korean war on the basis of the *status quo ante bellum*.

It is therefore incumbent upon the government of the United States to determine with all possible precision the extent of the American interest in South Vietnam. The extent of our military commitment must depend upon that political determination. Is South Vietnam as important to us, or more or less so, than Korea or Cuba? Or is it as important as Berlin? The answer to political questions such as these must determine the extent of our military commitment.

Once South Vietnam is assigned its place in the hierarchy of American interests throughout the world, the government of the United States can profitably raise the question of a diplomatic solution to the problem of South Vietnam. Such a solution could be envisaged after the model of the diplomatic solution of the Geneva agreement of 1954, to which South Vietnam after all owes its very existence as an independent state. The United States is not the only country that has interests in Vietnam. So do the Soviet Union and Communist China, and so do our allies. The possibility of a negotiated settlement within the context of the over-all interests of the major parties concerned is certainly worth exploring, and it is an open question whether the chances for such a settlement are greater now than they would be at the conclusion of a drawn-out, inconclusive war.

A purely military policy is popular with the officials in the field because it frees them from the burden of political manipulation to which they are unaccustomed and from which they almost instinctively shy away because of the political risks involved. It is also popular with large segments of the American people because it promises a clear-cut solution to an irksome problem in the form of victory. Yet, in truth, this purely military policy is fraught with enormous risks and dangers for the United States. For it raises acutely the fundamental issue of our Asian policy: the peripheral containment of Communist China by military means. It conjures up the possibility, if not the likelihood, of a repetition of the Korean war, perhaps even more drawn-out and less conclusive in its results than that war was. It should not be forgotten that, fought under much more favorable political conditions, the guerrilla war in Greece lasted five years and the one in Malaya lasted twelve.

It is an illusion to think that Communist China is being contained today by the military power which the United States can bring to bear locally in Laos, Thailand, South Vietnam, or Taiwan, or that it has thus been contained in the past. Communist China can if it wishes increase the challenges locally with little cost to itself and thereby force the United States to increase its military commitments far beyond its own. It will stop, as it has stopped in the past, at the point where the escalation of American conventional military commitments conjures up the possibility of an all-out war initiated by the United States. It is at that point that containment becomes effective. In other words, what contains Communist China is its over-all weakness vis-à-vis the United States. Yet, barring a catastrophe within Communist China, this weakness is likely to be replaced in the foreseeable future by a strength which will make Communist China the foremost military power in Asia. It is from the perspective of this actual source of the containment of Communist China and of the prospect of China's future military strength that the current military policy of the United States in South Vietnam must be viewed.

If the present primarily military approach is persisted in, we are likely to be drawn ever more deeply into a Korean-type war, fought under political and military conditions much more unfavorable than those that prevailed in Korea and in the world a decade ago. Such a war cannot be won quickly, if it can be won at all, and may well last, like its Greek and Malayan counterparts, five or ten years, perhaps only to end again in a stalemate, as did the Korean war. Aside from the military risks to which it will give rise, in view of the distribution of military power which exists today and is likely to exist five or ten years hence, such a war would certainly have a profound impact upon the political health of the nation. McCarthyism and the change in the political complexion of the nation which the elections of 1952 brought about resulted directly from the frustrations of the Korean war. The American people are bound to be at least as deeply affected by the frustrations of a Vietnamese war.

The present primarily military approach has been undertaken without sufficient regard for its own military implications and its likely impact upon American politics at home and the American position in the world. The only viable alternative to that approach is the subordination of our military commitments to, and thus their limitation by, our political objectives in South

Vietnam. These objectives must be defined as the restoration of a viable political order, which constitutes the only effective defense against Communist subversion. It is obvious that such a political order can be established only through American intervention. It would be infantile to argue against such a policy on the ground that it is intervention; for if we had not intervened consistently since 1954 in the affairs of South Vietnam, Mr. Diem would not be its President today and South Vietnam itself would not exist. The choices before us are not between intervention and non-intervention, but between an intervention which serves our political interests and thereby limits our military commitments, and an intervention which supports to the bitter end the powers-that-be, even if their policies, by being counterproductive, jeopardize the interests of the United States.

We Should Go Over to the Offensive*

Thomas Dodd

It is difficult to discuss neutralization in the context of southeast Asia, because of the vagueness with which the proposition is advanced; but let us try to do so, nonetheless.

If neutralization of the current conflict means that both North Vietnam and South Vietnam should be disarmed and placed under some kind of international supervision which effectively removes both from the cold war, then it is futile and absurd even to discuss it.

It is futile and absurd because the Communists reject it utterly, openly, and contemptuously, both as an abstract concept and as a practical solution to any conflict in which they are involved. They have specifically and violently condemned it as a solution to the current conflict in Vietnam.

True neutralization can thus be dismissed; it has never been a possibility. Only false neutralization has any chance of being considered.

Under false neutralization, South Vietnam would be disarmed, given a half-Communist government probably, and placed under the so-called protection of some international body which has no substance, and exists only on paper.

The victim of aggression, not the aggressor, is to be neutralized; and this

* From a speech to the U.S. Senate on March 11, 1964. *Congressional Record*, March 11, 1964, pp. 4814–4818. Mr. Dodd is a U.S. Senator from Connecticut.

neutralization serves only to delay for a short time complete Communist enslavement.

So let us be candid about neutralization. If we use the term, let us define what we mean by it.

If we mean that both the Communist aggressor and its victim are to be neutralized—and even this would be an injustice on the face of it, since it treats equally the aggressor and the victim—let us immediately dismiss it until we receive some indication that the Communists have totally abandoned their philosophy and their tactics and are willing to entertain a suggestion so contrary to their doctrine and their history.

The above situation would be similar to that of a quarrel between two men, in which one of them was entirely innocent and had not been doing any wrong; if, when he was attacked by a hoodlum, the police rushed up and said, "We are going to punish both of you"—obviously an injustice.

And if we mean by neutralization that only the victim of aggression is to be neutralized, let us call this term what it is—a dishonest substitute for unconditional surrender. . . .

Over and over again we hear it said that the key to victory is the morale of the South Vietnamese people; their belief in their way of life; their willingness to stand up and fight for it.

This is a vast oversimplification. Obviously, the morale of a people under attack is a very important element. But in this war, in which South Vietnam is actually a battleground between the Communist world and the free world, the morale of the people should not be the key to victory or defeat.

The real key is our capacity to respond effectively to the method of guerrilla warfare supplied and directed from the privileged sanctuary of North Vietnam.

Were it not for this one-sided method of warfare, which gives all the initiative to the enemy, which permits hardened guerrilla soldiers to terrorize an entire people for years on end, to turn a whole nation into a series of barbed-wire encampments—were it not for all this, the durability of the South Vietnamese would not even be in question.

Armies exist for the purpose of saving civilian populations from having to fight. It is the failure to deal effectively with the military threat that makes the morale and courage of the people a vital element in the war.

Let us be frank. Let us ask ourselves how our own people would stand up in such a contest if they were subjected to ceaseless attack year in and year out, from which their own army seemed powerless to protect them.

Does anyone suppose that under the same conditions the people of North Vietnam would fight to protect their status? Of course not. But that does not prevent their enslavers from successfully carrying forward aggression against their neighbors.

Our task is to change the nature of this conflict.

If we continue to permit the war in South Vietnam to be, in considerable measure, a contest between professional guerrillas against helpless civilians, most certainly we are in grave danger of losing. But what a monumental abdication of responsibility it would be to attribute our defeat, if we suffer such, not to our own unwillingness to change the terms of battle, but to the morale of the people whom we are asking to live in constant danger by day and by night for a period that is apparently to have no end.

Those who are entrusted with the responsibility for the defense of South Vietnam can reverse this situation almost overnight by carrying the struggle to its source: North Vietnam.

The key to victory in South Vietnam is the effective carrying of the war into North Vietnam until the forces of Ho Chi Minh have sustained such terrible attrition that they cease their aggression against the South. How can it be done?

I fully recognize here the limitations of Members of the Senate; I do not present myself as a military tactician. Yet, those who believe that we should push on in Vietnam—as I do—have as much information at our disposal and as much occasion for speaking up as those who believe we should pull out.

One does not have to be an architect to know that a house is falling down, and one does not have to be a military expert or a foreign service officer to know that our military and political effort in South Vietnam is going badly and that the course of our efforts must be changed if we are to succeed.

Our first task is to stabilize the rapidly deteriorating political situation in South Vietnam. There are a number of ways in which we can help to bring this about and I shall cite only three:

First, we must make clear our irrevocable determination to see this struggle through to victory, as long as the South Vietnamese carry their part of the burden. . . . .

Second, we should help the present Government of South Vietnam, under General Khanh, to ride out its present difficulties. We have no choice but to support this Government as it is, with its strengths and its weaknesses.

In doing so, we must seek to help it overcome its shortcomings, through persuasion and example, not only for the immediate purpose of strengthening its resistance to communism, but so that it may ultimately become a beacon of justice and progress for all the peoples of southeast Asia.

General Khanh is probably as good a man as can be found in the Vietnamese armed forces, and we may count ourselves fortunate that the second coup was not instigated by a man of less stature. He has a reputation as a capable and aggressive commander and as a careful planner.

According to all the reports I have heard, he is also a man of integrity and strong personal loyalty. He has displayed sound political instinct in retaining the popular Gen. Duong Van Minh as Chief of State and in bringing certain prominent political leaders and intellectuals into his Cabinet, while his energetic visiting to villages and to soldiers at the front suggests that Vietnam may at last have found the benevolent strong man it so sorely needs. His initial pronouncements, moreover, suggest that he recognizes the imperative need for constructive village programs if the people's loyalty is to be won and retained.

Instead of standing on the sidelines, waiting to see how General Khanh will shape up, we must do everything in our power to help the government of General Khanh stabilize itself and to help the general himself develop the popular image that is essential to effective national government.

We must make it unmistakably clear to the other officers in the Vietnamese Army that we are opposed to any more coups and that we shall support the government against any attempted coup. This is mandatory because another coup or two and even the Marines will be unable to save South Vietnam. Secretary McNamara has performed admirably in this regard during his visit.

Third, we must use our influence and our aid to assist the new Vietnam government to build upon a beginning that has already been made in encouraging the development of village democracy; in improving agriculture, education, and public health; and in giving the Vietnamese people the feeling that they have something to fight for and something worth daily risking their lives for. The plan announced by General Khanh last Saturday, if properly implemented through our aid, will mark a significant step forward.

We must help turn the war against North Vietnam.

We must explain to our own people, to our allies, and to the world the reasons which impel us to carry the fighting to the home base of the aggressor.

One method of doing this would be the publication of a white paper on North Vietnamese and Red Chinese aggression in South Vietnam, setting forth in detail all the massive information that has been accumulated about guerrilla infiltration and the smuggling of arms from the North, the evidence that the war is in fact directed from the North, and the evidence of Red Chinese involvement.

We have the truth; and we have the means to disseminate the truth to all who are disposed to believe it. Having made this attempt to solicit favorable world opinion, we must go forward and do what the facts of the situation require of us.

We now come to the critical point of our policy. What should be the nature of our attempt to take the offensive in this war which has been forced upon South Vietnam from the North?

It is, of course, for our military leaders to decide upon the tactics and for our diplomatic leaders to assess the possible repercussions.

But it is the direction of our efforts, not the details, that is my principal concern.

As a minimum, I believe we must permit, train, and assist South Vietnamese guerrilla forces to begin hit-and-run raids along the coast of North Vietnam, directed against targets like marshaling yards, harbor facilities, refineries, factories, bridges, dams, and so on. As experience and confidence are gained, it should be our goal to assist the South Vietnamese to open up sustained guerrilla operations in North Vietnam and give the Communists a full taste of their own medicine.

Every day that this war continues, the Red regime in Hanoi should be hurt in a very material way. And every day that we allow them to ravage South Vietnam with complete impunity to their home base, we give them an advantage which they should not have and which could be decisive in the war.

That is the minimum.

The maximum operation against North Vietnam would be to build up South Vietnamese air and sea forces so that they could launch air strikes against industrial and military targets and conduct naval blockades against commerce.

We have all read that this alternative is under serious consideration by the administration. We know that action of this kind would be a very bold step and that there are many reasons why any administration would be reluctant to undertake it. But if it is necessary it should be done, and I believe that the Congress and the American people will support this action if our best advice tells us that it is the quickest and most effective way to end the agony of South Vietnam and redeem our commitments in southeast Asia.

Three years ago, upon my return from Laos and South Vietnam, I urged that we not continue a purely defensive war but that we enable the forces of freedom to go over to the offensive. I stated the objectives of such an approach in words which I should like to repeat now:

> The best way for us to stop Communist guerrilla action in Laos and in South Vietnam is to send guerrillas in force into North Vietnam; to equip and supply those patriots already in the field; to make every Communist official fear the just retribution of an outraged humanity; to make every Communist arsenal, government building, communications center and transportation facility a target for sabotage; to provide a rallying point for the great masses of oppressed people who hate communism because they have known it.
>
> Only when we give the Communists more trouble than they can handle at home, will they cease their aggression against the outposts of freedom.

I think these words are even more applicable today than they were when I first spoke them three years ago.

Finally, I believe that we should make an effort to involve the other nations of the area in the task of keeping South Vietnam free.

As late as April of 1961, the SEATO nations in the immediate area, the Philippines, Thailand, Australia, New Zealand, and Pakistan, all favored common action against the Communist menace in Laos. But the British and French were opposed to such action, and we ourselves sat on the fence; and the result was that nothing was done.

In the absence of American leadership, SEATO has inevitably become an organization of questionable effectiveness. When I was in the Philippines in May of 1961, Foreign Minister Serano made a statement to me which I shall never forget. "We are prepared to fight and die with you if necessary," he said, "but we cannot fight without American leadership." Our failure to react to the challenge in Laos is one of the chief reasons for Pakistan's loss of confidence and her consequent erratic behavior.

Given American leadership and given the evidence of our determination to defend southeast Asia, it is not too much to hope that SEATO can be reactivated. Certainly it would be salutary and helpful to have other Asians fighting alongside the South Vietnamese and Laotians, in defense of their common freedom.

Conceivably, France might object to the reactivation of SEATO, now that De Gaulle seems bent on the appeasement of Mao Tse-tung. But if France should take this stand, then in my opinion she no longer belongs in SEATO, and we should ask for her withdrawal. . . . My view is that if we should back out, or give up in South Vietnam, all of Asia ultimately would be lost; and I do not believe that fateful day would be too far away. That is, of course, of the gravest importance.

But besides that, I believe the rest of the world would lose confidence in us. Whether we like it or not, we are the leaders of the free world. I believe it is true, as I have tried to say, that there is not a free country in the world that we have not helped. There is not an enslaved country in the world whose hope for freedom does not rest with us. We have friends and we have allies who help us; nevertheless, it rests with us. If we pull out, if we take the advice of those whom I call "the fainthearted ones," I believe one disaster after another will attend us, and we shall face a time and an hour when we shall be alone. There will be no allies to help us and we shall face the accumulated might of a foe the like of which has never been seen on earth.

I know it is much easier to say, "Let us get out."

All of us are conscious of the sacrifices of American boys there.

I have four sons, and all of them are of military age. Two are in the Army Reserve. I do not want my boys in a war any more than I want the boys of others to be in a war. But I believe the surest way to be certain that my sons and the sons of others will not be involved in a war is to do what is required of us, and to do it now. If we do not, our sons will be in that war, and what will be worse, the chances of their surviving it will be greatly reduced. . . .

Our Options in Vietnam*

Bernard B. Fall

With the fall of Dienbienphu on May 7, 1954, the first western attempt to save Laos and the northern provinces of Vietnam from Communist-led revolutionary warfare came to an end. Today the same conditions that impelled the French to make the bitter choice between broadening the scope of the war or cutting their losses face the United States and the South Vietnamese government we are committed to support. And once again the choices must be evaluated primarily on the basis of available military facts and figures.

The situation in South Vietnam today is militarily serious but by no means desperate, if you look only at the numerical balance sheets. On the South Vietnamese side, there are forces of some 530,000 men that include the Army of the Republic of Vietnam (ARVN, known among the Americans as "the Arvins"), probably the best-equipped army of its size in the non-Communist world; a militarized Civil Guard; local militiamen grouped in the Self-Defense Corps (SDC); and various police and special units. In addition, there are at least 15,500 American military "advisers."

The Communist insurgent forces, or Vietcong as they are called by the South Vietnamese, are both smaller in number and far poorer in terms of equipment. There are three types of combat units: a hard-core body known as Chu-Luc (Main Force), regional units, and the local militia. The hard-core units, used for all major attacks against the ARVN, are composed of those veterans of the war against the French who stayed in South Vietnam after 1954 or who went north for additional training and later reinfiltrated southward. Some Chu-Luc units operate as regiments of about 2,500 men, but most are in 500-man mobile battalions that may be shifted from province to province or even from region to region—from the mountain plateau area to the Mekong Delta, for example, as happened throughout 1963.

The regional units operate in company strength within a given province that they know well. They carry out small combat missions of their own, such as ambushes or sabotage; but their key mission is to serve as "protective coloration" when a hard-core unit arrives in their area. One or several companies of the regional units join the Chu-Luc for the duration of its operation in the province and thus provide the larger unit with local eyes and ears, food

* From *The Reporter,* March 12, 1964, pp. 17–22. Copyright 1964 by The Reporter Magazine Company. Reprinted by permission. Bernard B. Fall is Professor of International Relations at Howard University. He is the author of *The Two Viet-Nams* and of many other studies of the Indochina region.

or medical supplies requisitioned on the spot, and also with fairly well-trained replacements. When the hard-core unit strikes, the local militia levies come into their own. They act as guides and lookouts for the regulars and regionals. It is the local levies that give the Vietcong units their frightening ability to be at home almost everywhere. If the attack succeeds, the local Vietcong militiamen will "clean up" the battlefield, hide the booty, bury the dead of their own side, and care for its wounded before the ARVN can take an accurate count of enemy losses. And if, by rare chance, the regular Vietcong unit falls into a trap, the militia are expected to bear the brunt of the rear-guard fighting until the regulars have again disappeared into the jungle or into the impenetrable maze of canals and swamps. The elite of the militia eventually "graduate" into the regional units. Much later, after years of fighting and political indoctrination, the onetime peasant may become a hard-bitten Chu-Luc—if he lives that long.

Intelligence estimates of the exact number of Vietcong operating in South Vietnam have hardly varied over the past four years. A figure of between 22,000 to 25,000 regulars is generally admitted, supplemented by perhaps 60,000 to 80,000 irregulars. These figures are the basis for the optimism displayed by senior American officers both in Saigon and in the Pentagon. During the Indochina war, the French were fighting at a "tie-down ratio" of 1.5 to 1, which is notoriously insufficient to win against guerrillas. In South Vietnam today, the proportions are 16 to 1 if one counts the hard-core Vietcong only, and still 5 to 1 in favor of the ARVN when one includes all the Communist guerrillas.

For Secretary McNamara and his entourage, the slide rule and the computer are articles of faith in measuring "success" or "failure." In Vietnam, that familiar military yardstick, the front line, is disconcertingly absent. In Korea, when the U.S. forces were compressed into the Pusan perimeter, there were no possible pretexts for optimistic headlines; after two years of military stalemate, the need for some sort of political accommodation became obvious. In Vietnam, success or failure must be measured by far more controversial standards. There is, first of all, the "kill count" or "body count," i.e., the number of enemy bodies actually counted on the battlefield. The trouble with the body count is that the Vietcong have the habit of picking up their casualties, dead or wounded, under all but the direst of circumstances—precisely to prevent an accurate estimate of how badly they have been hurt. Often many of the dead, particularly those killed by strafing or bombing, are innocent civilians. Their numbers inflate the kill counts of Pentagon briefers but in no way affect the Vietcong combat potential. The kill count, though discredited, is being used religiously to this day. The official (and largely meaningless) estimate of Vietcong killed from mid-1957 up to January, 1964, is about 125,000.

Another standard of measurement, and one that is perhaps slightly more representative of the real situation, is the "incident count," that is, the number of hostile acts in a given month. Incidents are classified into four categories: armed attacks, terrorism, sabotage, and propaganda; and the shift of emphasis from one category to the other is in itself considered significant. Where the incident count proves itself unreliable is in lumping together the isolated shooting of a village guard and the battalion-size attack against a whole government garrison. Very often, a numerical decrease of Vietcong activities is more than compensated by the fact that each individual action is far larger than in previous weeks, or that the enemy places emphasis on more violent incidents: for example, of the 738 incidents reported for the week of February 7–14, 1964, close to 70 per cent involved acts of terrorism. In any event, judging by the British experience in Malaya, where a total incident count of thirty a month was considered the equivalent of "victory," South Vietnam still has a long way to go.

Air operations have two yardsticks of success. One is called the "structure count," and the other is simply the tonnage of bombs or the amount of cannon or machine-gun ammunition expended. The structure count records the number of houses destroyed by bombing or napalm. Any house designated by the Forward Air Controller as a target automatically becomes a Vietcong house and any village burned to the ground a Vietcong village, regardless of actual political allegiance.

Finally, there are such conventional criteria as the number of weapons lost by either side. Here again, the record shows that South Vietnamese commanders, for fear of loss of face or reprimand, have tended to understate their own losses and overstate those of the Vietcong. This has become a great deal less likely now that American advisers can be found even at the lowest unit levels. How disastrously bad the situation was in past years can only be guessed at—one educated guess is 125,000 light weapons lost to the Vietcong in the past two years—but the Pentagon officially admitted a loss rate of 234 weapons a week for the last three months of 1963, or more than 12,000 weapons for the year, as against average weekly Vietcong losses of ninety-seven weapons. The terms of comparison are relatively meaningless: "our" Vietnamese lose brand-new supermodern American weapons and the Vietcong lose homemade zip guns, although in recent months the ARVN have been recapturing American weapons. The huge amount of U.S. weapons available to the Vietcong through capture, theft, or even sale reduces the importance of the Ho Chi Minh Trail as a supply line from North Vietnam. It was important much earlier in the insurrection when organized units came south to become the nucleus of the hard-core battalions. Now the insurgency has reached the point where to a large extent it feeds on the enemy, in true Mao Tse-tung fashion. The trail, however, can still be useful for funneling in special replacements (saboteurs, anti-aircraft gunners, political cadres) and will be difficult to cut altogether.

As this picture of the military aspects of the South Vietnamese war unfolds, it becomes abundantly clear that in a war without fronts and without hard-and-fast criteria of success, victory in the accepted sense of the word, or even in accordance with some new counterinsurgency abstraction such as "effective control" of 90 percent of the population, becomes an elusive target.

This realization, which has belatedly come to Washington, has finally brought pressure on the administration for a re-examination of the various possibilities (the official term is "options") to resolve the Vietnamese conflict. Added to this pressure is a desire to do something to prevent the situation from becoming a political liability for the Democrats in November.

In brief, the four major options can be defined as follows:

(1) Let South Vietnam go down the drain by pulling American troops out at a given date, regardless of the situation on the ground.

(2) Continue the present type of "proxy war" for as long as another ten years if necessary, and try to win under the present ground rules, with perhaps both a larger South Vietnamese and American commitment. . . . this seems to be the official administration line.

(3) "Conventionalize" the war by escalating it from a counterguerrilla operation in South Vietnam to full-size combat operations against North Vietnam and, if necessary eventually, Red China. This is the new "hard" line advocated by less cautious officials in Washington.

(4) Negotiate with the enemy—*not* from the present position of weakness but from a position of strength created out of a sober-minded appraisal of Communist weaknesses and Western strength in the Far East as a whole. This alternative is often conveniently confused with the first option by those who fear that any settlement whatsoever would mean neutralization, followed by a Communist takeover.

Ironically, the Communist planners in North Vietnam seem to agree on the alternatives. They were described to the North Vietnamese higher cadres in the January, 1964, issue of *Hoc Tap* ("Studies"), the North Vietnamese Communist Party's theoretical monthly, as follows:

> (1) The United States must withdraw from South Vietnam and let the South Vietnamese people settle their affairs by themselves.
>
> (2) The United States will introduce into South Vietnam hundreds of thousands of more troops and large quantities of arms, and apply new techniques to carry on the war for some more years.
>
> (3) The United States will broaden its present special war (i.e., counterinsurgency operations), and invade North Vietnam in an attempt to win victory in South Vietnam.

Needless to say, Hanoi has no reason to publicize the fourth option, which from its standpoint is the least desirable course for the United States to adopt; and for entirely different reasons, Washington seems to agree with Hanoi.

Of the four U.S. options, the first two are temptingly the simplest and may well be advocated by the same people at different times. It would appear that the first one was implied in McNamara's testimony released by the House Armed Services Committee on February 18, in which he reiterated his intention to pull out the bulk of the American advisers stationed in Vietnam by

1965 because "I don't believe that we as a nation should assume the primary responsibility for the war in South Vietnam. It is a counterguerrilla war, it is a war that can only be won by the Vietnamese themselves."

The text is not clear on whether 1965 is still considered a decisive cutoff date. But, presumably, if it is obvious by then that the South Vietnamese are not pulling their own weight militarily and politically, the United States would simply get out of the war by refusing to increase its commitments while at the same time refusing to have any part of a negotiated settlement. That solution, it should be remembered, was in effect the course followed by the Eisenhower administration at the end of the French-Indochinese war in 1954. When it became obvious that the French would not or could not win the war as the Dienbienphu disaster took shape, Eisenhower, with the support of General Matthew Ridgway, then Chief of Staff of the U.S. Army, prevailed over the counsel of Vice-President Nixon and Admiral Radford, who advocated the use of American troops to save the French in Indo-China. And the late Secretary of State John Foster Dulles at the ensuing Geneva conference of April–July, 1954, steadfastly refused to sign "any treaty that makes anybody a slave."

In short, by refusing to accept a full measure of participation in the Geneva negotiations in 1954, the United States lost the opportunity to help shape the terms of the settlement and to use its power effectively in implementing the pact. Such an abdication of responsibility is of course unthinkable in 1964.

The second option—winning the war under present ground rules—would entail, on the basis of experience in other such wars, either doubling the number of South Vietnamese men under arms to one million or putting in two or three American army corps (about 200,000 men, with all attached services). In either case, civilian counterinsurgency programs would also have to be increased by substantial financial aid. These troop figures are not pulled out of thin air. As has been shown, the present ratio of friendly vs. hostile fighters is 5 to 1. Experience from Malaya to Algeria to Cyprus has shown that in order to break even (let alone win) militarily, a ratio of at least 15 to 1 is required. As for the use of American fighting troops in constituted units rather than as isolated "advisers," it would probably give the South Vietnamese Army the same lift in morale it gave the South Korean troops in 1950. The argument that the presence of American field troops would give substance to Communist charges of American imperialism can be considered baseless—the Communists are using the argument anyhow, and even the popular French magazine *Paris Match* recently termed that argument a "convention whose hypocrisy is only matched by its absurdity."

There remains the problem of feasibility. To double the number of armed Vietnamese would mean to boost American expenditures in Vietnam far over a billion dollars a year. It would also entail sending far more American advisers to the area. As for the alternative step of sending, say, six U.S. divisions to Vietnam, that would almost deplete the whole American strategic reserve, unless the draft is radically increased. What all this would do in terms of increased budget expenditures, the dollar gap, and mounting casualty lists can easily be guessed at. And, as the French demonstrated in Algeria or the British in Cyprus and Palestine, there is no ironclad guarantee of victory even through the massive military approach.

To "escalate" the Vietnamese war into a Korea-type operation extending into the North Vietnamese sanctuary, as outlined in Option No. 3, would combine the expenses of the second option with the tempting possibility of much quicker and greater rewards. North Vietnam is no longer the guerrilla country the French knew. Ho Chi Minh's regime now controls cities, builds industries and irrigation systems, runs railroads and airlines—all through the toil and sweat of the Vietnamese themselves over the past decade and the fairly large amounts of Soviet-bloc economic aid. All this provides very vulnerable conventional targets for American airpower. The rulers in Hanoi are fully aware of this and are obviously worried about it. I recall seeing unmuzzled anti-aircraft guns pointing skyward near industrial installations north of Hanoi in 1962; and Georges Chaffard, a reporter of *Le Monde,* recently noted similar anti-aircraft installations near the coastal city of Haiphong.

"We must be vigilant," said his North Vietnamese guide to him. "We're not at peace yet. The American aggressors fight against our brothers in the South and may well attack us here."

It is a matter of debate whether such an attack on the North Vietnamese heartland, the Red River Delta, would yield the desired dividends in terms of South Vietnamese pacification. As has been shown before, the Vietcong in South Vietnam do not depend to a very great extent upon North Vietnamese supplies and even less upon North Vietnamese manpower. If we expand the war to North Vietnam, we simply return to the French situation before 1954—assuming that Red China would not join the fray and expand the war even further. Furthermore, it is military idiocy to believe that the South Vietnamese Army, which cannot even hold on to major communication lines fifteen miles outside Saigon, could provide the backbone for a northern invasion. As in the case of Korea, where there also was an initial attempt to limit the American commitment to naval and air support, large American ground units would have to be thrown into the battle.

Such considerations doubtless explain the urgent attention Washington is now giving to the less risky proposition of mounting major guerilla operations across the border against North Vietnam. This would not represent a wholly new departure. South Vietnamese saboteurs have been parachuted periodically into North Vietnam from U.S. aircraft, at least one of which was shot down. But the North Vietnamese regime is quite familiar with this kind of warfare, and with its pervasive police-state system has thus far succeeded in capturing most parachuted or infiltrated agents. There is an iron rule in the counterinfiltration business: it's pretty hard to do if one's own bases are penetrated—and in South Vietnam today hardly an airplane can take off without being immediately spotted by pro-Communist elements.

In short, a guerrilla operation in the north, designed to dry up the Ho Chi Minh Trail, has little likelihood of making a dent in operations in the Mekong Delta in time to be useful. But it would, in turn, give the Hanoi regime a good pretext for opening the floodgates for large-scale infiltration of the south, thus far kept in check by the almost but not quite dead International Control Commission left over from the 1954 Geneva cease-fire. And this, too, would return us to the French situation of a generalized war.

Yet, carrying the war to North Vietnam in some form cannot be ruled out as a logical possibility. The North Vietnamese themselves, as evidenced in the previously cited *Hoc Tap* article, consider such a situation a distinct possibility, up to and including the use of nuclear weapons by the United States.

In fact, much has been made in recent weeks about statements from Hanoi that apparently reject almost any kind of peaceable solution except on its own terms, thus justifying the position of the bitter-enders in the United States who see salvation only in Option 2 or 3. Another interpretation of the *Hoc Tap* articles is that Ho Chi Minh's regime now has definitively thrown in its lot with Peking and is willing to pursue the war against South Vietnam no matter how great the risk.

A careful reading of the whole article and subsequent comments from Hanoi, Peking, and Moscow makes this far from crystal clear. The North Vietnamese prose is just as obscure as ever. For example, extracts rebroadcast by Peking contain the following passage:

> Taking strategic offense against the enemy does not mean pursuance of an adventurist policy by the socialist camp to eliminate imperialism by means of a world war, nor the start of armed uprisings and revolutionary wars to eliminate imperialism by the people of capitalist countries before a situation favorable to imminent revolution has emerged.

And in the next paragraph, the Hanoi text speaks of making "strategic attacks on the enemy politically" rather than through outright military operations. To be sure, the text pays obeisance to the Peking line condemning cooperation with "U.S. imperialism" as an "illusion," but another key text published on January 21 in the Vietnamese Communist Party's official newspaper *Nhan Dan* ("Humanity") also condemns "dogmatism and sectarianism," which are the sins Moscow accuses Peking of. In other words, Hanoi may well prefer to pursue what a knowledgeable British diplomat once called a "straight zigzag line" between its Communist masters. As for the struggle of the Vietcong guerrillas in South Vietnam, *Hoc Tap* warned that their war would be "long, hard, *self-supporting* (my italics), but . . . certainly victorious." To be sure, all the Communist powers have stressed the point that any attack against North Vietnam might bring Red China, and possibly the Soviet Union, into the fight, but that is neither new nor particularly revealing. In simple terms, Hanoi does not now seem keenly interested in escalating the war in South Vietnam to the point where it would have to provide the real estate for a slugging match between Red China and the United States; the more so as the Vietcong in South Vietnam seem to be doing reasonably well on a "self-supporting" basis.

All this leaves ample room for maneuver around the fourth option: negotiating a settlement from a position of strength. Over the last few years Hanoi has substantially lowered its sights: where it once insisted on early reunification as its minimum goal, it is now prepared to acknowledge the temporary existence of two Vietnams as separate states with "separate social systems." In fact, some French observers, notably Chaffard, assert that there is even a difference of view on the subject between Hanoi and the Vietcong civilian arm, the Southern Liberation Front, with the latter apparently willing to be even more accommodating to the West. This perhaps explains the unequivocal admission made by Mme. Ngo Dinh Nhu to the right-wing Paris weekly *Candide* of February 13 [1964] that her husband had indeed been negotiating with the Communists—but not via the French and not with Hanoi, but with the Liberation Front on the spot. His motive was "to seek ways to bring them back into the fold," says Mme. Nhu, but in all likelihood Nhu had concluded that a coalition government was the only way out of the military cul-de-sac.

It is also noteworthy that Hanoi recently disinterred the long-dead Geneva Agreement and asked for its "correct implementation" as a means of settling the "South Vietnam issue." The suggestion is disingenuous on the face of it. The application of an agreement that the United States never signed scarcely offers an acceptable solution to the present problem, and preachment from Hanoi about "correct implementation" would seem to exceed even Communist standards of cynicism. Nevertheless, the suggestion opens up interesting possibilities. For the Geneva Agreement, it will be recalled, allowed the presence of over six hundred American advisers, the number there at the time of the cease-fire. It also provided for two Vietnamese zones that would not be tied to any power bloc. All this suggests that Hanoi has not entirely made up its mind as to what it wants, or how to go about getting it without a major war.

Another area for maneuver favorable to the West centers on Red China's present weaknesses, both economic and military. The Chinese have had to get along for quite a while without Soviet spare parts and maintenance help. To supply, say, twenty Chinese divisions southward across Yunnan's chaotic terrain would by no means be as easy as it was to supply Chinese People's Volunteers in Korea from the excellent Manchurian rail and road net and from nearby Soviet supply depots. Finally, there is the handicap of two thousand years of Vietnamese distrust of the Chinese. The North Vietnamese in particular still recall with a shudder their VJ-Day "liberation" by the Yunnanese hordes.

The United States has other valuable cards to play. For one, South Vietnam has the surplus rice Hanoi needs. For another, while a major guerrilla offensive from North Vietnam would simply face Saigon with more of the same, a "counterescalation" by the United States of the war into North Vietnam, even if confined to one single saturation raid, could destroy the fruits of eight years' fighting against the French and ten years' backbreaking labor since 1954. To be sure, Chinese planes might appear in North Vietnamese skies the next day, but that would be small consolation to North Vietnamese leaders surrounded by devastation. In short, Hanoi cannot really afford a total "victory" in South Vietnam if the price is the destruction of its own economic base, for that would bring about total dependence on Red China. Furthermore, every new Communist military success along the Mekong may speed the day of both American and Chinese intervention in North Vietnam. This is a paradox that Hanoi will find hard to escape, unless it is willing to accept far less than its present demands.

The United States has yet another trump: whether to push Hanoi into Peking's hands or allow it to retain or even improve its present "straight zigzag line" is largely an American decision to make. A normalization of trade relations between the two Vietnams—bringing southern foodstuffs and rubber northward and northern minerals and manufactured goods southward—would allow Hanoi to depend less on China and to adopt a policy of national self-determination within the Communist bloc. That Moscow cannot do, but Washington can.

When all is said and done, the real American deterrent to Chinese military intervention in Vietnam is not the 15,000-odd American advisers wading around in the jungles of South Vietnam in search of an ever-elusive enemy (only two hundred out of a total of 3,450 weekly operations in South Vietnam make any enemy contact at all) but the U.S. Seventh Fleet with its aircraft carriers. That force can be brought to bear on the Vietnamese situation at any time as long as even a small American "tripwire" exists in South Vietnam. That deterrent has worked effectively on the Chinese at Quemoy and Taiwan. There is no reason to believe that it could not be used effectively in a Vietnamese settlement.

What special advantages might accrue from this fourth option? First, it would buy time for South Vietnam to establish at least some sort of durable political structure and to strengthen an economy ravaged by more than a decade of civil war. This sort of reconstruction, impossible under Option 2 or 3, offers the only sound defense against the inroads of Communist subversion, which can be expected to remain a major threat to the country for years to come. Second, a settlement based not on an abdication of our responsibility but on a determined application of our power and influence in the area would permit the West to increase North Vietnamese independence of Red China in exchange for an end to the guerrilla warfare, thus barring Red China from its most convenient avenue of domination of Southeast Asia. And third, it would disengage the United States from a secondary theatre of conflict that now absorbs an ever-increasing share of our resources and attention, but would not weaken our ability to save South Vietnam from outside subversion. Force could always be brought to bear on short notice should North Vietnam violate the terms of the settlement and challenge the U.S. guarantees that would necessarily underwrite it.

There must be negotiation and settlement sooner or later, unless the Johnson administration wishes to leave the Vietnamese war in what has been called the shadowland between unattainable victory and unacceptable surrender.

part five
Latin America

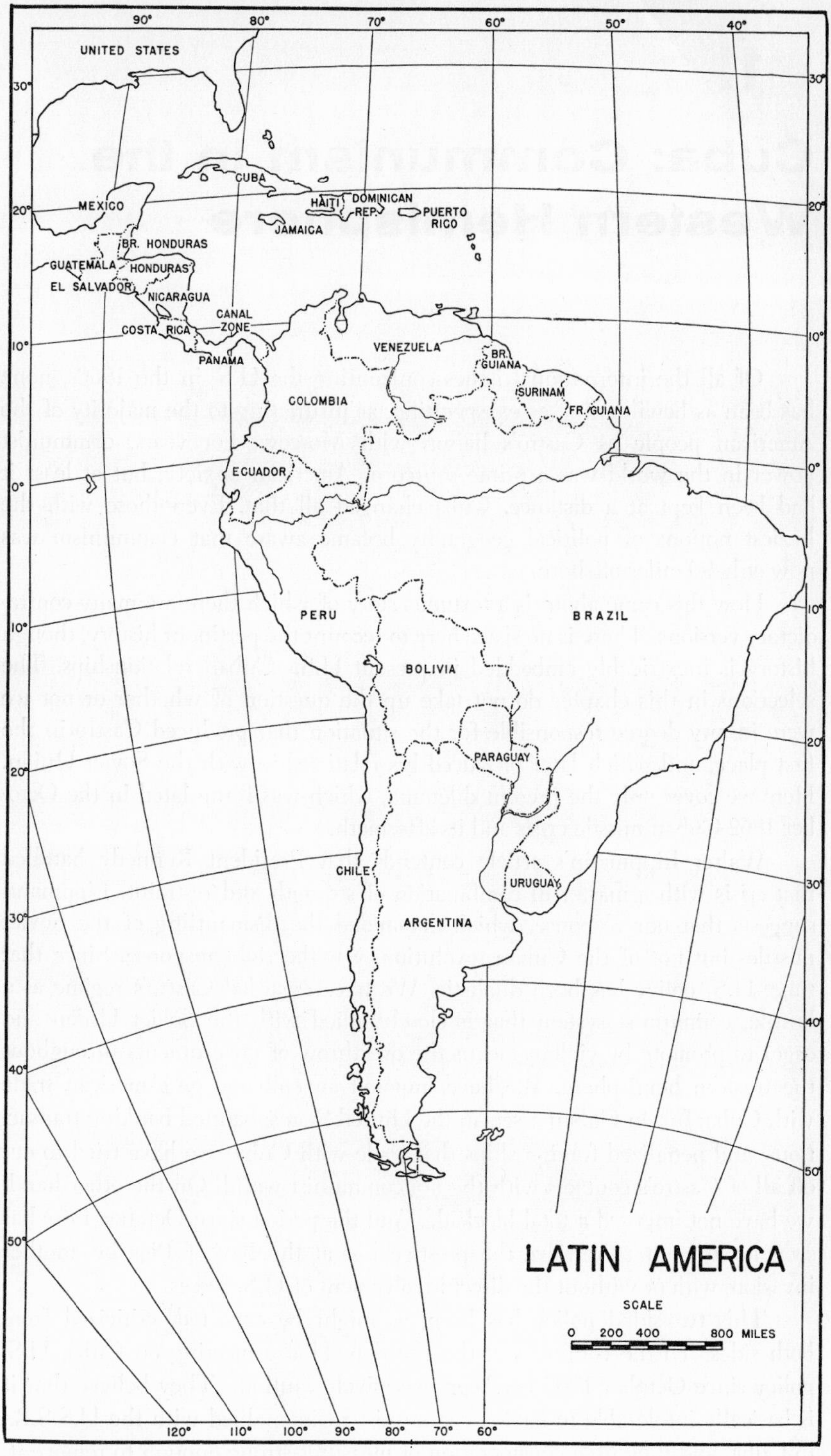

UNITED STATES
MEXICO
CUBA
HAITI
DOMINICAN REP.
PUERTO RICO
JAMAICA
BR. HONDURAS
GUATEMALA
HONDURAS
EL SALVADOR
NICARAGUA
CANAL ZONE
COSTA RICA
PANAMA
VENEZUELA
BR. GUIANA
SURINAM
FR. GUIANA
COLOMBIA
ECUADOR
PERU
BRAZIL
BOLIVIA
PARAGUAY
CHILE
URUGUAY
ARGENTINA
LATIN AMERICA
SCALE
0 200 400 800 MILES

11

Cuba: Communism in the Western Hemisphere

Of all the international issues confronting the U.S. in the 1960s, none has been as bewildering, as exasperating, as infuriating to the majority of the American people as Castro's liaison with Moscow. For years, communist power in the world was a prime source of American anxiety; but at least it had been kept at a distance. Cuba changed all that. Even those with the haziest notions of political geography became aware that communism was now only 90 miles offshore.

How this came about is a tortuous story of which there are many contradictory versions. There is no space here to recount the pertinent history, though history is inextricably embedded in present U.S.–Cuban relationships. The selections in this chapter do not take up the question of whether or not we were in any degree responsible for the situation that produced Castro in the first place, and which later produced his relationship with the Soviet Union. Here we cover only the present dilemma, which was formulated in the October 1962 Cuban missile crisis and its aftermath.

Walter Lippmann's article contends that President Kennedy handled that crisis with a masterful combination of strength and restraint. Lippmann suggests that our response, which demanded the dismantling of the Soviet missiles but not of the Cuban revolution, was the right response. Since that time, U.S. policy has been dualistic. We have regarded Castro's regime as a hostile, communist system that is closely allied with the Soviet Union and eager to promote by violent means the overthrow of governments throughout the western hemisphere. We have imposed an embargo on American trade with Cuba; frozen Cuban assets in the United States; banned banking transactions; and penalized foreign ships that trade with Cuba: we have tried to cut off all of Castro's contacts with the noncommunist world. On the other hand, we have not imposed a total blockade. And the period since October 1962 has seen no attempt to retrieve the prestige lost at the Bay of Pigs by another invasion, with or without the direct involvement of U.S. forces.

This two-sided policy has been, as might be expected, criticized from both sides. To the conferees at the Freedom House meeting on Cuba, U.S. policy since October 1962 has been excessively cautious. They believe that it is basically intolerable to have a communist regime, allied with the U.S.S.R., in Cuba, and they urge consideration of measures strong enough to remove it. Since the Freedom House report appeared, critics of Administration policy have lessened their emphasis on the possible use of Cuba as a Soviet base directed against the U.S. The report insists that we have no final proof that all the missiles that provoked the October controversy have been withdrawn; but there is a general assumption that they are gone. Moreover, U.S. officials claim that most of the 22,000 Russian troops present in Cuba in October 1962 have been withdrawn, and this issue no longer arouses widespread anxiety.[1]

The most persistent concern about Castro has revolved around his alleged subversive activities in Latin America. Venezuela charged in November 1963 that Cuba had tried to overthrow the Venezuelan government, and Venezuelan officials said that they had uncovered a 3-ton cache of arms shipped from Cuba. A committee of the Organization of American States endorsed the charges, and Venezuela called for the "rupture of diplomatic and consular relations by all American republics with Cuba," the "suspension of all commercial exchanges on the part of the American republics with Cuba, except for foodstuffs, medicines, and medical equipment," and "the suspension of all air and maritime traffic between the American republics and Cuba, except for traffic that must be maintained for reasons of emergency of humanitarian nature." These steps would simply bring the Latin-American states into harmony with U.S. policy. But the Venezuelans also called for authorization for the American states, acting collectively or individually, to employ measures, including the use of armed force, "in the event that the government of Cuba continues its aggression against any American state." This request comes close to some of the alternatives suggested by the Freedom House report.

Opposed to this view is that of Maurice Zeitlin and Robert Scheer. They see U.S. policy as intransigent, and they argue in their article that, by isolating Castro, we are forcing him irrevocably into the world communist camp. They propose a policy of conciliation, which might lead to the development of a political system in Cuba with which we could live comfortably. This thesis has subsequently been supported by the French journalist Jean Daniel, who visited Cuba and interviewed Castro in November 1963. In Daniel's judgment (concurred in by some, disputed by other correspondents who have visited Cuba recently) the embargo was causing shortages and some hardship, but not desperation or danger to the regime. If it is maintained, said Daniel, the Cuban people will eventually "adapt completely to a life based on Soviet economic aid."

Evidently, Soviet trade and aid will continue. At the same time, Castro has increased his trade with noncommunist countries. Britain, Spain, and others are willing to deal with Castro despite U.S. opposition, and it is clear

[1] The withdrawal of the Soviet troops did, however, introduce a source of anxiety. President Johnson insisted that "it is essential that we maintain surveillance and know whether any missiles are being shipped into Cuba. We will have to maintain our reconnaissance and our flights." But the Cubans declared that the overflights of U-2 reconnaissance planes constituted "flagrant violations of national sovereignty." There was concern in Washington that defense anti-aircraft missile installations would come under Cuban control, and that the Cubans might be less likely than the Soviet troops to refrain from using them.

that Western Europe does not share the American attitude toward Castro. Senator William Fulbright has argued, in consequence, that "it is simply not within our power to compel our allies to cut off their trade with Cuba unless we are prepared to take drastic sanctions against them such as closing our own market to any foreign company that does business in Cuba."[2]

A further complication is that Castro's links with communism are not limited to Russia. Ernst Halperin discusses the strong Cuban kinship with Chinese communist views on some important issues. Economically, Castro needs the Russians much more than he needs the Chinese, and he reaffirmed this relation by his January 1964 visit to Moscow, which apparently led to his support of the Soviet Union in its ideological battle with China. But it took him several months to come around to this position, and, as Halperin points out, the Soviets can never assume that Castro is unequivocally in their camp.

[2] Fulbright's general view is that "Castro is a nuisance but not a grave threat to the United States, and he cannot be got rid of except by means that are wholly disproportionate to the objective." Walter Lippmann has used much the same language.

Cuba and the Nuclear Risk*

Walter Lippmann

We have begun to live in the first years of the nuclear age. Ours is an epoch when the rivalry of two great social orders includes a rivalry in nuclear arms. We were very conscious of that fact during the crisis over Cuba. For in Cuba there was, for the first time in history, the kind of grim and deadly confrontation which could have led to thermonuclear war.

As a scientific phenomenon, the nuclear age began in 1945 with the explosion of the first nuclear bomb. But in world relations the nuclear age really began about ten years later. Until nearly the end of the forties, the United States was the only nuclear power in the world. In 1949, the Soviet Union exploded a nuclear device. But it was not until the middle of the fifties that the Soviet Union began to have an armory of nuclear weapons. Beginning about 1955, the West had ceased to have a monopoly of nuclear weapons, and by the end of the 1950s, the Soviet Union had become a very formidable nuclear power.

Since 1955 there have existed in the world two rival and conflicting coalitions armed with nuclear weapons. They are in conflict at many points on the globe. They distrust profoundly each other's purposes.

* From *The Atlantic Monthly*, February 1963, pp. 55–57. Reprinted by permission. Mr. Lippmann is a well-known political analyst and journalist.

The essential and novel fact in the contemporary conflict, which distinguishes it radically from the great conflicts of the past—as, for example, that between Islam and Christendom—is that the two coalitions possess nuclear weapons. These weapons differ from all other weapons, even those used as recently as the Second World War, in that they carry with them not only a greater quantity of violence but violence of a radically different order and kind.

In the wars of the prenuclear age, which ended with the bomb on Hiroshima, a victorious power was an organized state which could impose its terms on the vanquished. War damage, though great, was not irreparable, as we can see in the recovery of Europe and of the Soviet Union.

But after a full nuclear exchange, such as the United States and the Soviet Union are now capable of, there might well be over a hundred million dead. After the destruction of the great urban centers of the northern hemisphere, with the contamination of the earth, the water, and the air, there would be no such recovery as we have known after the two world wars of this century.

For all practical purposes, the devastation would be irreparable. The United States has the power to reduce Soviet society to a smoldering ruin, leaving the survivors shocked and starving and diseased. In an exchange of nuclear weapons, it is estimated coolly by our American experts that the Soviet Union could kill between thirty and seventy million Americans. I hesitate to say what would happen to Europe, whether or not it had a nuclear force of its own. But it is a fact that the Soviet Union has far more medium-range missiles capable of reaching Europe than it has long-range missiles capable of reaching the United States.

A war of that kind would be followed by a savage struggle for existence as people crawled out of their cellars, and all the democracies would have to be converted into military dictatorships in order to keep some semblance of order among the desperate survivors.

All that I have said has been said before. But it has not been said by men who have lived through an actual confrontation which could have produced such a catastrophe. If anyone wishes to understand the American position in the Cuban crisis and the American attitude toward military power in the world today, he must remember that responsible Americans do not dare to forget the reality of the nuclear age. I know some of these men. They live with these realities. For that reason, they do not find themselves in close sympathy with those Europeans who talk as if nuclear weapons were merely a bigger and better kind of artillery, and who think that the new weapons are subject to the same rules of warfare and of diplomacy as were the old.

Because nuclear weapons mean mutual suicide, the paramount rule of policy in this age is that, as between the nuclear powers, there can be no important change in the status quo brought about by the threat of force or by the use of force. Nuclear war cannot be used, as war has been used in the past, as an instrument of national policy. The Cuban affair has much to teach us about the nature of diplomacy in the nuclear age.

The United States has for some time possessed a marked superiority in nuclear weapons. This superiority was quite sufficient to deter the Soviet Union from using or from threatening to use nuclear weapons to enforce its purposes in Cuba. But our superiority was not sufficient to permit the United States to use or threaten to use nuclear weapons to enforce all of our own purposes in Cuba.

President Kennedy was able to prevail because, having the power to achieve a limited objective, he had the wisdom to narrow his objective to what he had the power to achieve.

Thus, he had the power to deter the Soviet Union from attempting to break the blockade by Soviet naval action and by the threat of Soviet nuclear missiles. But the President himself could not use America's nuclear power to bring about the overthrow of Castro and the liquidation of a Communist regime in Cuba.

It was manifestly unthinkable to use nuclear weapons against Cuba. They had no relevance to the Cuban problem. It would have been an incalculable risk to invade and occupy Cuba at the risk of retaliatory military action against Berlin, action which could have escalated into nuclear war. The President adopted limited objectives which could be achieved by limited means. He demanded the removal of the Soviet strategic missiles. He did not demand the removal of the Castro regime or even of the Cuban defensive missiles.

The President was able to achieve the objectives to which he limited himself. Soviet nuclear power was neutralized by American nuclear power, and in the Cuban area, the United States also had overwhelming land, sea, and air forces which were quite capable of destroying or capturing the Soviet missiles. The Soviet government had no conventional forces in the Caribbean area, and once its nuclear power was neutralized, it had no other force it could use.

This was, as I see it, the military rationale of the Cuban affair. But I hasten to add that, while the confrontation ended peaceably, it was possible that things might have got out of hand in Moscow or in Washington. There were rash men in both places. But for several reasons things did not get out of hand. First of all, Mr. Khrushchev and Mr. Kennedy have intimate knowledge of nuclear weapons, and they have a poignant personal realization of the meaning of nuclear war. For another reason, throughout the crisis, the two heads of government kept channels of personal and official communication open.

Finally, and decisively, the United States, which had overall nuclear superiority and conventional superiority around Cuba, was careful to avoid the ultimate catastrophic mistake of nuclear diplomacy, which would be to surround the adversary and to leave him no way to retreat.

Washington did not forget that while nuclear war would be suicidal lunacy, it is an ever-present possibility. Nuclear war will not be prevented by fear of nuclear war. For, however lunatic it might be to commit suicide, a great power, if it is cornered, if all the exits are barred, if it is forced to choose between suicide and unconditional surrender, is quite likely to go to war.

This is one of the facts of life in the middle of the twentieth century. It is as much a fact as the existence of the megaton bomb itself, and it is a fact which must be given weight in the calculation of national policy. It was kept constantly in mind in the calculation of our Cuban policy.

There is a line of intolerable provocation and humiliation beyond which popular and governmental reactions are likely to become uncontrollable. It is the business of the governments to find out where that line is, and to stay well back of it.

Those who do not understand the nature of war in the nuclear age, those who think that war today is what war was in the past, regard these careful attempts of statesmen not to carry provocation beyond the tolerable limits as weakness and softness and appeasement.

The Chinese do not understand the nuclear age, and they charge the Russians with appeasement for drawing back in Cuba. There are a good many people in the West who do not understand the nuclear age, and they are forever charging us with appeasement because we do not brandish the nuclear bomb in all our controversies with the Soviet Union. But prudence in seeking not to drive your opponent into a corner is not weakness and softness and appeasement. It is sanity and common sense and a due regard for human life.

It has, I know, been said in Europe that the United States has always had a special interest in Cuba, and that therefore the firm stand of the President is no proof that the United States would be equally firm in, let us say, Berlin.

Our answer to these skeptics must begin, I think, by asking them to look at what the United States was actually firm about in Cuba. It was firm, as I have already pointed out, about the Soviet strategic weapons in Cuba, which, in the American view, were offensive because they were good only for a first strike. Had the missiles been put in place, they would have changed seriously the balance of nuclear power in the world.

The United States deployed its whole military power, nuclear and conventional, against such an alteration of the status quo. It would do the same, and for the same kind of reason, if the Soviet Union moved with military force against Berlin or against any other point which is critically important to the maintenance of the status quo in the balance of strategic power.

But the United States did not use its power to unseat Castro or to crusade against Communism. It did not use its power for political or ideological ends. In my opinion, it will not risk a nuclear war in Europe over anything less than that for which it risked war in Cuba—that is to say, a radical move against the balance of strategic power. That is why the United States will defend the physical freedom of West Berlin. But it will not risk a nuclear war over political and juridical issues. . . .

Cuba Must Be Freed*

Freedom House

Communism's conquest of Cuba must be viewed in the context of the world-wide expansionist drive conducted by the Kremlin which has already led to totalitarian control over a third of the human race. At this point in history, simple solutions are no longer possible. The problem of resisting Communist expansionism is growing more complex and less manageable all the time. Any plan of action in the Caribbean has to take into account conditions and potential developments around the globe. Since we have committed ourselves to the defense of allies in all the continents, our Cuban policy must be consistent with those commitments, or at least must avoid jeopardizing them.

Participants in the Freedom House Conference [April 25–27, 1963] saw this fact as a major preoccupation in the thinking of those responsible for American policy. In an effort to define Washington's current approach, several conferees used role-playing procedures to present what might be the views of high government officials. In substance, they said:

> Our policy on Cuba must necessarily fit into the larger U.S. policy of defending the free world against Communism while avoiding war. Where certain common interests are shared by the U.S. and the Soviet Union, we must press for an agreement with the Soviets. In this context, other problems may have priority—such as reconstituting the troika coalition in Laos to prevent a serious collapse that would have dire consequences for Vietnam, Indonesia and others; the urgent need for concluding a nuclear test ban in Geneva; and preventing the military use of outer space. In such a framework Cuba is not the most pressing issue. We are concerned not only with restoring freedom to Cuba but also with maintaining and enlarging freedom in Berlin. A victory on any given front would hardly be worth while if the price turned out to be the loss of Berlin, Iran, Vietnam or some other sector of the global struggle. What we do about Cuba may precipitate reactions elsewhere that could seriously injure our wider interests.
>
> Nor can we forget the implications of the rift between Moscow

* From "What Can We Do about Cuba?" a report from Freedom House, 1963, pp. 5–14. Freedom House is an organization whose purpose is: "To advance the goals of a free society and oppose all forms of totalitarianism." Roscoe Drummond is Chairman of the Board.

and Peking. At this juncture it would hardly be wise to increase the pressure on Khrushchev and possibly make him look worse than he did when we forced him to pack up his missiles and go home. The prospect of another such defeat might force him, for example, to move into Iran in order to salvage his already shaky position as leader of the world Communist movement.

As realists, we know there is no automatic virtue in just doing something: consider the Bay of Pigs and the trouble we're having in Vietnam. And we have to take cognizance of the handicaps imposed by our very strength—the restraints on our freedom of action that flow from our giant size in comparison with the Cuban pigmy. Rough action would alienate world opinion. In any case, even our friends in Latin America are opposed to what they call "intervention." Certainly, the reaction during the Bay of Pigs misadventure demonstrates that a program of direct action by U.S. forces would be even less palatable than action by the Cuban freedom fighters—and that would be so despite a quick success and moderate casualties on both sides.

We are committed to getting Soviet troops out of Cuba as fast as possible. Some Sovietologists tell us we can probably do it more quickly by *reducing* rather than *increasing* the pressure on Khrushchev. Meanwhile, we are isolating Cuba from the rest of the hemisphere and discrediting its "revolutionary" image among Latin Americans. We are slowly strengthening our OAS allies and reinforcing their ability to maintain internal security. Over the long haul, we hope to achieve our goals through a successful Alliance for Progress.

Those who demand a commitment to immediate Cuban liberation are simply ignoring the unacceptable risks that would be involved. After all, we have a commitment to the eventual liberation of Eastern Europe, but those who pledged in campaign speeches to make good on it soon found out that they couldn't fulfill this promise without risking a global war. In 1956, Radio Free Europe and even the official Voice of America were criticized for having encouraged the Hungarians to revolt under the misconception that outside help would be forthcoming.

The risks of precipitant action cannot be dismissed. To go to the brink and then be forced to retreat rather than accept the dreaded next step would be disastrous. Even the political opposition which condemns a policy of caution, does not advocate military action in Cuba. Its leaders have been quick to disavow the few who call for blockade and invasion.

Such is the point of view apparently prevailing in Washington, as the conferees reconstructed it. It represents the considerations that seem to trouble the Administration as it picks its way across the heavily mined terrain of foreign policy.

Opinion at the conference was predominantly pessimistic that such consideration could get anywhere. As one participant put it: "the United States wants Cuba to *be* free, but does not want Cuba to *become* free. We are eager for the result that is sought; but we have no stomach for the actions needed to achieve it." Concededly, there was good reason during the first part of 1962 (before October) for U.S. officials to be apprehensive over the effect on Berlin, Laos and Vietnam if this country challenged Soviet arms shipments to Cuba. The most significant aspect of the brilliantly executed confrontation in October-November, however, was that it did *not* trigger Soviet actions in Berlin or in other places where Soviet capability existed.

The lesson of October-November confirms the thesis that action in the Caribbean ripples out to distant shores and sensitive regions. But even more important, it emphasizes dramatically that indecisiveness in the Caribbean can have the most deleterious effects on our alliances, especially NATO and SEATO. Inaction on the Cuban front will only be taken to mean a U.S. unwillingness to run risks in defense of others. If the U.S. accepts Russian intrusion at its own doorstep, where the Soviet military posture is weakest, how can Europeans expect the U.S. to risk nuclear devastation to repel a Soviet attack in Europe where Soviet military power is greatest?

Indeed, American resistance to Soviet military penetration in the Caribbean is a prerequisite to restraining the Soviets from an adventure in West Berlin. Defend our interests close to home, and we *reinforce* rather than endanger our outposts in more distant places. Blur our purpose and commitment in our own hemisphere, sow confusion between words and deeds about Cuba and we can only *damage* American objectives around the world.

Cuba in Context: Latin America's Future

Thoughtful observers are by now aware that Cuba is the Western Hemisphere base from which the Communist knife is aimed at the soft underbelly of the hemisphere—Latin America. A long history of economic and political errors has filled Central and South America with internal discontent, thus making it vulnerable to conquest by external forces. How many more Cubas can we sustain?

Time is a vital factor. There are hopeful, pro-democratic forces at work, but they are in a deadly race with the destructive, totalitarian forces. Decisive to the outcome will be the length of time it takes to dislodge not only the Russian troops but Communism itself from Cuba. The mere survival of the Castro regime is a factor of great importance. It strengthens the Communists in other Latin American countries and creates an image of Communist invincibility. It encourages the trend toward neutralism, already pronounced in some countries, with increasing numbers of Latin Americans saying, "If the United States is willing to tolerate or co-exist with a Communist Cuba, why shouldn't we?" It also encourages an equally dangerous trend toward extreme rightist dictatorship.

The spawning of more neutralist or militarist governments in Latin America, in reaction to the continued existence of the Castro regime in Cuba, can threaten the United States' objectives of preserving and enlarging freedom. "Co-existence," on the one hand, may lead to "coalitions" which ultimately produce one-party rule, while rightist dictatorship gives the Communists a moral pretext for carrying out their tactics of conspiracy and helps polarize public support in their direction.

History does not operate in smooth uni-directional lines. Developments are the product of a given equilibrium between rival forces. The presence of Castroism, viewed as a temporary phenomenon, has generated some wholesome reactions in Latin America, which should not be dismissed. The delivery of Cuba to Khrushchev as a military base added considerably to the disenchantment of many Latin Americans who had originally considered Castro a genuine patriot fighting foreign economic exploitation. Even before October Castro had paid some price for his betrayals—ranging from unfulfilled promises to hold elections to the public confession that he had been a Communist all along but had concealed the fact while seeking popular support. But now Soviet domination of Cuba has made it plain that Castroism is not a nationalist liberation movement. Political, labor and business leaders, editors, intellectuals and students whose hostility to Batista's dictatorship made them sympathetic to Castro, have been disabused. Military officers who might have been tempted to seek a deal with "the wave of the future" have been sobered by the purges and executions that followed Castro's accession to power.

The volatility of the poverty-stricken Latin American masses is another matter. It is difficult to predict the direction in which their pent-up resentments are likely to explode in a period when old institutions are disintegrating and new claimants are demanding power. Army take-overs, like those in Peru and Guatemala, are in the historical Latin American pattern. They are the traditional response when power centers are threatened or when chaos seems imminent. To be sure, in some situations the military play a legitimate role in preventing a minority from seizing power. But U.S. policy must take into account the fact that the Communists often find oppressive rightist regimes more useful than liberal or anti-Communist leftist governments.

The ultimate success of the Alliance for Progress may hinge on whether Latin America can be persuaded that Castro is not here to stay, and Communism will not spread to other Latin republics. Unfortunately, the Communist challenge has not yet convinced a majority of the more conservative Latin Americans to accept the reforms essential to the success of the Alliance. The effect of that challenge has been, rather, to encourage a massive flight of capital from Latin America and to discourage new investment there, thus contributing to further economic deterioration and reducing the Alliance's chances of success.

American policy seems geared to the thesis that we can defeat Communism by defeating hunger, poverty and disease in Latin America, and that all we need is time to accomplish the latter. The reality is that the attainment of a higher standard of living does not necessarily preclude Communism, as demonstrated by the very case of Cuba, which before Castro was one of the two or three most advanced countries in Latin America. At bottom, we are engaged in a two-front struggle against both Communism and poverty, at the same time. If Communism remains in control of Cuba indefinitely, it will have proved its permanency in the Western Hemisphere before the reform battle can be won. On the other hand, the mere erasure of Communism from Cuba would not, by itself, automatically insure orderly social and economic progress. . . .

The Fear of Escalation

Undoubtedly, much of American policy is based on genuine fears—not only the fear of consequences in other areas of the cold war, or of the reactions in Latin American countries, but also the fear that decisive action might escalate into a global, nuclear war. This is not an irrational fear, and it cannot lightly be dismissed. But it is precisely because we are living in a world of risks that leadership is necessary. Whoever would give guidance to others must be capable of assessing the risks, and then of *acting*. In a risk-less world there would be no need for leadership.

In his speech of October 22, 1962, President Kennedy said that the greater risk lay in *not* acting. He concluded that strong action involved the lesser risk.

Whatever happens, the same task will remain: to follow the line of the lesser, more manageable risk. In evaluating the hazards of weak versus strong action, the Freedom House conferees cited the following questions as most relevant:

1. To what extent will the risk of nuclear war increase with the passage of time, in view of the relative increase of Soviet nuclear capabilities?
2. What will be the effect of American vacillation in Cuba on other sensitive fronts of the cold war?
3. What will be the world-wide psychological impact of continued taunting propaganda by Castro and the Soviets?
4. What are the probabilities that the Cuban Communist base will be used against us in the future under unpredictably changed circumstances?
5. What will be the probable effectiveness of the Cuban Communist base in undermining other Latin American governments, with a consequent spread of Communism in the hemisphere?

The net effect of examining such factors is to suggest that a simple policy of risk-avoidance can lead only to the certainty of a worsening position for the United States. Indeed, it is more likely that an improvement of our position will occur only from a process of intelligent risk-taking.

This was demonstrated in the October confrontation. The Administration took manageable risks rather than accept the certainty that the nuclear balance would swing in Russia's direction and that Khrushchev's capabilities for blackmail and attack would be increased by the presence of Soviet missiles in Cuba. Unfortunately, while it was clearly willing to take risks in order to obtain a Soviet pledge of an inspected withdrawal of the missiles, there was no willingness to take the risk of a follow-through. Is there any practical value in running risks to gain a pledge, and running no risks to enforce it?

The fear of escalation, while it might logically deter certain types of all-out action, has distorted the judgment of our decision-makers on more limited action and narrower sectors of strategy and tactics.

U.S. Policy on Exile Activity

The conferees were especially troubled by the deterioration in the relations between the U.S. government and the Cuban exiles, whose principal concern is to find ways and means of liberating their country. Does this development foreshadow an ultimate conflict between the freedom-fighters' objective of liberation and an American policy of containment? This disturbing question underlay the discussion of American policy toward the Cuban exiles.

Arguing that there has been no consistency of purpose or action in our government's relations with Cuban activists in exile, conferees cited these specific items:

> . . . We can understand the legal and technical reasons for withholding the use of U.S. territory as a base for launching raids against Cuba and against Soviet shipping bound for Havana. But why was it considered necessary to deprecate as "irresponsible, ineffective and dangerous" the raids and supplying missions that originated *outside* the U.S.? Is this not inconsistent with our official position that the Cubans themselves must get rid of the Castro dictatorship? Does it mean that the Administration disapproves of the rebel action in the mountains and their use of sabotage against Castro? If we favor such action, can we expect the Cubans to proceed without our help and in the face of our public condemnation? In any case, what are anti-Castro Cubans in exile or inside Cuba to conclude?
>
> . . . Miro Cardona and his Council had urged Cuban exiles to enlist in the U.S. Army for training. Thousands of young Cuban exiles, including many of the Bay of Pigs veterans, did so. Why? What official representations led them to believe that joining the U.S. Army would offer them the best way of fighting for a free Cuba?
>
> . . . Reports of Central Intelligence Agency collaboration with the exiles seem to suggest a conflict of policies and activities within the Administration. Has CIA at times followed an independent line in conflict with that of the State Department?
>
> . . . Attorney General Robert Kennedy appealed to the Cuban exiles to unite in one organization with which the U.S. government could consult. Does this mean that the Administration disapproves of CIA's experiment in favoring certain Cuban factions which has

merely increased the disunity? Does the Attorney General's statement look towards the recognition of a government-in-exile?

The answers to these questions are uncertain, but they sustain the impression that American policy toward the Cuban exiles has lacked consistency and has not contributed toward the unity essential for their fight against Castro. . . .

The Soviet Presence in Cuba

Despite the political retreat by Khrushchev during the October-November crisis, there is no reason to believe that the Russian dictator has abandoned his hopes of maintaining a Soviet base only 90 miles from U.S. shores. That "Fortress Cuba" is a military threat in the Western Hemisphere is beyond question: it is operating as the training ground for guerilla warfare against Latin American republics and as a center for the spread of subversion, terror and sabotage.

The latest Soviet aim in Cuba is to use the island as a base for medium-range missiles which could completely circumvent U.S. warning systems and keep a large part of the hemisphere and the U.S. under the constant threat of nuclear attack. . . . In the absence of verified and precise knowledge of the conditions inside Cuba, American policy must be predicated on the assumption that the danger is real and will persist.

Other Soviet aims in Cuba have been achieved:

1. Castro has been supplied with the latest weapons to fend off an invasion from without or an uprising of the people from within. What still remains is for the Russian experts to train Cuban Communists in handling these weapons. According to some military opinion, this will take four to six years. The Castro regime argues that it has the right, as a sovereign power, to invite military assistance from a foreign country.

2. Cuba has been converted into a Communist West Point for the training of officers intended to lead military attacks on existing regimes. The island will eventually be the arsenal of Latin American revolutions, from which swift military support can be given to the creation of "new Cubas."

3. With its 150 operational jet fighter bombers, which have a substantial range, Cuba is in a position to control the air over a number of small, near-by countries. (It is reported that some policy-makers in Washington find comfort in the fact that all this lethal equipment is under the control of Soviet officers rather than the hard-core Castro-Communists who incline toward the more reckless views of the Chinese.)

American policy at the present time is focused, however, on the issue of the missile build-up in Cuba. There is little confidence that Khrushchev has actually carried out his pledge of last October-November. Russian credibility was completely destroyed by the fact that the prelude to the crisis was a direct face-to-face lie by Foreign Secretary Andrei Gromyko to President Kennedy on the very subject of missiles in Cuba. In the absence of on-site inspection, there can be no certainty that all the missiles and nuclear warheads have been removed. Some could have been installed in caves from which they can be fired with perhaps as great precision as missiles from an underwater Polaris. Moreover, the Soviet troops and technical advisers, even if we accept the lowest estimate of their numbers, can accomplish significant secret preparations, partly protected by darkness, cloud formations and other similar impediments to aerial surveillance. . . .

Continuance of the status quo—the uncertainty about the missiles and the absolute certainty of the Soviet Army presence—obviously has strong implications about our global position and could lead to even more serious consequences than we have already suffered. Both President Eisenhower and President Kennedy have categorically declared that a Communist base in this hemisphere would never be tolerated. The fact that a Soviet base is now being tolerated can lead the enemy to the kind of miscalculation that might be disastrous. A misreading of our equivocation could induce probing adventures elsewhere. Also, our acceptance of the situation could be taken as some justification for the Chinese view that strong-arm methods do work in dealing with the "degenerate democracies."

But most serious of all, the continued presence of Soviet military forces in Cuba could provide the very spark that ignites a nuclear war. The U.S. has warned that it will not stand by and allow Soviet forces to quell an uprising in Cuba as they did in Hungary. Any incident—a bar-room brawl with Soviet soldiers in Havana, a flare-up of tempers over a child run down by a Soviet jeep—could lead to Russian shooting, even in self-defense. As long as Russian troops are in Cuba, peace is endangered by the possibility of an accident. Emotions in this country might well make it impossible for any administration to control the consequences, which could escalate into nuclear war.

Precisely because the situation endangers peace, and because it threatens Khrushchev's policy of coexistence, there is some leverage in persuading the Russians to withdraw. But this can be done only if the U.S. persists in applying pressure. . . .

Definition of the American Commitment

Both political parties seem to be united on the objective—freedom for Cuba. To carry out appropriate measures will call for a national unity such as prevailed in the October crisis. But we must be prepared for the fact that future measures will have to be more numerous, more involved, perhaps more onerous and surely less dramatic, requiring a longer period of application than the quarantine during the Fall of 1962. Bi-partisan consultations are needed now to reach a broad, long-range understanding.

This is possible, however, only if the Administration recognizes that it is responsible for providing leadership in a national discussion of the Cuban problem. It must supply the needed facts and it must clearly articulate the country's objectives.

No responsible American doubts the desire of the Administration to see Cuba ultimately free and meanwhile to prevent Castro from spreading Communist dictatorship to other parts of the hemisphere. It can certainly be assumed that Washington is committed to eliminating the Soviet political and military base from Cuba *eventually* and to blocking Sino-Soviet ambitions in Latin America. What is needed is a commitment to urgent and immediate action, unambiguously expressed to the nation and the world. It is imperative that our people, our allies, and especially our enemies, clearly understand that this government intends to use all its power to achieve the objective.

All must know that we not only want a free Cuba but we are determined to help it *become* free—without undue delays. Any doubts on this score must be dispelled—for example, by publication of the correspondence between Khrushchev and the President during and following the October confrontation. So long as the record is withheld, there will be rumors and apprehensions at home and abroad, about our Cuban commitment. There must be no gap between word and deed. . . .

Aid to the Cuban Exiles

Cuba's proudest hope is the resistance of its patriots to Communist domination. No act of the American government should downgrade their courage; every pronouncement should aim to uplift the morale of freedom-loving Cubans everywhere.

We have a considerable responsibility for helping the exiles to achieve unity in their own ranks. We injure such unity if we play favorites among factions. We must encourage all groups to select responsible leaders with whom the U.S. government can cooperate for the common cause. Through every possible channel, we must assist the organized underground inside Cuba, bringing to bear our extensive resources and experience.

Exile and underground activity has many values. Not the least is the fact that it warns the Soviet interventionists that seizure of other men's countries will bring inevitable retaliatory action. If Communists can promote phony "wars of liberation," we can and should support real ones.

The presence of Cuban refugees in the United States, now numbering about 250,000, presents us with a rare opportunity. These men and women are the only major group of exiles since World War II who have any reasonable prospect of an early return to a liberated homeland.

Cuba's problems will not end with the overthrow of the Communists. If those problems are solved by a future democratic regime, a powerful blow will have been struck for liberation everywhere behind the Iron Curtain. Thus, we contribute to the oppressed people in Cuba and all the satellites when we provide special study opportunities to the refugees now within our shores. By training them in the fields of democratic government, public administration, industrial and agricultural management, defense, public safety and order, public education, we can lay the foundations for a wholesome future.

The Taking of Risks

Underlying the discussion of policy and action was the question: What risks are Americans willing to take in response to Communist expansionism and which policy is likely to minimize the risks?

We are most in danger of Communist attack, whether from Peking or Moscow, when our indecision suggests fear, weakness or ineptness. We are safest when our adversary realizes that we are clear about our objectives and determined in pursuing them.

Timing is, of course, a crucial factor in assessing risk. The Freedom House conferees tended to the view that *the risks later will be more formidable than the risks now.* Even on the assumption that time is inevitably on our side, which we do not accept, one cannot be sanguine about a Sovietized Cuba that brings a large portion of the U.S. and the Western Hemisphere within easy range of Communist missiles and nuclear warheads.

The conference was aware that the major premise of present policy is the assumption that action on Cuba must be delayed because of risks to our position elsewhere in the world. But the conferees were impressed by the fact that the U.S. position in October, far from provoking Communist adventures, forced the Soviet leaders to act with greater caution everywhere. In the context of the Sino-Soviet dispute, American toughness justifies Khrushchev's position of restraint, while any evidence that the U.S. is a "paper tiger" would strengthen Mao's call for aggression.

In any case, if choices must be made as to where we should take bold stands, Cuba is the most logical place. The Soviet Union has over-extended itself geographically by reaching into the Caribbean. Of all the fronts on which we face each other, Cuba is militarily Russia's weakest, and our strongest. The only Russian chance for success in such a contest would be to convert the local conflict into a general war—clearly too fearful a price for so small a prize. Moreover, military opinion considers the risk of general war in the near future relatively small because the Kremlin knows that it could not win. The record already shows that the Soviets have almost always backed away from action that might lead to general war when the U.S. has taken a firm stand, as in Cuba last October and in Berlin since Khrushchev issued his original ultimatum in November 1958.

The risks of inaction, however, must be spelled out also in terms of the impact on the non-Communist world. There is the risk—indeed, almost a certainty—that inaction will encourage neutralism. If the U.S. can accommodate itself to the indefinite perpetuation of a Communist regime in Cuba, why should not the rest of Latin America? And the consequence will be a steady seepage of Communism into the other islands of the Caribbean and the other Latin countries of the hemisphere. At the same time, in Europe and Asia, countries contiguous with the Iron Curtain will have every reason to ask: If the U.S. dare not uproot Communism from its own doorstep, how can we expect it to risk anything on our behalf?

The freeing of Cuba, not ultimately but soon, must be the aim of U.S. policy implemented by a practical program of action.

A Panorama of Alternatives

. . . a frank facing of our position reveals many directions—of varying merit, to be sure—in which we can go. Many of the proposals are contradictory in some respects or even mutually exclusive. They nevertheless help to illuminate *the areas in which decisions must be made consciously rather than by default.*

Top-Level Decisions

1. Insist as a basic premise that Castro-Communism must go or be defeated.

2. Seek to co-exist with a Communist Cuba headed by Castro or some other ruler.

Hemispheric Policy

1. Reassert the Monroe Doctrine, or a modernized version.

2. Announce U.S. support for all dedicated democrats who fight for freedom against dictatorship anywhere in the hemisphere.

3. Proclaim a hemisphere-wide right of self-determination, accepting any democratic decision on the form of government and social system so long as "human rights and fundamental freedoms" are observed.

4. Help to organize a Latin American Treaty Organization (LATO) outside the OAS, which would welcome all non-dictatorial states willing to ally themselves for purposes of military defense after the pattern of NATO. (It is assumed that several of the larger Latin American states would be reluctant to join, and that dictatorships like Haiti, Paraguay, etc., would be barred.)

5. Rally non-governmental organizations throughout the hemisphere, including business groups and labor unions, for freedom and social justice.

6. Declare that the U.S. opposes Communist penetration but not revolutionary social change in Latin America.

Direct Pressure on Cuba

1. Assert a policy of collective measures against Cuba based on a rigorous implementation of the Rio Treaty, the Bogota Pact and the Punta del Este Resolutions.

2. Repeal or amend the U.S. Neutrality Acts.

3. Organize a tight OAS embargo against trade, communications and

travel between member states and Cuba—any states rejecting participation to forfeit U.S. aid.

4. In cooperation with Venezuela, exert effective pressure on the five OAS members still maintaining diplomatic relations with Cuba to sever their ties.

5. Withdraw U.S. recognition of the Castro government.

6. Propose an OAS study of the steps deemed necessary to achieve the objective of a free Cuba.

7. Impose comprehensive sanctions on shipping to include all vessels of any line that uses as much as one of its ships in the Cuban trade.

8. Use pre-emptive buying to tighten the noose on Castro's economy.

9. Press OAS to impose the same quarantine on Communist Cuba as it did on Trujillo's Dominican Republic.

10. Citizen groups in this country should cooperate with Free Cuba Committees in our sister republics.

11. Press NATO countries to curtail the sale of any goods to the Iron Curtain countries of the type being supplied to Cuba by the Communists.

12. Quarantine Cuba against receiving any weapons, whether called offensive or defensive.

13. Quarantine all shipments of petroleum to Cuba.

14. Promote the organization of an OAS task force and prepare an OAS invasion force to be use as a last resort.

Aid to Anti-Castro Cubans

1. Arm and assist Cuban freedom fighters inside and outside of Cuba; encourage sabotage and raids.

2. Help establish bases for Cuban rebels outside U.S. territory.

3. Publicize the extent and character of current Cuban resistance.

4. Launch a major propaganda effort through all media, calling for public support of a Radio Free Cuba.

5. In cooperation with Cuban exiles, start OAS work on "winning the peace" in a free Cuba.

6. Help to organize a Cuban government-in-exile.

Post-Castro Cuba

1. Create OAS machinery for governing liberated countries and conducting elections under pre-planned rules, to be available for action in Cuba, Haiti and elsewhere.

2. Provide opportunities for qualified Cuban refugees to receive advanced training in their fields and to conduct studies on problems they will face in a liberated Cuba.

3. Prepare plans for the political, social and economic future of a free Cuba.

4. Declare that Cubans must and will choose their own form of government.

Removing the Russians

1. Announce that the removal of Soviet troops from Cuba has first priority in America's agenda.

2. Adopt a formal decision that Soviet troops and "technicians" must be repatriated within a stated time or face measures of expulsion.

3. Impose an OAS "quarantine" or blockade if necessary to expel Soviet forces or bring down the Cuban Communist regime—any states rejecting participation to forfeit U.S. aid.

4. Establish OAS teams to inspect all ships bound for Cuba. . . .

The Case for Reconciliation*

Maurice Zeitlin and Robert Scheer

What kind of a political system will eventually emerge in Cuba is still an open question. The possibility remains of a new, dynamic, and intimate political democracy close to the people, flexible and answering to their needs. The experimentalism and openness of the Cuban revolutionaries to conflicting viewpoints and the range of radical thought (leninist, anarchist, libertarian, syndicalist, etc.) is inseparable from the potential success of a new democratic political system; their youth and their energy, combined with their devotion—almost slavish—to public opinion, may allow them to create a political system in which the people *do* participate in controlling the decisions which affect them. Perhaps an undreamed-of unity between people and leaders, as has existed throughout the phases of revolutionary transformation in Cuba so far, may become a routine way of life.

The majority of the Cuban people apparently have continued in their support of Fidel Castro and the revolution. . . .

But a fine line separates mass support for the revolution (revolutionary democracy) from dictatorship. The spur-of-the-moment, impetuous, arbitrary decisions of the revolutionary leaders—especially the few immediately around Fidel Castro—Ernesto "Che" Guevara, Raúl Castro, Osvaldo Dorticós, Armando Hart, Antonio Nuñez Jiménez—control the destinies of the Cuban people. That has been a necessity, for "revolution" means change—rapid, thorough, fundamental. And to accomplish that, the revolutionaries had to act quickly. To transfer power to the people, the old regime had to be transformed. It was the prerequisite for establishing a democratic society.

* From *Cuba: Tragedy in Our Hemisphere,* by Maurice Zeitlin and Robert Scheer. © Copyright 1963 by Maurice Zeitlin and Robert Scheer, published by Grove Press, Inc. Pp. 209–214, 217–223. Reprinted by permission. Mr. Zeitlin is on the faculty of Sociology and Anthropology at Princeton University. Mr. Scheer is a free-lance writer.

That is what the revolution has been doing since 1959. The military apparatus was destroyed and a popular militia has replaced it. The mass of the people have gained a greater measure of economic security than before; they are becoming familiar with political problems and have gained political skills—organizational ability, confidence, education. The old ideology is being replaced with a philosophy that the people must rule their society, while many of the necessary conditions are being created toward that end. The economic and political power of the former ruling class and old government apparatus has been eliminated, and new, young, honest and dedicated personnel run the government—young people almost romantic in their desire to communicate and remain close with the masses. The mass assemblies have been methods of more of less direct communication between the people and their leaders. The assemblies have served to make people aware of and to teach them about the course of the revolution and the needs of Cuban society. Fidel Castro's "long, didactic speeches on television . . ." as *The London Observer* (April 23, 1961) correctly pointed out, "give his mostly illiterate compatriots a sort of lecture-course on the theory and practice of Socialism." The belief in popular government has been made into a passionate creed.

For all these reasons, the Cuban Revolution has been a fundamentally democratic experience for the Cuban people. The essential preconditions for their participation in the conduct of public affairs, and an ideology which insists on their participation, have been created. Fidel Castro said on May Day 1961:

> A revolution expressing the will of the people is an election every day, not every four years; it is a constant meeting with the people, like this meeting. The old politicians could never have gathered as many votes as there are people here tonight to support the revolution. . . . What do they (in the U.S.) want? Elections with pictures on the posts. The Revolution has changed the conception of pseudodemocracy for direct government by the people. There had to be a period for abolition of the privileges.

The last sentence is the most significant, for the period for the "abolition of the privileges" is well past. Without those steps being taken all talk of system was premature. But revolution cannot be a permanent form of society. The revolutionaries must begin immediately to create a political system—to establish institutions to secure the gains of the revolution. Mechanisms to assure the participation of the people in major decisions both in the economic and political realms are now necessary. The mass assemblies, whatever their undoubted educational value, cannot be the basis of the political system, although they may continue alongside of other institutions which become basic. The revolution cannot continue to depend on the whims of the revolutionaries, nor the accuracy of an assassin's bullet. Methods of choosing and replacing competing political leaders have to be decided on and established. Channels for the communication of minority opinion, criticism, and dissent must be formed. At the moment, complete political power is in the hands of the revolutionary leaders. There is the militia, of course, which has served as a potential source of censure. But the militia cannot serve as any permanent guarantee that the present closeness of popular will and the government will continue. At most, if a consistent series of policies becomes sufficiently distasteful to the people, the militia allows them the alternative of civil war.

Cuba has entered a phase in which she will be developing permanent institutions. There are all sorts of organizations in Cuba, but no real system of organization. The revolutionaries do not yet seem to have an entirely clear idea, for instance, about how the nationalized industries are to be run, how planning is to be done, priorities decided, and plans implemented. The extent of worker control and participation, the selection of administrative personnel, their replacement, and so on, remain open to suggestion. The sugar cooperatives are now being reorganized into Granjas del Pueblo, people's farms, in which the workers are employees rather than participants in a cooperative enterprise. Yet in the fishing industry, cooperatives apparently are planned to continue.

The mass media, though increasingly centralized, are still in diverse hands. There is no central control of programming on radio or TV, or in the determination of news coverage or editorial policy—although no significant differences in point of view are expressed. The Cuban Confederation of Labor, the National Institute of Agrarian Reform, the Ministry of Education, the various provinces and ministries, cultural and political organizations still own and run newspapers, periodicals, radio and TV stations. Organizational lines and administrative authority and responsibility throughout the country have yet to be decided.

The Cubans are still searching for methods of organizing their society—but they need a relatively calm atmosphere to carry on a fruitful search. The April 1961 invasion signifies the extent to which the establishment of a system of political democracy is not in their control alone. Whether or not the United States will let them alone will be crucial. The ability and the will to experiment with new forms cannot survive in an atmosphere of siege.

The Cuban revolutionaries dreamed of putting through a revolution that would be an inspiration—a classic—to democratic revolutionaries elsewhere: a symbol and a reality of a revolution going forward with full popular support and the people's liberties protected. Despite the harassment to which their country has been subjected, and despite the 1961 invasion attempt, and threats of future ones, the revolutionaries seem still to have retained that dream. In his May Day speech of 1961, shortly after the failed invasion, Fidel Castro again repeated the determination of the revolutionaries to be "generous" to opponents of the revolution:

> The revolution has already passed its basic measures. Nobody need worry. This is the hour in which we, far from using the moment against those who do not understand, should ask them if the

> time has not come for them to join us. . . . The revolution does not want to use its force against a minority. The revolution wants all Cubans to understand. We do not want all this happiness and emotion to ourselves. It is the glory of the people. We say this to those who have lived in the past and have not understood. We frankly say that our revolution should not be lessened by severe sanctions against all the mercenaries. We say this because we tell the people all that will benefit the revolution. We have had a moral victory and it will be greater if we do not besmirch our victory.

. . . . One of the most compelling qualities of the Cuban Revolution has been its attachment to the people, its concern for their immediate material and cultural gain, and its experimentalism and pragmatism. The unspoken principle of the revolution in its first years might be summed up in a paraphrase of the German socialist Rosa Luxemburg's famous revolutionary axiom: "Mistakes committed by a genuine revolutionary government are much more fruitful and worthwhile historically than the infallibility of the very best central committee."

By the fall of 1961, however, it was apparent that the leaders of the revolution had begun to think differently. A new political party, the United Party of the Socialist Revolution, formed according to principles of "democratic centralism" was being planned; its official ideology was to be "Marxism-Leninism" and decisions were to be taken in the name of this ideology.

The growth of Marxism-Leninism into the official ideology of the Cuban Revolution has been both cause and consequence of the increased strength of the Communists. The former *Partido Socialista Popular* (PSP) membership will probably form the core of the new United Party when it is formed from the present loose Integrated Revolutionary Organizations (ORI)—consisting of the 26th of July Movement, the Revolutionary Directorate, and the PSP. Today there can be no doubt of the immense influence in Cuba of the "old Communists" as Fidel Castro refers to them. Despite a series of denunciations by Castro of their "sectarianism" and authoritarianism, and of their apparent attempt to usurp control from the Fidelistas, the Communists are still, as individuals, in important positions throughout the Government structure.[1]

[1] . . . It might be worthwhile noting here that although it was reported in many newspapers and magazines that Fidel Castro, in his speech of December 2, 1961, said he had always been a Communist, this is not correct. The speech is quite long, and Castro makes many allusions to his own political development, but nowhere does he say that he had always been a Marxist-Leninist, or a Communist. On the contrary, he was at great pains to indicate why he had been opposed to the Communists:

> Did I have prejudices? I believe it is good to talk about that. Did I have prejudices about the Communists? Yes. Was I ever influenced by imperialist and reactionary propaganda against the Communists? Yes. What did I think about the Communists? Did I think they were thieves? No. Never. I always regarded the Communists—at the University and elsewhere—as honorable and honest people. . . . Why did I have such opinions about the Communists? Simply, I am absolutely convinced that the ideas I had about the Communists, not about Marxism, about the Communist Party, were like the ideas of many people, a product of propaganda and prejudices inculcated in my mind ever since I was a little boy, almost from my school days. . . . In short, I

Nevertheless, the revolutionaries have tried, while taking measures necessary to protect the revolution, to instill by example and precept a respect for dissent. It remains to be seen whether continued U.S. pressures will force them to severely limit civil liberties and other personal freedoms. We have, by our determined hostility, impelled the development in Cuba of an atmosphere which cannot accept dissent. By attacking Cuba in the name of democracy, the United States has also damaged democracy's meaning, and is increasingly alienating the revolutionaries from what is valuable in the Western tradition. Central to that tradition is the belief that individuals can and should make the decisions which affect them, and that having the right and ability to make those decisions is itself essential—whatever decisions emerge. The individual shall judge the effect of social policy upon himself, and have the power to determine that policy. Life becomes meaningful insofar as the individual creates his own link with reality, his own purpose for existence. The individual's ability to have a creative impact on his existence is the most vital aspect of being "human."

To make meaningful decisions, the individual must have accurate knowledge bearing upon the decisions to be made: knowledge of the situation and the choices open to him. He must be able to understand and deal creatively with his own existence. To say that is to recall immediately to ourselves that human beings can be manipulated, can be made to believe nonexistent "facts," to make decisions to their own detriment, and be gulled into satisfaction with their lot. Excluded from the reality of freedom, they cannot recognize its possibilities.

The freedoms of dissent, debate, criticism, press and assembly in the United States were fought for to open and keep open the channels of information and to allow the ever-enlarging utilization of man's potential. It is precisely to make human choice meaningful and majority rule possible that there should be concern with elections, political parties, legislatures, and independent judiciaries which constitute our representative democracy. Those

---

was prejudiced against the Partido Socialista, prejudices stemming fundamentally from the (political) campaigns. I admit it with the honesty one ought to have when admitting such things. . . .

On certain occasions, on certain occasions early in the revolutionary process, there was some friction between us, probably due to different conceptions of certain things, but, basically, because we did not discuss matters.

I must also say that there were people here who fell victim to the intrigue of the early days, when every time something happened, it was said there was a group of Communists stirring up trouble, provoking a riot. I must say that at one time I even believed it was the Communists who had provoked a riot at a certain place, when a group of citizens with sticks attacked a citizen there. I was led to believe it; I must admit it here. And later I discovered it wasn't the Communists who staged the riot, but divisionist elements who had armed the whole mob with sticks to beat up citizens. . . .

I believe that one of the errors of those first days was the lack of any major exchange of views between the different organizations. Each of us was acting more or less on our own account. It was the revolutionary struggle itself which brought us more and more into contact, more and more into common discussion, more and more into an exchange of views, and steadily promoted our unification.

mechanisms should be used to facilitate majority rule. If they are not, then they are no longer democratic.

Generally, Cuba's critics in the United States have seen fit to remonstrate about forms—parties, elections, separation of powers—but have not been willing to grapple with the problems—or at least recognize them as valid—of socialist democracy. Are economic planning and government ownership of the means of production compatible with the traditional separation of powers, or with a parliamentary system? Can a free press be guaranteed when there is no private ownership, and how? How are the technical requirements of expertise and authority in a planned economy to be reconciled with popular election of government officials? What forms will prevent bureaucratic control of the new society? What form of popular representation is best adapted to a society that is not based on competing private economic interests? Questions such as these are the kind to which Cubans must find the answers in the immediate future.

Intellectuals in our country have asked these and similar questions about the possibilities and dangers of socialism. Off our shores, there is a socialist economy led by young, fresh and flexible revolutionaries of strong democratic convictions. What shall we offer them? If our intellectuals, whether of the right or of the left, repeat the old clichés, if they ask that Cuba adopt U.S. institutions, or that she fulfill their own left sectarian theories, they will succeed only in making democracy appear irrelevant.

The aid that the Soviet Union has given Cuba has been crucial to the survival of the revolution. The Cubans originally received their impressions of Soviet society from the United States and its news agencies. Their counterrevolutionaries have been called "freedom fighters" by our political leaders and intellectuals. No wonder that the Hungarian revolt loses its meaning to them. At home and abroad, the Communists have supported their revolution, while the same people who attack the Communists now attack the revolution. Is it difficult to understand, therefore, why anti-Soviet opinion is as absent from Cuba's mass media now as is pro-Soviet opinion from our own? Or why the Cuban Communists have increased in prestige and influence? At the same time, while the United States seems to be unable to offer Cuba any meaningful example for her own development, Soviet institutions based on government ownership of the means of production and a planned economy, must appear relevant. There is much in Soviet society that *is* relevant to Cuba: certain techniques of public planning and management, concern for the provision of social goods and the satisfaction of broad community needs, a dynamic state involvement in the extension of education and culture to the people. In these areas, the Soviet Union has been a vital innovator and is worthy of emulation. The danger is that because of our policies, the Soviet impact may be greater than necessary—that Cuba will adopt Soviet institutions wholesale and uncritically. The revolutionaries were receptive to the consideration of diverse radical traditions and forms of socialist and Marxian thought. The question is, how long can they continue to be so, faced with U.S. pressure, Communist influence, and the reliance on the Soviet bloc that was forced on them?

Unlike the Soviet Union and China, Cuba has no need to require great sacrifices of personal freedom to attain economic development. The country has an exceedingly small population compared to its available resources, a fertile and arable land, and the possibilities of vast economic and technical aid, if this is not prevented by our government. Cuba is small and the complexities of planning are less cumbersome and difficult to perfect. Her small population and territorial size allow extensive and intensive communication between the government and people, and mass participation in public affairs. The prerevolution agricultural structure prepared the way for relatively easy and rapid modernization and socialization, and for the solution of agricultural problems that have plagued planners in the Soviet bloc and China.

Unlike the Communists in China and Russia, the Cuban revolutionaries came to power in a society relatively free of chaos. The spirit and the energies of the people were not exhausted, but were, in fact, simply waiting to be tapped.

Cuba still has a unique opportunity to develop institutions which allow government ownership and planning to lead both to economic growth and to the development of diversity, intellectual freedom and meaningful majority rule. But infatuation with the Soviet example, probably inevitable as a result of American policies, may make it impossible for Cuba to grasp her opportunity. The increased power of the Cuban Communists, whose history shows little concern for experimentation, either theoretical or practical, cannot help matters. Communist governments have not shown themselves to be particularly sensitive to the need for freedom of dissent and criticism—of free and easy access to conflicting ideas and points of view—for democratic rule.

At home, can it be maintained that the United States has made *effective* minority dissent possible and provided meaningful intellectual freedom and genuine majority rule? Yet the United States does have a long written and oral tradition of commitment to such ideals. *That tradition is entirely relevant to Cuba.* It contains the essential message of Western civilization's concern for man, as man, and for the development of his fullest potential and creativity, his fullest humanity. The tragic paradox is that the United States Government itself may be responsible for the death of that tradition if it continues to pursue the policies it has pursued in the past.

But if the United States Government wants to act as heir to that democratic heritage and to regain Cuba's friendship as a sovereign nation, it is still possible, despite the hostility of the past few years. Certainly, for example, the Algerian struggle for independence, which involved incomparably more destruction of life and property, did not prevent France and the new Algerian Government from establishing cordial political and commercial relations.

Given the present situation, what can our government do to best serve our interests and be fair to the Cuban people? Two important steps have already been taken: First, the Cuban Government's release of the Bay of Pigs invaders in return for United States' shipments of drugs and medicines to Cuba equivalent in value to the "fines" levied against the invaders. This has helped to establish an atmosphere conducive to further reciprocal acts. So has the continuing prisoner exchange between the two countries. Second, the United States has both declared its intention to prevent and acted to prevent Cuban exile raids against the Cuban Government launched from our territory. This has been of mutual advantage to both countries. It has decreased harassment of the Revolutionary Government and decreased as well the likelihood of our becoming involved in a conflict precipitated by the exiles. In turn, the Cubans have tacitly accepted our aerial reconnaissance of their country.

The United States took these steps in its national interest, but they also helped to create a more relaxed atmosphere. We can now take several other simple steps which do not in any way weaken our security but which could lead to reconciliation:

1. Relax travel restrictions to Cuba by American citizens. This might ensure more reliable reporting about internal conditions in Cuba and certainly would increase the information available to our government on which to base sound policy. If the Cubans reciprocated by loosening their own restrictions concerning the issuance of visas to our citizens, this would tend to encourage further diplomatic initiatives.

2. Relax our pressures on our allies against their trading with Cuba. This would reduce Cuban dependence on the Communist countries and thereby make it more likely that Cuba could negotiate with us flexibly. Simultaneously, it would increase the flow of much-needed goods to Cuba from non-Communist countries.

3. Let it be known that the United States is considering relaxing its own restrictions on trade with Cuba by United States businessmen. The Cubans might be asked in return to consider negotiating new terms of compensation for nationalized United States' property.

If these steps are taken, the next steps would come more easily.

4. Announce that the United States intends to convert Guantanamo Naval Base (in any case militarily obsolete) into an inter-American University (a suggestion made by Charles E. Osgood in *The Nation*). In return the United States would expect Cuba to send home all Soviet military personnel and/or to join in an agreement for turning Latin America into an "atom free" zone (the latter proposal has already been made by several important Latin American countries).

Such steps as these would lead to decreased tension between the two countries and open the way to possible resumption of diplomatic and commercial relations between them under conditions of equality. If the United States were to attempt such policies and the Cubans were not to reciprocate, we would have lost nothing whatsoever in national dignity or security. On the contrary we would have demonstrated that the United States was concerned with encouraging an equitable resolution of Cuba–United States differences and could not do so because of Cuban intransigence. But that such steps would lead to the resumption of cordial relations seems more likely given the background of the conflict.

Such a reconciliation would be to the long-run interests of the United States in this hemisphere. For there will be other revolutions in Latin America in our lifetime. And such a reconciliation with Cuba would make clear to the leaders of those revolutions that they need not engage the Colossus of the North in a life and death struggle in order to bring their own countries independence and economic development.

Castro, Latin America, and the Sino-Soviet Conflict*

Ernst Halperin

Relying upon his position as the head of the first Communist regime of the Western hemisphere, Castro demands the leadership of the whole Communist movement of Latin America. But to subordinate themselves to the leadership of Castro and to change over from the strategy of cooperation and infiltration to that of terrorism and armed rising would be political suicide for Latin American Communist leaders. They must reject his demand even though they risk a split in the movement in the course of which they would not only lose the overwhelming majority of the sympathizers and new members but also a part of the old party cadres.

True, the cohesiveness of Communist parties in Latin America is less than in Europe; splits on the basis of tactical differences of opinion are frequent but are not considered a catastrophe. They are even tolerated by Moscow in case the splinter group is as unconditionally loyal to the Soviet Union as the official Communist party. Thus, for example, Moscow recognizes the Mexican Vicente Lombardo Toledano as one of the leaders of Latin American communism although he is the head of a splinter group and never belonged to the official Communist party in Mexico.

The split which now threatens Latin American communism through the leadership claim of Fidel Castro, however, is more serious than all previous internal conflicts and splits. Today it is not a matter of tactical differences of

* Reprinted from Ernst Halperin, "Castro and Latin American Communism" (mimeo), Center for International Studies, Massachusetts Institute of Technology, 1963, pp. 9–14, by permission of the Center for International Studies. Mr. Halperin is a Swiss journalist who writes on Eastern European affairs for Swiss and German newspapers. He is the author of *The Triumphant Heretic*.

opinion in individual Latin American countries but a question of the general line of the Communist movement in the whole Latin American continent. Furthermore, it is also a question of the authority of Moscow over the Latin American Communist parties. The present struggle of tendencies in Latin American communism is very closely bound together with the Sino-Soviet conflict about the leadership of world communism.

Direct Chinese influence on Latin American Communists is amazingly small. There is not a "Chinese" group in Latin American communism, no matter what one may read to this effect in inaccurate press reports. Certainly from the beginning of the Sino-Soviet conflict, particularly among the older party cadres, there has been strong sympathy for Peking, above all because these circles do not have a high opinion of Khrushchev and cannot forgive him his destruction of the Stalin myth. However, Chinese propaganda in Latin America remains ineffective; it is too doctrinaire for the Latin Americans.

Abstract thought, the manipulation of concepts and categories, is not thought highly of generally in Latin America, and this is true for Latin American Communists. They have little understanding for dogmatic hair-splitting, and their speeches and writings are much more concrete and easily understandable than those of the Communists of other countries.

As a result, the Chinese tracts, with their scholastic way of demonstrating all kinds of revisionist deviations of their Soviet enemies on the basis of the writings of Lenin, are incomprehensible to Latin American Communists. Proving that Khrushchev represents the policy of Bernstein or Kautsky and not that of Lenin seems meaningless even to that extremely small number of them who have ever heard the names of Bernstein or Kautsky and read any of the writings of Lenin. On the other hand, Fidel Castro's undogmatic way of arguing is entirely in accord with the Latin American mentality. He fights against Khrushchev's thesis of the possibility of a peaceful transition to socialism not, like the Chinese, with the argument that Lenin said otherwise; on the contrary, he simply refers to the practical situation. Thus he declared in his speech of January 16, 1963: "We are no dogmatists. We do not deny the possibility of the peaceful transition, but we are still waiting for the first such case."

The fact that Castro in purely a theoretical manner recognizes the possibility of a peaceful transition to socialism does not change the fact that in practice and in the Latin American continent, the only one which interests him, he supports revolution by force just as decisively as the Chinese.

This is the decisive point for the Latin American Communists. It is exactly in respect to this question, on which the Cuban and Chinese positions agree, that opinion is divided in Latin America. Thus the split which today threatens Latin American communism is not one between a Soviet and a Chinese group; what threatens is much more a split between the party leaderships supported by the Soviet Union, who support a policy of infiltration and cooperation with non-Communist groups, and the supporters of Castro, who support a revolution by force and naturally therefore sympathize with Peking.

Thus the Chinese have in Fidel Castro an important ally in their attempt to break the Soviet hegemony over the international Communist movement. Of course Castro is something entirely else than a tool of the Chinese. He is only their ally insofar as his interests coincide with theirs. In the case of an open break between Moscow and Peking he would probably support the Chinese side only if Moscow acted extremely clumsily toward him. His aim is to seize the leadership of the Communist movement of Latin America not in order to subordinate it to the orders of Peking but to use it as a motor for the speeded-up victory of the revolution.

One may ask why the Soviets tolerate these moves of Castro at all in view of the fact that he is economically and militarily entirely dependent upon them.

The conduct of Moscow is in fact incomprehensible as long as one does not consider that the relations between Castro and the Soviet government almost from the beginning have been very closely tied to and in fact determined by the development of the Sino-Soviet conflict. Any analysis of Soviet-Cuban relations which does not begin with this relationship will be incorrect from the beginning.

In the conflict between Moscow and Peking, the Soviet help to Cuba has always served to refute the Chinese charge of treason to the world revolution. This is the most serious charge which a Communist can ever raise against a party comrade. The Soviets could demonstrate by the concrete example of their revolutionary help to Cuba that it was not a true one. But, exactly because of this reason, the Soviets cannot possibly shut off this help. Certainly they can threaten to do so, but they cannot turn their threat into reality, and Castro is not the man who can be intimidated by mere threats.

Help for Cuba has become a serious problem for the Soviets. Certainly the decision of Moscow to establish missile bases in Cuba was taken not the least because of its desire to obtain, in addition to morale, capital, a genuine power gain from its Cuban investments. But this adventure ended with a failure which Peking immediately and very effectively utilized for its propaganda purposes.

In the meantime the position of Moscow in the international Communist movement has worsened. The number of Peking supporters is increasing and, as a result, the Soviets can less than ever afford a fight with Castro. They must literally handle him with kid gloves.

This is why Castro has been invited to Moscow. He will probably be overwhelmed there with honors, but he will hardly be handed the leadership he demands over the Communist movement of Latin America; and it is extremely questionable whether he will be satisfied with anything less.

12

The Alliance for Progress

"It is safe to say that the Alliance has grown roots," said Teodoro Moscoso, then the U.S. Coordinator of the Alliance for Progress, in August 1963. By the end of 1963 it was apparent that the roots were shallow indeed. Reorganization of the U.S. Latin-American policy structure early in 1964 placed Alliance matters in the hands of Thomas Mann, Assistant Secretary of State for Latin-American Affairs, who would report directly to the White House as well as to the State Department. This reorganization reflected widespread dissatisfaction with the progress of the Alliance. The Alliance for Progress, however, is not being abandoned by the United States. One of Lyndon Johnson's first acts as President was to call together the representatives of the Latin-American countries to "reaffirm that Alliance and pledge all the energies of my Government to our common goals." Even so, the ringing phrases of the "Declaration to the Peoples of America" uttered at Punta del Este in August 1961 seem to have lost their resonance.

First, the pace of economic change in most of Latin America has been slow. The charter of the Alliance called for a per capita growth rate of 2½ per cent per annum; but, because of surging population figures, the modest gains in productivity could not raise the standards per capita in 1962 by even 1 per cent. Moreover, thoroughgoing land reforms and significant changes in antiquated tax systems were under way in only a few of the Alliance countries. The selection here by Peter R. Nehemkis, Jr., expresses the skepticism about the prospects for thorough reforms that has been reiterated by Senator Morse and other critics of the Alliance, who complain about the incredible obtuseness of Latin-American oligarchs.

Second, where drastic changes have been made in the economic status quo it has sometimes gone in directions least palatable to U.S. interests—such as nationalization and expropriation of foreign oil companies in Peru and Argentina.

Third, in many Latin-American countries, democracy is an exceedingly frail structure. The Punta del Este charter insists that the Alliance is based on "free men working through the institution of representative democracy." President Kennedy felt that economic development must be carried out along with democratic rule or, ideologically, we would have no case against the communists. Yet military regimes continue to be a part of Latin-American life, and military coups are commonplace. And, if the appeal of Castro was somewhat reduced after the October 1962 Cuban missile crisis, the extreme Left was still a potent factor in some of the Latin-American countries.[1]

On their side, Latin-American leaders offer a different set of reasons for the Alliance's troubles: deteriorating terms of trade for their raw materials that might cost more than the Alliance could bring; alleged bureaucratic clumsiness and timidity on the part of the U.S.; aid on a scale much too limited for the dimensions of the problems to be surmounted; continued exploitation by U.S. economic interests; and United States' insensitivity to the national pride of the other countries.

All sides offer solutions. John Paton Davies, Jr., argues here that talk about social reform is absurd when the harsh requirement is a forced economic growth that can only be accomplished by relatively untrammeled business operations. At the other extreme, Carlos Fuentes says that revolution is the only answer, and that the Alliance is at best a pathetic misreading of the necessities of Latin America, at worst (and more likely) a cover for U.S. economic imperialism. Between these two extremes fall a vast number of proposals that try to retain the spirit of the Punta del Este charter. These proposals mostly concern the administration of the Alliance, and seek to bring the Latin-American countries more directly into its decision-making process; to this end, an eight-man inter-American Committee for the Alliance for Progress has been established to give guidance to Washington.

But the problems of the Alliance are more than administrative and procedural. So vast are the difficulties, so resistant are many of the Latin-American social structures to the advances of technology, that we can only avoid despair if our expectations are substantially reduced. In this respect, Teodoro A. Moscoso comments that transformation of Latin-American society can hardly be accomplished overnight. Albert O. Hirschman argues here that reform and revolution are not necessarily mutually exclusive and that the case for reform may be stronger than have been the arguments of the reformers. If Hirschman is right, the Alliance for Progress may not be quite in such perilous condition as the depressing recitations of its shortcomings, which are so frequently heard in both parts of the hemisphere, would make it appear.

[1] The U.S. Administration quickly gave its approval when, in April 1964, the Brazilian government of President João Goulart was overthrown by the military in cooperation with a group of civilian state governors. Despite the involvement of the military, Washington assumed that this coup would bolster the cause of democratic moderation in Latin America and set back the prospects of Castroism and other extreme Left-wing movements.

Objectives of the Alliance for Progress*

Charter of Punta del Este

It is the purpose of the Alliance for Progress to enlist the full energies of the peoples and governments of the American republics in a great cooperative effort to accelerate the economic and social development of the participating countries of Latin America, so that they may achieve maximum levels of well-being, with equal opportunities for all, in democratic societies adapted to their own needs and desires.

The American republics hereby agree to work toward the achievement of the following fundamental goals in the present decade:

1. To achieve in the participating Latin American countries a substantial and sustained growth of per capita income at a rate designed to attain, at the earliest possible date, levels of income capable of assuring self-sustaining development, and sufficient to make Latin American income levels constantly larger in relation to the levels of the more industrialized nations. In this way the gap between the living standards of Latin America and those of the more developed countries can be narrowed. Similarly, presently existing differences in income levels among the Latin American countries will be reduced by accelerating the development of the relatively less developed countries and granting them maximum priority in the distribution of resources and in international cooperation in general. In evaluating the degree of relative development, account will be taken not only of average levels of real income and gross product per capita, but also of indices of infant mortality, illiteracy, and per capita daily caloric intake.

It is recognized that, in order to reach these objectives within a reasonable time, the rate of economic growth in any country of Latin America should be not less than 2.5 per cent per capita per year, and that each participating country should determine its own growth target in the light of its stage of social and economic evolution, resource endowment, and ability to mobilize national efforts for development.

2. To make the benefits of economic progress available to all citizens of

* Title I of the Charter of Punta del Este. Published in *Alianza para el Progreso: The Record of Punta del Este* (Washington, D.C.: Pan American Union and U.S. Department of State, 1961), pp. 4–5. The charter emanated from a meeting of American states in Uruguay on August 5–17, 1961, which established the Alliance for Progress.

all economic and social groups through a more equitable distribution of national income, raising more rapidly the income and standard of living of the needier sectors of the population, at the same time that a higher proportion of the national product is devoted to investment.

3. To achieve balanced diversification in national economic structures, both regional and functional, making them increasingly free from dependence on the export of a limited number of primary products and the importation of capital goods while attaining stability in the prices of exports or in income derived from exports.

4. To accelerate the process of rational industrialization so as to increase the productivity of the economy as a whole, taking full advantage of the talents and energies of both the private and public sectors, utilizing the natural resources of the country and providing productive and remunerative employment for unemployed or part-time workers. Within this process of industrialization, special attention should be given to the establishment and development of capital-goods industries.

5. To raise greatly the level of agricultural productivity and output and to improve related storage, transportation, and marketing services.

6. To encourage, in accordance with the characteristics of each country, programs of comprehensive agrarian reform leading to the effective transformation, where required, of unjust structures and systems of land tenure and use, with a view to replacing latifundia and dwarf holdings by an equitable system of land tenure so that, with the help of timely and adequate credit, technical assistance and facilities for the marketing and distribution of products, the land will become for the man who works it the basis of his economic stability, the foundation of his increasing welfare, and the guarantee of his freedom and dignity.

7. To eliminate adult illiteracy and by 1970 to assure, as a minimum, access to six years of primary education for each school-age child in Latin America; to modernize and expand vocational, technical, secondary and higher educational and training facilities, to strengthen the capacity for basic and applied research; and to provide the competent personnel required in rapidly growing societies.

8. To increase life expectancy at birth by a minimum of five years, and to increase the ability to learn and produce, by improving individual and public health. To attain this goal it will be necessary, among other measures, to provide adequate potable water supply and sewage disposal to not less than 70 per cent of the urban and 50 per cent of the rural population; to reduce the present mortality rate of children less than five years of age by at least one-half; to control the more serious communicable diseases, according to their importance as a cause of sickness, disability, and death; to eradicate those illnesses, especially malaria, for which effective techniques are known; to improve nutrition; to train medical and health personnel to meet at least minimum requirements; to improve basic health services at national and local

levels; and to intensify scientific research and apply its result more fully and effectively to the prevention and cure of illness.

9. To increase the construction of low-cost houses for low-income families in order to replace inadequate and deficient housing and to reduce housing shortages; and to provide necessary public services to both urban and rural centers of population.

10. To maintain stable price levels, avoiding inflation or deflation and the consequent social hardships and maldistribution of resources, always bearing in mind the necessity of maintaining an adequate rate of economic growth.

11. To strengthen existing agreements on economic integration, with a view to the ultimate fulfillment of aspirations for a Latin American common market that will expand and diversify trade among the Latin American countries and thus contribute to the economic growth of the region.

12. To develop cooperative programs designed to prevent the harmful effects of excessive fluctuations in the foreign exchange earnings derived from exports of primary products, which are of vital importance to economic and social development; and to adopt the measures necessary to facilitate the access of Latin American exports to international markets.

The Alliance and Its Accomplishments*

Teodoro A. Moscoso

It is no longer necessary today to give a reason for discussing the problems of Latin America. Events there in the past three or four years have had a powerful impact on the American public. The area has moved from virtual oblivion to the front pages of our newspapers. The image of the sleepy Latino, of the tourist paradise, of the fiesta that yields good pictures for home movies, has radically and rudely changed. Now we think of Latin America as a hotbed of Castro-communism, of feudal rule and unreasonable reluctance to go along with us in policies that we believe are good for the region. The trouble is that these current notions are just as oversimplified as the superficial romanticism that colored our thinking about Latin America in the past. The one thing that is unquestionably true is the simple but immensely meaningful statement

* "Results of the Alliance for Progress in Latin America." Address to the Commonwealth Club of California in San Francisco, California on August 23, 1963. Mr. Moscoso, formerly the Coordinator of the Alliance for Progress, is now serving as a member of the Puerto Rican–U.S. commission that is studying Puerto Rico's status.

President Kennedy made a few months ago: "I regard Latin America as the most critical area in the world today."

I hope today to trace some of the reasons why this is so, to analyze what we are doing about it, and what more we can do.

The Latin America with which we deal today is nineteen different countries, with nineteen different sets of problems and opportunities. Most of the people speak Spanish. The single largest nation—with a third of Latin America's population—Brazil, uses Portuguese. But millions of people in these countries don't speak either of these languages. Guarani is the Indian language of Paraguay, Quechua and Aymara the major languages of the Andean countries, and many other dialects are spoken by smaller groups of indigenous people, most of whom do not figure in the money economy and hardly are aware that they are citizens of the countries in which they live.

Some of the Republics have long traditions of constitutional democracy, while others are only now emerging from a succession of strongman dictatorships. Some have firmly rooted private and public institutions, which need reshaping under the impact of social ferment and economic pressures. Others have as yet no firm institutional base. Some are industrially developed, thanks in large measure to immigrants from Europe—from the same countries who sent us millions that helped build our nation—Italy, Yugoslavia, Germany, England, Spain and Portugal. Most are essentially agricultural—with too many people working too hard to produce too little. A few Latin American countries boast highly developed educational systems, with literacy rates comparing favorably with our own. Most are struggling to reduce the waste resulting from mass illiteracy and to give their people the skills so vitally needed for modern development work. Some have gone through deep political and social revolutions. Most are now at a pre-revolutionary stage, bent on massive change, and challenging their own leaders and us to help them do the job in freedom and with a minimum of violence. But changes they want and they will get—either with us, or without, and, in that case, possibly against us. The man with the hoe will make his voice heard.

Since the early years of our Republic, the United States has had a deep and unique commitment to the struggle of our fellow Americans to the south for political independence, economic growth and social justice. This commitment has been embodied in the Monroe Doctrine, the Pan American Regional Organization and the Good Neighbor Policy. It symbolizes the brotherhood of the Western Hemisphere—the common interest of the American peoples for building societies capable of providing solutions to popular demands.

But since World War II, none of these policies has been adequate to deal with the rapidly growing problems of Latin America. An industrial ferment which began in the postwar years—a ferment induced in part by the near stagnation of rural communities—brought new millions of unskilled workers to the burgeoning cities. Since the end of the war, Sao Paulo's population has doubled. Mexico City's population increased by 58 percent between 1950 and 1960. City after city has grown and in the cities, the process of the "revolution of rising expectations" has accelerated. The back windows of some plush apartment houses in Rio de Janeiro open out on a hillside of huts—the favelas, homes without water, light or sewers. The favela dwellers, as well as more fortunate citizens with a social conscience, began to ask "Why?" The answer: Because this has always been so!—no longer is good enough.

Political and economic thinkers in Latin America have understood the seriousness of the problem for a good many years. The United Nations Economic Commission for Latin America, under Dr. Paul Prebisch, proposed comprehensive approaches to the problems of social and economic development in the hemisphere early in the fifties. In 1954, the Latin American countries proposed to the United States the establishment of an Inter-American Development Bank—a regional equivalent of the World Bank—to concentrate on planning and financing the modernization of Latin America. We said "no." It took the disastrous events of the Nixon trip four years later to change our attitude. The Bank became a reality in 1960 and has done a fine job ever since.

But the Bank was only a partial answer. In 1958, President Kubitschek of Brazil proposed a comprehensive program of social and economic development under the title "Operation Panamerica."Again, we failed to pick up a plan of action that a Latin American leader who knew the urgency of the situation offered us. Another two years later, reacting to the incidents involving then Vice President Nixon, we moved ahead another step, with the Act of Bogota, in which we committed ourselves to a major attack on Latin America's social ills. But it was not until 1961, when John F. Kennedy became President, that we faced up to the problem in all its complex and deep-rooted aspects.

On March 13, 1961, in an address to the Latin American ambassadors in the White House, the President proposed "that the American Republics begin on a vast 10-year plan for the Americas, a plan to transform the 1960's into a historic decade of democratic progress." He called it the Alliance for Progress. On August 17, [1961], nineteen Latin American republics and the United States signed the Charter of Punta del Este to give birth to the Alliance.

The Alliance represents a totally new approach to United States cooperation with our Latin American neighbors. It is not a projection of the bilateral technical assistance programs which were initiated during World War II under the Coordinator of Inter-American Affairs and continued under Point IV. These former activities were programs designed to transmit technical know-how through demonstration projects and training of Latin American technicians.

The Alliance calls for major development efforts by all the Latin American countries in which national and international financial, technical and moral resources are committed to attack the causes of economic underdevelopment, social injustice and political instability. It is an attempt to change the status quo, and to make change itself the hallmark of a new way of life.

Under the Charter of Punta del Este, the primary responsibility for such basic development is placed on the Latin American countries themselves. Each country has agreed to improve and strengthen democratic institutions through the principles of self-determination of its people, to carry out social and economic reform programs and to accelerate the integration of Latin America, and to provide the bulk—an estimated four-fifths—of the total resources required.

The progress achieved during the two years since the Charter was signed shows more action by the Latin Americans in the enactment of basic reforms than in the preceding half-century. The picture of tax, agrarian, administrative, and other reforms is encouraging. But it is also uneven. Some countries have made giant strides while others have only made superficial efforts. In many cases, reform laws have been adopted in good faith, but the countries do not have the trained administrators and specialists to implement them and make them effective.

To help the Latin American governments do this job, we assist them in such areas as national planning, improved revenues collection and better public administration. To this technical assistance we add development loans under terms which they can afford. But we cannot do the job for them. Only the governments of Latin America can bring about the basic reforms which, soundly conceived and implemented, will ultimately help to make democratic government secure.

Unfortunately, the history of Latin America is full of unhappy experiences with corrupt and irresponsible government which have bred disillusionment and cynicism among the people, especially the youth. Lack of confidence in their government has made it doubly difficult for Latin Americans to modernize. In less than two years, the Alliance could not possibly reverse the trend, which has such deep historical roots. But a beginning has been made.

In the two years since Punta del Este, planning for development has got under way in every member country of the Alliance. Seven countries have submitted blueprints for marshaling their internal resources and effectively utilizing external assistance.

In eleven Latin American countries, tax reforms are under way. In many cases, income and property taxes are being applied for the first time in a country's history. We have made it a policy to work with Latin American governments in generating internal sources of financing for government programs rather than [have them] seek from us non-productive budget support.

In this context, an agreement between our Agency for International Development and the Internal Revenue Service warrants special mention. The IRS is undertaking not only to train Latin American officials here but also to provide technical assistance on the spot in improving tax administration. Cooperation between AID and IRS has already achieved some notable results.

Tax administrators from Chile who were trained by the IRS were instrumental in increasing that country's revenues under existing laws and in bringing two tax evaders to justice—the first such cases in Chile's history.

In the last two years, landholding problems have received more attention than at any time since the Wars of Independence of Latin America. Prior to the signing of the Alliance Charter, only Mexico, Bolivia, and Venezuela had basic agrarian reform legislation. Since its signing, five more countries have adopted laws and started on land redistribution schemes. Five other countries are now studying the most effective and appropriate methods to raise both productivity and living standards on the land. We do not look on land reform as the splitting up of large estates and the distribution of the land to peasants per se. We see it as a complex problem. Aside from changes in landholding patterns—and these need not necessarily be changed in every case—adequate and supervised credit, marketing facilities, technical assistance and many elements go into the development of a healthy agricultural economy which can produce abundant food for fast growing populations.

Perhaps the most fundamental series of reforms carried out in Latin America during the past two years has been in education. The Latin American countries have substantially increased their budget allocations to education and have taken other significant stages to develop their most valuable resource: people.

All of the Hemisphere's resources could be poured into primary education without coming to grips with its need for qualified engineers, economists, professionals and technicians needed to staff government and industry, to draft and execute national plans and to develop a productive agriculture. Latin America has an estimated 50,000 engineers and technicians in a population larger than our own, while we have over a million and feel we suffer from a shortage.

In husbanding national and inter-American resources for education under the Alliance, we are seeking a balance between primary and higher education. In the first two years of the Alliance, more than 8,000 new classrooms have been built—and teachers trained to use them. Nearly 4,000,000 textbooks have been distributed—often the first books of their kind ever received by the children. We are supporting technical training programs for workers in a score of countries, ranging from apprenticeship in El Salvador and industrial training in Chile to vocational education in Brazil and Ecuador. Some 40 major U.S. universities are working with 60 institutions in Latin America to help prepare the future professional, technical, administrative, academic and political leadership of Latin America.

Basic reforms and sound public administration of those reforms are essential building blocks of the Alliance. But the success of the Alliance will depend not only on governmental action but also on involving the people of Latin America directly and intimately in the development process.

Within the AID program, special efforts are being made to this end.

Individual projects in community development are under way in many countries to make the people themselves protagonists in social, economic and political development. In Central America and Panama, the rural mobile health project combines minimum medical care for 600 villages with community development efforts. The health teams, made up of local personnel, travelling by jeep, boat and mule-back, collect a nominal and voluntary fee of 25 to 50 cents for treatment and cost of medicine; the fees collected are turned over to committees in each community, which invest these fees in community projects of the villagers' choice. The possibilities for involving the people in their own development under such a project is unlimited, and the response of the people so far has been most encouraging.

On a hemisphere-wide basis, AID had also set in motion programs which harness the resources of United States private enterprise, the leading United States unions, cooperatives and voluntary agencies to work on a people-to-people basis.

The Alliance cannot succeed without a healthy and vigorous private sector in Latin America. This is so, not for reasons of verbal convention, but because our economies prove the point pragmatically. An effective market economy must be created, and preserved, and the forces of individual initiative allowed to play their creative role in Latin America as they have in Europe, North American and Japan. Thus, Latin American business must feel that it has a stake in the Alliance.

United States investment has not moved into Latin America of late at the rate at which it is needed. But things are not as bad as some have recently suggested. United States firms and investments are already playing a role in the development programs of the Alliance, especially in the key area of manufacturing. But we are not satisfied. AID has developed a number of programs to assist the private sector to play its due role in the development effort. These include direct loans; loans to intermediate credit institutions; investment guaranties and proposed tax credits on investments in developing countries. Particularly promising are joint ventures of United States companies with local businessmen.

Such joint ventures can be mutually advantageous to the business partners themselves, as well as helpful in knitting closer ties among the individuals working together in such firms.

On the labor side, the AFL-CIO has lent its support through the Labor Advisory Committee for the Alliance for Progress. Under its guidance, AID has contracted with the American Institute for Free Labor Development to carry out a Hemisphere-wide effort to combine United States and Latin American union resources in training democratic union leaders and in developing social projects needed by workers to raise their living standards. In little more than a year of operations, the Institute has helped establish labor leader training centers in four countries as well as a regional training center in Washington; it is now setting up centers in seven other countries. In the social projects area, the Institute is working with unions in a score of countries on housing, cooperative and other activities.

Another area of people-to-people action is in the field of cooperatives. In collaboration with the Credit Union National Association, a center for training credit union technicians is being set up in Peru and will be working with groups in 16 countries to develop credit unions which will provide the common people of Latin America with the means to save and to borrow at reasonable rates. In cooperation with the National Farmers Union, a people-to-people exchange of 75 farm leaders from six Latin American countries has been started to provide agricultural and cooperative leadership training.

One program that has given us particular satisfaction and that has opened up a whole new field for people-to-people participation in the Alliance is the association formed between [California] and Chile. As you know, your state government and leaders in key sectors of California's economic life—especially in agriculture—are doing pioneering work today. They are exploring the possibility of making the accumulated experience and the research and development resources of California available to Chile, which is confronted with problems and opportunities of geography, soil and climate similar to those that California faced long ago and has solved so successfully. There are also some special historical ties between these two West Coast frontier regions—going back all the way to California gold rush days when Chileans came north to this state to work as miners and settle here.

Success in these California-Chile ventures would undoubtedly lead to other such associations between states or regions of the United States and our Latin American sister-republics under the Alliance. It would be another large field for people-to-people action—for the involvement of individuals in this country and in the Latin American countries in a program that must be rooted in understanding and cooperation among our *peoples* and not just in agreements of governments if it is to have lasting effects.

Today, two years after the signing of the Alliance Charter, it is safe to say that the Alliance has grown roots. Throughout Latin America, the housing projects, hospitals, water systems and schools that have been built under its banner are tangible evidence that it has got under way. More importantly, the Alliance has made its impact on political, economic and social discussion and conduct in the hemisphere.

Elections have been held where, without the influence of Alliance objectives and Charter principles, they might not have been held. Constitutional governments are more secure from *coups d'état* today—though far from inviolate as yet—because the subtle pressure of the Alliance Charter and of the policies it imposes on all its signers is making would-be strongmen think twice before they roll their tanks up to the Presidential Palace. And even where unconstitutional changes have occurred, the new rulers are likely to pledge new elections and support for economic and social reform when in the not distant past they could not have cared less.

This represents the real progress that the Alliance has made. Men and women in Latin America today are arguing about policies and programs when in the past they dismissed such subjects as political responsibility, economic growth, and social reform as ivory tower debates.

Our free system of life and government precludes the imposition of social and economic change from above. We have to act within the framework of consent, and of change through acceptance rather than fiat. This is a long-term process. But not as long as to be endless. I believe that by 1970 much of Latin America will be sustaining its own growth, equipped with the institutions and human resources to transform itself into a modern society.

But the job will by no means be finished by 1970. The political, economic and social transformation of a continent is not accomplished overnight. What we must seek to provide rapidly is evidence of progress which can sustain the hopes of the people and thus provide the opportunity to complete the long-term task.

The impatience with which some of us view the realization of this program is sometimes inspired by an excessive sense of panic, or by unrealistic expectations of what is possible even in the best circumstances. On the other hand, impatience designed to keep up the pressure is healthy and welcome. Working with the dedication that people connected with this program have displayed in the first two years, I am confident that we shall accomplish what we set out to do.

The Latin-American Oligarchy*

Peter R. Nehemkis, Jr.

I am very pessimistic about the prospects of achieving the kind of social revolution which the United States has agreed to underwrite. The crucial issue in Latin America, the issue on which Latin Americans must make up their minds before the Alliance for Progress has any meaning, was articulated with brutal candor by a feminine representative of Latin America's ruling and governing class. Speaking in Washington a year ago last spring, Madame Prado, the wife of the President of Peru, put the dilemma of her own oligarchic class this way: "Either we give; or they take."

The Latin American oligarchy is unable to resolve this dilemma because it is incapable of accommodating itself to a revolutionary situation. Latin

* "Economic Developments in South America." Hearings before the Subcommittee on Inter-American Economic Relationships of the Joint Economic Committee, Congress of the United States, May 10–11, 1962 (Washington, D.C.: Government Printing Office, 1962), pp. 49–60. Mr. Nehemkis is Washington Counsel for the Whirlpool Corporation.

America's oligarchy does not yet grasp the hard fact of life that either it moves over and shares its power with the democratic parties of the left, or it invites having its collective throat slit from ear to ear by a machete made in Havana.

Unlike the English Tories, who successfully made their accommodation by capturing the Labor Party's "welfare state," Latin America's oligarchy does not yet comprehend that its survival depends upon its willingness to preside over the liquidation of its own economic and social empires.

I am also bound in all candor to say to you that the majority of Latin America's business elite (whose true interests are not tied to the preservation of the status quo) have been astonishingly shortsighted. With few, notable exceptions, they have not shown any sense of noblesse oblige; any pronounced willingness to accept public responsibilities, to furnish progressive leadership, or to exert an enlightened leverage on their governments. Parenthetically, I suspect that much of the mistrust for American business throughout Latin America stems from the mistrust of most Latin Americans for their own rich. Guilt by association thereby attaches to U. S. business.

We should ask ourselves whether the structure of the Alliance for Progress—as now constituted—is geared to dealing with Latin America's impending revolutionary upheaval. What we have by way of organization is an establishment ready to implement the Marshall plan with the techniques so successfully employed in Europe during the late forties and early fifties. But Latin America in 1962, with its feudal land system, its few oases of industrialization surrounded by a vast desert of indigenous poverty, is not the war-shattered industrial plant of Europe whose technicians knew their needs down to the last industrial nut and bolt.

By 1963, when the U. S. managers of the Alliance say they will have completed their organizational retooling, we shall in all probability be confronted with so deep a revolutionary situation as to render the revamped organization inapposite.

Another major difficulty with the Alliance for Progress is the notion that we can erect sophisticated economic superstructures upon jerry-built democratic political foundations. If a social revolution in Latin America is to be accomplished peaceably—and the operative word here is "peaceably"—it requires a literate people. It requires that the representatives of the people be sent to the national parliaments. Throughout Latin America—with a few, notable exceptions—we have only a mass of inchoate illiteracy, and unrepresentative governments. President Ayub [Khan] of Pakistan once made the wise observation that for democratic planning to prevail in his country, you had to have literacy and communication. Without these essentials, [he] pointed out, economic planning was sheer hypocrisy.

I venture to suggest that we have invited our own disillusionment by a mistaken belief that Latin America's governments can—and will—speedily produce the economic reforms which were agreed to at Punta del Este.

We merely indulge in self-deception when we assume that the majority of the present Latin American governments have either the technical skills, or the administrative organizations, or that they are going to rid themselves of a paralysis of the will, to accomplish their necessary basic reforms.

We shall continue to deceive ourselves if we mistakenly assume that when most—not all—Latin American governments submit a beautifully drawn plan replete with charts and statistics for implementing the Alliance for Progress they have thereby placed themselves on the road to salvation.

I hope my Latin American friends will forgive me if I say that they have two commodities which are in oversupply. These are talk and paper plans.

A beautifully conceived plan is one thing. Making it work is quite another thing. Our Latin American friends are long on plans but woefully short on how to get the plan off the paper.

Increasingly, I am driven to the conclusion that the Latin American "problem" is primarily political and only secondarily economic. We've put the cart before the horse in our preoccupation with the economics of development to the exclusion of the politics of development. Our economists have evolved a masterful strategy of economic development. What we need with compelling urgency is a master strategy for the political development of Latin America, along with the political tactics for its execution.

If you accept my premises, would it not be far wiser for us to concentrate our efforts in building stronger democratically based political movements, solidly supported by democratic traditions? In devising methods of preventing the political arc of the democratic middle from being pulverized by the extremists of the right and left? In strengthening the trade union movements? In encouraging the growth of cooperatives? In short, can we achieve social justice throughout Latin America unless there first exists the political environment which is capable of accommodating democracy?

In our preoccupation with economic development, it seems to me that we are ignoring at our own jeopardy Latin America's intellectual world. Perhaps as much as 50 per cent of Latin America's university students are already lost to the democratic ideals of the West. But what of the 50 per cent who have not embraced Marxism? If they, too, become disillusioned we will have totally lost the mind, the spirit, and the heart of all that is best in Latin America. At that point of no return, the battle will be finished. The continent can be transferred to Moscow and Peiping without the need of landing one Chinese or Russian soldier.

A critical gap in the Latin American university is the absence of good texts in current economics. What are we doing to make available a steady flow of economics materials?

What are we doing to export cheap paperback editions of the world's finest literature to the university students?

What are we doing to publish the works of Latin America's intellectuals who, lacking any creative outlet for their talent, drift into the Communist ranks?

What are we doing to make certain that democratic newspapers do not fold for lack of funds with which to buy newsprint?

What are we doing to provide financial and technical support to the true voice of progress in Latin America which reposes in the 23 liberal democratic parties? It was these parties, under the leadership of that dynamic hemisphere statesman, wise counselor, and great friend of the United States, President José Figueres, who presented to President Kennedy their joint resolution in support of the Alliance for Progress.

While you are fielding my questions, will you indulge me if I throw you still another? Assuming for the moment that a major decision of policy were reached with the objective of executing action in these various areas upon which passing mention has been made, what institutions do we have in the U. S. Government which possess the capability and the skill to implement the tactics of this strategy of political development?

Can an agency of the U. S. Government—even assuming the requisite talents were on hand—undertake such missions in Latin America without imparting to the undertaking the kiss of death? If not, how can this job of work be done? I believe—perhaps I should say, I hope—you will agree that the questions come easier than answers. But answers there must be—and soon.

Development before Reform*

John Paton Davies, Jr.

A lot of effort and money has gone into the attempt to make a better life for the people of Latin America. Yet there is a general feeling that little progress is being made, even that ground is being lost.

The U. S. Government furnished about a billion dollars last year to the fight against poverty, ignorance and disease in the Good Neighborhood. The Congress is now being asked for nearly as much again. In addition, there is our human contribution: more than 1,400 scientists, teachers, technicians and other specialists in the aid programs throughout Latin America, and 1,300 more in the Peace Corps.

Nor have the Latin Americans been idle, as some critics imply. From the Rio Grande to Tierra del Fuego, governments, private organizations and individuals are working in their own fashion to develop their countries.

Still, with all that has been and is being done, the poor remain piteously

* "Another View of the Latin American Problem," *The New York Times Magazine,* August 25, 1963, pp. 15, 68–70. © 1963 by The New York Times Company. Reprinted by permission. Mr. Davies is a former U.S. Foreign Service officer with wide experience abroad, including Latin America. He is now a businessman in Lima, Peru.

poor, and ignorant, and diseased—and multiplying. And the rich—most of them are still rich. The gap between the poor and the rich is the most publicized characteristic of the Latin-American scene. Although such disparities exist in other parts of the world, it is the Latin-American gap which arouses our greatest indignation. Someone must be the villain of the piece. Who but the rich, the "oligarchs"?

This excited generalization is more misleading than enlightening. What are we talking about?

The rich, assumably, are that 5 per cent of the Latin-American population which, we are told, accounts for some 30 per cent of the area's consumption. The aggregate consumption being low, this ratio is theatric rather than genuinely dramatic. For in that 5 per cent are not only the relatively few millionaires with great haciendas, yachts and polo ponies, but also many more who are what we would consider well-off rather than very wealthy.

Implying that the rich are an oligarchy is to misrepresent the power structure of Latin America. No country in the area is governed exclusively by a few wealthy men or families. Ecuador and Guatemala, for example, currently have governments of the few. But the few are military men, not plutocrats. The truth is that power in Latin America is usually shared in fluctuating combinations among the very rich, the military, politically inclined professional men, and a growing number of variegated Marxists from all classes.

Still, it is argued, the rich are an obstacle to progress. There is that tiny minority among them, living lavishly, almost like foreigners on the fringe of their own countries, parasites on their national economies, stashing away their ill-gotten, feudal extortions in Swiss banks and, when not cavorting on the beach at Copacabana, jet-setting to the fanciest spas of the old world.

There are indeed some who live more or less in this colorful fashion, trying to keep up with their kind elsewhere. But it is correct that they are a tiny minority. And they are not as important in the total scene as they are popularly represented. Latin America's fate does not lie in their manicured hands.

Most of the rich are very much a part of their countries. They are the most productive part. They live well, some luxuriously. But so did the men who laid the groundwork of American economic strength: the Astors, the Goulds, the Armours, the Carnegies, the Harrimans and the Rockefellers.

The rich pay their labor the wages of the country, which are low, but steadily rising. Whether it be growing crops or mining or manufacturing, they are in business with the incentive of profit. Many export their products to compete in the world market against commodity producers on other continents, also paying low, or lower wages. Or they must compete against subsidized production—for example, against American export cotton with its 8½ cents per pound subsidy.

These Latin employers can recognize that raising all wages voluntarily would be, theoretically, enlightened self-interest. But unless productivity also rises, which they have good reason to doubt, wage increases might well price their exports out of the market, with disastrous consequences to themselves and their workers. They therefore tend, like businessmen elsewhere, to make across-the-board wage raises only when unions or the government cause them to do so.

Being the product of traditional Latin civilization, most of the wealthy live by the Latin conception of civic and business ethics, which differs from the Anglo-Saxon—as from the Hindu, the Japanese or the Arab. In their relations with individuals and the government, they are more personal than the Anglo-Saxons. Matters are more likely to be arranged and compromised rather than enacted and enforced.

This does not contribute to administrative efficiency in the Harvard Business School or Bureau of the Budget sense. But it is the way things are done. And the torrent of foreign advice to straighten themselves out is received with more patience and tolerance than one could imagine being mustered by the National Association of Manufacturers, were it subjected to moralistic nagging by European Socialists, insisting that free enterprise does not meet America's need to move ahead on social reform.

The rich are accused of being "not overly enthusiastic about . . . domestic investment" and of putting money away in American and European banks for a rainy day. So far as this is true, it is because in most of Latin America it looks politically stormy—from showers of redistributed wealth to cloudbursts of revolutionary confiscation. And everything that the Latins hear from north of the Rio Grande heightens this apprehension. They would not be prudent custodians of their children's futures if they did not tuck away something abroad for all of them.

That there are so many children (for the rich generally share with the poor a wealth of babies) means that the assets of the prosperous are automatically being redistributed among its progeny. As almost none of the fortunes are really all that grand by American standards, even the very rich are in a process of spreading their wealth thinner.

The hope of Latin America should lie with those privileged men who were sent by discerning fathers (as they are now sending their own sons) to M.I.T., to the London School of Economics or to Oklahoma State. These are the ones who would seem best equipped to make a workable synthesis of the three worlds which they know: the traditional Latin American, the computerized, socially tranquilized Yankee, and the uncomputed, untranquil Latin America now aborning. These men have made a contribution far out of proportion to their numbers. But there are not enough of them. And it is asking a bit too much to expect them to transform a society in a hurry.

So it is perhaps not wrong to say that they who should be the architects of the Latin future may not be so—excepting as they forget or abandon many of their inclinations toward and lessons in rationality and efficiency. For a society out of balance and maladjusted, in a near-revolutionary situation, reason is usually a faint, fading voice. In such a body politic, the spleen and the fist often take over from the brain.

What are the evidences of maladjustment in Latin America?

The population of the area is some 200 million, with the world's highest growth rate—nearly 3 per cent per year. This projects to 600 million by the end of the century.

Because Latin America has ample space, even this extreme rate of human multiplication would be supportable were economic development keeping pace. But the annual economic growth rate per capita, as calculated by the United Nations Economic Commission for Latin America, is 1 per cent. To foster economic growth, according to Secretary of the Treasury Douglas Dillon, it should be at least 2½ per cent.

Half of the population, says the commission, has an average annual income of $120 and accounts for only 20 per cent of consumption. And in exports, vital to earning foreign exchange, Latin America advanced during the period 1953–1960 a mere 13 per cent in contrast to a world increase of 56 per cent.

Nearly two-thirds of the Western Hemisphere is, then, an area of lagging growth—in everything but more mouths to feed. There is a lag in capital formation, a reported flight of domestic capital and a decline in American investments. With the fall of commodity prices on the world market, the Latin Americans earn less for what they produce. And with the rise in cost of manufactured goods, they pay more for the farm tractors, mine compressors and other machinery to produce the commodities they need to earn their way in the world.

None of these countries are highly industrialized. Nor can they industrialize rapidly. They do not have enough capital and, even though others were to supply it, neither do they have sufficient trained manpower to do the job speedily.

How has it been proposed to deal with this staggering problem? There are, basically, two approaches to moving a society from underdeveloped to developed. One is the old-fashioned do-it-yourself process. This is the tougher of the two. For the other is to do it with foreign aid.

England was the forerunner of self-help development. Through the innovation of the Industrial Revolution, it progressed to the most advanced and powerful position of the 19th century.

The Japanese, following the same prescription, transformed themselves in about one generation from archaic feudalism, from being the subject of sentimental opera and the butt of Gilbert and Sullivan spoofs, to the status of world power.

The Russians also did it, essentially on their own. They operated on the basis of ideological superstitions and were, therefore, spectacularly inefficient. Nevertheless, they were able to make the grade, with a slowly rising standard of living, because of their unusually rich endowment of natural resources.

In the transition of these three to developed societies, there were certain conditions in common. There was a ruling group which, notwithstanding internal differences, instinctively or by disciplined plan, forced the development of the country and the creation of wealth. Of the wealth created, a trickle was tapped off into good living by the small élite which managed the process. The mainstream was reinvested in economic expansion and arms. The wealth was not shared with the general population. On the contrary, the poor not only remained impoverished, but capital formation was in part extracted from the needy.

Because this was a painful process for the majority, repressions and controls were necessary. The peasantry and the factory workers were held down to a subsistence level, at least in the early stage of development. This tough solution can now be attempted only by dictatorships. Modern free societies will not countenance the sacrifice of two or three generations to forced national development.

So, for a democratic Latin America, the harshly proven course is unacceptable. A new, indulgent formula is needed to move a society from underdeveloped to developed. The Alliance for Progress is represented as that modern formula.

Its charter portrays a broad offensive on a sweeping front: capital formation, production, education, public health, housing—plus social justice, democratic processes, land reform, tax reform and a rising standard of living. The commitment is to change more than the structure of Latin society; it is to change also its ethics. This is to be progress free of exploitations, the birth without pain of affluent, upright democratic societies. The timetable set is ten years from 1962.

Obviously, such a transformation could not be wrought on a do-it-yourself basis. Foreign help is thus an integral part of the program.

It was reckoned at Punta del Este that the Latin countries themselves would in a decade have to generate $80 billion. Foreign sources, governmental and private (both primarily American), were to contribute $20 billion.

The feeling of urgency about the *Alianza* and dedication to reform of the Latin social structure originated essentially in Washington. They grew out of acute anxiety over the spread of Castroism. We felt that we had to force through democratic evolution before the *Fidelistas* took over by revolution.

Social reform and economic development were supposed to proceed in tandem in the *Alianza*. The general impression in Latin America, however, is that social reform takes precedence, a reversal of the historic order.

The Kennedy Administration's resolve to push reform is unexceptionable in moral intent. But it is politically naive and inoperable. The determination to make over the Latin-American social structure has aroused suspicion, when not hostility, without attracting in the area a strong alignment of supporters. The two most powerful elements—the rich and the military—suspect that the *Alianza* is a Yankee maneuver to diminish their influence. In this they are not far wrong.

As for an upsurge of popular support, Dr. Lleras Camargo, former

President of Colombia and an ardent supporter of the *Alianza,* summed it up: "The truth is that one cannot see anywhere in Latin America the spirit of enthusiasm that should precede and go along with such a formidable adventure."

The Administration, apparently, had not thought through the implications of its policy. If one advocates a crash program to upset an established social order, resistance should be anticipated. And if the undertaking is serious, then one should be willing and prepared to follow through to overcome the resistance when encountered. But this, on belated second thought, our Government seems unwilling to do. And quite rightly so. For to try to force through the reforms would reduce our relations with the rest of the hemisphere to a shambles, without attaining the ends sought.

What can be done about our faltering policy of a better life for the people of Latin America?

First, to be able to work effectively, quietly de-emphasize social reform. We only get ourselves into trouble by trying to make Latin America a little bit pregnant with revolution. Our Government is in no position to denounce the flight of Latin capital and the reluctance of American investors to enter the area when the Administration urges drastic changes in the social system, with unforeseeable results.

"Ah," it will be countered, "but to back away from social reform will deepen anti-American feeling throughout Latin America and give the Communists valuable ammunition for their propaganda." As it happens, pushing social reform has created precious little pro-American feeling, certainly not nearly enough to offset the irritation and resentment it has generated. And as for Communist propaganda, it is not likely to be any more persuasive when distorting a program limited to economic development which creates jobs than when distorting a reformist one involving even greater gringo intervention in internal Latin affairs. In any event, fear of what the Communists might say should not be a limitless inhibition on the formulation of sensible American policy.

The problem of social reform as a criterion for aid may be eased by a proposed inter-American committee to allocate aid according to the receiving country's efforts toward self-help. Whether this body will be established and, if it is, how successful it will be remains to be seen.

Second, Washington should stop feuding with the Latin military. Our attempts to chastise juntas are self-defeating, as has been embarrassingly demonstrated. They are also economically unsettling. The slack cliché that a military dictatorship necessarily produces a Castro-type successor is contradicted by events since the Cuban revolution. In fact, the Latin-American country most threatened by internal Communism is one of the most democratic and most progressive, with the highest gross national product, and a near model in compliance with the *Alianza* program—Venezuela.

We have to adjust ourselves to the reality of continuing political influence by the military in Latin America. Beyond this, we should recognize that in the convulsive transition through which the area is passing, the situation can degenerate piecemeal into chaos. In the face of such extremities, the armed forces are the ultimate hope for maintaining order, without which even a semblance of economic development is not possible.

Furthermore, we would do well to appreciate that the military has a passionate tradition of patriotism and has recently developed a feeling for civic contribution: public works, and teaching conscripts the three R's and trade skills. All of this can go sour, for the Communists are working to infiltrate the armed forces. We only contribute to that and make the military actively anti-American by lecturing it on its proper role in society and cracking down on juntas that seize power.

Third, our primary emphasis had best be on aiding economic development. This means, essentially, helping to create and increase productivity, and thus wealth and jobs, wherever we can and are wanted.

Many democratic Latin-American governments have legislated generous social-security and fringe benefits for labor; as examples, one month's paid vacation per year and early retirement on full pay. This is indeed progressive, leaving the *Alianza* really little more progress to register on this front. Yet nearly all of these governments have neglected the importance of increasing productivity, essential to the welfare of both the individual worker and the state.

So our main role in Latin America is the traditional aid function that we have been performing for years. It is demonstrating how two stalks can be made to grow where one grew and how skills and machines can produce more.

It is also fostering, with modesty and tact, education in management and in labor organization. American unionists are now trying to offset the powerful Communist influence in Latin labor and to help the workers to understand the importance to themselves of advancing productivity. This is a practical step in the right direction. As for development loans, they had best be phased over to international banks and their affiliates.

Fourth, we should do everything that we can to make it possible for the Latin Americans to earn their own way in international trade. When we can help remove a block on the road to their making a respectable living, we do something solidly constructive. That is why something like the recent international agreement on coffee prices is so important. One such compact is worth millions of dollars in aid. For Latin America's greatest hope is, perhaps, an improvement of its position in the international commodity market. If this does not happen, our whole aid program may well prove to be futile.

Finally, we shall have to be uncommonly patient. For Latin America is in for a long time of trouble, the end of which cannot be foretold. At best, the gap between the rich and the poor will remain wide at the close of the Decade of Progress. There will be disorder and violence, demagoguery and subversion. But there will also be constructive advance, and statesmanship.

The main thing for us to remember is that there are humbling limitations on what we can do to help in so turbulent and alien a situation.

Revolution, Yes!*

Carlos Fuentes

South of your border, my North American friends, lies a continent in revolutionary ferment—a continent that possesses immense wealth and nevertheless lives in a misery and a desolation you have never known and barely imagine. Two hundred million persons live in Latin America. One hundred and forty million of them work virtually as serfs. Seventy million are outside the monetary economy. One hundred million are illiterate. One hundred million suffer from endemic diseases. One hundred and forty million are poorly fed.

Today, these miserable masses have decided to put an end to this situation. Latin America, for centuries nothing more than an object of historical exploitation, has decided to change—into a subject of historical action.

You will ask yourselves: what has caused this Latin American backwardness? Why, if we won political independence more or less at the same time, are North Americans prosperous, free, democratic—and Latin Americans poor, subjugated, unable to govern themselves? You will sigh with relief: now, everything is going to change, thanks to American generosity. The Alliance for Progress will solve all the problems afflicting Latin America. Thanks to those $20 billion, Latin Americans will forget the spectre of revolution so stained with blood and destructive of democracy and human rights, will manage to develop peacefully and, in a short time, will set up democratic societies, twins of the United States.

You are much given to good wishes, to what you call "wishful thinking." You have always believed that what is valid for you is valid for all men in all nations and at all times. You forget the existence of specific historical factors. You fail to realize that in reality there are two worlds, one of rich countries and one of poor countries. You fail to recognize that, of necessity, the poor countries require solutions different from yours. You have had four centuries of uninterrupted development within the capitalistic structure. We have had four centuries of underdevelopment within a feudal structure. . . .

During the nineteenth century, economic liberalism—laissez faire—was superimposed on the feudal structure in Latin America. Side by side with the landlord class of the colonial period, a new class of entrepreneurs sprang up to deal in the business of exploitation. Those capitalists turned us into single-

* "The Argument of Latin America: Words for the North Americans," *Monthly Review,* January 1963, pp. 487–496, 499–501. Reprinted with permission of *Monthly Review*. Carlos Fuentes is a young Mexican novelist.

product countries, exporters of raw materials to the occidental marketplace. The utopia of these entrepreneurs was the following: because of the international division of labor, it was appropriate for some regions to produce raw materials and for others to refine them; such an exchange would produce welfare for everyone. Now we know this is not true; now we know that, in the long run, the price of manufactured goods will always be higher than that of raw materials. Now we know that, in a depression of the central economy, those who suffer most are the satellite economies, the producers of raw materials. Between 1929 and 1938, Latin American exports decreased by 70 percent. In that time, hunger *did* exist in Cuba: 50 percent of her labor force was unemployed, the national banks failed, the sugar lands were bought at bargain prices by Americans. The myth collapsed. If economies were complementary, as the classical theory states, our standard of living should be equal to yours.

In order to overcome the effects of economic liberalism, many Latin American countries entered another phase after 1930: protectionist capitalism, with the aim of encouraging the internal industrialization of Latin America and making it less dependent on the export of raw materials. But this naive and liberal capitalism was also superimposed on the feudal structure without destroying it. It abandoned to their fate the great masses of peasants and workers, and reserved progress for an urban minority. It ended by crystallizing a dual society in Latin America: the modern capitalistic society of cities and the feudal society of the countryside. The minority society became richer at every turn, face-to-face with a majority society becoming more miserable at every turn. In the last few years, the abyss between the two has done nothing but grow. This is why capitalism has not succeeded in solving the problems of Latin America. It has been unable to destroy the legacy of feudalism. It has been unable to promote true collective development in Latin America.

This is what Latin America is: a collapsed feudal castle with a cardboard capitalistic facade.

This is the panorama of the historical failure of capitalism in Latin America:

Continuous monoproductive dependence. In Brazil, coffee constitutes 74 percent of the exports; tin in Bolivia, 60 percent; copper in Chile, 63 percent; bananas in Costa Rica, 60 percent; coffee in Colombia, 82 percent; bananas in Honduras, 75 percent; coffee in Haiti, 63 percent; oil in Venezuela, 95 percent; coffee in Nicaragua, 51 percent; sugar in the Dominican Republic, 60 percent.

A continuous system of "latifundio." In Chile and Brazil, 2 percent of the population owns 50 percent of the workable land. In Venezuela, 3 percent of the population owns 90 percent of the land. In general, in Latin America, with the exception of Mexico and Cuba, 5 percent of the population owns half of the land. More than half of all Latin Americans are peasants who work under conditions close to slavery. However, only 24 percent of the land in Latin America can be cultivated. Of this percentage, enormous expanses are out of active production, either to maintain the earnings of the owners or through pure irrationality. Most Latin American countries must import a good part of their food; only Uruguay and Argentina are relatively self-sufficient. The productivity of agriculture is extremely low in relation to the manpower employed. And international prices of the agricultural products fluctuate and are constantly declining.

Continuous underdevelopment. The present systems are unable to increase production and use natural resources in the rhythm required by our increase in population. As a result, the average annual increase in production per inhabitant in Latin America, which in 1955 was 2.2 percent, declined in 1959 to 1 percent, and in 1960 to 0.0 percent. In other words, at present, in its double feudal-capitalistic system, Latin America *does not progress.*

Continuous political stagnation. The continued existence of the feudal structure forbids the masses access to education and assures the concentration of political power in the hands of a fistful of landlords and city capitalists. Latin American armies financed and equipped by the United States, support this system, as we have just seen in Argentina, Ecuador, and Guatemala.

Continuous general injustices. At present, 4 percent of the Latin American population receives 50 percent of the combined national incomes. The higher classes have hoarded more than 14 billion dollars in foreign banks. A great percentage of their local investments are unproductive ones: fixed-income securities, real estate, luxury goods.

Continuous dependence on foreign capital. At present, a good part of the Latin American economy is not serving its own development, but is nothing more than an extension of foreign economies, particularly that of the United States. Iron and oil in Venezuela, copper in Chile, Peruvian minerals, do not remain in those countries to promote economic development: they are a possession of the American economy and benefit only that economy. But since this is a topic very closely related to you, we will talk about it later.

The key question is this: How can the causes of underdevelopment in Latin America be chopped away? There is no room for doubt in the answer: stabilization of prices of raw materials in the short run, and economic diversification—industrialization—in the long run. But you want it to be done through peaceful evolution and the Alliance for Progress. And we think: through revolution. Let us examine both solutions.

The Alliance for Progress

The only structural reform foreseen in the Alliance for Progress is agrarian reform. Now, please consider that in Latin America the base of political power is the landlords. Do you sincerely believe that a leading class whose roots are in the ownership of land is going to let go of its reason for being? Agrarian feudalism is the basis of the wealth and political dominion of the governing classes in Central America, Chile, Peru, Argentina, Brazil, Venezuela, Colombia, Ecuador; do you believe these classes are going to commit suicide voluntarily? A Peruvian oligarch recently told me: "If the gringos force us to divide the land, we will answer by expropriating their mining companies." No, my American friends: an agrarian reform in Latin America, as demonstrated by Mexico and Cuba, is only made through revolution, with weapons in hand. This is what the sharecroppers of Peru, the peasants of northeastern Brazil, the pariahs of Chile, Ecuador, and Colombia are beginning to do. They are not allowing themselves to be cheated by "false" agrarian reforms: the distribution of sterile lands, without credit, without machinery, without schools or hospitals. Those governing classes can deceive you, but they are not going to swindle the peasant masses or stifle their revolutionary impetus.

The Alliance is going to be used by governments that do not truly represent their people, by governments representing the old feudal order whose only interest is to keep its privileges. Look where your dollars are going to go: as in South Vietnam, as in South Korea, as in Iran and Spain—to the bank accounts of a handful of people, to the importation of luxurious automobiles, to the construction of apartment houses.

The Alliance does not even mention one of the basic factors of backwardness in Latin America: the economic deformation imposed by foreign domination of our economies. Ah, you jump at this point. You refuse to admit this. You have helped the development (what development?) of Latin America. You unselfishly give us dollars and technical aid.

We have already spoken about the domination of natural resources: iron ore, copper, tin, coal, lead, zinc, oil. These resources, in your hands, enter your economy: they are not employed in the internal development of our countries. The Alliance does not even speak of that. It does not foresee that the iron and oil of Venezuela may contribute to creation of heavy industry there, that the copper of Chile or the lead of Peru may be motors of national industrialization. At any rate, our industrialization must be light, for transformation, but nothing more.

You are also proprietors of Latin American foreign trade. Sixty percent of our foreign trade is with you, in accordance with the prices you set. American companies manage 75 percent of our commercial movement. You impose the conditions and the prices. Last year, the Alliance gave 150 million dollars to Colombia; but in that same year, Colombia lost 450 million dollars because of the decrease in coffee prices.

Ask the great cotton concerns how much they pay for a bale of Mexican cotton, at what price they resell it to the English monopoly in Hong Kong, and how much they charge the Communist government of China, which you detest, for it. The Anderson Clayton in this operation makes five times the amount that the Mexican grower does. And ask the Department of State why it forbids Mexico to sell its excess oranges to Czechoslovakia in exchange for machinery we need, machinery you either do not sell us or sell us for too high a price; ask the Department why the whole crop went rotten on the docks of Tampico while you traded happily with Communist countries and allowed

Adenauer's Germany to be the principal Western market of that very same Czechoslovakia.

Investments? Yes, you have invested 10 billion dollars in Latin America. It is a curious thing: we have always received your investments, and we are still poor. You speak about *your* property in Latin America and call us thieves when we expropriate it. But why don't you ask your investors? Ask them how much they invest and how much they take back to the United States in profits. Do you want to know? Between 1950 and 1955, you invested 2 billion dollars, made three and a half billion, and took back to the States one and a half billion. In a single year, 1959, you made 775 million, only reinvested 200 million and sent 575 million back to the United States. In the last 7 years, Latin America lost, because of these shipments of money, $2,679,000,000. You take out too much, leave too little, and even this little is distributed unfairly: where is the real benefit for our economies? Is it just that these profits do nothing, not a single thing, to alleviate the horrible misery, ignorance, and illness of the great majority of the Latin Americans who, with their slavery, made them possible? You, as Americans, tell me if that is just.

And tell me also whether you have not recovered more than your investments, whether it is not right that this squandered wealth should be recovered and directed towards improving the lot of everyone, because it was created by the work of everyone though today it benefits only a dozen corporations.

Finally, in its year of life, the Alliance for Progress has been accompanied by acts of political aggression that prostitute it completely. These acts are the Cuban invasion in April, 1961, and the violation of the inter-American law in Punta del Este in January, 1962.

Playa Giron and Punta del Este

American responsibility in the invasion of the Bay of Pigs is not debatable: President Kennedy assumed it completely, with full knowledge that in this way he was violating not only inter-American treaties but the internal laws of the United States itself: the Neutrality Act and the U.S. Code. You pride yourselves on living in a State of Law. Why did you allow your government to violate it? Don't you count on representatives of the people to defend it? Is there not a process to call to account—impeach—the president who violates it? Why do you permit an apparently irrational act by your government, your CIA and a band of mercenaries recruited from the assassins and sadists of the Batista government? Or do you agree with your government in considering the law a dead letter when faced by political necessities? In this case you yourselves are justifying Goldwater, the John Birch Society, and all the fascist forces that, beginning with McCarthy, have been growing in the United States of America.

You killed women and children in Playa Giron. You bombed the first decent houses, the first schools, the first hospitals of Cubans who never before, during the long American protectorate over Cuba, had a roof, an alphabet, or their health. And you did it in the name of liberty, democracy, and free enterprise. What do you want us to think of these nice-sounding words when in their names a population is murdered and the first proofs of concrete welfare are destroyed? We think the same as Simon Bolivar did 150 years ago: "The U.S.A. seems destined by Providence to plague us with all kinds of evils in the name of liberty."

In Punta del Este, the second aggressive act in the name of the Alliance took place. Maybe for you the standards of inter-American law are not important, but for us they are the result of a long struggle. It took us a whole century to win these standards. We won them with the invasion of Mexico and the annexation of half our territory, with the mutilation of Colombia, with the Platt Amendment, with the murder of Madero, with the occupation of Veracruz and the punitive Pershing expedition, with the interventions in Haiti, Nicaragua, and Santo Domingo, with the death of Sandino, with the campaign and the pressure against the Mexican Revolution, with the violation of Guatemala. It cost us a great deal of blood to set these standards: self-determination, non-intervention, respect for territorial integrity, equal rights for natives and foreigners, peaceful solutions of controversies, the right of each American state to organize as it thinks best. In Punta del Este, all these standards were violated by your government. A century of judicial construction collapsed. It does not matter, said Secretary Rusk: "It is not the role of foreign ministers to discuss judicial matters, but to make decisions in the field of politics." The OAS ceased to be a legal organization because it was converted, now without any disguise, into a political weapon of the United States of America.

And the Alliance for Progress looked like the soft loincloth of naked intervention in favor of the concrete political and economic interest of the United States in Latin America.

Revolution, Yes

For years, many Latin Americans put faith in a gradual change of American policies towards Latin America; they also put their faith in the ability of the inter-American organization to support the minimum principles of our sovereignty. It is necessary to thank President Kennedy who, in only a year, has destroyed those illusions. The New Frontier turned out to be identical to the Republican Old Guard. Today, Latin Americans know they must no longer trust in the possibility of a change in the American government or in the OAS: they must trust only in themselves, in their capacity to destroy, by themselves, the old feudal structure and replace it with a radically new society, from which they can build for themselves. . . .

Revolution, yes! Don't be deceived, Americans. Open your eyes. Ask the Peruvian farmer who chews coca and eats rats if he wants fake elections or revolutions. Ask the Chilean miner who crawls through the tunnels of Lota if he believes in free enterprise or in revolution. Ask the northeast Brazilian farmer if he wants capitalism or revolution. Ask the student castrated by the Paraguayan dictator if he wants Stroessner's free press or revolution. Ask the Guatemalan farmer "freed" by Castillo Armas if he wants Alliance for Progress or revolution. Ask the Latin Americans who corrupts the press and the unions, who supports the armies and the oligarchies, who pays miserable salaries, who owns the mines and the oil wells. Ask them who gets the Alliance for Progress money, and ask what they use it for. Ask them if we believe in the free world of Franco, Salazar, Chiang Kai-shek and Ngo Dinh Diem. Ask them and they will tell you why people spat on Nixon.

Ask the men living in "misery village" in Buenos Aires, in the "favela" of Rio, in the "cayampa population" of Santiago, if they are afraid of Communism. These beggars, these pariahs, will answer that they are afraid only of their present oppressors, of those who exploit them in the name of capitalism and representative democracy, and that they prefer anything that might mean a change.

Ask these men if they are against Cuba, if they believe the lies they read in the "free press" of our countries, if they do not know that the old American colony of the Caribbean is our hope because there the caste army, the *latifundio*, the administrative corruption, the official cheating are over and everybody works together, with weapons ready, Americans, with weapons ready to defend the Revolution; tell Ydigoras or Somoza to arm their people with the weapons you give them—and then to move forward together despite aggression and boycott.

Ask these men if they are afraid of help from the Soviet Union. Ask them if there is a single Soviet company in Cuba that exploits the Cuban economy for its own gain.

Do you see, Americans? The world has changed. Latin America is no longer your preserve. The world moves ahead. And you are standing on the rim. Are you going to help these inevitable revolutions or are you going to antagonize them with invasions, press campaigns, and economic aggressions? It does not matter. Revolutions are going to progress. The world has changed. You will not be able to put out all the fires in Latin America, Africa, and Asia.

But try to understand. Try to understand that a revolution in Latin America can affect only a handful of Yankee enterprises, but never the concrete welfare you enjoy. Try to understand that our real development, which can be achieved only through revolution, far from hurting you will help you. Do not let yourselves be fooled by this handful of enterprises and investors. Try to understand that the sooner we start our basic development, which can come only through revolution, the more buyers you will have, and we will all be closer to a planned world economy, rational and interdependent. . . .

The Contriving of Reform*

Albert O. Hirschman

Faced with the claims of the Cuban revolution on the one hand, and with the demands and promises of the Alliance for Progress on the other, Latin Americans appear to have been placed squarely before the familiar, if stark, alternative: change through violent revolution or through peaceful reform?

. . . this traditional dichotomy does very poorly at catching the reality of social and economic change. But first it should perhaps be explained that, contrary to what might be expected, a strong initial advantage for the advocates of revolution results from formulating the choice facing the developing countries of Latin America in this bipolar fashion.

Social reform and social revolution are usually distinguished by the manner in which a given change is brought about as well as by the extent of that change. But they have in common the nature of the change, since both propose a shift in power and wealth from one group to another. Hence they are varieties of what we shall call *antagonistic* solutions to problems in contrast to *non-antagonistic* solutions which consist of measures that are expected to leave each group better or at least as well off as before.

A proposed change can be thought of as non-antagonistic by its advocates, but may turn out to be antagonistic and to be perceived as such. In fact, any "progress," however non-antagonistic it was meant to be, will almost always hurt the absolute or relative position of *some* social group, at least initially. Anthropologists have shown that all aspects of the status quo, even those that seem wholly undesirable, have their defenders and profiteers who are going to fight the proffered improvements. Unrealistic expectation of universal cooperation with measures which in the mind of their sponsors had no antagonistic component has spelled the failure of many a technical assistance project. Such disappointments have been well documented even in the ostensibly most non-antagonistic field of public health. Thus we tend consistently to *underestimate* the difficulties of change in the case of (subjectively) non-antagonistic measures and we are constantly surprised and chagrined by the resistances which they encounter.

The opposite bias—overestimate of the difficulties of change—frequently

* From *Journeys toward Progress: Studies of Economic Policy-Making in Latin America,* The Twentieth Century Fund, New York, 1963, pp. 251–261. Reprinted by permission. Mr. Hirschman is Professor of International Economic Relations at Columbia University, the author of *The Strategy of Economic Development,* and editor of *Latin American Issues.*

affects measures which are openly and avowedly antagonistic. We know and expect that land expropriation, nationalization of industries or progressive income taxation will be strongly opposed by well-entrenched groups. Hence, when it comes to such measures, the revolutionary who is out to ridicule the peaceful reformer has an easy task indeed. He will show that a basic transformation of existing power relationships is a prerequisite to adopting and enforcing any measure that threatens the interests and privileges of the ruling class. He will deride the argument that the establishment of democratic institutions and of universal suffrage will allow basic reforms to be adopted legally since, so he will argue, democratic trappings will be discarded as soon as the real powerholders find them no longer convenient. . . .

The idea of revolution as a prerequisite to any progress draws immense strength from the very limited human ability to visualize change and from the fact that it makes only minimal demands on that ability. All we are asked to imagine by the revolutionary is the tumbling down of the old regime in a total upheaval which will give birth to the new order. Revolution thus conceived is essentially a quite brief, though cataclysmic, interlude between two static societies: one, unjust and rotten, which is incapable of being improved, and the other, rational and harmonious, which has no further need to be improved upon. Sorel, the apostle of the violent general strike as an energizing myth, clearly had this concept of revolution in mind when he wrote:

> . . . the general strike must be considered as an undivided whole; consequently, no detail about ways and means is of the slightest help for the understanding of socialism. It must even be added that there is always danger of losing something of this understanding, if one attempts to split this whole into parts . . . the transition from capitalism to socialism must be conceived as a catastrophe whose process defies description.[1]

Sorel thus understood perfectly the dual function of the idea of revolution: to gratify the desire for change and to dispense with the need to visualize the process of change in its intricate and perhaps unpleasant details by telescoping it into an "undivided whole."

The neat trick involved in this operation, while intellectually not very respectable, goes far toward explaining the drawing power of the idea of revolution. But the reformers are also to blame. They have made themselves particularly vulnerable to the charge of being unrealistic by failing to explore how social change short of cataclysmic revolution actually happens. Thus they have permitted the revolutionists to set up a caricature of "change via reform" where the latter follows smoothly (and unbelievably) upon the 51 per cent election victory of the Reform Party or, more modernly though even more naively, upon the recommendations of international experts or the offer of finance. Actually there are a good many intermediate stations between this

[1] Georges Sorel, *Réflexions sur la violence,* 11th ed. (Paris: Marcel Riviere, 1950), pp. 185, 217.

kind of effortless and painless reform at one extreme and total revolution at the other . . .

Events of recent years have created a somewhat similar continuum between total peace and total war (cold, phony, brushfire, limited war), and political scientists have identified various types of political regimes (tutelary democracy, modernizing oligarchies) filling the void between Western-type parliamentary democracy and totalitarian autocracy. In contrast to these efforts, our observations do not lead to the firm establishment of a typology. Rather, . . . elements of both reform and revolution are present in the sequences of policy-making which we have studied. . . . Our argument, as developed so far, does not mean to imply that any reform whatever can always be introduced without revolution, i.e., without the prior, violent, wholesale overthrow of the current power holders. Certainly many situations have existed and still exist in Latin America as elsewhere in which power is so concentrated, opposition to change so fierce, and the social and political structure so rigid that any non-revolutionary change is, short of a miracle, impossible, *besides* being inconceivable. The point we have been trying to make is that there are many other, less rigid situations in which change by methods short of revolution is or has become possible, but where, because of the force of habit or some similar cultural lag, change is still visualized primarily as something that requires a prior revolution. This contrast between reality and the widely entertained image of reality seems to the writer to prevail in much of Latin America today. A similar contrast with opposite content characterizes the present intellectual and political climate in the United States where, as a result of positive experience with gradualism, a majority appears to have come to the unwarranted conclusion that any progressive change whatever can and must be achieved exclusively by a succession of moderate reforms or cannot be achieved at all. This can be just as much an illusion as the opposite belief of many Latin Americans that any "real" change can only come through revolution.

Our statement that reform and revolution are not nearly as far apart as language would make us believe holds up well when we consider the role of violence. The received idea is that revolutions are violent and reforms peaceful. But if we applied this criterion for distinguishing between reform and revolution to the history of land tenure problems in Colombia, we would immediately have to conclude that Colombia has passed not through one but through several agrarian revolutions. Yet the historical record knows of no such revolution.

On reflection it will be realized that even if violence is a necessary condition for revolution it is not a sufficient one, and that it is also a common element of reform. To qualify as revolutionary, violence must be *centralized;* it must attack and conquer the central seats of political and administrative power. In Colombia, violence has been scattered, local, decentralized. For the past hundred years, peasants have occupied and are still occupying today lands that are not theirs. Sometimes they have used force and force has occasionally been used against them by those who claim ownership. But eventually forcible appropriation of large areas has been sanctioned by the state through *ad hoc* intervention or general legislation. Thus, the willingness of the peasants to occupy uncultivated lands—a kind of entrepreneurial spirit—has powerfully contributed to reform legislation. Without the past experience of mass squatting and the threat of more to come, neither Law 200 of 1936 nor the land reform of 1961 would ever have been passed by the Congress.

In Brazil's Northeast, decentralized violence appears in a different guise. It is first unloosened by nature itself which, through its droughts, periodically chases hundreds of thousands of nordestinos from their homes in search of food, water and work. Relief shipments and the organization of emergency public works are an automatic response to the overriding need of social and physical survival so that it may well be said that, whenever a drought strikes, minimal needs of subsistence are "appropriated" by the Northeastern refugees. When the relief funds are not forthcoming with sufficient promptness, looting of food stores in the cities by the drought refugees serves as a reminder. This sudden and forcible appropriation of public monies by the Northeast leads subsequently to a whole chain of attempts to disburse the monies in such a way as to limit the damage that will be wrought by future droughts.

Since violence has in part the function of signalling protest to the central authorities, an improvement in the signalling mechanism serves to increase pressure as much as an intensification of the problem. Something of this kind happened in the Northeast when better and more numerous highways (built largely during droughts) and the availability of trucks permitted the miserable drought refugees to reach the coastal cities more rapidly and in greater numbers and thereby increased the threat to public order consequent upon the droughts.

As though the violent immediate reactions to the violence of nature were not enough, Northeasterners have been casting around for additional stimulants to action in the form of threatened violence. The traditional threat has been that of secession. Yet the threat of this particular violence always remained a bit rhetorical and ineffectual for lack of credibility. For one, it seemed an irrational move since it would cut off the Northeast from the principal source of relief and investment funds. Secondly, the threat is really one of an all-out centralized clash; it cannot be graduated, since a region cannot secede "just a little bit." In both respects, the Colombian squatter's kind of violence is more efficient, and its Brazilian counterpart has recently come into prominence in the Northeast through the activities of the peasant leagues. The creation of the new development agency in the Northeast (SUDENE) was originally rather a response to the 1958 drought, but the threat implicit in the rise of the peasant leagues strengthened the agency, which could now claim that its reform program represented the only alternative to a violent and disorderly change in the existing power structure in the Northeast.

In addition to being decentralized rather than centralized, the violence we have encountered in Colombia and Brazil is distinguished from revolutionary violence by the fact that it is not immediately countered by the aggrieved party. The violence one meets with is unilateral, sequential, *temporarily unrequited.* Land is "grabbed" by peasants, but ordinarily no immediate resistance follows. There may be action in the local courts and eventually forcible eviction of the squatters by the police and occasionally the army. Or again nothing may happen for a long time; and when the state believes it important that uncertainty be removed, but does not wish to use force to evict the peasants, it may buy the property from the owner and then attempt to sell it back to the peasant who already holds it, but still is ready to pay something for the much-coveted title, which, among other advantages, makes it possible to obtain credit.

Thus the violence that is compatible with reform and frequently appears to be part and parcel of it is not the kind of decisive clash—force meets force in the principal square of the capital—which is usually associated with revolutionary violence. Rather it is a violence akin to guerrilla warfare, with the ability of the groups practicing it to now advance, now retreat, now lie low and now come forward with a new thrust. . . .

The Latin American scene thus appears to be replete with mechanisms and sequences which permit the exertion of powerful pressures and the venting and adjudication of conflicts by means equally far removed from traditional concepts of either reform or revolution. Policy-makers usually act as a result and in the midst of such situations. To paraphrase Marx, decentralized, unrequited violence is frequently found in the role of indispensable midwife to *reform.* To advocate reforms in Latin America without tolerating, accepting and sometimes even welcoming and promoting the only kinds of pressures which have proven to be effective in getting reforms through is to risk being accused of hypocrisy and deception: now that the United States has declared itself in favor of a variety of reforms in Latin America, it should perhaps be apprised of the circumstances and hazards usually associated with such an enterprise. . . .

